92-2664

In all Western countries, people are leaving work earlier than ever before – at a time when their life expectancy keeps increasing. How has this paradoxical process been brought about? What is the impact of labor markets and social policy? And what will be the effects of this massive lengthening of retirement? *Time for Retirement* addresses the "aging of society" and the restructuring of the life course in terms of the changing relationship between work and retirement. Based on a comparative analysis of seven different national regimes, it assesses the range of possible political answers to this process. The editors and contributors are among the leading social scientists in the field of life-course studies, aging, and social policy.

TIME FOR RETIREMENT

TIME FOR RETIREMENT

COMPARATIVE STUDIES
OF EARLY EXIT FROM THE LABOR FORCE

Edited by

MARTIN KOHLI
Free University of Berlin

MARTIN REIN
Massachusetts Institute of Technology

ANNE-MARIE GUILLEMARD
University of Paris I

HERMAN VAN GUNSTEREN
University of Leyden

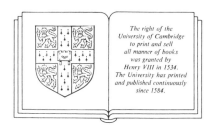

*The right of the
University of Cambridge
to print and sell
all manner of books
was granted by
Henry VIII in 1534.
The University has printed
and published continuously
since 1584.*

CAMBRIDGE UNIVERSITY PRESS
Cambridge

New York   Port Chester   Melbourne   Sydney

Published by the Press Syndicate of the University of Cambridge
The Pitt Building, Trumpington Street, Cambridge CB2 1RP
40 West 20th Street, New York, NY 10011, USA
10 Stamford Road, Oakleigh, Melbourne 3166, Australia

© Cambridge University Press 1991

First published 1991

Printed in the United States of America

Library of Congress Cataloging-in-Publication Data
Time for retirement / Martin Kohli . . . [et al.].
        p.   cm.
    ISBN 0-521-40053-8. – ISBN 0-521-42364-3 (pbk.)
1. Early retirement.   2. Early retirement – Government policy.
                I. Kohli, Martin.
HD7110.T56   1991   91-10462
331.25′2–dc20   CIP

British Library Cataloguing in Publication Data
Time for retirement.
1. Retirement
I. Kohli, Martin
306.38

ISBN 0-521-40053-8 hardback
ISBN 0-521-42364-3 paperback

Contributors

MARTIN BLOMSMA
Netherlands Scientific Council for Government Policy
The Hague, The Netherlands

BERT DE VROOM
Leyden Institute for Law and Public Policy
University of Leyden, The Netherlands

ANNE-MARIE GUILLEMARD
University of Paris I and Centre d'Etudes des Mouvements Sociaux
Paris, France

KLAUS JACOBS
IGES (Institute of Health and Social Research, Berlin)
Germany

MARTIN KOHLI
Institute of Sociology
Free University of Berlin, Germany

FRANK LACZKO
Department of Social Science and Policy Studies
Coventry Polytechnic, England

CHRIS PHILLIPSON
Department of Applied Social Studies and Social Work
University of Keele, England

MARTIN REIN
Department of Urban Studies and Planning
Massachusetts Institute of Technology, USA

HAROLD L. SHEPPARD
International Exchange Center on Gerontology
USA

JULIA SZALAI
Institute of Sociology of the Hungarian Academy of Sciences
Hungary

HERMAN VAN GUNSTEREN
Faculty of Law
University of Leyden, The Netherlands

ESKIL WADENSJÖ
Swedish Institute for Social Research
University of Stockholm, Sweden

Acknowledgments

This book is an outgrowth of a research project on welfare state exit and entry patterns (WEEP), initiated by Martin Rein and Lee Rainwater in 1985. Gösta Esping-Anderson was the director of the project until he left for the European University Institute, Florence. The project was financed and administered by the Science Center Berlin (Wissenschaftszentrum Berlin, WZB). Throughout its history, Frieder Naschhold sponsored and nourished the project, giving it intellectual support and leadership. Konstanza Prinzessin zu Löwenstein handled the administrative complexity of the project with skill and good humor. The WZB was a superb base from which to conduct this cross-national research. The study on early exit was initiated by Martin Rein, with Klaus Jacobs as the principal research associate.

The data for the book were provided through the kind assistance of a number of colleagues in various universities, including Walter Müller (University of Mannheim), and through the support of the Department of Urban Studies and Planning at MIT, with the able secretarial help of Debbie Kunz. At the Free University of Berlin the secretarial tasks were competently handled by Cornelia Heinz. Completion of the book was greatly helped by an invitation to Martin Kohli to serve as guest professor at the Department of Sociology of Harvard University during the spring term 1989.

As the project unfolded, financial support was provided by the Centre National de la Recherche Scientifique (CNRS) - especially the French-German Program headed by Hinnerk Bruhns - and the Maison des Sciences de l'Homme under the direction of Clemens Heller. In addition, support was provided by the Deutsche Forschungsgemeinschaft, the Center for the Steering of Society at the University of Leyden, and the International Exchange Center on Gerontology at the University of South Florida, Tampa. These organizations made it possible for us to meet several times during the course of our study.

Throughout these meetings, the contributors did much more than report on their countries. By spelling out the peculiarities on their cases, and also by arguing from their specific viewpoints, they shaped our common agenda and forged a unified approach. As a result, the book represents a team effort.

M.K./M.R./A.-M.G./H.v.G.

CHAPTER 1

The changing balance of work and retirement

MARTIN KOHLI AND MARTIN REIN

1.1 THE PROBLEM

THE decrease in the age of exit from gainful work has been one of the most profound structural changes in the past 25 years. It has occurred – albeit to differing degrees – in all Western societies, irrespective of their institutional regimes. In the recent history of these societies, few trends are as consistent and homogeneous as this one. The period spent in gainful work is shrinking, with early exit at the upper end and the extension of schooling at the lower end of the work life contributing to this outcome from both directions. The period spent in retirement is also expanding in both directions as a result of early exit at the lower end and increasing life expectancy at the upper end. Thus, what has been the "normal life course" is being massively reorganized, and the relations between age groups and generations are being redefined.

Moreover, the trend is (on first sight at least) highly perplexing and even paradoxical. In a period of increasing life expectancy, of increasing concern with the financial viability of the public pension systems, and of increasing admonitions from gerontologists about the fallacy of age stereotypes regarding work performance and productivity, why should there be such a pervasive tendency to leave work earlier and earlier? The paradox defies easy explanations; by posing the question of how life phases and the boundaries between them – especially the all-important boundaries between work and nonwork periods – are socially constructed, it is perhaps the most explicit challenge for life-course theory. It also challenges most current assumptions about the effects of social policy by contrasting the explanatory potential of theories that focus on the state as the key actor and those that focus on actors in the economic sphere. The trend toward early exit thus not only presents an explanatory task by itself but is also a theoretical window on the social construction of aging and the life course in general, and on the articulation of the economy and the polity.

1

The consequences of this trend can be observed both at the level of the individual and at that of policy-making. In important respects, Western societies are still "work societies" (as discussed later). For individuals, being or not being part of the labor force is critical in terms of life chances and social participation. For policy-making, the consequences concern not only the public old-age insurance system but also some of the other welfare programs that have been created to cover the financial risks associated with not being able to work, such as unemployment and disability insurance. With the decreasing age of exit from work, these programs that were originally aimed at exceptional risks are now increasingly being used to manage the normal transition phase, and are therefore put under increasing strain.

The strain for the welfare state is intensified by the process of population aging that all Western societies face. Old-age insurance – which has long been the most popular and least controversial part of modern social security, and thus a cornerstone of the "moral economy" of these societies (cf. Kohli 1987) – is becoming a focus of political controversy. The questions of intergenerational equity take on a new urgency, and some observers predict that the competition for resources between age groups or generations will emerge as one of the main arenas of social conflict (cf. Johnson, Conrad, and Thomson 1989). In this situation, reversing the trend of early exit seems to offer an easy solution. In the United States, Germany, and Japan, measures to raise the age limit of eligibility for public pensions have been passed, and in other countries, they are under discussion. But the knowledge base of this discussion is still inadequate. For delineating the possibilities and the likely consequences of raising the pension age, it is necessary to get a clear picture of how the trend toward early exit has come about.

This is what we propose to do in this book. We document the evolution of early exit, analyze the conditions, actors, and institutions that have produced it, and assess its effects on the life course. The book thus has a theoretical and a practical goal. Theoretically, it addresses the restructuring of the life course and of the "generational contract" in terms of the changing relation between work and retirement, and by doing so, highlights the relation between labor markets and welfare institutions. Practically, it addresses these issues in the context of population aging and examines the range of possible political answers that are currently being debated. To those who expect everything from manipulating the public pension age limit, the results of our examination may appear to be rather impractical: They caution against a reliance on social policy alone by pointing to structural conditions of the organization of work and economic actors as the main driving forces. But such caution is indispensable to keep burden sharing equitable, and in the long run, it will also prove to be more efficient for social policy than poorly informed interventions.

1.2 THE COMPARATIVE APPROACH

Our approach is rigorously comparative. The questions that we address have been unnecessarily muddled by studies examining them only within specific national regimes.[1] Few studies have paid attention to the more general features of exit trends.[2] By implicitly assuming that the phenomenon is one of their particular country, most studies have been misled into searching for explanations on too small a scale. The logic of comparison requires identification of differential conditions and outcomes as well as of lines of structural convergence. Thus, the comparative approach shows to what extent the process is similar across national labor market and social policy regimes, and to what extent the latter do make a difference.

The starting point of our study has been an attempt to systematically analyze the articulation between social policy and the labor market (Rein 1985; Rainwater and Rein, in preparation), resulting in a project on welfare state entry and exit patterns (or, conversely, exit from and entry into the labor market).[3] In the course of this work, it became evident that the transition from work to retirement was a particularly apt topic for an in-depth comparative study of the social policy–labor market interface and, moreover, promised to relate these issues to those of the social construction of the life course (Kohli 1986) and of intergenerational redistribution (Kohli 1987).

---

[1] The few good comparative studies of social security (e.g., Gordon 1988; Pampel and Williamson, 1989) do not go sufficiently deep into our issues. This is true even for the most ambitious and largest comparative undertaking to date, the five-volume study of Western European welfare states directed by Flora (1986ff). Esping-Andersen (1990) forcefully addresses the general questions of relating social policy and labor markets (cf. section 1.4.1), but again does not give a detailed examination of early exit.

[2] Notable among them are the studies by Pampel and Weiss (1983) and Pampel (1985), who, however, restrict themselves to the decline in labor force participation of men over 65, and by Inkeles and Usui (1988), who in addition to a general overview give some comparative data on individual preferences but lack in institutional detail (e.g., about pathways for early exit outside the public pension system). A very useful overview of the types of programs available for early exit has been provided by Mirkin (1987).

[3] The Welfare Exit and Entry Project (WEEP) was financed by the Science Center Berlin. Gosta Esping-Andersen was the first Project Director until he left for the European University Institute, Florence, and was replaced successively by Martin Rein and then Lee Rainwater, who saw the project through its final phase.

The next two chapters present comparative analyses of aggregate data: one on the evolution of labor force participation among the elderly,[4] and the other on exit patterns by industry. The remaining chapters are detailed reports on individual countries designed to provide an institutional account of how and why the exit trends developed. The rationale for selecting the countries of our study has been both conceptual and practical. We first focused on those countries in which the trend toward early exit is most pronounced – the Netherlands, France, and Germany, where less than half of all men aged 55 to 64 are still employed (compared with nine-tenths in the "prime" ages). The interesting point for comparison here lies in the fact that although the outcomes in these countries are similar, the institutional processes that have brought them about are quite different. Sweden presents the contrasting outcome of a still rather high rate of employment among the elderly (and is also the model case of the "social-democratic" welfare-state regime, to use Esping-Andersen's [1990] term). With the United States and Great Britain, it is possible to examine more closely the role of private-sector arrangements in the exit process (which in the course of the study have turned out to be increasingly important in the Netherlands as well). Finally, Hungary provides a comparison of Eastern European and Western experiences.[5]

The country chapters follow a common framework that has been developed and tested in the course of several meetings among the authors. The decision to make each country the focus of a specific chapter, rather than restricting ourselves to analyzing dimensions across countries, is a decision for an institutional (and against a purely correlational) approach. It was prompted partly by the large number of institutional peculiarities that had to be covered in each case. (In fact, the profusion of institutional details has often threatened to overwhelm us; after completing this book, we understand even better why comparative work of this scale is so rarely undertaken!) But we also wanted to put the transition from work to retirement into proper context: into the overarching

---

[4] The analysis is based on the OECD labor force participation and unemployment data, supplemented by data from our country contributors and by data on long-term participation trends. The data were assembled and put into a common format by Klaus Jacobs.

[5] Among the other countries for which the OECD publishes the requisite data, Finland's labor force participation among males aged 55 to 64 is almost as low as that of France. Australia, Portugal, and Spain are in the middle range. Canada is on the level of the United States, and Ireland on that of Sweden. Japan is highest, with still almost four-fifths of this age group in employment; but even here, there is a clear trend toward earlier exit (although more pronounced above 65 than for ages 55 to 64). Some of these cases have fairly obvious parallels to the countries in our study; others would require a more detailed analysis.

features of the respective national labor-market and social-policy regimes and of their evolution.

Some differences between the country chapters are due to the differential availability of specific data and also to the different disciplinary backgrounds and intellectual inclinations of the authors. The latter have been more a source of inspiration than of concern. We hope to have succeeded in securing comparability while at the same time allowing each author to do what he or she is best at.

In sum, while each country chapter is a case study of a specific national experience undertaken from a specific analytical viewpoint, it is nevertheless comparative by virtue of being informed by a common conceptual framework and by an understanding of how other countries address the same issues. This approach of comparative case studies has been essential for securing our results.

1.3 THE CONCEPTS: RETIREMENT, EXIT, PATHWAY

Clarifying our concepts is not a straightforward task because, as part of the story that we are covering, the concepts themselves have changed and become more differentiated. "Retirement" has always been an ambiguous term; it can refer to an event, a process, a role or status, or a phase of life (Atchley 1976; Palmore et al. 1985); and it can be indexed on several different criteria, including objective criteria of work, income, or pension receipt, and subjective ones based on self-assessment (Ekerdt and DeViney 1990). In this book, "retirement" refers to the event of entering into the public old-age pension scheme (i.e., of beginning to draw an old-age pension) or, in some cases, to the phase of life beginning at that point.[6] Other authors have used definitions based on labor force participation, or on a combination of the latter with drawing an old-age pension (cf. Palmore et al. 1985:3; Burkhauser and Quinn 1989; Reimers and Honig 1989). These definitions result in highly divergent proportions of retirees and also allow for the possibility of transitions back out of retirement, whereas with our definition, there are no such countertransitions (as all public old-age pension programs provide for continu-

---

[6] There is some evidence that retirement in this objective sense – in terms of entering the public old-age pension system – and subjective retirement tend to coincide: People who have exited from work but have not yet entered the public pension system usually do not define themselves as "retired" (e.g., Kohli et al. 1989). But there are also cases of people drawing pensions and still being active who refuse this category as a label for themselves, and there seems to be an increasing unwillingness to use it as a symbolic resource because of its implications of inactivity and withdrawal from social participation.

ous coverage until death). To avoid conceptual confusion, we clearly distinguish between program participation and labor force participation, using the term "exit from work" to refer to the latter.[7]

It is essential for our argument that "retirement" and "exit" do not necessarily coincide; the decreasing age of exit from work has been brought about partly by lower retirement limits, but mostly by the emergence of an intermediary phase between exit and retirement, and it is the institutional management and the meaning of this intermediary phase that is the topic of much of this book.

"Early" exit or retirement is again an ambiguous term, which can only be clarified by giving a precise reference point. In the following discussions, the reference point will usually be the regime of age boundaries that was effective in the mid-1960s. For Western societies, this turns out to have been surprisingly uniform. In most of these societies, the normal retirement limit for men was at that time set at (or around) age 65. And as is shown in Chapter 2, the labor force participation data suggest that age 65 had by the mid-1960s also widely become the age around which exit from work clustered. Thus, 65 was effective both as a legal or programmatic reference point and as a behavioral or labor force reference point.

To deal with the emergence of a gap between retirement and exit, we develop the concept of "pathways" of exit. A pathway is an institutional arrangement or – in most cases – a combination of different institutional arrangements that are sequentially linked to manage the transition process, that is, the period between exit from work and entry into the normal old-age pension system. In the limiting case, a pathway is thus constituted by one institution only, such as a preretirement program, or disability leading into normal retirement at age 65 (as in the British case), or occupational pensions used to cover the period until normal retirement age. More often, however, pathways consist of sequences of institutional arrangements, with rules providing for a specific program to be followed by a specific second (and third, etc.) one. Sometimes there are two institutions; for example, unemployment insurance is followed by a special pension provision (as in Germany, where the long-term unemployed can enter the public pension system already at age 60). Sometimes there are even more; for example, unemployment may last longer than the period covered by unemployment benefits, and the latter are followed by a

---

[7] The OECD measurement convention that we follow in our comparative data analysis treats any gainful work above one hour per week as a case of labor force participation; in some instances, however, we will speak of "exit" in terms of leaving the last full-time job.

period of social assistance, or disability for labor market reasons (as in Sweden).

According to our conceptual distinctions, lowering the normal age of entry into the public pension system – as has been done in Sweden and France – is not a pathway of exit (although it obviously does facilitate a lower age of exit).[8] It should also be noted that pathways for us are *institutionalized* routes of exit. This includes collectively regulated private arrangements (such as regularly available occupational pensions); if, however, an individual patches together his or her own sources of personal support, we speak of personal routes of exit but not of pathways.

1.4   THE THEORETICAL FRAMEWORK

In setting out our theoretical framework, our objective is to lay the groundwork for explaining the early-exit trend and for assessing its consequences. We first deal with the interplay of social policy and labor market (or, more broadly, of the social organization of work) and then discuss how it is shaped by the relevant institutions and actors. Next, we examine what early exit means in terms of the patterning of the life course, which in modern societies has emerged as an important institutional reality sui generis, and finally we turn to the questions of social stratification and intergenerational redistribution. Our arguments are informed by the material presented in the comparative chapters, and partly also in the country chapters without, however, aiming at a comprehensive review of their results or at questions of future evolution and policy.

1.4.1   *Social policy and labor market*

Explanations for the patterns of transition from work to retirement tend to focus either on the individuals making the transition or on institutional and societal processes, with very few studies attempting to bridge the two. In the tradition of social and psychological gerontology, individual retirement behavior is accounted for by characteristics such as

---

[8] In speaking of "normal" pension age, we follow the legal–administrative terms. They can be quite misleading in terms of behavioral frequency, especially where an age limit is coupled to certain conditions of eligibility that are fulfilled not by all but by a majority of participants. A case in point is the German "flexible age boundary" at 63, available to those with at least thirty-five insurance years, which has become a much more prevalent route of entering the public pension system than what in legal terms is still the "normal" boundary of 65. A similar program available in the United States has a high take-up in spite of the fact that benefit levels are actuarially reduced.

health, income, job conditions and career history, and attitudes (e.g., Palmore et al. 1985; Talaga and Beehr 1989). In the microeconomic approach, which has gained much prominence in recent years, individual retirement decisions are modeled as the result of the work and transfer income situation, and of the work–leisure trade-off (e.g., Burkhauser 1980; Tuma and Sandefur 1988; cf. Hurd 1990 for an overview). The relationship between social policy and work supply is seen as antagonistic; since any rational person chooses leisure over work in the effort to maximize his or her personal utility, the more generous the benefits of the transfer system, the weaker must be the inclination to work. In these individual-level studies, institutional factors are considered only in terms of incentives or disincentives in the personal decision-making process. Much of the American research literature follows this approach, often to the point where it is implicitly presented as the only possible way of conceptualizing the transition to retirement.[9] In our view, it is deficient in two respects: It is not able to explain how the institutions themselves have changed (in other words, its chains of causality are much too short), and even when treating the institutions as given, it is insufficient as an explanation of the massive shift toward early exit[10] because of its overly narrow model of decision making. To mention just one important point, decisions are not simply the product of the retiring individuals themselves but also of the firms from which they retire (as becomes evident in the frequent cases of forced unemployment and in the widespread conflicts about who controls the exit process, which are discussed later).

In contrast, the approach known as the "political economy of aging" focuses on institutional and societal processes (e.g., Phillipson 1982; Myles 1984; Guillemard 1986; Pampel and Williamson 1989). This level is also addressed by some studies in labor economics (e.g., Casey and

---

[9]   This theoretical preference (or bias) may have something to do with the U.S. retirement system, which has always given more room to individual decisions than most European systems. As argued later, the trend toward early exit also runs in this direction: It amounts to an increasing individualization – and in this sense to a partial "Americanization" – of the retirement process. It is, however, far from eliminating all elements of institutional and normative structuring.

[10] Thus, Boaz (1988) finds that early exit is the result not only of pension incentives but also of the constraints posed by diminished employment opportunities. Hurd (1990:605) concludes from his review of the economic literature that the research on the effects of (public and private) pension incentives has produced somewhat disappointing results: "the models have not been able to explain the large drop in labor force participation in the past 30 years." He at first attributes this disappointment to data limitations, but then concedes, "We particularly need to be able to describe the employment opportunities an older worker faces (the demand side of the labor market)" (1990:630).

Bruche 1983).[11] It is these approaches that we follow here with our analysis of the institutional pathways for early exit and of the actors that have produced them. The pathways as such obviously do not provide a complete explanation of the exit process, since they do not systematically follow the institutional structure down to the level of firms and individuals. But by documenting how the institutions have been created and changed by the aggregate actors in the field of industrial relations and of labor-market and social policy, our analysis shows how the process is regulated and to what economic and political conditions it responds.

The most general issue in the debate on early exit is about the role of pull and push factors. On the institutional level, this refers above all to pension policy incentives and labor-market constraints. Accordingly, there are two contrasting theories. The pull view – the one underlying most studies so far – assumes that early exit is the result of social policies that have created attractive exit possibilities, for example, by lowering the age boundaries and opening new institutional pathways. There are two variants to this view: Proponents of the welfare state tend to see the process as an achievement, in line with long-standing demands (e.g., of unions), whereas neoclassical economists tend to see it as the undesirable outcome of a perverse incentive system that undermines the willingness to work. According to this theory, we should expect substantial differences between national policy regimes: Countries that have not developed the necessary social-policy infrastructure will have low rates of early exit. But the data falsify this assumption. Countries like Sweden have almost all the supporting legislation needed to produce early exit but, nevertheless, do not show the same rates as, for example, Germany, France, and the Netherlands. On the other hand, the United States has explicit legislation forbidding age discrimination and much less well developed social-policy arrangements for early exit;[12] nevertheless, the

---

[11] One might also mention here some studies that extend the microeconomic framework to account for structural properties of internal labor markets, such as the theory of efficiency wages, according to which workers – in order to increase their long-term effort and commitment to the firm – are paid less than their marginal product when young and more when old. It is therefore profitable for firms to terminate the employment of their elderly workers through the help of mandatory retirement rules (cf. Lazear 1979) or through special pension incentives. A few other studies combine microeconomic reasoning with structural arguments (e.g., Boaz 1988).

[12] Researchers often point out that the United States, too, has encouraged early exit, e.g., by extending tax privileges for company and individual pension plans, and by a work penalty that reduces the value of public pensions for those who still receive work incomes. But in a comparative perspective, these incentives are rather modest; there is for instance no long-term unemployment insurance that can serve as a pathway for early exit, nor are there public preretirement programs.

United States has – although on a somewhat higher level – still managed to produce a sharp decline in labor force participation of the elderly. So the theory of social-policy dominance of early exit is clearly inadequate.

The theoretical alternative is the structural perspective focusing on the push factors generated by the social organization of work. It assumes that the process of early exit is driven by the evolution of the labor market, especially by the high rates of unemployment that have become endemic in most Western economies since the early 1970s (having persisted even after each successive period of economic recovery), and by deeper structural features such as rationalization and the decline of internal labor markets, accompanied by the growth of subcontracting and the increased use of temporary workers. In this view, early exit takes place regardless of what institutional pathways are available. Social policy cannot stop early exit from occurring. It may be important in other respects, by molding the exit process so that it is more acceptable to some actors than others. Thus, social policy can alter the distribution of costs among actors, but it cannot altogether undo the process. Central to the structural view is the belief that if some actors are able to block access to early exit through one social-policy pathway, this will force other actors to open other pathways. There is a process of instrument substitution (Casey 1989) – If one instrument is eliminated, another will be used to bring about the same ends.

The structural perspective is better able to deal with the empirical data, but in the simplified form stated above it is misleading. The availability of institutions, and thus of legitimate pathways out of the labor force, clearly has an impact: It makes early exit attractive for individual workers, and it makes it easier for firms to deal with an oversupply of labor and with efforts to increase productivity. If no institutional pathways were available, early exit would occur on a much smaller scale. But institutions need not be well developed to produce early exit; even in rather restrictive public welfare regimes, such as the United States and (increasingly) Great Britain, early exit continues. Blocking all institutions that make early exit possible would pose major risks for industrial relations and the "social contract" more generally; hence it is unlikely to be attempted, much less to succeed.

A more detailed picture of the exit process can be obtained by examining its temporal pattern (see Chapter 2). For labor force participation over age 65, where the decrease has been fairly continuous, the modernization or "industrialism" thesis (cf. Pampel and Williamson 1989) seems most pertinent. It views the institutionalization of retirement as a result of the adaptation of the work force to the requirements of economic modernization and rationalization (which evidently encompasses a substantial number of factors), and of a societal "decision" about how to allocate the benefits of improved economic productivity. For the age groups below 65, on the other hand, the labor force participation patterns are more in line with short- and middle-term economic development, especially with the decreasing GNP growth and the increasing unemployment rates after 1974 (in the wake of the first oil shock) and again in the early 1980s.

These patterns thus reflect the sharp and persistent rise of unemployment. The early exit of older workers from the labor force has been one of the "bloodless" ways of coping with unemployment, while at the same time avoiding inflation. This has been valid for retirement more generally; one of the most important functions of retirement is "control of unemployment" (Atchley 1985). And it is by no means a new strategy; as we know from historical records (e.g., Achenbaum 1986) – and as is suggested by the long-term data on labor force participation reported in Chapter 2 – it was already promoted during the depression years, with slogans such as "Make room for the young!" in Germany or "Incomes for the old, jobs for the young!" in the United States. But with the expansion of the welfare state in the meantime, the potential for such a strategy has multiplied; at the same time, the problems encountered by Keynesian economic regulation have put policies of employment stimulation in disrepute, so that early exit has become one of the few remaining alternatives for aggregate labor-market management (Esping-Andersen 1990). In other words, since economic policy is less and less able to increase the demand for work, it falls to social policy to reduce the work supply.

The correspondence between the exit trend and unemployment is, however, far from perfect, even for ages below 65. To the extent that the downward trend began in the early 1970s, it cannot be explained simply by macroeconomic indicators. Other aspects are of importance too, such as institutional changes in the pension system that can be shown – especially with participation data for single age years – to have had immediate consequences in terms of labor force participation. On the other hand, many of these changes have an economic background as well. In France between 1968 and 1971, aging workers experienced high levels of unemployment for the first time. Unions campaigned intensively to lower the retirement age to 60. While they were unable to achieve this objective, they did manage in 1971 to obtain legislation that provided opportunities for aging workers with some incapacity to receive a social security old-age pension at 60 without an economic penalty. The threat of unemployment may have been influential long before it became evident on a mass scale. In Germany, the (rather modest) recession of 1967 hit the elderly especially hard: The unemployment rate of men aged 60 to 64 jumped to 4 percent in 1968, which – although not particularly dramatic by present standards – contrasted sharply with the rate of 0.2 to 0.3 percent of the age groups from 15 to 44. This experience was crucial not only for the attempt of the unions to contractually secure job-maintenance provisions for the elderly, but also for the introduction of "flexible retirement" in 1972, with the possibility for men of obtaining a full pension at age 63. Early exit promised a way out of this specific plight of the elderly workers even though it still took some years for overall unemployment rates to rise. Thus, unemployment is relevant for early exit not only as a direct push factor, but also through the initiation of public exit pathways as a response to it.

To qualify these general statements, it is important to call attention to some of the differences among countries. The sharpest contrast is perhaps between the Netherlands and Sweden. The Netherlands has a low labor force participation over the whole life course, with no five-year age group (in 1985) over 90 percent. The highest participation rate is that for men aged 35 to 39 (89 percent), and thereafter for every five-year age group the rate declines slowly. In Sweden, by contrast, from 94 to 97 percent of men aged 25 to 54 and 88 percent of those aged 55 to 59 work. In other words, the labor force participation of men aged 55 to 59 in Sweden is as high as that of the group aged 35 to 39 in the Netherlands. These striking differences can only be accounted for by examining the national regimes of labor organization and social policy as systems in which all parts are articulated with one another. The country chapters make it clear how Sweden has systematically pursued a work principle, whereas the Netherlands has tended to follow more the cash support principle in its social and labor market policies.

Going back to the initial question of the weight of the economy and the polity, we thus find that the system of state policies can make a difference: It can produce substantial contrasts between national regimes. But on the whole, our results are anticyclical: For our topic, the currently fashionable emphasis in welfare-state research (and in macrosociological research more generally) on the state as the main societal actor is not borne out. It seems that the state has not so much acted as reacted; state activity has to a considerable extent been a response to changing economic pressures – a response that has followed an incremental policy style or, to use a less up-graded term, has consisted largely in attempts at muddling through.

1.4.2   *Institutions and actors*

For a more complete assessment of these issues, we need to focus on all of the main actors that are involved in the exit process. It is for a closer examination of the dynamics of institutions and actors that we have developed our concept of pathways of early exit. As mentioned before, many pathways make use of institutional arrangements that were originally constructed for purposes other than early exit – usually to cover specific risks that were thought to be the exception rather than the rule (such as unemployment or disability). Incorporating them into pathways of early exit means that they are now used to deal not with specific risks but with the burden of a whole age group. The old instruments came to be transformed into new tools for labor-market regulation. The unusual became the usual, and the special became the general. This again suggests that the political process has been one of muddling through;[13] the actors have liberally recombined and reconverted elements of the transfer system, resulting in a highly eclectic mix of institutions.

Such eclecticism can be interpreted in different ways, either as the policy drift and distortion associated with the well-known phenomenon of "unintended effects," or as a flexible adaptation to context shifts. The former interpretation is certainly valid in some instances, but most of our analysis speaks for the latter one. There was a broad consensus among the key actors that some form of adaptation to the changing economic environment was both necessary and desirable. Early exit was a new social invention. There was a willingness to create polite social fictions by using disability and unemployment as substitutes for programs of early exit that did not exist or were not sufficient.

This subtle process of institutional "bricolage" was fueled by cultural norms and public opinion stressing both the responsibility for full employment in society and the belief that, given a scarcity of jobs, priority should be given to younger workers. Some unions used collective-bargaining agreements to forsake general wage increases in favor of pre-retirement programs.

As the country chapters show, the form that these beliefs took has unfolded over time in close correspondence with the shifting agenda of economic problems, resulting in a changing political discourse on the exit of older workers. In other words, similar behavioral outcomes have been motivated and consolidated by different legitimations. Each historical period emphasized a somewhat different theme. Taking Great Britain as an example, we find that the 1950s was the only time when the integration of older workers into the labor force was emphasized. In France and Germany, this continued into the early 1960s. In the context of high economic growth and of a (real or anticipated) labor shortage, older workers were considered essential to maintain an adequate labor supply. Corre-

---

[13] For the United States, this has been well demonstrated by Achenbaum (1986).

spondingly, there was a thrust of psycho-gerontological studies stressing the potential of older workers and advising the firms on how to maximize their productivity.

From the 1960s onward, the tide turned. Now each decade produced another rationale for early exit. In Great Britain in the 1960s, the emphasis was on the overmanning of the economy. It was widely believed that a labor force shakeout was necessary in order to improve productivity and technical efficiency. Redundancy payments were introduced as a way of shedding older workers. In the 1970s, the emphasis shifted from overmanning to mass unemployment. Unemployment benefits, combined with public assistance, became an important exit route, with the goal of reducing some of the excess labor supply. In the 1980s, the emphasis has shifted again, now to the impending crisis of welfare spending in the context of an aging society. At the center of public discussion is the introduction of flexible retirement provisions in the public pension system. The continuing pressure of the labor market, however, inhibits the short-term realization of this objective. But the discussion does illustrate the energy that keeps the discourse on early exit alive.

The British example documents the kind of societal dynamic that contributes to an unbroken exit trend. As public policy shifts its emphasis and as the institutional pathways for exit are creatively changed over time, the labor force participation outcome goes on, but for different reasons, with different legitimations, and through different institutional mechanisms. The result is a change of form and meaning and a continuity of substance of the process.

Shifting from a comparative time perspective within a country to a comparative country perspective, we can again see similar outcomes produced by a wide variety of processes and pathways. In France, unemployment has been the central institutional mechanism producing early exit, and the extensive use of this mechanism has finally forced a lowering of the public pension age to 60. In Germany, too, the unemployment pathway has been prominent, with unemployment insurance sequentially linked to a special provision permitting long-term unemployed older workers to enter the public pension system at age 60; but unlike France, other pathways such as disability have also been relied upon. The Netherlands shows a double pattern. On the one hand, early exit was, and still is, made possible by combinations of public social security programs, especially disability and unemployment. On the other hand, this sytem has now been extended and partly replaced by private contractual preretirement schemes. By contrast, in the United States, private pensions are the main early-exit pathway; there is no public program, other than disability, that permits early exit, and unemployment benefits last for only 26 weeks.

Although different pathways may produce the same basic outcome in terms of labor force participation, they differ greatly in who controls them, who bears the costs, how they stratify the elderly, and what moral meaning they carry. In the public discourse among actors, while the explicit level may be about changing the trend of labor force participation (e.g., by raising the age limit of the public pension system), the real issue is often about who controls the process and who bears the burden. In Great Britain, the failure to develop an adequate public pension program meant that the cost of early exit was shifted to the individual, leading to a high degree of poverty and stigma associated with the use of means-tested programs. In Germany, the cost-shifting controversy centered primarily on the state and the firms. The state tried to shift the cost back to the firms when it introduced the preretirement program. The effort failed because it led to a process of pathway cumulation rather than substitution, as both the old and the new program were used. In France, the decision to lower the retirement age to 60 was largely motivated by cost-shifting considerations. The preretirement programs that were sponsored by the social partners tended to higher replacement levels (more generous benefits in relation to former earnings) than the old-age pension system. Thus, the cost shifting occurred not only between the unemployment fund, which financed preretirement, and the old-age fund, which financed pensions, but affected the individual workers as well.

Pathways are thus constructed by, and contested among, the relevant institutional actors (state, firms and employers' associations, and unions). The picture that emerges from our country chapters is one of cooperative antagonism among the actors. The actors cooperate because they have a common stake in making early exit work; they do so antagonistically because their institutional interests are different.

On a descriptive level, it is obvious that the firms have been important participants in this process, and have thus massively contributed to early exit. Why this is so remains a matter of heated discussion (cf. Kohli [forthcoming] for a more detailed account). We should, of course, not assume complete rationality of decision making in firms.[14] Many gerontological researchers have argued that the firms, in trying to rid themselves of their older workers, do not act in their objective self-interest but are instead acting on the commonly held deficit model of aging – that is,

---

[14] For example, from his study of private pensions in the United States David Wise (forthcoming) observes: "Conversations with pension managers reveal that in some instances the incentives of the plans are not fully understood and many plans have been introduced without consideration of their effects on retirement." Wise concludes, "I believe that the typical plan was established without much attention to the incentive effects that it might create."

on deeply entrenched but faulty stereotypes or "labels" – and hence practice unfounded age discrimination. This argument is, however, based on too narrow a view of the employment contract. There are indeed good reasons for such an interest on the part of the firms.

The most controversial reasons – and the ones that the gerontologists have mainly concentrated on – are those pertaining to the work performance of older workers. The empirical evidence here is somewhat mixed. But this is only part of the picture; it has to be complemented by the issues of costs and job deployment. First, it has been broadly documented that older workers usually earn more than comparable younger ones because of formal or informal seniority arrangements, and thus are more costly for their employers. Relative earnings usually peak at ages 45 to 50 and then decline, but still tend to remain above those of younger workers (Habib 1990:332). Older workers also enjoy a series of other seniority-based prerogatives, making them less easy to move around or to fire as the interests of the firm change; in other words, they present higher transaction costs. Economists have used these age-earning profiles to refute the neoclassical spot-market model of employment, replacing it with an efficiency wage model, that is, with the notion of a lifetime earnings contract consisting of subproductivity earnings at the beginning and above-productivity earnings toward the end of work life, which makes it profitable for firms to terminate their older workers early (e.g., Lazear 1979; Kotlikoff 1988). Second, older workers are on the average less well educated – and are educated on technologies that have long since become obsolete. In spite of all the exhortations, since the 1960s, for "recurrent education" during the whole life course, there has been no regular requalification of middle- and lower-level workers after their initial training – even in countries (such as Germany) where turnover is comparatively low and where good occupational training is considered important for the productivity of the work force. As a consequence, older workers are also less flexible; given the amount of time that has elapsed since their last formal training, they cannot easily be requalified when the need arises. Third, the costs of requalification would have to be discounted more rapidly because of the shorter period of usability as retirement approaches. And fourth, the structure of the internal labor market may also contribute to the interests of firms in terminating their older workers, such as for clearing the vacancy chains (cf. Sorensen, forthcoming).

There is another reason, one that has nothing to do with productivity or costs and is often overlooked: The "control of unemployment" aspect of early exit applies to the firms as well. The availability of institutional pathways and the fact that retirement is an expected part of one's life course make early exit the most legitimate way of shrinking the work force.

This last reason applies to those firms that face pressure to reduce their work force. The other reasons also apply to those that maintain or even expand the number of their workers. Replacing older workers by younger ones is reasonable in terms of the cost issues just mentioned, and it becomes even more so if new job qualifications are required.[15] The overall result of this configuration of interests is that early exit takes place in almost all industries – not only in the declining ones but also in the expanding ones (see Chapter 3).

Of special relevance is the part that the elderly workers themselves play in the exit process, in other words, the articulation of pathways and individual choice. The question of whether early exit represents an involuntary exclusion and "marginalization" of the elderly is a key political issue and is, moreover, critical for some theoretical claims (e.g., for some variants of the "political economy of aging"). At this point, a comprehensive answer is not possible, but several elements can be mentioned.

Generally, there is a conflict between the principle of early exit and the principle of (formal or informal) seniority, that is, of giving elderly workers special protection. In some instances, early exit is enforced without regard to seniority claims; the elderly are (partly) "pushed out" of the labor market and thus deprived of their control over the process. However, this is not the case everywhere. For example, in France from 1977 to 1986 early retirement was not based on dismissal but on voluntary resignation. Individual choice was greatly "helped along" by attractive offers from the employers, of close to or even more than 100 percent of wages. (The provision for individual choice was removed in 1986; today the only way to enter a public early retirement scheme is through dismissal by the employer.) In Germany, the contracts – negotiated for the most part in the early 1970s – about special protection for elderly workers remain valid up to now, so that it remains impossible for employers to dismiss elderly workers on normal grounds. The only grounds allowed are either plant closings or failure of the workers to fulfill their contractual duties. The "normal" dismissal – already rather difficult for employers under the standard provisions of German work law – is precluded. This means that even under the preretirement program, elderly workers

---

[15] As an example, in the German chemical industry – whose preretirement program we have studied in detail (Kohli et al. 1989) – there has been no decline of the overall size of the work force, but there has been a large structural shift toward jobs demanding more highly qualified workers, both within production-line work and away from the latter toward laboratory work, making for a strong interest of firms in early exit.

could not be pushed out against their declared will, and the same applied (and still applies) to the unemployment pathway. Where early exit has not been more or less enforced by plant closings, it has been brought about by making the pathways advantageous to the workers. The available studies show that early exit is indeed very popular – a great majority of people want to exit early if given an acceptable way (both financially and morally) for doing so.

The fact that the protection for the elderly is still in place means that the incentives in terms of exit pathways have to be more convincing. Thus, control over the process is crucial. This has also been demonstrated with the opposition by employers to the preretirement program, which contributed to its not being renewed after its first five-year period. The resistance of the employers was motivated not only by the high direct costs that accrued to them but also by the fact that the workers were totally in control; they could not only resist exit but could also insist on it (if they were entitled to it under the rules) without the firm being able to deny it. If the firm wanted to retain a particular worker, it could do so only by making an offer that was so attractive that the worker himself or herself decided to stay on (cf. Kohli et al. 1989). Control by the workers translates into better conditions for them, and into higher transaction costs for the employers – both for early exit and for continued employment.

The same applies to the attempts to raise the normal retirement age. It is more advantageous for the workers to have it remain low, so that if the employers really need them, they have to make appropriate offers (in terms of income and attractive work places and working conditions). Where the limit is raised (as will be the case in Germany and the United States), the control shifts more to the employers; they can still shed their older workers (or – as far as the latter remain protected – buy them out) if they do not need them, but to the extent that they do need them, they have no difficulties (and no additional costs) in retaining them.

1.4.3   *Changing life-course patterns*

The changing patterns of exit from the labor force are redefining the boundary between work life and retirement, and thus the social meaning of old age. Accounting for early exit requires a theoretical framework that does not treat age boundaries as given; interest is directed at what goes on within these boundaries. What has in recent years become more generally evident in studies of youth, middle age, and old age is here put into focus: the necessity of contextualizing all such studies in a life-course framework.

The emerging sociology of the life course (cf. the overviews by Kohli and Meyer 1986 and Sorensen, Weinert, and Sherrod 1986) has already succeeded in denoting some of the ways by which the life course is socially constructed, and by which the various social actors contribute to this process. The new patterns of early exit from the labor force present a new challenge to this field; they draw attention to the changing organization of work in society, and thus call for concepts that are articulated with the key dimensions of social structure.

These dimensions relate to the modern ("capitalist" or "industrial") organization of work and its impact on all aspects of social life, in other words, to the fact that modern societies can be theoretically conceived as "work societies" (e.g., Offe 1983). The impact of work is highlighted by contrasting the basic perspectives of economics and sociology (cf. Kohli 1988). For the former, the economy is a system that organizes labor and capital with a view toward the production of goods, and accordingly effects the distribution of income and well-being. For sociology, the economy is a system that "socializes" people by providing them with income and corresponding chances for consumption, but also by confronting them with systematic tasks and challenging their competence, by structuring their everyday routines, by integrating them into social relations (of cooperation as well as of dependence and conflict), by locating them in the social fabric, and by shaping their identity. This is why the distribution of gainful work – who takes part in it and how – is of critical importance.

As shown in Chapter 2, retirement as a stage of life is a rather new historical phenomenon: It slowly became generalized since the end of the nineteenth century and only attained its full expansion in the 1960s. This evolution is part of the broader historical process of the past two centuries that we have termed the "institutionalization of the life course" (Kohli 1986). This process, witnessed by Western societies in a surprisingly uniform fashion, basically consists of three aspects: (1) the emergence of continuity in the sense of a reliable life span with material security; (2) the emergence of an orderly and chronologically standardized sequence of life phases and transitions; and (3) the emergence of a code of personal agency and development, in other words, a culturally objectified set of biographical perspectives.

The life course has become an important social institution – not in the sense of a social grouping (an aggregate of individuals) but in the sense of a pattern of social rules ordering a key dimension of life. The descriptive evidence for this process comes from a wide range of fields, from the demographic and family regime to work careers, to the age-grading produced by the state (e.g., by the systems of schooling and social security), and finally, to the history of mentalities and discourse, including the history of literary genres such as autobiographical writing.

The modern life course thus consists of a standardization of life events, keyed to chronological age. There are formal rules about the chronology of life, such as those linked with citizenship and public welfare; but there is also a decreasing age variance of other events such as those of the family cycle. Moreover, these events have become more prevalent, applying to increasingly larger parts of the population. The result has been a comprehensive life-course regime with a well-ordered sequential life program that is rather homogeneous and general, even though still stratified according to class and especially gender.

In a sociological perspective, the growing importance of chronological age is an unexpected and puzzling trend. Whatever our quarrels with modernization theory, we are used to viewing modernization in terms of a replacement of criteria of ascription by criteria of achievement; and age, like gender, is (mostly) an ascriptive criterion. On a normative level, this is clearly at odds with the modern emphasis on universalism – a contradiction that has become the basis for the age-discrimination legislation in the United States. It is even more at odds with the (postmodern) dislike for any chronological "prison" and the preference for "flexible life scheduling" (Best 1980) or "time sovereignty."

The institutionalization of the life course is an essential part of the societal process of individualization, that is, the process in which the individuals have become the main units of social life. Social order has become less a matter of being attached to the bonds of status and locality, and more a matter of the newly emerging life-course programs. In other words, persons have become much more mobile in all respects, but their passage through the social structure follows a predictable course, at least as concerns the basic temporal markers of life.

This account of the historical institutionalization of the life course, although very general and thus rather crude, is basically supported by a large number of studies on various dimensions and with various methodologies. But while there is wide agreement as to the description of this process, there is some disagreement as to its explanation, centering again on the relative importance of the economy and the polity. On the one hand, emphasis is put on the state as the key producer of the institutionalization of the life course (Mayer and Müller 1986). On the other hand, and this seems more plausible to us (Kohli 1986), the change in life-course regime is explained by referring to the basic change in the organization of production, that is, the transition from a household economy to an economy based on free labor recruited from labor markets. This means, among other things, that work and family career are no longer one, and that the succession to positions in the economy is no longer confined to the personnel available in the household but has to be organized in terms of the interface between internal and external labor markets. For the firm, the problem becomes one of integrating its own organizational timetable with the life course of the individual. The result has been a normalized biography, produced by the institutions of work and welfare and at the same time representing the model to which they are keyed. In this view, the emergence of the public systems of schooling and retirement – systems that define and standardize childhood, adolescence, and old age – is a response to these structural changes in economic production.

By the 1960s, retirement for men had become a normal feature of the life course, a taken-for-granted part of one's biography. The modern tripartition of the life course into a period of preparation, one of "active" work, and one of retirement had become firmly established. Old age had become synonymous with the period of retirement: a life phase structurally set apart from "active" work life and with a relatively uniform beginning defined by the retirement age limit as set by the public old-age pension system. With the increasing labor force participation of women, they too have increasingly been incorporated into this life-course regime.[16]

Early exit from the labor force has changed this schedule considerably and thus has led to new lifetime budgets. As an example, the median age of exit (as measured by the aggregate labor force participation rates) for men in Germany between 1960 and 1986 has dropped by about five years (from 65 to 60) (see Chapter 2). During the same period, their mean life expectancy at age 60 has increased by almost two years (from 15.5 to 17.3 years), with the result that the mean duration of retirement has increased by about two-thirds.

The consequences of this change of schedule can be traced in a number of issues. The first is whether the change amounts to a "de-institutionalization" of the later half of life, in other words, to a reversal of the secular trend toward increasing chronological standardization that occurred until the mid-1960s. If so, it would correspond to changes in other domains; there is mounting evidence that, beginning in the late

---

[16] There is also a moral dimension to this process, referring to the basic conceptions of justice and reciprocity that underly the normal labor contract. It is in this sense that one may speak of retirement as a cornerstone of the "moral economy" of modern Western societies (cf. Kohli 1987). Retirement is not viewed as a "risk" of the labor market, to be avoided as long as possible, but has come to be viewed as a right that can legitimately be claimed after a long working life. Public pension systems now guarantee this right to some extent by providing for an old-age income that is (more or less) continuous with former work income, usually clearly above the levels of minimal social assistance.

1960s, the process of institutionalization of the life course has come to a halt or even been reversed – a process most dramatically evident in the domain of family life events. In some respects, such de-institutionalization is clearly occurring here: The variation in the timing of the transition to retirement has increased, and the transition is less clear-cut not only on the aggregate level but also on that of the individual. This is especially obvious where individual-level data have been studied, that is, for the United States (cf. Hayward, Grady, and McLaughlin 1988). The transition is now less a matter of following a well-institutionalized and largely self-evident normative schedule, and becomes more a matter of personal timing. Also, transitions from "retirement" back into some form of gainful work seem to increase, although there is still considerable disagreement on the frequency of such countertransitions, depending not only on the data source but also on how "retirement" is defined, with some authors stressing that countertransitions are fairly frequent (e.g., Burkhauser and Quinn 1989), whereas others find them to be so rare as to be negligible (e.g., Tuma and Sandefur 1988).[17]

What are the consequences for overall life-course scheduling? Such consequences are less obvious than for the transitional period itself, and more open to controversy. In contrast to the assessment given in the concluding chapter, it seems to us that the basic tripartition of the life course is still firmly in place. The transition to retirement has become longer and fuzzier,[18] but it is still a transition between two very distinct states. Most

[17] The American pattern of reentry into work can be contrasted with the Japanese pattern of institutionally defined reemployment after exit from "lifetime" employment in the core segment of the labor market, that is, the large firms (cf. Jacobs and Rein 1990). In most of the large firms, there is a mandatory retirement age, which is usually five years below the age at which an individual is eligible for a public pension. At this so-called "teinen" age, the firms release virtually all regular workers and pay them a lump-sum retirement allowance as compensation, which, however, is almost never sufficient to live on by itself. For most workers there is therefore a strong economic need to continue working after the "teinen" age (a need that is supplemented by a strong normative commitment to work). In 1982, about half of the firms with mandatory retirement rules had some sort of reemployment system where workers are reassigned – albeit with lower job and wage levels than before – to other jobs in the same firm or to an affiliate of the firm. The other two possibilities for continued working after the "teinen" age are self-employment or employment in smaller firms with no association to the former employer.

[18] The same applies to the transition between education and work. In countries like the United States, the labor force participation of men aged 16 to 24 has changed very little between 1965 and 1988, although the proportion of men continuing their education has increased strongly. Part of the explanation is that more men have to combine work and schooling because the opportunities for public subsidies have declined. By contrast, in France, for example, the labor force participation of men aged 16 to 24 has declined from almost 70 percent to well below 50 percent. This suggests that more men have managed to postpone work, and to pursue a full-time educational career.

people at age 55 and below still work, and most people at age 65 and beyond do not; most people below 55 gain most of their income from work, and most people beyond 65 gain most their income from retirement pensions. Thus, there is little evidence so far that the "education-work-retirement-lockstep" (Best 1980) is breaking up. One can even argue that life-course segmentation has become more important in relation to other lines of segmentation such as gender. The work life has been shortened, but at the same time it has become more pervasive as regards women. In Germany, for example, the overall (ages 15 to 65) labor force participation rate of women has remained about the same during the last 20 years, but this masks the fact of a substantial increase (by about a third) during the core adult period (ages 25 to 55). Thus, the labor-market regime has become more inclusive and homogeneous in terms of gender, while at the same time it has become more exclusive and heterogeneous in life-course terms, with longer periods wholly outside of gainful work.

This is not to say that there is no change of retirement in general. With the lengthening of retirement, it is not only the transitional phase that is "individualized" to some extent but the period of retirement as a whole. It becomes more of a personal challenge: It changes from a restricted left-over period, to be lived through without much ambition, to a significant new period of life, to be filled by new projects (for which there are as yet few valid cultural guidelines). This can be seen as the ultimate achievement of the right to retirement. There is a range of activity patterns open to individual choice; even reentry into work becomes an option. At the same time, however, the idea of continuity of income guaranteed by public pensions becomes more difficult to realize (and to legitimate).

Another change concerns the impact of the lengthening of retirement on productivity. This is a multifaceted problem that cannot be fully treated here, but one point can be made: Retirement need not be seen as wholly irrelevant to economic production. The labor force participation data mark the boundary of taking part in the *formal* economy, but do not indicate economically relevant activity as such. An interesting case in this respect is that of Hungary (cf. Chapter 10): Before the recent changes, "retirement" basically meant a transition from the first (state-controlled) to the second (private, less-institutionalized) economy. This transition has mostly been viewed as a positive event, resulting in more autonomy as well as a chance to gain more money, with the state conceding the possibility to make the transition rather early as a measure of social pacification. In many Western countries, informal production – referred to by terms such as "gray" or "shadow economy" – is also considerable, and its relevance seems to be growing. In addition, there is a wide range of unpaid activities, from home and neighborhood production to volunteer work in formal organizations, that are to some extent similar to gainful work. While this similarity is sometimes exaggerated, the former disregard for the productive value of these activities is now being rectified, most clearly for the work done by housewives, and increasingly also for that done by the elderly (cf. Herzog et al. 1989). And the structural importance of these activities is growing as the time taken up by gainful work is shrinking. Thus, early exit itself is likely to contribute to a higher salience of nongainful work, thereby blurring somewhat the qualitative boundary between work and retirement.

The second issue, which needs to be discussed in greater detail, is whether there is some replacement of age criteria for retirement by functional criteria (cf. Neugarten 1982), which would again mean a decreased role of chronological age in organizing the life course. The pension system has made it easier to withdraw from work in three different ways.[19] The first and most obvious way is by lowering the pension age. Sweden has lowered the normal age of retirement from 67 to 65, and France has lowered it from 65 to 60. Of course, this process is reversible, and in some countries, like the United States, Japan, and Germany, a gradual raising of the retirement age spaced out over the next decades has been decided on. In most countries the normal legal age for retirement, however, remains 65.

Another way is through the introduction of early old-age public pensions. Sweden, Germany, and the United States introduced legislation in the 1970s to make it possible for individuals to retire below the normal retirement age: at age 63 in Germany, 62 in the United States, and 60 in Sweden. Thus, what is still "normal" in legal–administrative terms has become rather exceptional in behavioral terms. In Sweden and the United States, using this early-exit route leads to an actuarial reduction for the entire duration of the receipt of the pension. In Germany, there is also some financial penalty for using the flexible retirement route – as

---

[19] A key question in this respect is how retirement (in the sense of receiving an old-age pension) and work (in the sense of gaining a work income) can or cannot be combined. In some countries (such as France), pensioners were permitted to work without penalty, while in others (such as the United States) there were work tests that permitted only some part-time work without loss of benefits. These rules have changed. In the United States, work tests have been liberalized, and there is pressure to eliminate them altogether. In 1989 Great Britain introduced a rule change that permits retirees to work without loss of benefits. France has moved in the opposite direction by imposing a work test that now denies or limits benefits to those who gain work incomes. In the Netherlands and Germany, those who retire at age 65 are free to work as much as they want without financial penalty. It is, however, customary for work contracts to end when retirement formally begins, so that the "life jobs" can usually not be continued into retirement. Still, the fact that so few retirees work despite the absence of any work test is highly significant.

it is called – but it is much lower than what would correspond to an actuarial reduction (see the chapters on individual countries for details).

The third way is to create special groups that can retire below the legally defined normal retirement age. For example, in Germany, three groups are identified: women (whose flexible retirement starts at age 60), the handicapped, and the unemployed. If older workers are severely handicapped, or have been unemployed for at least one year, they can enter the pension system at age 60. In some countries, there is at present a pressure to equalize the treatment of women, in line with the more general questioning of gender inequality. To achieve equity, a country must either raise the age of retirement for women or lower it for men.

Even though these rule changes have contributed to lowering the age of access to public pensions, the trend toward earlier exit has also had the effect that individuals spend more time in transitional programs outside of the normal (or flexible) old-age pension system. Such intermediary programs become more important for managing the exit process, which in itself may be interpreted as a transformation of the meaning of chronological age. If, however, one examines each intermediary program in context, some countertendencies also emerge.

The main intermediary public programs include disability, sickness, preretirement, unemployment, and means-tested public assistance (sometimes referred to as social help, supplementary benefits, or welfare). Chronological age remains, of course, directly relevant in preretirement. But age is also increasingly important in unemployment and disability. For example, in Great Britain, an unemployed man over 60 who has received unemployment benefits and is in need is entitled to receive public assistance (now called income support). Since 1982, the benefits he receives are based on the assumption that his age automatically determines his status as a long-term beneficiary, by which he is entitled to substantially higher benefits than those who are short-term recipients (such as the young unemployed). These older individuals are no longer required to register as unemployed in order to obtain credits toward their retirement pension at age 65. In Germany, the older long-term unemployed can enter the public pension system at age 60. In the Netherlands, an older unemployed worker is able to move from unemployment insurance for six months to unemployment assistance at the minimum wage level for two years. In all these examples, older unemployed workers are treated as a separate category as age becomes the decisive factor in redefining eligibility. Age is thus combined with functional criteria in regulating the exit process.

Age also enters into the disability programs by way of special rules for older workers. In Sweden, for example, since 1972 the receipt of a disability pension no longer requires medical justification for unemployed persons above age 63 (and since 1974, above age 60). Older workers who have exhausted their unemployment benefits and are unable to find a job in the work they customarily did can also be eligible for a disability pension. On the other hand, the local social insurance program can take the initiative for securing a disability pension for those who are sick, since the sickness benefits are more generous than the disability benefits, and this is most likely to happen with older workers. In other countries, there are retraining programs to reintegrate the disabled into work, and they usually have an implicit age standard: Older workers are seldom eligible to participate.

A further example is provided by Germany, where a rule change introduced by the courts has resulted in elderly workers being considered "disabled" for all practical purposes of the labor market with even fairly minimal impairments. It has not really been a return to the old assumption (valid at the time of Bismarck) that age per se is a disabling condition, but the relation to work capacity has been eased by assuming that with some disability, the elderly will no longer be able to find work. Thus, functional criteria certainly remain important in disability, but with disability becoming a major pathway of early exit from work, these criteria have been eased in favor of introducing some age criteria. In other words, to accommodate disability to early exit, age criteria have been grafted onto it.[20]

It is thus not entirely clear that the fact that the institutions of retirement proper are losing some of their control of the exit process will result in the destruction of the tripartite model of the life course. The process of instrument substitution can be viewed in a different perspective: as a story not of institutional breakdown and failure but of institutional success – success in keeping up the sequential program of the life course at least in its basic structure by creatively using welfare instruments other than merely old-age pensions. To take up a term used before, the process is one of institutional "bricolage" which redefines these other instruments so that they are able to manage the exit process.

---

[20] The extensive use of disability as an exit pathway has now led some countries to attempt to discourage its long-term use. In the Netherlands until now, a disabled worker could get 70 percent of the last gross income, which meant that he or she was assured of a similar net income when at work or in receipt of disability. This has been a strong incentive to become disabled. In new disability legislation introduced in 1990, the structure of disability benefits will become similar to that of unemployment benefits – the longer the lower, until an individual reaches the level of the minimum wage. The new ruling is however still age-related: current beneficiaries over age 45 are exempt from it.

A final issue concerns the moral dimensions of early exit. They are obviously more difficult to measure than behavioral variables such as labor force participation, but are nonetheless an essential part of reality. Some individuals seem to comply closely with the economists' model of humanity by being interested in material resources only, but for many others, questions of moral legitimacy also are crucial. The three most important transitional pathways – unemployment, disability, and pre-retirement – seem to have very different personal and social meaning. Preretirement programs are usually voluntary, and although there may have been some initial hesitation about their advantages and disadvantages, their legitimacy has been reinforced as they have become "normalized," so that participation has strongly increased. Exit through unemployment can be very demoralizing, especially for individuals who have never been unemployed before and take pride in that fact. They face the end of their career with a sense of not having satisfactorily completed their work life, in other words, of being denied a decent ending. On the other hand, some individuals quit voluntarily because they feel the work situation is too frustrating and unrewarding. The disability pathway often involves emotional as well as physical exhaustion; on the other hand, poor health is a legitimate rationale for retirement, even in work-oriented societies.

It is thus not only the adequacy of resources, but also the legitimacy of the pathway, in other words, its potential for stigmatization or social respect, that determine its impact on later well-being. Moreover, many studies of the exit process demonstrate the importance of the age boundary as a point of reference in the life course. For most individuals, there is a "normal" time to end one's working career, and exit before this standardized point of reference creates uncertainty and apprehension. When more and more people leave before the standardized age, however, a process of social redefinition of the appropriate age boundary is set in motion.

1.4.4   *Social stratification: class and gender*

The preceding discussion has shown that the early-exit pathways have different outcomes in terms of income and moral meaning. To the extent that access to the pathways is distributed unevenly, the outcomes are also pertinent to social stratification. The effects of early exit on social stratification are visible most sharply in those countries where there is a rather low baseline of social protection, and supplements by firms for private pension arrangements are widespread. A system of stratification arises when some groups receive only the baseline and others receive the supplement – the "two nations" of the elderly, as they have been called in the British case (e.g., Walker 1986). In some countries, like the United States, a substantial proportion of older workers who have stopped working before 62 (the age of eligibility for public old-age pensions) have neither a private nor a public pension; they have no visible sources of income other than their own private savings, gray work, or the income of their families (Rein, unpublished CPS 1988 data). In those countries, on the other hand, where the exit pathways provide for a replacement rate of public benefits relative to previous work incomes, as in Germany, there is probably less stratification because there is less reliance upon private supplementary programs.

The exit process, moreover, affects stratification according to who exits early. In Great Britain, it appears to be primarily concentrated among blue-collar workers. This is not surprising because the main exit program makes extensive use of low benefits and means-tested programs. In the Netherlands, a more heterogeneous combination of stratified exit pathways is found. Two-thirds of blue-collar workers exit through disability, while among civil servants and white-collar workers, exit occurs mainly by way of supplementary schemes contracted through collective bargaining.

Another dimension of stratification that needs to be stressed is gender – a topic long neglected in retirement research (cf. Gordon 1988:102). We have said that the labor-market regime has become more inclusive and homogeneous in this respect, but "more" does not mean "completely"; gender differences remain important, especially among the older cohorts of women (cf. O'Rand 1988; Allmendinger, Brückner, and Brückner 1989). On the one hand, early-exit pathways are less important for women because of the practice in most countries of a split pension-age regime, with women often being eligible to draw a retirement pension five years earlier than men. Split pension-age regimes, which were first introduced in the 1940s,[21] are mainly based on the argument that given the mean age difference in marriage, this would allow working couples to enter retirement together (Ehmer 1990:116f). The desire to avoid role reversal – husband at home and wife at work – has evidently been very strong. (In fact, with the five-year difference a substantial error margin was introduced, since the mean age difference between marriage partners is usually less.) The introduction of preretirement schemes has often meant an equalization of age of eligibility, which for many couples has posed new difficulties in their attempts to synchronize their exit from

---

[21] In 1944, the International Labor Organisation recommended to its member states that the normal pension age be set at 65 for men and 60 for women.

work, and has forced some of them into unintended experiments in role reversal, with pressure to change the division of labor in the household (Kohli et al. 1989). In the United States, where there is no split pension-age regime, it has been amply demonstrated that a major determinant of retirement age for married women is the link to their husband's retirement, again documenting the widespread wish to avoid role reversal (see Chapter 8).

On the other hand, women's work careers have been, and continue to be, characterized by lower incomes, more interruptions, and more part-time work, which in many systems has severely negative consequences for their pension claims. This also may affect their eligibility for a lower pension age and their access to early-exit pathways. Before women can retire early with a public pension, they must earn some entitlement. In most systems this means some minimum number of years of work, often including recent work experience. A cohort perspective is essential here. Younger cohorts of women increasingly follow the male life-course model. They enter training and then work without substantial interruption during their prime years, much as the men do. An important reason for not exiting from work for long periods to raise children is that the opportunities to reenter work in a tight labor market are restricted. With such continuous work, they gain the eligibility to retire early. By contrast, older cohorts have followed more the traditional "M" curve of exit and reentry after the child rearing years. They need then to work longer before having access to retirement pensions or to some other exit pathway. This may explain the cohort crossover pattern of exit that holds, for example, in Germany and France (cf. Chapter 2).

1.4.5   *Intergenerational redistribution and conflict*

In conclusion, it should be recalled that early exit sharpens the issues of intergenerational exchange and redistribution – issues whose salience has become dramatically evident with the prospect of population aging and the financial squeeze of the welfare state. In the public discourse, these issues are increasingly greeted with alarming overtones: "The rapid ageing of the populations of all industrial countries over the next forty years will be an economic and social transformation of vastly greater magnitude than the 1970s oil price shock or the 1980s recession" (Johnson et al. 1989:1).

In the light of these prospects, early exit on first sight seems highly undesirable. As we have seen, several countries are now attempting to reverse the trend by raising the age limits of their public pension systems. However, the pressures of the labor market have so far counteracted these attempts. As noted above, there are conflicting views on how to evaluate this situation. On the one hand, early exit is seen as an involuntary exclusion and "marginalization" of the elderly resulting from practices of age discrimination. This view is widespread among old-age interest groups and among the gerontological research community. On the other hand, early exit under some conditions is highly popular among the older workers themselves, and there is, moreover, a widespread sentiment that the redistribution of work from the elderly to the young is indeed a legitimate and even positive goal if coupled with adequate social security provisions, in other words, with a matching redistribution of income from the young to the old. The issues of early exit thus lead into the heart of the "generational contract" of our societies (cf. Kohli 1987) – which is a "contract" first about access to and obligation to work, and only secondly about resource transfers.

Of course, this poses the question of its viability – of whether the required resource transfers are and will be still possible. Accordingly, one way that the issue of intergenerational conflict surfaces is in terms of welfare-state spending. This debate has been spurred especially by Preston (1984), who has argued that old people have been getting a larger and larger share of social spending, leaving fewer and fewer resources for other age groups, especially families with children. According to Preston, this is not only a threat to intergenerational equity but to our whole societal future; in order to invest more in children, the spending for the retired has to be cut down.

Although Preston's argument has been challenged in terms of causation (Easterlin 1987), his descriptive evidence has been supported by a more thorough examination (Palmer, Smeeding, and Torrey 1988), but the issue remains complicated and no single set of facts can resolve the debate. It is worth noting that the picture for Europe – as suggested by social protection statistics provided by the European community[22] – is somewhat different. Total social protection, including public and private spending for sickness, old age, family benefits, and unemployment insurance, is divided by the number of persons in the population, producing a measure of total benefits per head. We find that in Germany, 30.3 percent of benefits per head in 1975 were distributed for old age, 29.3 percent in 1980, and 28.7 percent in 1984. A similar decline is found in Great Britain where the figures were 43 percent in 1975, 40.6 percent in 1980, and rose slightly to 41.4 percent in 1984. In the Netherlands,

---

[22] Social Protection, Theme 3: Population and social conditions, Series F, Rapid Reports 2 (1986). Eurostat, European system of integrated social protection statistics (ESSPROS).

between 1975 and 1980 there was a decline from 29.4 percent to 28.2 percent. These data suggest that the Preston hypothesis about the increasingly privileged position of the aged may not apply. Evidently, if the data were more adequate and included a measure of the cost of early exit, this conclusion might have to be revised; but as far as the data go, they lend little support to the thesis of increasing intergenerational inequity.

Moreover, participants in the debate tend to overlook the issue of intergenerational redistribution of work; it would seem to make little sense in terms of the purported goals of raising the welfare of the young to keep older workers at work longer if this means fewer jobs for the young. This again shifts the terms of the debate to the labor market (cf. Kohli, forthcoming). In all aging societies, the supply of potential young entrants into the labor market is declining rapidly. It is usually argued that this will lead to a labor shortage – if not in aggregate numbers, then at least for some segments of the market. However, whether the elderly workers would indeed be absorbed by the labor market up to a substantially higher age than now is still an open question. It remains to be seen whether the effects of the demographic change will outweigh the effects of job loss through rationalization. And a possible labor shortage may be offset in other ways than by raising the age of exit from work, most notably, by migration: internal "migration" of women into the labor force (which is likely to continue), and immigration of workers from outside. In Germany, the events of the past two years have demonstrated the fragility of the assumption of a closed system (see Chapter 6); and Western Europe more generally is slowly coming to realize how difficult it will be to insulate these aging and rich populations from the pressures of mass migration.

If this perspective seems to offer little hope for integrating the growing elderly population into the main societal concerns, and at the same time for keeping the "generational contract" balanced, two points need to be recalled. On the one hand, early exit from formal work is not tantamount to exclusion from all meaningful activities; it may create the room for increasing rates of activities such as unpaid volunteer work, self-help activities, intensified household production, or more demanding "hobby" work. On the other hand, changing the intergenerational distribution of formal work by raising the age limit may become more easily possible in the long run through changes in labor policy over the whole life course, with shorter weekly and yearly working hours (reducing the labor supply) and regular schedules of requalification (increasing the human capital value of older workers); by these same changes, it may also become more generally acceptable.

REFERENCES

Achenbaum, W. Andrew. 1986. *Social Security: Visions and Revisions.* Cambridge/New York: Cambridge University Press.

Allmendinger, Jutta, Hannah Brückner, and Erika Brückner. 1989. *The Production of Gender Disparities in Old Age.* Frankfurt/Mannheim: Sonderforschungsbereich 3 (Working Paper No. 262).

Atchley, Robert C. 1976. *The Sociology of Retirement.* Cambridge: Schenkman.

—— 1985. "Social Security-Type Retirement Policies." In: Zena Smith Blau (ed.), *Current Perspectives on Aging and the Life Cycle.* Greenwich: JAI-Press, pp. 275–93.

Best, Fred. 1980. *Flexible Life Scheduling.* New York: Praeger.

Boaz, Rachel F. 1988. "Early Withdrawal from the Labor Force." *Research on Aging* 9:530–47.

Burkhauser, Richard V. 1980. "The Early Acceptance of Social Security: An Asset-Maximization Approach." *Industrial and Labor Relations Review* 33:484–92.

Burkhauser, Richard, and Joseph Quinn. 1989. "Work and Retirement: The American Experience." In: Winfried Schmähl (ed.), *Redefining the Process of Retirement: An International Perspective.* Berlin: Springer, pp. 91–113.

Casey, Bernard. 1989. "Early Retirement: The Problems of 'Instrument Substitution' and 'Cost Shifting' and Their Implications for Restructuring the Process of Retirement." In: Winfried Schmähl (ed.), *Redefining the Process of Retirement: An International Perspective.* Berlin: Springer, pp. 133–50.

Casey, Bernard, and Gert Bruche. 1983. *Work or Retirement? Labour Market and Social Policy for Older Workers in France, Great Britain, the Netherlands, Sweden and the USA.* Aldershot: Gower.

Easterlin, Richard A. 1987. "The New Age Structure of Poverty in America: Permanent or Transient?" *Population and Development Review* 13:195–208.

Ehmer, Josef. 1990. *Sozialgeschichte des Alters.* Frankfurt: Suhrkamp.

Ekerdt, David I., and Stanley Deviney. 1990. "On Defining Persons as Retired." *Journal of Aging Studies* 4:211–29.

Esping-Andersen, Gösta. 1990. *The Three Worlds of Welfare Capitalism.* Oxford: Polity Press.

Flora, Peter (ed.). 1986ff. *Growth to Limits: The Western European Welfare States since World War II,* 5 vols. Berlin: De Gruyter.

Gordon, Margaret S. 1988. *Social Security Policies in Industrial Countries: A Comparative Analysis.* Cambridge/New York: Cambridge University Press.

Guillemard, Anne-Marie. 1986. *Le déclin du social.* Paris: Presses Universitaires de France.

Habib, Jack. 1990. "Population Aging and the Economy." In: Robert B. Binstock and Linda K. George (eds.), *Handbook of Aging and the Social Sciences,* 3rd edition. New York: Academic Press, pp. 328–45.

Hayward, Mark D., William R. Grady, and Stephen D. McLaughlin. 1988.

"Recent Changes in Mortality and Labor Force Behavior among Older Americans." *Demography* 25:371–86.

Herzog, A. Regula, Robert L. Kahn, James N. Morgan, James S. Jackson, and Toni C. Antonucci. 1989. "Age differences in productive activities." *Journal of Gerontology* 44:S129–S138.

Hurd, Michael D. 1990. "Research on the Elderly: Economic Status, Retirement, and Consumption and Saving." *Journal of Economic Literature* 28:565–637.

Inkeles, Alex, and Chikako Usui. 1988. "The Retirement Decision in Cross-National Perspective." In: Rita Ricardo-Campbell and Edward P. Lazear (eds.), *Issues in Contemporary Retirement*. Stanford: Hoover Institution Press, pp. 273–311.

Jacobs, Klaus, and Martin Rein. 1990. *Labor markets and the process of early retirement*. Manuscript.

Johnson, Paul, Christoph Conrad, and David Thomson (eds.). 1989. "Introduction." In: *Workers versus Pensioners: Intergenerational Justice in an Aging World*. Manchester: Manchester University Press, pp. 1–16.

Kohli, Martin. 1986. "The World We Forgot: A Historical Review of the Life Course." In: Victor W. Marshall (ed.), *Later Life: The Social Psychology of Aging*. Beverly Hills: Sage, pp. 271–303.

1987. "Retirement and the Moral Economy: A Historical Interpretation of the German Case." *Journal of Aging Studies* 1:125–44.

1988. "Ageing as a Challenge for Sociological Theory." *Ageing and Society* 8:367–94.

Forthcoming. "Labor Market Perspectives and Activity Patterns of the Elderly in an Aging Society." In: Wim Van den Heuvel et al. (eds.), *Opportunities and Challenges in an Aging Society*. Amsterdam: Elsevier.

Kohli, Martin, Claudia Gather, Harald Künemund, Beate Mücke, Martina Schürkmann, Wolfgang Voges, and Jürgen Wolf. 1989. *Je früher – desto besser? Die Verkürzung des Erwerbslebens am Beispiel des Vorruhestandes in der chemischen Industrie*. Berlin: Edition Sigma.

Kohli, Martin, and John W. Meyer (eds.). 1986. "Social Structure and Social Construction of Life Stages." *Human Development* 29:145–80.

Kotlikoff, Laurence J. 1988. "The Relationship of Productivity to Age." In: Rita Ricardo-Campbell and Edward P. Lazear (eds.), *Issues in Contemporary Retirement*. Stanford: Hoover Institution Press, pp. 100–31.

Lazear, Edward P. 1979. "Why Is There Mandatory Retirement?" *Journal of Political Economy* 87:1261–84.

Mayer, Karl-Ulrich, and Walter Müller. 1986. "The State and the Structure of the Life Course." In: Aage B. Sorensen, Franz Weinert, and Lonnie R. Sherrod (eds.), *Human Development and the Life Course: Multidisciplinary Perspectives*. Hillsdale: Erlbaum, pp. 217–45.

Mirkin, Barry A. 1987. "Early Retirement as a Labor Force Policy: An International Overview." *Monthly Labor Review*, March, pp. 19–33.

Myles, John. 1984. *Old Age in the Welfare State: The Political Economy of Public Pensions*. Boston: Little, Brown.

Neugarten, Bernice (ed.). 1982. *Age or Need? Public Policies for Older People.* Beverly Hills: Sage.

Offe, Claus. 1983. "Arbeit als soziologische Schlüsselkategorie?" In: Joachim Matthes (ed.), *Krise der Arbeitsgesellschaft?* Frankfurt: Campus, S. 38–65.

O'Rand, Angela M. 1988. "Convergence, Institutionalization, and Bifurcation: Gender and the Pension Acquisition Process." *Annual Review of Gerontology and Geriatrics* 8:132–55.

Palmer, John L., Timothy Smeeding, and Barbara Boyle Torrey (eds.). 1988. *The Vulnerable.* Washington: The Urban Institute Press.

Palmore, Erdman, B., et al. 1985. *Retirement: Causes and Consequences.* New York: Springer.

Pampel, Fred C. 1985. "Determinants of Labor Force Participation Rates of Aged Males in Developed and Developing Nations, 1965–1975." In: Zena Smith Blau (ed.), *Current Perspectives on Aging and the Life Course,* vol. 1. Greenwich: JAI Press, pp. 243–74.

Pampel, Fred C., and Jane A. Weiss. 1983. "Economic Development, Pension Policies, and the Labor Force Participation of Aged Males: A Cross-National, Longitudinal Approach." *American Journal of Sociology* 89:350–72.

Pampel, Fred C., and John B. Williamson. 1989. *Age, Class, Politics, and the Welfare State.* Cambridge/New York: Cambridge University Press.

Phillipson, Chris. 1982. *Capitalism and the Construction of Old Age.* London: Macmillan.

Preston, Samuel H. 1984. "Children and the Elderly: Divergent Paths for America's Dependents." *Demography* 21:435–57.

Rainwater, Lee, and Martin Rein (eds.). Forthcoming. *Social Policy and Labor Markets.* Boston: Sharpe.

Reimers, C., and M. Honig. 1989. "The Retirement Process in the United States: Mobility Among Full-Time Work, Partial Retirement, and Full Retirement." In: Winfried Schmähl (ed.), *Redefining the Process of Retirement: An International Perspective.* Berlin: Springer, pp. 115–31.

Rein, Martin. 1985. *Women in the Social Welfare Labor Market.* Berlin: WZB working papers.

Sorensen, Aage B. Forthcoming. "Retirement, Individual Performance and Labor Market Structures." In: Wim Van den Heuvel et al. (eds.), *Opportunities and Challenges in an Aging Society.* Amsterdam: Elsevier.

Sorensen, Aage B., Franz Weinert, and Lonnie R. Sherrod (eds.). 1986. *Human Development and the Life Course: Multidisciplinary Perspectives.* Hillsdale: Erlbaum.

Talaga, Jean, and Terry A. Beehr. 1989. "Retirement: A Psychological Perspective." In: C. L. Cooper and I. Robertson (eds.), *International Review of Industrial and Organizational Psychology.* New York: Wiley, pp. 185–211.

Tuma, Nancy B., and Gary D. Sandefur. 1988. "Trends in the Labor Force Activity of the Elderly in the United States, 1940–1980." In: Rita Ricardo-Campbell and Edward P. Lazear (eds.), *Issues in Contemporary Retirement.* Stanford: Hoover Institution Press, pp. 38–83.

Walker, Alan. 1986. "Pensions and the Production of Poverty in Old Age." In: Chris Phillipson and Alan Walker (eds.), *Ageing and Social Policy. A Critical Assessment.* Aldershot: Gower, pp. 184–216.

Wise, David A. Forthcoming. "A Firm Pension Policy in Early Retirement." In: Tony Atkinson and Martin Rein (eds.), *Age, Work, and Social Security.* New York: Macmillan.

CHAPTER 2

The evolution of early exit: A comparative analysis of labor force participation patterns

KLAUS JACOBS, MARTIN KOHLI, AND MARTIN REIN

2.1 INTRODUCTION

OVER the past two decades, the age of exit from the labor force in Western societies has decreased dramatically. In this chapter, we document this evolution in detail to provide the empirical background for the following chapters on individual countries. We first take a look at the long-term development of labor force participation in the six Western countries that are included in our study; then we examine the process of early exit since the late 1960s on the basis of year-to-year data. Since many older workers leave their work life via unemployment, labor force participation rates (which include the unemployed) still underestimate the real extent of exit, which makes it necessary, as a third step, to describe the process of exit in terms of age-specific employment activity rates (excluding the unemployed). For reasons of demographic discontinuity, cross-sectional data may lead to somewhat distorted results; as a final step, we therefore analyze the exit process in a cohort perspective for countries where the appropriate data are available. The cohort analysis also is indispensable for clarifying the more complicated picture for women.

2.2 LONG-TERM EXIT TRENDS

Before going into the analysis of exit patterns over the past two decades, it is necessary to take a look at their long-term evolution. Data on labor force participation in the first half of this century (or even earlier) are scarce. Because of different definitions and age brackets, they do not exist in a form that allows easy comparison across countries. Even for single

36

countries, they are available only in rough age breakdowns, and these have sometimes been changed over time. Nevertheless, these data allow some broad conclusions.

The long-term development of labor force participation rates in France, Germany, Sweden, the United Kingdom, and the United States is shown in Table 2.1. For all of these countries, we can see that from the beginning of the century until about 1970, retirement among men has become much more prevalent, and the age of exit has increasingly clustered around 65. Labor force participation of men over 65 dropped from 66.6 percent (France, 1896), 47.4 percent (Germany, 1925), 62.1 percent (Sweden, 1910), 56.8 percent (United Kingdom, 1911), and 68.4 percent (United States, 1990) to around 20 percent in 1970 (about 25 percent in Sweden and the United States).[1] During this period, labor force participation of men aged 60 to 64 has – with some fluctuation – remained fairly high. The largest decline for this age group was in France (from 85.1 percent in 1906 to 68.0 percent in 1970), but there were only small declines in Germany, Sweden, and the United States (from 79.7 percent in 1925, 85.5 percent in 1930, and 79.0 percent in 1940, respectively, to still clearly above 70 percent in these three countries in 1970), and no decline at all in the United Kingdom (with a high rate of 86.7 percent in 1970). In countries for which appropriate measurement points are available, the downward fluctuations were largest during the Great Depression (France in 1936, Germany in 1933).

Thus, up to the end of the 1960s, retirement for men had become a normal feature of the life course, a taken-for-granted part of one's biography. The modern tripartition of the life course into a period of preparation, one of "active" work, and one of retirement had become firmly established. Old age had become synonymous with the period of retirement: a life phase structurally set apart from active work life, with a relatively uniform beginning defined by the retirement age limit as set by the public old-age pension scheme.[2] This is part of a much broader historical process – what we have termed the "institutionalization of the life course" (Kohli 1986a, 1986b): a process of chronologically standardizing

---

[1] In the Netherlands (which is not included in Table 2.1 because of missing data for the age groups below 65), the labor force participation of men over 65 dropped from 57.8 percent in 1909 to 19.9 percent in 1960 and to less than 10 percent in the early 1970s.

[2] In Germany, for example, the first statutory retirement age was established with the Bismarckian old-age and disability pension scheme for blue-collar and low-earning white-collar workers in 1891; the age limit for receiving an old-age pension was set at 70 years. A new pension insurance scheme for all white-collar workers became effective in 1913, with an age limit of 65; in 1916, the retirement age for all workers was generally set at age 65, which seems to have been adopted by most other nations as well.

Table 2.1. Long-term development of labor force participation rates

France

Year	Men 50–54	55–59	60–64	65–69	65+	Women 50–54	55–59	60–64	65–69	65+
1896	/[a]	——86.4——		/	66.6	/	——32.2——		/	24.9
1901	/	——88.1——		/	65.6	/	——39.6——		/	23.5
1906	——91.8——		85.1	78.0	/	——50.4——		44.4	37.8	/
1911	93.5	89.2	83.4	/	65.6	51.0	48.3	43.4	/	27.7
1921	95.1	91.7	85.7	78.6	/	54.0	51.6	47.0	41.0	/
1926	94.2	89.2	82.4	73.8	/	47.8	44.8	39.9	33.5	/
1931	93.8	88.4	80.7	71.9	/	48.0	44.8	38.9	32.2	/
1936	91.0	83.2	74.0	65.4	/	46.1	42.2	36.4	29.0	/
1946	93.1	85.4	76.3	66.5	/	50.2	46.1	40.1	31.3	/
1954	94.0	82.0	69.6	49.3	/	46.8	42.0	33.5	20.2	/
1962	93.0	83.5	67.9	36.5	/	45.3	41.5	31.9	16.9	/
1970	/	82.9	68.0	/	19.5	/	46.0	34.3	/	8.6
1985	/	67.8	30.8	/	5.3	/	42.8	18.9	/	2.2

Germany

Men

Year	50–54	55–59	60–64	65–69	65+
1882	91.5	(91.5)	79.3	(79.3)	/
1895	92.4	(92.4)	75.3	(75.3)	/
1907	90.4	(90.4)	71.2	(71.2)	/
1925	92.4	(92.4)	79.7	/	47.4
1933	86.9	(86.9)	67.0	/	29.7
1939	89.7	(89.7)	71.4	/	29.5
1950	93.4	87.4	73.0	/	26.8
1961	93.9	88.9	73.0	/	22.9
1970	/	88.4	71.8	/	17.2
1985	/	76.2	32.4	/	5.1

Women

Year	50–54	55–59	60–64	65–69	65+
1882	24.9	(24.9)	22.2	(22.2)	/
1895	26.5	(26.5)	22.5	(22.5)	/
1907	36.6	(36.6)	30.1	(30.1)	/
1925	37.3	(37.3)	31.9	/	17.6
1933	34.8	(34.8)	27.0	/	13.1
1939	36.9	(36.9)	28.0	/	14.0
1950	33.9	29.4	21.2	/	9.7
1961	37.8	32.5	21.1	/	8.4
1970	/	36.4	20.4	/	6.1
1985	/	35.9	10.1	/	2.3

Sweden

Men

Year	50–54	55–59	60–64	65–69	70–74	75+
1910	91.8	(91.8)	82.7	(82.7)	62.1	(62.1)
1920	95.3	(95.3)			47.1	(47.1)
1930	94.7	(94.7)	84.5	71.5	41.5	(41.5)
1940	94.9	91.5	79.8	59.8	/	/
1950	94.1	(94.1)	69.2	(69.2)	23.7	(23.7)
1960	/	92.3	82.5	50.6	20.3	7.3
1970	/	90.8	79.5		28.9	
1985	/	87.6	65.1		11.0	

Women

Year	50–54	55–59	60–64	65–69	70–74	75+
1910	17.2	(17.2)	18.0	(18.0)	11.3	(11.3)
1920	23.6	(23.6)			10.6	(10.6)
1930	26.0	(26.0)	21.0	17.0	11.0	(11.0)
1940	25.1	22.1	17.1	12.9	/	/
1950	28.1	(28.1)	15.7	(15.7)	5.4	(5.4)
1960	/	31.3	21.1	9.6	2.8	1.0
1970	/	52.8	35.8		8.7	
1985	/	74.5	46.6		3.2	

Table 2.1. (cont.)

	United Kingdom									
	Men					Women				
	45–54	55–59	60–64	65–69	70+	45–54	55–59	60–64	65–69	70+
1911		——94.1——		——56.8——			——21.6——		——11.5——	
1921	96.8	——91.9——		79.8	41.2	20.7	——19.1——		15.1	6.5
1931	96.7	94.1	87.6	65.4	33.4	21.0	18.8	16.3	12.2	5.5
1951	97.9	95.4	87.8	48.7	20.9	34.0	27.7	14.4	9.0	3.2
1961	98.6	97.1	91.0	39.9	15.2	43.3	36.9	20.4	10.3	3.1
1970	97.5	95.3	86.7	——20.1——		59.4	50.1	27.9	——6.4——	
1985	92.1	81.8	54.5	——8.2——		69.1	51.6	18.6	——3.0——	

United States

	Men				Women			
	45–54	55–59	60–64	65+	45–54	55–59	60–64	65+
1890		——95.2——		73.8	——12.6——			8.3
1900	95.5	——90.0——		68.4	14.7	——13.2——		9.1
1910		——92.1——		63.5	——16.2——			8.9
1920		——93.8——		60.2	——17.1——			8.0
1930	96.5	——90.2——		58.3	20.4	——16.1——		8.0
1940	92.0	87.9	79.0	41.8	22.5	18.5	14.8	6.1
1950	92.0	86.7	79.4	41.4	32.9	25.9	20.6	7.8
1960	93.3	87.7	77.8	30.6	46.7	39.7	29.4	10.4
1970	93.2	88.3	71.7	25.7	54.2	48.8	34.8	9.0
1985	90.4	78.9	55.1	15.2	64.2	50.1	33.2	6.8

^aData not available.

Sources: Until the early 1960s: "The Working Population and its Structure", Brussels, 1968 (the German data for 1939 are taken from "Bevölkerung und Wirtschaft 1872–1972"); from 1970 onward: OECD Labour Force Statistics, Paris, 1989.

the sequence of life events, and of creating regularized biographical perspectives (see Chapter 1).

For women, the levels and long-term trends are less uniform. For women over 65, labor force participation has never been an important factor. The only exception here is France, where in the first half of the century about 30 to 40 percent of women aged 65 to 69 were part of the labor force. Since then, however, the participation rate for women over 65 has declined to almost zero, as in Germany, the United Kingdom, and (although still slightly higher) Sweden and the United States.

For women below 65, the exit trends are masked by their generally increasing labor force participation (see section 2.3.4), which makes for a rather heterogeneous pattern. In France the participation rates of women aged 50 to 64 were already relatively high in 1911–21; since then, they have – with some fluctuation – declined. In Germany age 60 marks an important boundary: For women below this age, labor force participation has slowly but more or less steadily increased, but it has gone down for those aged 60 to 64 – especially since 1970. In the other three countries, the long-term trend is one of considerable increase. In Sweden it has continued until now, whereas in the United States and the United Kingdom it came to a halt after 1970 and has even been reversed for the group aged 60 to 64.

2.3 EXIT TRENDS OVER THE LAST TWO DECADES

2.3.1 A general view

Over the past two decades, as we show in detail in the next section, the labor force participation of men over 65 has further decreased, but more importantly, that between the ages of 55 and 64 has also dropped considerably. This pattern is valid for all Western countries for which we have data. The drop of the age of exit from gainful work has come at a time when many factors seemed to point in the opposite direction. The "hardest" one is that life expectancy (even at age 60) has substantially increased during this period. Also, the newer cohorts of aged people have increasingly better health and better educational resources. But there have also been dramatic changes in the cultural "software" of aging. One is the steady stream of (psycho-)gerontological research literature that – starting around 1960 – has been arguing over and over again that the process of aging is not necessarily associated with a loss of functional capacity and productivity (at least not in the age bracket that is at issue here), and that the commonly held "deficit model" of aging should therefore be abolished. Another is the increasing emphasis on activity and social participation as beneficial for "successful" aging. And finally, fixed age limits as criteria for the exit from gainful work and for the allocation of welfare benefits are increasingly seen as alien to the universalistic normative regime of modern societies, with their emphasis on achievement instead of ascription. In the countries of Western Europe this notion has not had any immediate institutional impact, but in the United States it has become institutionalized in the legislation against mandatory retirement as well as in a broad discourse on whether to replace chronological age by "functional" age as a basic criterion (cf. Neugarten 1982).

In spite of these factors, people have been leaving the work force at increasingly earlier ages – and this has occurred in all Western countries, irrespective of their institutional regimes. Obviously, the shortening of the work life has been a key mechanism of adapting to the shrinking demand for and/or the increasing supply of work. In Germany this process has been paralleled by a shortening of yearly work time: Between 1960 and 1985 the mean number of hours worked decreased by more than 20 percent, from 2,144 hours to 1,705 hours (Reyher and Kohler 1986:47). In Sweden the total labor force increased by 16 percent between 1970 and 1988; at the same time, the total number of hours worked increased by only 4 percent.[3] But the tripartition of the life course has been retained, even though the transitional period has become longer and fuzzier. The early exit of older workers has made it possible to conserve this basic structure of the life course. It should be added that in some countries, the work phase has also been shortened from below, by extending the period of schooling.[4] The trend is even stronger if we turn to employment activity rates instead of labor force participation rates (see next section), which include unemployment; the latter is usually highest at the beginning and partly also at the end of the work phase.

2.3.2 Results in detail

Labor force participation rates by age – defined as the ratio between the labor force and the total population of a given age group – have already been used in section 2.2 to document the long-term trends. They are a widely used index for the exit of older workers from active work life. It should be noted, however, that they are aggregate data that do not directly measure the individual transitions from work to retirement.

---

[3] See Chapter 9 for a more detailed account.
[4] Cf. the data for the group aged 16 to 24 presented in Tables 2.2 and 2.3. The pattern of a decrease in labor force participation would be clearer if we were to focus only on the group aged 16 to 19.

Table 2.2. *Labor force participation rates of men*

Age group	Year	France	Germany	Netherlands	Sweden	U.K.	U.S.
16–24	1965	65.3	78.1	—	71.7	77.4	70.9
	1966	66.0	76.7	—	70.3	77.7	71.7
	1967	64.3	73.6	—	68.0	77.4	72.4
	1968	61.5	73.0	—	68.4	76.5	72.0
	1969	59.6	72.3	—	68.1	80.1	72.0
	1970	60.3	75.4	—	67.0	80.0	71.8
	1971	59.0	74.4	65.3	66.9	80.0[a]	71.1
	1972	57.9	71.5	62.6	67.1	78.0	73.4
	1973	57.0	69.5	59.0	67.9	77.5	74.7
	1974	56.3	67.9	56.6	70.6	76.2	74.5
	1975	55.6	66.4	54.7	72.4	75.4	73.2
	1976	54.7	64.5	52.5	72.9	78.7	73.7
	1977	54.2	63.5	50.9	71.9	78.2	74.5
	1978	52.9	63.7	50.0	70.8	79.2	75.1
	1979	52.9	63.5	49.2	71.8	80.2	75.2
	1980	52.5	62.2	49.4	71.5	80.1	74.5
	1981	51.0	61.0	54.1[a]	67.9	79.2	73.8
	1982	51.4[a]	60.5	53.1	67.0	78.1	74.0
	1983	50.9	60.5	52.3	65.7	77.2	72.9
	1984	49.3	50.8	51.3	64.6	79.2	73.1
	1985	49.0	61.8	50.5	65.7	79.8	73.3
	1986	47.7	61.9	50.4	65.2	79.2	73.3
	1987	46.3	64.3	50.9	66.1[a]	81.7	72.6
	1988	43.5	64.5	50.6	67.9	82.7	72.7
25–54	1965	96.1	96.6	—	96.2	98.4	95.7
	1966	96.3	96.7	—	96.3	98.0	95.5
	1967	95.8	96.5	—	95.6	98.0	95.5
	1968	96.8	96.8	—	95.1	97.9	95.2
	1969	96.8	97.0	—	95.0	98.0	95.1
	1970	96.8	97.1	—	94.8	97.9	94.8
	1971	96.8	97.0	94.9	94.7	95.5[a]	94.7
	1972	97.0	96.0	94.9	94.2	95.6	93.9
	1973	96.8	95.7	94.8	94.3	95.6	93.9
	1974	96.7	95.2	94.6	94.5	95.7	94.1
	1975	96.4	95.1	94.2	95.2	95.8	93.8
	1976	96.5	94.8	93.9	95.7	95.8	93.6
	1977	96.3	94.6	93.6	95.5	95.9	93.7
	1978	96.3	94.5	93.0	95.3	95.7	93.6
	1979	95.3	94.3	93.0	95.3	95.6	93.7
	1980	96.4	93.6	93.1	95.4	95.4	93.4
	1981	96.2	92.9	92.5[a]	94.9	95.3	93.3
	1982	96.1[a]	92.3	92.3	94.9	94.7	94.2
	1983	96.1	91.9	92.2	95.0	93.9	93.0
	1984	95.9	91.5	92.0	94.9	93.7	93.1
	1985	95.9	91.5	91.7	95.2	93.7	93.1
	1986	95.9	90.8	91.4	95.3	93.2	93.0
	1987	95.9	89.4	91.2	94.7[a]	93.3	92.9
	1988	95.7	91.6	92.0	94.7	93.7	92.7

Age group	Year	France	Germany	Netherlands	Sweden	U.K.	U.S.
55–59	1965	82.9	90.5	—	92.8	95.7	85.7
	1966	83.9	90.4	—	93.3	95.4	85.6
	1967	82.8	90.4	—	94.2	95.4	86.5
	1968	84.3	90.0	—	93.6	95.2	87.2
	1969	84.6	89.9	—	91.9	95.1	87.9
	1970	82.9	88.4	—	90.8	95.3	88.3
	1971	82.4	87.4	86.6	90.9	93.0[a]	87.9
	1972	82.4	85.4	85.5	90.2	93.0	86.4
	1973	82.7	85.1	84.6	89.3	93.0	85.3
	1974	82.4	84.7	82.4	89.2	93.0	84.7
	1975	83.3	84.5	78.9	89.7	93.0	83.3
	1976	82.7	84.4	78.9	89.1	92.4	82.6
	1977	83.9	83.6	79.0	88.7	91.8	82.2
	1978	82.6	82.0	78.0	88.1	91.3	81.1
	1979	82.3	80.9	74.5	88.1	90.8	81.1
	1980	80.9	80.0	74.8	87.7	90.1	80.9
	1981	79.5	79.4	71.6[a]	87.8	89.2	80.5
	1982	75.6[a]	78.9	69.8	87.2	86.6	81.9
	1983	71.0	78.1	69.2	87.2	83.9	80.1
	1984	68.1	76.7	67.1	87.5	81.9	79.6
	1985	67.8	76.2	64.8	87.6	81.8	78.9
	1986	69.4	75.7	63.2	86.4	80.9	78.4
	1987	67.3	76.3	61.3	85.9[a]	81.0	79.1
	1988	67.3	76.6	60.0	85.9	81.6	78.7
60–64	1965	68.8	78.1	—	83.0	89.2	79.2
	1966	70.1	78.2	—	82.7	88.7	78.6
	1967	63.0	77.7	—	83.2	88.3	76.9
	1968	68.7	76.1	—	83.7	87.7	75.3
	1969	69.6	75.4	—	80.6	87.2	72.9
	1970	68.0	71.8	—	79.5	86.7	71.7
	1971	67.4	68.8	73.7	78.1	82.9[a]	70.7
	1972	66.1	66.6	71.0	76.6	82.7	70.7
	1973	64.4	64.8	69.1	76.0	82.6	67.3
	1974	63.0	60.7	66.1	74.6	82.4	66.6
	1975	56.7	56.2	64.9	74.0	82.3	64.5
	1976	51.5	51.1	63.8	73.0	80.4	62.5
	1977	48.8	46.3	61.6	69.7	78.5	61.7
	1978	45.0	42.0	59.9	68.9	75.8	60.8
	1979	45.1	40.9	54.0	69.0	73.0	60.7
	1980	47.6	42.5	48.8	69.0	71.2	59.8
	1981	42.5	43.0	40.3[a]	68.2	69.2	57.8
	1982	40.0[a]	41.3	37.6	68.4	64.2	57.2
	1983	33.6	37.9	37.4	67.4	59.3	56.4
	1984	31.1	34.1	32.1	65.8	56.8	55.5
	1985	30.8	32.4	27.8	65.1	54.5	55.1
	1986	27.4	32.3	23.4	65.2	52.2	54.3
	1987	25.7	31.4	19.0	64.2[a]	53.3	54.3
	1988	25.4	31.5	14.6	64.1	55.1	53.8

Table 2.2. (*cont.*)

Age group	Year	France	Germany	Netherlands	Sweden	U.K.	U.S.
65+	1965	28.3	24.0	—	37.7	23.7	26.6
	1966	27.0	23.0	—	35.4	23.5	25.8
	1967	23.3	22.5	—	34.1	22.7	26.0
	1968	23.0	21.4	—	33.3	21.9	26.2
	1969	22.1	21.0	—	31.1	21.0	26.2
	1970	19.5	17.2	—	28.9	20.1	25.7
	1971	18.6	15.4	11.3	27.6	19.3[a]	24.4
	1972	17.7	14.4	10.5	25.9	18.4	23.2
	1973	15.8	14.1	9.7	23.9	17.5	21.6
	1974	14.8	12.5	8.9	22.1	16.6	21.4
	1975	13.9	10.8	8.0	19.9	15.6	20.7
	1976	12.7	9.7	7.1	15.0	14.5	19.3
	1977	11.5	8.9	6.2	13.0	13.4	19.2
	1978	10.6	8.0	5.2	13.7	11.8	19.5
	1979	9.0	7.4	5.4	14.0	10.3	19.1
	1980	7.5	7.0	4.8	14.2	10.3	18.3
	1981	7.3	6.5	3.8[a]	13.0	10.3	17.7
	1982	5.9[a]	6.2	3.9	13.2	9.3	17.8
	1983	5.3	5.9	3.9	12.0	8.2	16.8
	1984	5.5	5.4	3.7	11.1	8.3	15.7
	1985	5.3	5.1	3.5	11.0	8.2	15.2
	1986	5.0	4.8	3.3	12.7	7.6	15.4
	1987	4.7	4.7	3.0	15.4[a]	7.9	15.7
	1988	4.6	4.7	2.8	19.0	7.7	15.9

[a]Break in time series.
Source: OECD Labour Force Statistics, Paris, 1984–9.

They can be interpreted in these terms only to the extent that counter-transitions from "retirement" back to employment may be disregarded: Under this condition, they indicate what proportion of a cohort has not yet left the labor force. Where countertransitions are frequent, the labor force participation rates of the oldest age groups must be regarded as including a substantial number of individuals with some experience of exit.[5]

[5] For the United States, individual-level longitudinal data (from the Retirement History Survey) show that there is indeed a considerable amount of countertransition from "retirement" back into work (cf. Burkhauser and Quinn 1989; Reimers and Honig 1989). It is not clear how much of this would be found in other countries if longitudinal data were available for them as well. The amount depends, of course, on how "retirement" is defined: by leaving the labor force (fully or partly), by an income reduction, by receiving an old-age pension, or by a combination of these criteria. Our data on labor force participation refer to only the first criterion.

Table 2.3. *Labor force participation rates of women*

Age group	Year	France	Germany	Netherlands	Sweden	U.K.	U.S.
16–24	1965	49.8	69.3	—	60.5	61.0	43.6
	1966	51.5	67.7	—	60.2	61.0	46.1
	1967	49.1	65.0	—	57.5	60.0	47.2
	1968	48.3	64.0	—	59.7	58.9	48.1
	1969	47.5	63.2	—	58.8	61.0	49.9
	1970	47.2	65.0	—	59.4	60.6	50.7
	1971	45.9	64.1	53.3	50.2	62.2[a]	50.3
	1972	46.0	62.4	52.4	60.8	62.3	53.0
	1973	45.5	61.1	50.9	60.1	62.0	55.0
	1974	45.0	60.0	49.5	63.5	62.0	56.5
	1975	45.6	58.6	48.7	66.1	62.0	57.1
	1976	45.7	57.2	47.0	67.7	66.4	58.0
	1977	45.4	55.6	46.8	68.0	67.4	59.5
	1978	44.1	55.0	46.7	68.0	68.6	61.6
	1979	44.4	54.3	46.3	69.7	69.7	52.3
	1980	43.2	53.4	47.3	70.1	71.4	61.7
	1981	42.4	52.6	52.0[a]	67.8	69.4	61.9
	1982	42.3[a]	52.0	51.3	66.4	68.3	62.3
	1983	41.4	51.9	50.6	65.1	67.3	62.0
	1984	41.1	52.8	49.8	64.8	68.7	62.9
	1985	40.3	53.9	49.1	66.4	69.4	63.7
	1986	39.7	54.6	49.1	65.6	69.7	64.3
	1987	38.7	57.2	49.9	66.6[a]	71.6	64.6
	1988	36.1	58.0	49.8	67.8	72.7	64.5
25–54	1965	42.8	46.1	—	56.0	48.1	45.1
	1966	45.8	45.9	—	57.4	49.9	45.9
	1967	46.7	45.3	—	57.7	50.7	47.0
	1968	48.3	45.9	—	59.8	51.5	47.6
	1969	49.5	46.6	—	61.5	52.3	48.7
	1970	50.1	47.3	—	64.2	53.1	49.7
	1971	50.9	48.3	22.8	66.5	55.7[a]	50.1
	1972	52.5	49.5	24.3	67.7	56.9	50.7
	1973	54.1	50.5	25.7	68.9	58.6	52.0
	1974	55.8	51.2	27.2	71.4	60.4	53.8
	1975	57.3	51.6	28.5	74.3	61.0	55.0
	1976	58.5	51.9	29.8	75.6	62.1	56.7
	1977	60.0	52.0	30.9	77.5	63.3	58.4
	1978	60.5	52.3	32.0	79.3	63.3	60.5
	1979	62.0	52.7	34.0	81.1	63.3	62.2
	1980	63.0	53.6	36.7	82.9	63.4	63.8
	1981	64.1	54.5	38.6[a]	84.8	63.4	65.2
	1982	66.1[a]	55.1	40.6	85.9	63.6	66.4
	1983	67.1	55.3	42.4	87.0	63.7	67.0
	1984	68.2	55.8	43.4	88.1	66.0	68.1
	1985	68.9	56.6	44.4	88.9	66.9	69.5
	1986	70.5	57.4	45.3	89.8	67.8	70.6
	1987	70.6	57.4	46.2	90.4[a]	69.0	71.7
	1988	71.2	58.2	47.6	90.8	70.2	72.5

Table 2.3. (cont.)

Age group	Year	France	Germany	Netherlands	Sweden	U.K.	U.S.
55–59	1965	41.2	36.3	—	46.6	44.5	44.9
	1966	45.5	36.3	—	50.0	46.2	45.7
	1967	43.1	36.4	—	52.3	47.2	46.7
	1968	45.9	36.9	—	49.3	48.1	46.8
	1969	47.4	37.1	—	49.9	49.1	49.1
	1970	46.0	36.4	—	52.8	50.1	48.8
	1971	44.7	35.9	17.7	54.6	50.9[a]	48.7
	1972	45.2	35.8	18.0	56.7	51.1	48.3
	1973	43.1	36.3	18.2	57.4	51.4	47.7
	1974	43.8	37.2	18.1	59.3	51.9	47.1
	1975	43.5	37.9	17.5	60.8	52.4	47.5
	1976	44.8	38.3	17.5	62.3	54.3	47.8
	1977	46.4	38.3	17.3	64.2	56.1	47.6
	1978	45.7	37.8	17.0	66.6	54.9	48.0
	1979	45.9	37.3	17.6	67.9	53.8	48.2
	1980	47.3	37.4	18.5	68.8	53.6	48.1
	1981	46.6	37.7	17.7[a]	70.2	53.1	49.0
	1982	46.1[a]	38.0	18.0	72.1	51.7	49.6
	1983	43.7	37.9	19.2	73.6	50.3	48.5
	1984	42.9	36.8	18.8	73.6	50.9	49.6
	1985	42.8	35.9	18.3	74.5	51.6	50.1
	1986	43.1	36.8	17.8	76.3	52.1	51.1
	1987	44.6	38.0	17.2	78.9[a]	53.5	51.9
	1988	45.3	38.5	16.7	79.6	54.8	53.0
60–64	1965	31.7	23.3	—	30.9	25.8	34.5
	1966	35.1	24.1	—	33.5	27.1	35.2
	1967	30.4	23.6	—	33.6	27.2	35.1
	1968	35.9	23.5	—	35.8	27.4	35.2
	1969	34.4	23.4	—	38.2	27.6	34.1
	1970	34.3	20.4	—	35.8	27.9	34.8
	1971	33.3	18.1	11.8	34.5	28.8[a]	35.1
	1972	33.3	17.2	11.7	34.1	28.8	34.9
	1973	33.1	17.6	11.3	32.2	28.7	33.9
	1974	31.7	16.9	11.2	36.1	28.7	33.1
	1975	29.8	15.5	10.8	38.3	28.6	33.0
	1976	27.7	14.1	10.7	37.5	26.9	32.8
	1977	27.2	12.7	10.1	38.4	25.1	32.5
	1978	24.1	11.6	10.2	38.9	23.3	32.7
	1979	24.0	11.3	10.6	39.4	21.5	33.5
	1980	27.3	12.0	9.5	41.0	22.4	32.9
	1981	25.3	12.4	7.5[a]	44.8	23.3	32.3
	1982	23.3[a]	12.1	7.7	46.2	21.9	33.4
	1983	20.6	11.3	9.3	46.8	20.5	33.6
	1984	19.0	10.5	7.8	47.1	21.2	33.1
	1985	18.9	10.1	6.3	46.6	18.6	33.2
	1986	18.4	10.2	4.9	47.6	18.3	33.0
	1987	18.0	10.6	3.4	50.1[a]	18.2	32.9
	1988	17.9	10.8	1.9	50.5	19.3	33.6

Table 2.3. (*cont.*)

Age group	Year	France	Germany	Netherlands	Sweden	U.K.	U.S.
65+	1965	11.5	7.8	—	11.6	6.5	9.4
	1966	11.1	7.8	—	10.2	6.8	9.0
	1967	9.6	7.9	—	8.1	6.7	9.0
	1968	9.2	7.7	—	9.3	6.5	9.0
	1969	9.3	7.5	—	10.0	6.4	9.3
	1970	8.6	6.1	—	8.7	6.4	9.0
	1971	7.6	5.7	2.2	8.1	6.3[a]	8.8
	1972	7.3	5.7	2.0	7.8	6.0	8.8
	1973	6.8	5.6	2.0	7.4	5.6	8.4
	1974	6.2	5.1	1.8	6.4	5.2	7.7
	1975	5.8	4.5	1.8	6.1	4.9	7.8
	1976	5.3	4.1	1.5	6.2	4.6	7.7
	1977	4.8	3.7	1.2	4.8	4.4	7.6
	1978	4.4	3.4	1.0	4.3	3.9	7.8
	1979	4.3	3.2	1.1	4.0	3.4	7.8
	1980	3.3	3.1	0.9	3.7	3.6	7.6
	1981	2.9	2.9	0.7[a]	4.0	3.7	7.5
	1982	2.4[a]	2.9	0.8	4.1	3.5	7.9
	1983	2.2	2.8	0.8	4.1	3.2	7.3
	1984	2.4	2.5	0.7	3.8	3.0	7.0
	1985	1.1	2.3	0.6	3.2	3.0	6.8
	1986	2.0	2.2	0.6	2.9	2.8	6.9
	1987	1.9	2.2	0.5	3.4[a]	2.8	6.9
	1988	1.8	2.2	0.4	4.9	2.9	7.4

[a] Break in time series.
Source: OECD Labour Force Statistics, Paris, 1984–9.

From the mid-1960s onward, OECD has reported labor force participation rates of men and women by age groups in its Labour Force Statistics.[6] The following analysis is based on these data; it focuses on the six OECD countries that are considered in more detail in the individual country chapters (Chapters 4–9).

For men over age 65 (Figure 2.1), a steady decline in labor force participation can be observed in the past two decades in all of our countries.

---

[6] The OECD concept considers as employed all persons who gainfully work for at least one hour a week. There are some definitional differences between countries, among which are the temporal point of reference (e.g., monthly averages or a certain month of the year) and whether or not the armed forces are included (which for our focus on the elderly is not relevant). See McMahon (1986) for a discussion of the significance of these differences for a comparative analysis.

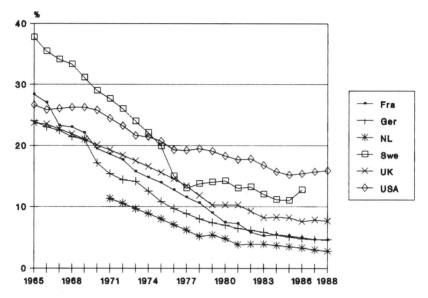

Figure 2.1. Labor force participation rates of men aged 65+. *Source:* OECD Labour Force Statistics, Paris, 1984–9.

It has dropped to about 10 to 15 percent (Sweden and the United States) or even clearly below this margin (France, Germany, the Netherlands, and the United Kingdom).

The group aged 60 to 64 (Figure 2.2) documents best how retirement has been redefined. Age 65 can no longer be regarded as the "normal" age limit when less than one-third (France, Germany, and the Netherlands) or only about one-half (the United Kingdom and the United States) of the male population between 60 and 64 are still part of the labor force. The highest rate – almost two-thirds – is found in Sweden, but it has shown a distinct decline as well, even if still moderate in comparison with the other countries. The decline is fairly steady over the whole period for Sweden and the United States, whereas for the Netherlands and the United Kingdom it gains momentum in the late 1970s and early 1980s. France and Germany show a strong decline in the mid-1970s, a slight reversal up to 1980, and another decline in the early 1980s.

The decline extends already to the group aged 55 to 59 (Figure 2.3), but its shape has been less uniform. In some countries it has been rather steady since the early 1970s (Germany, the Netherlands, and Sweden); in others it was very sharp during the early 1980s (France and the United

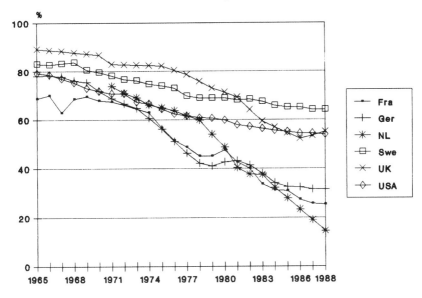

Figure 2.2. Labor force participation rates of men aged 60 to 64. *Source:* OECD Labour Force Statistics, Paris, 1984–9.

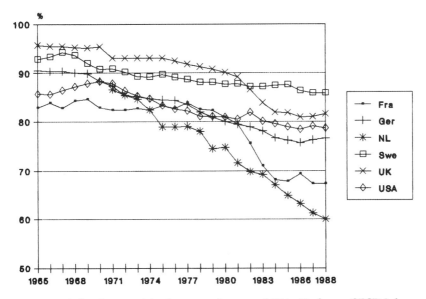

Figure 2.3. Labor force participation rates of men aged 55 to 59. *Source:* OECD Labour Force Statistics, Paris, 1984–9.

Kingdom). Sweden, again, is the country with the highest participation rate.

The temporal pattern of the decline allows for some hypotheses as to its determinants. Even without a formal time-series analysis, some links with economic development are obvious. All six countries experienced a collapse of GNP growth after 1974 in the wake of the first oil shock, a recovery with positive growth rates in the late 1970s, and a fall to zero or even negative growth again in the early 1980s. Aggregate unemployment rates have (except for Sweden) closely followed this course, with a sizable increase after 1974, a plateau phase in the late 1970s, and another large increase in the early 1980s. For the men above 65, the steady downward trend of labor force participation since the mid-1960s seems to be unrelated to these short-term economic ups and downs; it is more plausible to view it as completing the long-term institutionalization of retirement, and as the expression of a secular trend toward a general reduction of working hours and increased valuation of leisure time. For the age groups below 65, on the other hand, the links with economic growth are more evident. They are, however, far from perfect; to the extent that the downward trend began in the early 1970s, it cannot be explained simply by macroeconomic indicators. Other aspects are of importance, too. For instance, there have been institutional changes in the pension schemes, with immediate consequences in terms of labor force participation. To what extent these institutional changes were themselves motivated by economic factors cannot be assessed here in detail, but in some cases such an economic rationale – especially with reference to the labor market – was clearly the driving force. There also may have been some pressure toward earlier exit as a consequence of the growing size of the new cohorts entering the labor market. Labor force participation data alone are not sufficient to disentangle these different factors: the secular trend, the impact of economic crises, changed institutional mechanisms, and demographic changes. The difficulties are compounded by the fact that these factors are closely linked. More precise analyses need to examine their interaction in the context of institutionally well-grounded country-specific case studies such as those given in the following country chapters.

For older women, the trends of labor force participation at first sight differ considerably from those of men and are, moreover, quite different from country to country (see also Bach and Brinkmann 1986), with regard to both total levels and developments over time. Only above age 65 is there a homogeneous pattern: The participation rates have dropped to below 8 percent in the United States and even below 4 percent in the other countries (Figure 2.4).

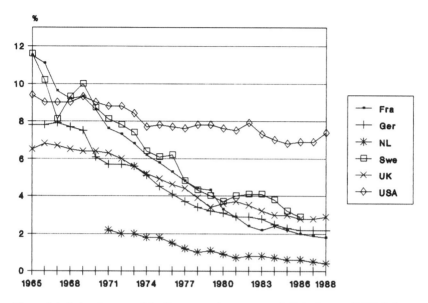

Figure 2.4. Labor force participation rates of women aged 65+. *Source:* OECD Labour Force Statistics, Paris, 1984–9.

For women below 65, there is great heterogeneity. Participation rates for the group aged 60 to 64 (Figure 2.5) have declined in the Central and Western European countries, remained stable in the United States, and increased in Sweden. The group aged 55 to 59 (Figure 2.6) shows no decline; the rates have again increased in Sweden and remained fairly stable in the other countries, but at very different levels: comparatively high in the United Kingdom and the United States (above 50 percent), somewhat lower in France (still clearly above 40 percent) and Germany (below 40 percent), and very low in the Netherlands (below 20 percent). If the age of exit has decreased for women as well, it has been compensated by a general growth in female labor force participation (see section 2.3.4).

2.3.3 *Accounting for unemployment: Employment activity rates*

Although participation rates for older age groups are a good first index of exit from the labor market, they still underestimate its real extent. The labor force includes a number of persons who, for all practical purposes, have already left the labor market. This is the case, for example, for most

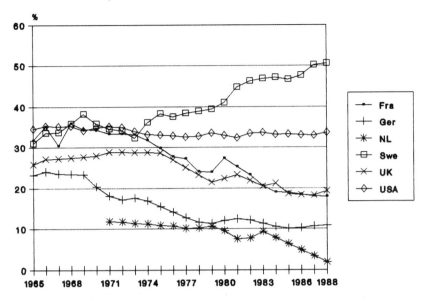

Figure 2.5. Labor force participation rates of women aged 60 to 64. *Source:* OECD Labour Force Statistics, Paris, 1984–9.

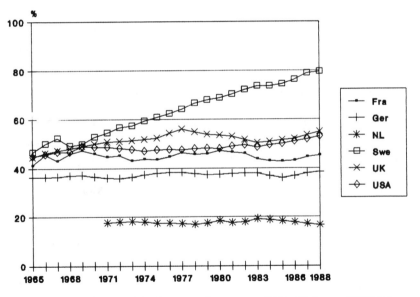

Figure 2.6. Labor force participation rates of women aged 55 to 59. *Source:* OECD Labour Force Statistics, Paris, 1984–9.

older unemployed workers. On the one hand, they represent a typical "problem group" of the labor market: Finding a new job is very difficult, if not impossible, for them. For Germany, this is documented by empirical studies of both the duration of unemployment and the period after unemployment of the elderly (e.g., Bäcker 1979; Preiser 1985). On the other hand, unemployment sometimes is a necessary precondition for being entitled to special old-age pensions. In Germany, for example, one kind of pension that becomes effective at age 60 requires a period of unemployment of at least 52 weeks within the last one and a half years.[7] Although these unemployed workers do not intend to become employed again, they are still included in the labor force and therefore also in the participation rates.

In its Labour Force Statistics, OECD also reports unemployment rates by age. They are defined as the number of unemployed divided by the total labor force for a given age. Differences in the definitions of unemployment across countries appear to be even greater than those for labor force participation (cf. McMahon 1986:11). There are also some changes in the definition of unemployment within individual countries over time.[8] Bearing in mind these conceptual problems, a comparison of labor force participation rates and employment activity rates (excluding the unemployed) leads to interesting results (Figures 2.7 and 2.8, Tables 2.4 and 2.5).[9] First, it is obvious that the real activity level of older workers is overestimated by participation rates. Second, the trend toward early exit may be underestimated by participation rates. When unemployment of older workers increases, the differences between both rates grow and intensify the process of early exit. For men, this has clearly been the case in Germany and – at least in the first half of the 1980s – in Sweden; in the United States unemployment rates have developed in a less uniform way. As already mentioned, the picture for older women is more complicated because of the two opposite and overlapping trends. But here again, excluding the unemployed affects not only the level of work activity but also its development over time: In Sweden, for example, the labor force participation rate of women aged 55 to 64 still increased by 2.5 percent between 1981 and 1985, but their employment activity rate remained fairly stable.

---

[7] For details, see Chapter 6.

[8] This is especially true for older workers in the case of administrative rule changes (e.g., about no longer being counted as unemployed if unemployment can be considered in terms of definitive exit) that have clearly been aimed at de-dramatizing the picture offered by public statistics.

[9] Because of significant changes in the definition of unemployment of the elderly in Germany (1986) and Sweden (1987), the employment activity data are given only up to 1985. Data for the years before 1970 are not available for all of the countries.

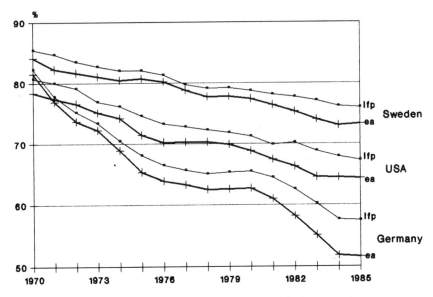

Figure 2.7. Labor force participation and employment activity rates of men aged 55 to 64.
Source: OECD Labour Force Statistics, Paris, 1986, and our own calculations.

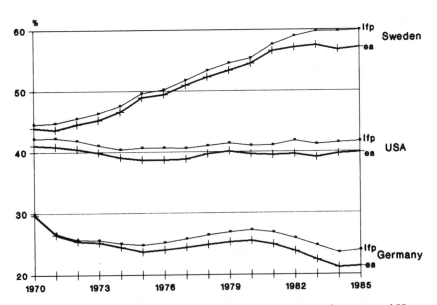

Figure 2.8. Labor force participation and employment activity rates of women aged 55 to 64. *Source:* OECD Labour Force Statistics, Paris, 1986, and our own calculations.

Table 2.4. *Employment activity rates of men aged 55 to 64*

	Year	France	Germany	Netherlands	Sweden	U.K.	U.S.
Labor force	1970	75.4	80.1	—	85.4	91.2	80.7
participation	1971	74.6	77.8	80.6	84.7	88.1[a]	80.0
rates	1972	73.6	75.2	78.7	83.5	88.0	79.1
	1973	72.1	73.4	77.2	82.7	87.7	76.9
	1974	70.8	70.5	74.6	82.0	87.6	76.2
	1975	68.9	68.1	72.2	82.0	87.6	74.6
	1976	67.9	66.5	71.8	81.3	86.5	73.3
	1977	69.4	65.7	70.9	79.7	85.5	72.8
	1978	68.8	65.1	69.8	79.1	84.3	72.3
	1979	69.9	65.4	65.3	79.2	83.2	71.8
	1980	68.5	65.5	63.2	78.7	81.6	72.2
	1981	64.3	64.5	57.3[a]	78.1	79.9	69.9
	1982	59.8[a]	62.6	54.8	77.7	75.9	70.2
	1983	53.6	60.2	54.2	77.0	71.7	68.8
	1984	50.3	57.8	50.3	76.2	69.2	67.9
	1985	50.1	57.0	47.0	75.9	68.2	67.3
Unemployment	1970	1.9	0.9	—	1.5	5.0	2.8
rates	1971	2.2	1.2	1.5	2.3	5.9[a]	3.3
	1972	2.6	2.0	2.3	2.3	6.6	3.2
	1973	1.9	1.6	2.5	2.1	5.7	2.4
	1974	2.1	2.3	2.6	1.9	5.4	2.6
	1975	2.6	3.9	3.3	1.5	6.3	4.3
	1976	3.1	3.9	3.7	1.4	7.6	4.2
	1977	3.6	3.7	3.5	1.1	7.8	3.5
	1978	4.3	4.0	3.3	1.8	8.2	2.8
	1979	4.0	4.3	3.3	1.8	8.1	2.7
	1980	4.7	4.3	3.5	1.6	9.5	3.4
	1981	4.8	5.4	4.4	2.2	15.2	3.6
	1982	5.3[a]	7.0	5.9	3.1	17.7[a]	5.5
	1983	6.0	8.5	14.9	4.0	13.9	6.1
	1984	6.2	10.0	13.1	4.2	13.5	5.0
	1985	6.7	10.1	6.0	3.5	13.8	4.3
Employment	1970	74.0	79.4	—	84.1	86.6	78.4
activity rates	1971	73.0	76.9	79.4	82.8	82.9[a]	77.4
	1972	71.7	73.7	76.9	81.6	82.2	76.6
	1973	70.7	72.2	75.3	81.0	82.7	75.1
	1974	69.3	68.9	72.7	80.4	82.9	74.2
	1975	67.1	65.4	69.8	80.8	82.1	71.4
	1976	65.8	63.9	69.1	80.2	79.9	70.2
	1977	66.9	63.3	68.4	78.8	78.8	70.3
	1978	65.8	62.5	67.5	77.7	77.4	70.3
	1979	67.1	62.6	63.1	77.8	76.5	69.9
	1980	65.3	62.7	61.0	77.4	73.8	68.8
	1981	61.2	61.0	54.8[a]	76.4	67.8	67.4
	1982	56.6[a]	58.2	51.6	75.3	62.5[a]	66.3
	1983	50.4	55.1	46.1	73.9	61.7	64.6
	1984	47.2	52.0	43.7	73.0	59.9	64.5
	1985	46.7	51.2	44.2	73.2	58.8	64.4

[a] Break in time series.
Source: OECD Labour Force Statistics, Paris, 1986, and our own calculations.

Table 2.5. *Employment activity rates of women aged 55 to 64*

	Year	France	Germany	Netherlands	Sweden	U.K.	U.S.
Labor force participation rates	1970	40.0	28.5	—	44.5	39.2	42.2
	1971	38.6	26.7	14.9	44.7	39.9[a]	42.3
	1972	38.4	25.7	15.0	45.5	39.9	41.9
	1973	37.2	25.6	14.8	46.3	39.8	41.1
	1974	36.4	25.1	14.7	47.7	39.0	40.4
	1975	35.9	24.8	14.2	49.6	40.1	40.7
	1976	36.4	25.2	14.2	50.2	40.5	40.7
	1977	38.1	25.8	13.9	51.7	41.0	40.6
	1978	37.4	26.4	13.8	53.4	40.2	41.0
	1979	38.4	26.9	14.4	54.5	39.4	41.4
	1980	39.7	27.2	14.4	55.3	39.1	41.0
	1981	37.6	26.8	12.9[a]	57.5	38.8	41.1
	1982	35.7[a]	25.9	13.1	58.8	36.9	41.8
	1983	32.6	24.7	14.4	59.7	35.1	41.2
	1984	31.0	23.3	13.4	59.6	35.4	41.5
	1985	31.0	22.6	12.3	59.9	34.7	41.7
Unemployment rates	1970	2.8	0.6	—	1.3	—	2.7
	1971	3.3	0.9	1.6	2.4	—	3.3
	1972	3.2	1.2	1.7	2.2	—	3.3
	1973	2.5	1.4	2.0	2.3	—	2.8
	1974	3.1	2.5	2.1	2.0	—	3.3
	1975	3.3	4.4	2.6	1.4	—	5.0
	1976	4.4	4.8	2.7	1.6	—	4.9
	1977	4.9	5.3	2.8	1.6	—	4.4
	1978	4.1	5.7	2.9	2.0	—	3.2
	1979	4.8	6.0	2.7	2.2	—	3.2
	1980	6.1	6.3	2.6	1.7	—	3.3
	1981	6.2	7.2	3.0	1.7	—	3.8
	1982	6.4[a]	8.2	3.2	3.1	—	5.2
	1983	6.9	9.4	8.2	3.8	—	5.0
	1984	7.7	10.5	7.4	5.1	—	4.3
	1985	7.6	11.7	4.5	4.6	—	4.3
Employment activity rates	1970	38.9	28.3	—	43.9	—	41.1
	1971	37.3	26.5	14.7	43.6	—	40.9
	1972	37.2	25.4	14.7	44.5	—	40.5
	1973	36.3	25.2	14.5	45.2	—	39.9
	1974	35.3	24.5	14.4	46.7	—	39.1
	1975	34.7	23.7	13.8	48.9	—	38.7
	1976	34.8	24.0	13.8	49.4	—	38.7
	1977	36.2	24.4	13.5	50.9	—	38.8
	1978	35.9	24.9	13.4	52.3	—	39.7
	1979	36.6	25.3	14.0	53.3	—	40.1
	1980	37.3	25.5	14.0	54.4	—	39.6
	1981	35.3	24.9	12.5[a]	56.5	—	39.5
	1982	33.4[a]	23.8	12.7	57.0	—	39.6
	1983	30.4	22.4	13.2	57.4	—	39.1
	1984	28.6	20.9	12.4	56.6	—	39.7
	1985	28.6	20.0	11.7	57.1	—	39.9

[a] Break in time series.
Source: OECD Labour Force Statistics, Paris, 1986, and our own calculations.

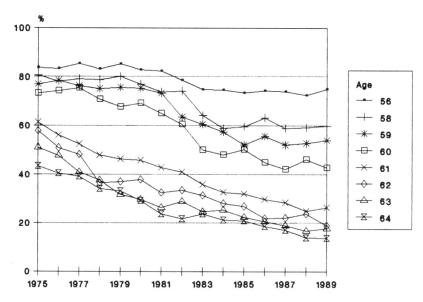

Figure 2.9. Labor force participation rates in France: Men by single years of age. *Source:* INSEE, Enquete d'Emploi, Collection D.

Another factor in the underestimation of exit from the labor market is picked up neither by participation rates nor by employment activity rates. In some countries there are special preretirement programs (in single firms or industries) for workers who have not yet reached the retirement age of the statutory pension scheme; they are often paid by their firms (sometimes with state subsidies) and are therefore still counted as regular wage or salary earners, although in fact they are not working and have no intention of working again.

2.3.4 *Participation rates for single age years and individual birth cohorts*

The sensitivity of the exit process to institutional changes can be analyzed more accurately by using data for single age years instead of five-year age groups (Figures 2.9–2.12). In Germany, for example, the introduction of "flexible retirement" (with a lower boundary of 63) in 1973 was followed by an immediate decline of the labor force participation of men aged 60 to 64 (see Figure 2.2). But to what extent this is a cause–effect relation remains unclear if only this aggregate information is available, since there is another causal candidate: the simultaneously occurring economic slowdown in the wake of the oil shock. The data for single

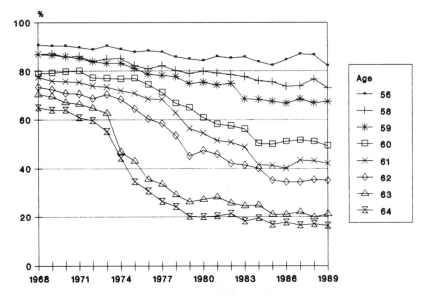

Figure 2.10. Labor force participation rates in Germany: Men by single years of age. *Source:* Mikrozensus; EC-Labor Force Survey, and our own calculations.

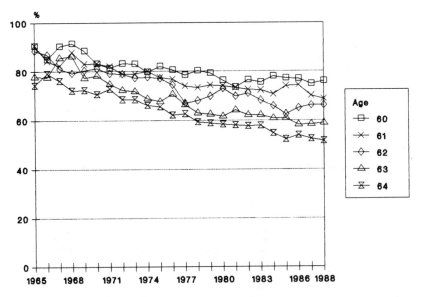

Figure 2.11. Labor force participation in Sweden: Men by single years of age. *Source:* Labor Force Survey.

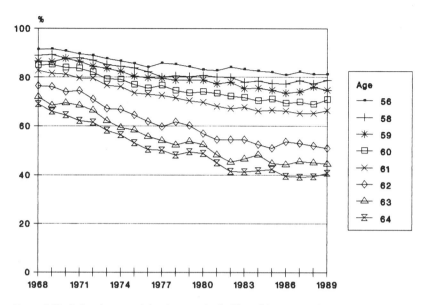

Figure 2.12. Labor force participation rates in the United States: Men by single years of age. *Source:* Current Population Survey, and our own calculations.

age years (Figure 2.10) show that the institutional change indeed has a direct effect: The decline becomes steeper for ages 63 and 64.[10] In the United States, (reduced) Social Security benefits can be received from age 62 onward. The data for single ages (Figure 2.12) again document the importance of this regulation: Labor force participation rates of men aged 62 have always been clearly lower than of those aged 61. Moreover, the difference between ages 61 and 62 has steadily increased since the early 1970s; in other words, the exit process for age 62 (and over) has become more pronounced than for age 61 (and below). These examples indicate that the group aged 60 to 64 may be very heterogeneous with respect to labor force participation. However, the data for single age years are not available in most countries (at least not over a long period) and therefore cannot be used for broad international comparisons.

In addition to cross-sectional analyses, data for single age years can also be rearranged so as to examine participation trends in a cohort perspective. This type of analysis has two advantages: It accounts for the size of individual birth cohorts which (for demographic reasons) may dif-

[10] It has to be noted that these data come from a different source (using a slightly different labor force participation concept) than the OECD data.

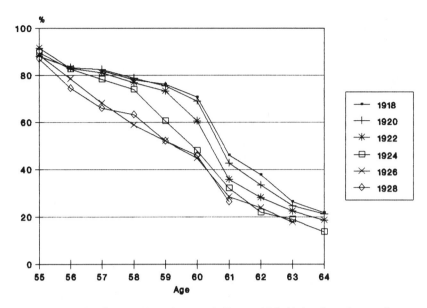

Figure 2.13. Labor force participation rates in France: Male birth cohorts by age. *Source:* INSEE, Enquete d'Emploi, Collection D, and our own calculations.

fer considerably, and it makes it possible to disentangle overlapping trends, which is particularly important for the analysis of female labor force participation.

Mainly as a consequence of World War I, the size of the French and German birth cohorts for 1915–19 is very small in comparison with both the older and the younger cohorts. In such a case, labor force participation rates for specific age groups are very sensitive with respect to the composition of these groups. In both countries, participation rates for men aged 60 to 64 increased from 1979 to 1980 (see Figure 2.2). This "increase," however, is a compositional effect – it is simply due to the entry of the large cohort for 1920 into the group aged 60 to 64: Labor force participation of men aged 60 (which is the highest within this age group) is weighted by the larger size of this cohort and raises the aggregate rate for the total age group.[11]

Cohort data show that in both countries, there has been no "real" increase for any individual birth cohort. On the contrary, the younger the cohort, the earlier and sharper the decline (see Figures 2.13 and 2.14). A

---

[11] The impact of differences in the size of individual birth cohorts on aggregate numbers has also been noted for data on entries into the German pension system (cf. Conradi et al. 1987:183).

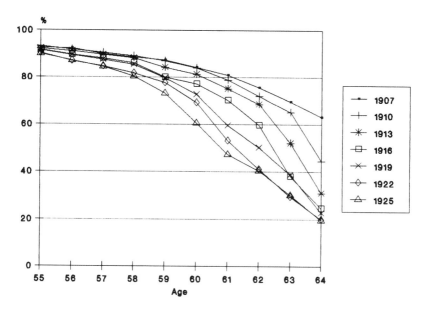

Figure 2.14. Labor force participations rates in Germany: Male birth cohorts by age. *Source:* Mikrozensus; EC-Labor Force Survey, and our own calculations.

similarly shaped decline can be seen in the United States (Figure 2.15). But whereas in France and Germany all cohorts at age 55 start at about the same level, this is not the case in the United States: Of the men born in 1910, 93 percent were still in the labor force at age 55 compared with only 85 percent of those born in 1925. Thus, the trend toward early exit is effective already at an earlier age.

Cohort data are also an absolute must for understanding the patterns of female labor force participation (Figures 2.16 and 2.17). For Germany, they clearly document the two overlapping trends (see Figure 2.17): Up to age 59, the participation rates of younger cohorts are higher than those of the older cohorts, indicating the general growth of female labor force participation. After this age, the participation rates of younger cohorts are lower than those of the older cohorts, indicating that early exit has increased for women as well. Each cohort starts on a higher level than the one before and has a steeper decline. For France, the same type of analysis leads to a similar picture (Figure 2.16), except that the age that marks the "turning point" between the older and younger cohorts has not remained constant over time as it did in Germany. In the United States the pattern is less clear (Figure 2.18).

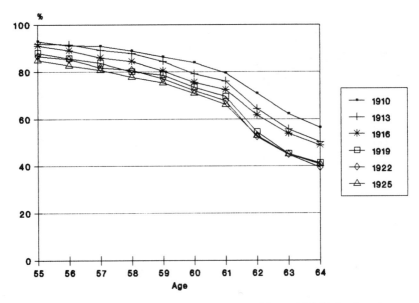

Figure 2.15. Labor force participation rates in the United States: Male birth cohorts by age.
Source: Current Population Survey, and our own calculations.

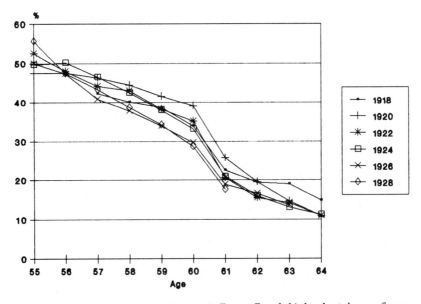

Figure 2.16. Labor force participation rates in France: Female birth cohorts by age. *Source:*
INSEE, Enquete d'Emploi, Collection D, and our own calculations.

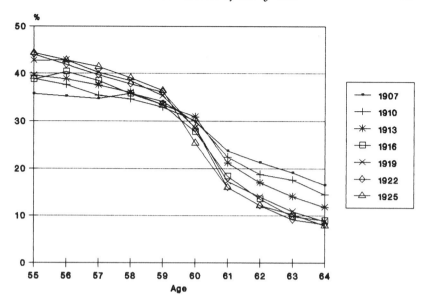

Figure 2.17. Labor force participation rates in Germany: Female birth cohorts by age. *Source:* Mikrozensus; EC-Labor Force Survey, and our own calculations.

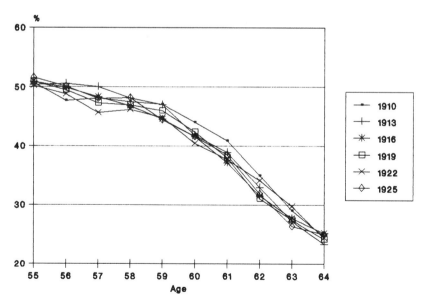

Figure 2.18. Labor force participation rates in the United States: Female birth cohorts by age. *Source:* Current Population Survey, and our own calculations.

As stressed before, further interpretation of the trends in labor force participation of the elderly require detailed knowledge of the socioeconomic, institutional, and cultural background. This cannot be provided in a comparative chapter but only in well-contextualized country reports such as the ones in the following chapters.

REFERENCES

Bach, H.-U., and C. Brinkmann. 1986. "Erwerbsbeteiligung von Frauen im internationalen Vergleich." *Mitteilungen aus der Arbeitsmarkt- und Berufsforschung* 19:356–61.

Bäcker, G. 1979. "Der ältere Arbeitnehmer auf Arbeitsplatz und Arbeitsmarkt." *Sozialer Fortschritt* 28:64–7, 85–92, 112–18, 135–7.

Burkhauser, R. V., and J. F. Quinn. 1989. "American Patterns of Work and Retirement." In: W. Schmähl (ed.), *Redefining the Process of Retirement. An International Perspective*. Berlin: Springer, pp. 91–113.

Conradi, H., K. Jacobs, and W. Schmähl. 1987. "Vorzeitiger Rentenbezug in der Bundesrepublik Deutschland." *Sozialer Fortschritt* 36:182–9.

Kohli, M. 1986a. "The World We Forgot: A Historical Review of the Life Course." In: V. M. Marshall (ed.), *Later Life: The Social Psychology of Aging*. Beverly Hills: Sage, pp. 271–303.

   1986b. "Gesellschaftszeit und Lebenszeit." In: J. Berger (ed.), *Die Moderne – Kontinuitäten und Zäsuren (Soziale Welt, Sonderband 4)*. Göttingen: Schwartz, pp. 183–208.

McMahon, P. J. 1986. "An International Comparison of Labor Force Participation, 1977–84." *Monthly Labor Review* 109(5):3–12.

Neugarten, B. L. (ed.). 1982. *Age or Need? Public Policies for Older People*. Beverly Hills: Sage.

Preiser, K. 1985. "Arbeitslosigkeit älterer Arbeitnehmer." *Zeitschrift für Gerontologie* 18:266–73.

Reimers, C., and M. Honig. 1989. "The Retirement Process in the United States: Mobility among Full-time Work, Partial Retirement, and Full Retirement." In: W. Schmähl (ed.), *Redefining the Process of Retirement. An International Perspective*. Berlin: Springer, pp. 115–31.

Reyher, L., and H. Kohler. 1986. "Arbeitszeit und Arbeitsvolumen: Die empirische Basis der Arbeitszeit-Politik." *Beiträge zur Arbeitsmarkt- und Berufsforschung* vol. 75, *Arbeitszeit und flexible Altersgrenze*, 2nd edition, pp. 29–55. Nürnberg: Institut für Arbeitsmarkt- und Berufsforschung.

CHAPTER 3

Testing the industry–mix
hypothesis of early exit

KLAUS JACOBS, MARTIN KOHLI, AND MARTIN REIN

3.1 INDUSTRY MIX AND AGE STRUCTURES
WITHIN INDUSTRIES IN SIX EUROPEAN COUNTRIES

THE usual way of accounting for the changing patterns of transition to retirement is to focus on social policy: on the changes in the public old-age pension regimes that have defined new pathways for early exit from work. In this perspective, the labor market may give the impetus for such social policy changes, but it is the latter that shape the exit process.

Our perspective here is different. We examine early exit as a consequence of the organization of work and, thus, of the specific industrial structure of each country. We focus on changes in the labor market and the labor process of industries. In our view, they not only define the problem that social policy then has to solve; they also contribute directly to shaping pathways of early exit from the labor force, or to using existing pathways for that purpose.

Thus, our way of explaining the differences in exit patterns between countries and the general trend valid for all countries is to analyze the patterns of exit by industries. In this chapter, we cannot go into detailed considerations of internal labor markets and of how they depend on the organization of production in the different industries. No attempt is made to perform a complete data analysis. Rather, our aim here is to present the available data on industry age structures in a form suitable for comparison and to present some results that show what can be obtained from such a comparison.

The industry-mix hypothesis assumes that early exit mainly takes place in certain industries. A first assumption is that there are systematic differences between economic sectors. The expansion of retirement has closely followed the pattern of the formal sector, and one could expect that participation rates of the elderly are still higher in the primary sector (or more precisely, agriculture), with its lower degree of wage labor. The share of agriculture in each country should be salient for explaining the

67

differences in exit patterns between countries, and the shrinkage of agriculture should have contributed to the decrease in the mean age of exit. Alternatively, the age of exit in agriculture itself might have become lower because the modernization of this sector would contribute to earlier exit. However, as the share of agriculture in the total work force is relatively low for the European countries that we consider, and has been so for some time, the evolution of agriculture alone will not be able to explain a large part of the differences between countries and between points in time. A second assumption is that early exit is especially high in industries that are under pressure to reduce their work force. Among these are industries that are affected by the economic downturn to an especially large extent (e.g., coal and steel), industries that are facing massive international competition (e.g., textile), and industries that are facing especially high rates of rationalization as a consequence of rapid technological change (e.g., some manufacturing of goods). Third, for some industries (e.g., the chemical industry), technological change means that even without a general reduction of their number, workers need to adapt to a changing qualification profile by shifting from older unskilled or blue-collar to younger skilled or white-collar workers. Finally, we might expect to find more early exit in industries that place particularly high physical strain on their workers (e.g., mining and construction).

The set of assumptions composing the industry-mix hypothesis of early exit can explain the differences between countries in observed exit patterns at a given time by higher shares of industries with a high age of exit (as already stated for agriculture). Explaining the decrease of the age of exit over time is more complicated. There are two possible changes that act in this direction – either alternatively or in conjunction. The first is a reduction in size of those industries that have particularly late exit (or an expansion of industries with early exit). The second is that (a large share of) industries have lowered their age of exit during the period under consideration.

It should be noted that the analysis also poses some formal problems. If we interpret changes in the proportion of older workers in a given industry in terms of changes in the age of exit, we run into difficulties that are well known from demography. The "aging" of an industry can be the result of two processes: changing exit and changing entry. Depending on the age profile of the population of workers of an industry, the proportion of older workers may be less sensitive to changes in the rate of exit ("mortality") than to changes in the rate of entry ("fertility"). In expanding industries that recruit large numbers of young workers, the proportion of older workers decreases even if the mean age of exit remains the same (and vice versa). Moreover, industry age structures can be very irregular, with some age groups being much more strongly represented than others. These difficulties can be solved by a cohort analysis of the exit process. Here, however, another problem appears: There is some mobility between industries, even among the older age groups. Its extent could be assessed only on the basis of individual longitudinal data. Because such data are not available, it is necessary to combine different types of analyses, each with its own limitations.

We will use two types of empirical evidence. The first is data on the present (1985) age structure of industries, which are available for six European Community countries, namely, Belgium, Denmark, France, the Federal Republic of Germany, the Netherlands, and the United Kingdom. Here we will examine how far the countries differ in their industry-age mix – that is, the composition of industries regarding their share of total employment and their age structures – and how these differences correspond to those between their patterns of early exit. We can also identify industries that deviate from the general age pattern, but such deviations cannot be readily interpreted in terms of early exit.

We therefore need a second type of evidence, namely, data on historical changes of industry age structures, which are available for three countries: Germany, the Netherlands, and Sweden. Here, we will proceed in three steps. The first is to assess globally to what extent the observed changes in the industry-age mix are due to changed employment shares between industries or to changed age structures within industries. The second is to look more closely at the evolution of single industries and sectors in terms of their age structures. Finally, in order to differentiate between possible explanations of this evolution, we set up the data in a cohort analysis form.

The data for the six European Community countries exist on a two-digit level of the NACE (Nomenclature générale des activités économiques dans la communauté européenne) code. In order to compare the industrial structure and the age structure within single industries, the 61 single categories of NACE are grouped into 16 economic sectors. Grouping of single industries always is somewhat arbitrary. Nevertheless, the international comparison of the industry-age mixes is possible because the basic employment data of all the six countries are given in the same industrial code and the grouping is done in the same way. The numbers include all wage and salary earners, the self-employed, and the family workers.

A first look at the employment data for men of the six countries (Table 3.1) shows some differences concerning the respective industry mixes of these countries, that is, the share of the total male employment that sin-

Table 3.1. *Industry-age mix for men in six European Community countries (1985)*

Sector	Employment of industry (1,000s)	Share of total employment (%)	<25	25–54	55–59	60–64	65+	55+
			\multicolumn{6}{c}{Proportion in industry by age (%)}					

Sector	Employment of industry (1,000s)	Share of total employment (%)	<25	25–54	55–59	60–64	65+	55+
\multicolumn{9}{c}{Belgium}								
1. Agr., for. & fishing	87	3.8	12.6	59.8	16.1	10.3	1.1	27.6
2. Mining & utilities	57	2.5	10.5	75.4	12.3	1.8	0.0	14.0
3. Construction	184	8.1	13.0	78.3	7.1	1.6	0.0	8.7
4. Food, drink, tobacco	75	3.3	14.7	74.7	8.0	2.7	0.0	10.7
5. Leather & textile	52	2.3	17.3	73.1	7.7	1.9	0.0	9.6
6. Chemical ind.	89	3.9	10.1	80.9	6.7	2.2	0.0	9.0
7. Basic metal ind.	61	2.7	8.2	88.5	3.3	0.0	0.0	3.3
8. Machinery/equipm.	295	13.0	15.6	78.6	4.7	1.0	0.0	5.8
9. Wood, paper, print.	93	4.1	16.1	76.3	5.4	2.2	0.0	7.5
10. Other manufact.	45	2.0	8.9	82.2	8.9	0.0	0.0	8.9
11. Transp. & communic.	230	10.2	7.8	80.4	9.1	2.6	0.0	11.7
12. Wholesale & retail	270	11.9	11.9	74.1	8.5	4.4	1.1	14.1
13. Business services	152	6.7	7.2	81.6	7.2	3.3	0.7	11.2
14. Personal services	67	3.0	16.4	73.1	6.0	3.0	1.5	10.4
15. Communal services	268	11.8	8.2	81.3	5.6	3.4	1.5	10.4
16. Publ. admin./defense	240	10.6	12.1	74.6	8.8	4.2	0.4	13.3
Total	2,265	100.0	11.6	77.4	7.5	3.0	0.5	10.9
\multicolumn{9}{c}{Denmark}								
1. Agr., for. & fishing	131	9.4	19.1	49.6	9.9	9.2	12.2	31.3
2. Mining & utilities	19	1.4	5.3	84.2	5.3	5.3	0.0	10.5
3. Construction	154	11.0	22.7	66.2	5.8	3.2	1.9	11.0
4. Food, drink, tobacco	61	4.4	23.0	62.3	8.2	4.9	1.6	14.8
5. Leather & textile	12	0.9	33.3	50.0	8.3	8.3	0.0	16.7
6. Chemical ind.	26	1.9	11.5	80.8	7.7	0.0	0.0	7.7
7. Basic metal ind.	5	0.4	40.0	60.0	0.0	0.0	0.0	0.0
8. Machinery/equipm.	188	13.5	25.5	64.4	6.4	2.1	1.6	10.1
9. Wood, paper, print.	69	4.9	26.1	62.3	5.8	2.9	2.9	11.6
10. Other manufact.	19	1.4	21.1	63.2	10.5	0.0	5.3	15.8
11. Transp. & communic.	131	9.4	17.6	71.8	6.1	3.1	1.5	10.7

Sector	Employment of industry (1,000s)	Share of total employment (%)	<25	25–54	55–59	60–64	65+	55+
12. Wholesale & retail	192	13.8	26.0	62.0	5.7	3.6	2.6	12.0
13. Business services	93	6.7	16.1	74.2	6.5	2.2	1.1	9.7
14. Personal services	30	2.2	26.7	66.7	6.7	0.0	0.0	6.7
15. Communal services	183	13.1	10.9	73.8	8.2	3.8	3.3	15.3
16. Publ. admin./ defense	82	5.9	14.6	70.7	7.3	4.9	2.4	14.6
Total	1,395	100.0	20.2	66.1	7.0	3.7	3.0	13.7

France

Sector	Employment of industry (1,000s)	Share of total employment (%)	<25	25–54	55–59	60–64	65+	55+
1. Agr., for. & fishing	1113	9.0	10.3	58.8	16.1	10.1	4.7	30.8
2. Mining & utilities	267	2.1	11.2	83.9	4.1	0.7	0.0	4.9
3. Construction	1450	11.7	14.6	78.3	5.9	1.1	0.1	7.2
4. Food, drink, tobacco	443	3.6	22.1	70.2	6.1	1.6	0.0	7.7
5. Leather & textile	205	1.6	13.2	77.6	7.3	2.0	0.0	9.3
6. Chemical ind.	431	3.5	9.5	84.0	6.0	0.5	0.0	6.5
7. Basic metal ind.	159	1.3	7.5	88.1	3.8	0.6	0.0	4.4
8. Machinery/ equipm.	1792	14.4	12.5	81.8	4.5	1.2	0.1	5.7
9. Wood, paper, print.	374	3.0	15.8	73.8	7.8	1.9	0.8	10.4
10. Other manufact.	206	1.7	10.7	82.5	5.3	1.5	0.0	6.8
11. Transp. & communic.	960	7.7	8.6	85.6	4.5	0.9	0.3	5.7
12. Wholesale & retail	1476	11.9	16.5	72.8	6.6	3.0	1.1	10.8
13. Business services	815	6.6	9.4	80.0	6.7	2.5	1.3	10.6
14. Personal services	384	3.1	21.1	65.6	6.5	4.9	1.8	13.3
15. Communal services	1360	10.9	9.7	81.4	5.3	2.7	0.9	8.9
16. Publ. admin./ defense	996	8.0	10.6	81.2	5.7	2.1	0.3	8.1
Total	12,431	100.0	12.6	77.3	6.6	2.6	0.9	10.1

Germany

Sector	Employment of industry (1,000s)	Share of total employment (%)	<25	25–54	55–59	60–64	65+	55+
1. Agr., for. & fishing	707	4.5	15.3	55.4	13.2	8.5	7.6	29.3
2. Mining & utilities	500	3.1	16.4	73.6	8.0	2.0	0.0	10.0
3. Construction	1,706	10.7	23.7	67.2	6.7	1.8	0.5	9.1
4. Food, drink, tobacco	383	2.4	21.1	67.4	7.3	3.1	1.0	11.5

Table 3.1. (*cont.*)

Sector	Employment of industry (1,000s)	Share of total employment (%)	Proportion in industry by age (%)					
			<25	25–54	55–59	60–64	65+	55+
5. Leather & textile	238	1.5	14.3	68.9	12.2	3.4	1.3	16.8
6. Chemical ind.	667	4.2	13.2	75.0	9.7	2.1	0.0	11.8
7. Basic metal ind.	380	2.4	15.5	75.3	8.2	1.1	0.0	9.2
8. Machinery/ equipm.	3,472	21.9	20.0	70.4	7.4	2.0	0.2	9.5
9. Wood, paper, print.	776	4.9	18.7	68.4	8.9	2.8	1.2	12.9
10. Other manufact.	260	1.6	13.5	74.2	10.0	1.9	0.4	12.3
11. Transp. & communic.	1,159	7.3	11.0	76.6	9.7	2.5	0.3	12.4
12. Wholesale & retail	1,521	9.6	18.5	68.2	7.8	3.4	2.0	13.2
13. Business services	999	6.3	10.6	77.1	7.8	3.1	1.4	12.3
14. Personal services	365	2.3	19.7	67.9	5.8	3.3	3.3	12.3
15. Communal services	1,257	7.9	6.5	80.0	8.3	3.4	1.8	13.5
16. Publ. admin./ defense	1,485	9.4	15.8	71.0	10.2	2.9	0.1	13.2
Total	15,875	100.0	16.6	71.1	8.4	2.8	1.1	12.3

Netherlands

Sector	Employment of industry (1,000s)	Share of total employment (%)	<25	25–54	55–59	60–64	65+	55+
1. Agr., for. & fishing	213	6.4	16.4	64.3	8.9	7.5	2.8	19.2
2. Mining & utilities	91	2.7	7.7	79.1	9.9	3.3	0.0	13.2
3. Construction	363	10.8	17.1	76.3	4.7	1.7	0.3	6.6
4. Food, drink, tobacco	129	3.9	18.6	71.3	7.0	3.1	0.0	10.1
5. Leather & textile	30	0.9	13.3	76.7	10.0	0.0	0.0	10.0
6. Chemical ind.	95	2.8	12.6	77.9	7.4	2.1	0.0	9.5
7. Basic metal ind.	0	0.0						
8. Machinery/ equipm.	380	11.3	16.6	75.5	6.1	1.6	0.3	7.9
9. Wood, paper, print.	118	3.5	18.6	73.7	5.9	1.7	0.0	7.6
10. Other manufact.	87	2.6	11.5	77.0	8.0	3.4	0.0	11.5
11. Transp. & communic.	274	8.2	11.3	79.6	6.9	1.8	0.4	9.1
12. Wholesale & retail	421	12.6	17.8	72.0	5.7	2.9	1.7	10.2
13. Business services	288	8.6	9.0	80.6	5.9	3.5	1.0	10.4
14. Personal services	88	2.6	21.6	69.3	4.5	2.3	2.3	9.1
15. Communal services	499	14.9	6.4	84.4	5.8	2.6	0.8	9.2
16. Publ. admin./ defense	273	8.2	11.4	79.5	6.6	2.2	0.4	9.2
Total	3,349	100.0	13.5	76.7	6.3	2.7	0.8	9.8

Sector	Employment of industry (1,000s)	Share of total employment (%)	Proportion in industry by age (%)					
			<25	25–54	55–59	60–64	65+	55+
		United Kingdom						
1. Agr., for. & fishing	445	3.1	20.4	55.3	9.9	7.4	7.0	24.3
2. Mining & utilities	603	4.3	13.1	74.3	8.8	3.8	0.0	12.6
3. Construction	1647	11.6	22.3	65.9	6.4	4.3	1.1	11.8
4. Food, drink, tobacco	389	2.7	21.6	64.8	7.2	5.7	0.8	13.6
5. Leather & textile	243	1.7	23.5	60.1	8.2	6.2	2.1	16.5
6. Chemical ind.	465	3.3	16.1	69.7	8.8	4.7	0.6	14.2
7. Basic metal ind.	170	1.2	17.1	65.9	11.2	4.7	1.2	17.1
8. Machinery/ equipm.	2,394	16.9	19.9	64.7	8.9	5.7	0.9	15.5
9. Wood, paper, print.	612	4.3	24.2	61.1	6.5	6.0	2.1	14.7
10. Other manufact.	224	1.6	20.1	65.2	8.0	4.5	2.2	14.7
11. Transp. & communic.	1,161	8.2	13.2	71.0	9.5	5.8	0.6	15.8
12. Wholesale & retail	1,668	11.8	30.5	55.7	6.4	4.6	2.9	13.8
13. Business services	1,208	8.5	17.7	69.2	6.3	4.4	2.4	13.1
14. Personal services	442	3.1	28.1	55.0	6.8	4.5	5.7	17.0
15. Communal services	1,633	11.5	12.1	70.2	9.0	6.4	2.3	17.6
16. Publ. admin./ defense	848	6.0	16.7	71.3	7.0	4.4	0.6	11.9
Total	14,152	100.0	19.7	65.5	7.8	5.2	1.8	14.8

Source: Unpublished data from eurostat (Statistical Office of the European Communities); our own calculations.

gle industries have. A rough grouping into the three categories of the primary sector (agriculture, mining, and utilities), the secondary sector (construction and manufacturing), and the tertiary sector (all kinds of services and public administration) illustrates these differences (Table 3.2).

Among the six countries, Germany and the Netherlands show the greatest contrast in employment structures. In Germany the secondary sector still has a comparatively great share, almost 50 percent, of the total male employment, whereas in the Netherlands construction and manufacturing come to only about 35 percent. Because construction has a

Table 3.2. *Share of male employment by sectors (in percent), 1985*

	Sector		
Country	I	II	III
Belgium	6.3	39.4	54.2
Denmark	10.8	38.4	51.1
France	11.1	40.8	48.2
Germany	7.6	49.6	42.8
Netherlands	9.1	35.8	55.1
United Kindgom	7.2	43.3	49.1

quite similar relative size in all six countries, differences in the employment shares of the secondary sector result mainly from differences in manufacturing. Germany has a very big metal manufacturing industry that accounts for more than 20 percent of the total male employment. On the other hand, this industrial division provides only about 11 percent of the total employment of men in the Netherlands.

The shares of the employment of the tertiary sector range from only 42.8 percent in Germany to 55.1 percent in the Netherlands. There are considerable differences for the category communal services, which contains sanitary services, education and research, and health, recreational, cultural, and other services provided to the general public. The share of the total employment of men for this category is below 8 percent in Germany, but clearly above 10 percent in the other countries, reaching almost 15 percent in the Netherlands (Table 3.1).

In addition to the differences in the relative sizes of the secondary and tertiary sectors, there are also clearly different employment shares for the primary sector across the six countries. This difference is mainly due to the differing relative size of agriculture (including forestry and fishing), which ranges from 9 percent and even more in France and Denmark down to less than 4 percent of the total male employment in Belgium and the United Kingdom.

As a first result, it can thus be noted that the industry mixes of the six countries are not very similar. There are considerable differences in the relative size of the three basic economic sectors as well as in their internal structures. These differences, however, are not reflected in the labor force participation of the elderly, as shown in Chapter 2. Despite their different industry mixes, France, Germany, and the Netherlands have similar participation rates of men aged 60 to 64; only in the United King-

Table 3.3. *Age structure of all employed men without agriculture*

Country	< 25	25–54	55–59	60–64	65+	55+
Belgium	11.6	78.2	7.2	2.7	0.5	10.4
Denmark	20.3	67.8	6.6	3.2	2.1	11.9
France	12.8	79.1	5.7	1.9	0.5	8.1
Germany	16.7	71.9	8.2	2.5	0.8	11.5
Netherlands	13.3	77.5	6.2	2.4	0.6	9.2
United Kingdom	19.7	65.8	7.8	5.1	1.6	14.5

dom does the labor force participation of this age group differ from that of the other countries.[1]

As a second point, we now have to consider the age structures within industries and their possible deviations from the overall age structure of the male labor force. The general age pattern of all employed men is not the same in each country, especially at the beginning of the age scale but also to some extent at its end; therefore we will examine differences among industries only within countries, not between countries.

In all six countries, the agricultural sector has a very special age structure (see Table 3.1). As we expected, the older age groups have a much bigger share of the total employment than in all other industries, and agriculture therefore accounts for a disproportionately large share of all older workers. If we examine all workers over 65, for instance, those in agriculture comprise 46.8 percent of this age group in France, 38.1 percent in Denmark, and 31.8 percent in Germany; only in Belgium is agriculture's share of the total work force over age 65 below 10 percent.

This special position of agriculture, as well as the differences in its weight between countries, poses a problem for the analysis of the remaining industries: It partly distorts the picture of the overall age structure, especially in those countries where its weight is high. Therefore the age structure of all employed men *without* the agricultural sector seems to be more adequate as a standard against which to compare the age structures within single industries (Table 3.3).

But even with these adjusted standards of comparison, it is not easy to identify those industries with strikingly different age structures. Table 3.4 shows the relative deviations from the adjusted overall age structures of each country within single industries for the older age groups. If we differentiate between the groups aged 55 to 59 and 60 to 64, there is no clear picture concerning the possible identification of certain industries

[1] OECD does not report participation rates for Belgium and Denmark.

Table 3.4. Relative deviations from overall proportion by age (without agriculture) in each country (in percent)

Category	Belgium 55–59	Belgium 60–64	Denmark 55–59	Denmark 60–64	France 55–59	France 60–64	Germany 55–59	Germany 60–64	Netherlands 55–59	Netherlands 60–64	U.K. 55–59	U.K. 60–64
2 Mining & utilities	70.6	−35.0	−20.3	64.5	−27.7	−60.6	−2.4	−20.0	59.5	37.4	12.7	−25.2
3 Construction	−1.9	−39.6	−11.5	1.5	4.1	−41.9	−17.8	−27.3	−24.5	−31.1	−17.5	−16.7
4 Chemical ind.	−6.4	−16.8	16.6	−100.0	5.8	−75.6	18.8	−16.0	18.8	−12.3	13.0	−7.2
5 Basic metal ind.	−54.5	−100.0	−100.0	−100.0	−33.8	−66.9	−0.5	−57.9	—	—	43.3	−7.7
6 Machinery/equipm.	−34.1	−62.3	−3.3	−33.5	−20.7	−38.3	−9.7	−21.7	−2.4	−34.2	13.5	11.4
7 Food, drink, tobacco	11.1	−1.2	24.2	53.7	6.9	−16.8	−10.8	25.3	12.5	29.2	−7.7	10.9
8 Leather & textile	6.8	−28.8	26.3	160.4	28.4	2.7	48.6	34.5	61.3	−100.0	5.5	21.0
9 Wood, paper, print.	−25.3	−20.4	−12.2	−9.4	36.0	−1.5	8.4	13.4	−4.3	−29.4	−16.2	18.5
10 Other manufact.	23.5	−100.0	59.5	−100.0	−6.3	−23.4	22.0	−23.1	29.8	43.7	3.0	−12.5
11 Transp. & communic.	26.8	−3.4	−7.5	−4.6	−21.4	−50.7	17.8	0.1	11.8	−24.0	21.5	13.2
12 Wholesale & retail	18.3	64.6	−13.2	13.9	16.5	60.5	−4.6	34.1	−8.1	18.8	−18.5	−10.7
13 Business services	0.5	21.8	−2.2	−32.8	18.4	29.2	−4.8	24.1	−4.8	44.7	−19.3	−14.0
14 Personal Services	−17.1	10.6	1.0	−100.0	14.2	160.4	−29.8	31.5	−26.7	−5.3	−13.0	−11.3
15 Communal services	−22.3	24.4	24.2	19.5	−7.1	43.2	0.9	36.8	−6.3	8.6	15.4	24.9
16 Publ. Admin/defense	21.5	54.3	10.9	52.4	0.4	11.0	24.8	15.8	6.3	−8.4	−10.8	−14.4

Source: eurostat; our own calculations.

as relatively "old" or "young" ones in all the observed countries. Even within single countries it is almost impossible to identify such industries. In some industries where the employment share of one of the two age groups is somewhat above or below the average, very often it is just the opposite for the other age group. However, since we are mainly interested in the general age profile of industries, we can also use the total proportion of workers over 55 as a composite index of how old the work force is. To facilitate the interpretation, we now mostly refer to this composite index, which makes it possible to identify some industries as "old" ones in almost every country. This is the case for leather and textile (with the exception of Belgium), for wholesale and retail and for public administration (both with the exception of the United Kingdom), for personal services (except in Denmark), and for communal services.

3.2 CHANGES OF THE INDUSTRY-AGE MIX IN GERMANY, THE NETHERLANDS, AND SWEDEN

The industries just mentioned are considered again later. However, even to the extent that clear age patterns for industries emerge, these cross-sectional data do not allow us a ready interpretation in terms of early exit. The information for just one point in time cannot measure the historical changes in employment patterns. Do lower employment shares of older age groups indicate "young" industries that have few older workers and therefore no problems concerning early exit, or are they the result of a process of early exit that has already taken place? Can high shares be interpreted as showing that the age of exit is higher, or is early exit taking place here also but starting from originally even higher employment shares of the respective older cohorts?

To answer these questions, we need employment data by industry and age for more than one point in time, but such data are difficult to obtain. It is also difficult, and sometimes impossible, to compare cross-sectional information for different points in time because of changes of the industrial codes within single countries. Nevertheless, we do have comparable data for two different points in time for Germany (1970 and 1982), the Netherlands (1971 and 1981), and Sweden (1970 and 1980).[2]

---

[2] The Dutch and the Swedish data do not create big problems: They come from identical sources (Labor Force Survey in the Netherlands, Census in Sweden) and are given in the same industrial categories for both time points. The German data are more difficult to handle: The 1970 data are taken from the Census (the last German census before May 1987), and the 1982 data come from the Mikrozensus, a 1 percent sample of the population. There was also a small change of the industrial classification from 1970 to 1982. The German employment data used in this section cannot easily be compared with the 1985 data from eurostat. Education, for example, is classified as a communal service by eurostat; here it is grouped under public administration and defense.

A comparison of these three countries is of interest because they represent different positions with regard to exit patterns. As shown in Chapter 2, Germany and the Netherlands can be regarded as early-exit countries, while Sweden in comparison has a pattern of late exit. Germany and the Netherlands have similar exit patterns but different industrial structures, as shown in section 3.1.

Table 3.5 shows the changes of the industrial structure and Table 3.6 shows the changed age structure across and within industries. Table 3.5 documents the big changes in the employment share of single industries during the relatively short period of 10 years (in Germany 12 years). The pattern of this change is quite similar in the three countries considered. Every country shows a decline of the employment share in agriculture, in mining and utilities, in construction, and in manufacturing. On the other hand, all three show a distinct increase in the tertiary (service) sector. This increase is particularly sharp in the public domain (communal services and public administration).[3]

Table 3.6 shows the age structure within single industries for the two points in time. For the age structure of all employed men in each country (last line for each country), there is a clear decline of the employment shares of the older age groups (55 to 59, 60 to 64, and 65+).

To test the industry-mix hypothesis of early exit, we first examine globally whether the decrease in the employment shares of men in older age groups is created more by the change of the industrial structure and a shrinkage of "old" industries or by the change of the age structure within industries. To decompose the decrease in the employment share of older age groups into these two components, we use a shift-share analysis (Table 3.7; for formula see appendix). Columns 1 and 2 of Table 3.7 contain real numbers: the initial share of the total male employment by age and the decline of this share. The numbers in columns 3 and 4 can be read as "as if" changes of the employment shares by age. The first of these numbers (column 3) shows the change in this share that can be attributed to the change of the industrial structure, assuming constant age structures within each industry. The second (column 4) reflects the change of the age structures within industries, assuming that the industrial structure of the country has remained the same. The last column contains the residual ("interaction effects") that is due to simultaneous changes of both the industry mix and the age structure within industries.

---

[3] At first sight the German picture looks slightly different from the two other countries because there is a substantial increase not only in communal services but also in public administration. But this category, as mentioned earlier, also contains some parts of employment, like education, that elsewhere are grouped in communal services.

Table 3.5. Changes of employment by industries in three countries

Sector	Germany 1970 100s	%	Germany 1982 100s	%	Netherlands 1971 100s	%	Netherlands 1981 100s	%	Sweden 1970 100s	%	Sweden 1980 100s	%
1. Agr., for. & fishing	10,429	6.14	6,754	4.16	3,138	8.84	2,311	6.58	2,210	10.05	1,525	7.10
2. Mining & utilities	7,482	4.40	6,714	4.13	999	2.81	831	2.37	412	1.87	430	2.00
3. Construction	19,228	11.32	16,845	10.36	5,418	15.26	4,493	12.80	3,192	14.51	2,508	11.67
4. Food, drink, tobacco	5,910	3.48	5,194	3.20	1,566	4.41	1,333	3.80	520	2.36	484	2.25
5. Leather & textile	4,460	2.63	2,583	1.59	872	2.46	373	1.06	338	1.54	196	0.91
6. Chemical industry	7,110	4.18	7,003	4.31	1,088	3.07	1,073	3.06	480	2.18	484	2.25
7. Basic metal ind.	9,903	5.83	9,223	5.67	303	0.85	322	0.95	624	2.84	531	2.47
8. Machinery/equipm.	33,631	19.80	31,196	19.19	4,750	13.38	4,210	11.99	3,915	17.80	3,747	17.44
9. Wood, paper, print.	7,851	4.62	7,051	4.34	1,467	4.13	1,239	3.53	1,705	7.75	1,562	7.27
10. Other manufact.	1,682	0.99	1,502	0.92	442	1.25	542	1.54	441	2.00	299	1.39
11. Transp. & communic.	11,817	6.96	11,694	7.19	2,680	7.55	2,808	8.00	1,990	9.05	2,014	9.37
12. Wholesale & retail	15,180	8.93	13,636	8.39	4,563	12.85	4,320	12.30	2,271	10.32	2,393	11.14
13. Business services	6,454	3.80	8,358	5.14	1,999	5.63	2,672	7.61	972	4.42	1,403	6.53
14. Personal services	4,488	2.64	4,607	2.83	987	2.78	1,087	3.10	298	1.36	312	1.45
15. Communal services	8,567	5.04	11,864	7.30	2,690	7.58	4,346	12.38	1,606	7.30	2,538	11.81
16. Public administr.	15,702	9.24	18,314	11.27	2,534	7.14	3,142	8.95	1,018	4.63	1,062	4.94
Total	169,894	100.00	162,538	100.00	35,496	100.00	35,112	100.00	21,992	100.00	21,487	100.00

Table 3.6. *Changed age structures within industries in three countries*

Sector	Initial proportion by age (%)						Changed proportion by age (%)					
	<25	25–54	55–59	60–64	65+	55+	<25	25–54	55–59	60–64	65+	55+
	Germany, 1970 and 1982											
1. Agr., for. & fishing	11.28	54.07	9.21	10.41	15.03	34.66	14.24	58.05	10.96	7.08	9.67	27.70
2. Mining & utilities	9.30	76.95	7.95	5.01	0.79	13.75	13.60	75.35	8.34	2.52	0.19	11.05
3. Construction	17.44	69.63	6.33	5.25	1.35	12.92	21.33	70.16	5.93	1.94	0.64	8.51
4. Food, drink, tobacco	18.00	65.89	7.75	6.23	2.13	16.11	21.64	66.49	7.24	3.47	1.16	11.86
5. Leather & textile	13.99	64.24	9.44	9.08	3.25	21.77	12.00	71.04	10.14	4.92	1.90	16.96
6. Chemical industry	13.05	72.87	7.48	5.78	0.82	14.08	12.18	76.25	8.65	2.68	0.24	11.58
7. Basic metal ind.	15.06	71.40	6.94	5.59	1.01	13.54	16.25	72.60	8.48	2.34	0.33	11.15
8. Machinery/equipm.	22.23	65.18	6.19	5.28	1.12	12.59	20.56	70.54	6.65	1.96	0.29	8.90
9. Wood, paper, print.	17.69	64.30	7.67	7.45	2.89	18.01	20.37	69.04	6.50	2.98	1.11	10.58
10. Other manufact.	15.58	67.95	7.73	6.90	1.84	16.47	14.91	72.45	8.85	3.26	0.53	12.65
11. Transp. & communic.	13.07	69.53	10.95	5.59	0.86	17.40	12.31	76.73	7.76	2.81	0.39	10.97
12. Wholesale & retail	19.80	60.37	7.71	7.19	4.93	19.83	18.28	68.31	7.25	3.62	2.54	13.41
13. Business services	16.61	66.06	7.16	6.23	3.94	17.32	10.94	75.74	7.42	3.95	1.95	13.32
14. Personal services	17.45	62.21	9.58	6.53	4.23	20.34	18.34	68.89	6.25	3.65	2.87	12.76
15. Communal services	6.34	71.31	10.13	7.69	4.53	22.35	7.16	79.05	7.43	3.92	2.44	13.79
16. Public administr.	28.40	54.64	9.87	6.48	0.61	16.96	28.84	60.31	7.82	2.86	0.17	10.86
Total	17.58	65.36	7.92	6.36	2.78	17.07	17.93	70.33	7.45	2.99	1.30	11.74
	Netherlands, 1971 and 1981											
1. Agr., for. & fishing	16.51	59.37	9.97	8.76	5.39	24.12	15.19	65.21	10.47	6.58	2.55	19.60
2. Mining & utilities	12.21	73.87	7.91	5.61	0.40	13.91	9.51	78.46	8.18	3.85	0.00	12.03
3. Construction	26.84	60.62	6.39	5.13	1.02	12.53	20.39	72.29	4.87	2.23	0.22	7.32
4. Food, drink, tobacco	20.56	63.67	8.17	6.45	1.15	15.77	18.15	70.52	7.80	3.30	0.23	11.33
5. Leather & textile	17.43	65.13	9.29	6.54	1.61	17.43	12.06	74.27	9.38	3.75	0.54	13.67

80

6. Chemical industry	15.53	73.35	6.34	4.14	0.64	11.12	11.74	78.94	7.55	1.77	0.00	9.32
7. Basic metal ind.	14.19	74.26	7.26	4.29	0.00	11.55	12.05	77.71	8.13	2.11	0.00	10.24
8. Machinery/equipm.	23.85	65.12	6.08	4.17	0.78	11.03	18.00	72.78	6.70	2.40	0.12	9.22
9. Wood, paper, print.	24.34	61.75	6.82	5.45	1.64	13.91	18.81	71.10	6.78	2.91	0.40	10.09
10. Other manufact.	15.84	64.03	9.95	9.28	0.90	20.14	12.92	74.72	8.12	4.06	0.18	12.36
11. Transp. & communic.	19.51	68.21	6.83	4.59	0.86	12.28	14.28	76.79	6.37	2.35	0.21	8.94
12. Wholesale & retail	21.21	62.68	7.23	5.46	3.42	16.11	18.73	70.47	5.97	3.70	1.13	10.81
13. Business services	21.51	62.94	6.35	5.35	3.85	15.56	13.66	75.19	6.55	3.29	1.31	11.15
14. Personal services	19.55	63.02	9.02	5.78	2.63	17.43	19.87	70.65	5.15	3.50	0.83	9.48
15. Communal services	11.64	71.45	8.29	6.13	2.49	16.91	9.32	80.61	6.30	3.13	0.64	10.08
16. Public administr.	30.15	57.58	7.38	4.50	0.39	12.27	27.50	62.76	6.27	3.31	0.16	9.74
Total	21.22	63.96	7.35	5.52	1.95	14.82	16.86	72.71	6.62	3.19	0.62	10.43

Sweden, 1970 and 1980

1. Agr., for. & fishing	8.27	55.19	14.07	13.18	9.29	36.54	11.01	55.83	13.04	11.55	8.57	33.16
2. Mining & utilities	10.84	66.75	11.86	8.73	1.82	22.41	9.76	71.44	10.89	7.37	0.54	18.80
3. Construction	16.06	63.32	10.26	7.79	2.57	20.61	14.98	70.12	8.19	6.05	0.66	14.90
4. Food, drink, tobacco	14.96	60.53	11.06	10.04	3.41	24.50	20.18	62.38	9.36	7.26	0.82	17.44
5. Leather & textile	12.15	57.05	13.23	12.78	4.79	30.80	14.69	58.80	13.10	11.37	2.04	26.52
6. Chemical industry	14.29	64.85	10.26	8.16	2.44	20.85	14.65	67.85	9.64	7.19	0.67	17.50
7. Basic metal ind.	14.33	62.96	11.27	9.16	2.28	22.71	14.39	67.04	10.16	8.02	0.39	18.57
8. Machinery/equipm.	17.34	65.86	8.44	6.25	2.11	16.80	16.14	67.02	9.46	6.61	0.59	16.66
9. Wood, paper, print.	15.39	59.93	10.96	9.81	3.91	24.67	15.59	65.35	10.15	7.83	1.08	19.07
10. Other manufact.	13.59	61.66	11.08	10.01	3.66	24.75	15.39	65.36	10.21	8.08	0.96	19.25
11. Transp. & communic.	12.58	71.02	9.82	5.04	1.54	16.40	11.73	71.62	10.53	5.51	0.61	16.65
12. Wholesale & retail	14.91	64.59	9.00	7.47	4.03	20.50	14.77	68.48	8.74	6.24	1.77	16.76
13. Business services	11.09	70.30	8.00	6.50	4.11	18.61	8.62	74.67	8.69	6.41	1.61	16.72
14. Personal services	16.36	62.55	9.80	7.74	3.55	21.09	16.92	68.66	7.25	5.15	2.02	14.42
15. Communal services	8.24	71.55	9.20	7.89	3.12	20.20	10.67	74.64	7.99	5.51	1.19	14.69
16. Public administr.	10.09	71.34	9.98	6.75	1.84	18.57	7.95	73.32	10.80	6.99	0.94	18.73
Total	13.64	64.68	10.15	8.07	3.46	21.68	13.37	68.72	9.54	6.84	1.53	17.90

81

Table 3.7. *Decomposition of the changing share of older age groups ("shift-share" analysis)*

Country and period	Age group	Initial share of total employment by age (1)	Actual change in share (2)	Fixed age structure in each industry/ changing industry distribution (3)	Fixed industry distribution/ varying age structure within industry (4)	Interaction (5)
Germany,						
1970–82	55–59	7.92	−0.47	−0.16	−0.24	−0.07
	60–64	6.36	−3.37	−0.33	−3.19	0.15
	65+	2.78	−1.48	−0.32	−1.28	0.12
	55+	17.07	−5.32	−0.86	−4.60	0.14
Netherlands,						
1971–81	55–59	7.35	−0.73	−0.08	−0.56	−0.09
	60–64	5.52	−2.33	−0.11	−2.24	0.02
	65+	1.95	−1.33	−0.02	−1.30	0.00
	55+	14.82	−4.39	−0.22	−4.10	−0.08
Sweden,						
1970–80	55–59	10.15	−0.61	−0.35	−0.31	0.05
	60–64	8.07	−1.23	−0.38	−0.88	0.03
	65+	3.46	−1.93	−0.23	−1.71	0.01
	55+	21.68	−3.78	−1.03	−2.85	0.10

Source: Our own calculations (see appendix for formula).

The first result seen from the shift-share analysis is that the decrease of employment shares of these age groups is due to both the change of the industry distribution and the changes of the age structure within industries. This is shown by the minus signs in columns 3 and 4: All these numbers are negative. The second result, however, is that the degree to which both these components can explain the general decrease in employment shares of older age groups differs between the age groups and across the countries. Germany and the Netherlands have already been identified as early-exit countries in terms of their low labor force participation of men over age 55 and particularly over age 60. This characterization is now supported. There is a remarkable decline of the employment share for the group aged 60 to 64 in these countries, especially considering the rather short time period. To a large extent, this decline is due to the changes in the employment share of this age group within all of the different industries. The change of the industry distribution alone would have led to only a comparatively small decrease. In Sweden, the decline in the employment share of this age group is smaller. The part of this decline that can be explained by the age-structure component is also somewhat smaller here, although it is still clearly higher than that of the industry-mix component.

For the group aged 55 to 59, the picture is more difficult to describe. The decrease in the employment share is clearly smaller than that of the group aged 60 to 64. In the Netherlands this decrease is again mainly due to the age-structure component. For Germany this component is still somewhat smaller than the industry-mix component, whereas for Sweden it is slightly larger.

In sum, the findings from the shift-share analysis show that a decrease in employment shares of older men within all the industries, rather than changes in industry distribution, is the main factor underlying the overall changes in the old-age share of male employment. This is particularly the case for those age groups and in those countries with a relatively large decrease, that is, for the group aged 60 to 64 more than for group aged 55 to 59 and in Germany and the Netherlands more than in Sweden.

As a second step, we now examine the difference between industries in terms of changes in their age structure (Table 3.6). The composite number for men aged 55 + gives the clearest picture. Initially, the proportion of older workers is especially high not only in the primary sector and in some traditional industries that are now under pressure, such as leather and textile, but in Germany and the Netherlands it is also high in the service sector. In both countries, the service sector becomes considerably "younger" in the period under study; its age proportion approaches that of the bulk in the secondary sector, with the concomitant result that the total variance between industries decreases. In agriculture and in leather and textile, on the other hand, the share of older workers is reduced to a lesser degree; at the second time point, these categories have the highest age proportion in all three countries. Thus, it is not the troubled industries that are the leaders in rejuvenating their age structure but rather the service industries, especially those of the public sector.

The relative employment changes by industry and age (left part of Table 3.8) allow a closer look at the change of the industry-age mix. Relative change in employment means that changes of absolute employment numbers by industry and age are taken as a percentage of the initial employment number. Information about the demographic structure of each country in terms of relative changes of the total male population by age is given as an additional standard of comparison.

Table 3.8. Employment changes by age in three countries

Sector	Relative changes in employment (%) — Germany, 1970–82							Employment changes in a "cohort perspective"					
	<25	25–54	55–59	60–64	65+	55+	Total	1970, 45–49	1982, 55–59	Change (%)	1970, 50–54	1982, 60–64	Change (%)
1. Agr., for. & fishing	−18.20	−30.45	−23.00	−55.99	−58.35	−48.24	−35.24	1,015	740	−27.09	564	478	−15.25
2. Mining & utilities	31.18	−12.12	−5.88	−54.93	−77.97	−27.89	−10.26	1,001	560	−44.06	576	169	−70.66
3. Construction	7.13	−11.73	−17.91	−67.69	−58.30	−42.33	−12.39	1,447	999	−30.96	765	326	−57.39
4. Food, drink, tobacco	5.64	−11.30	−17.90	−51.09	−52.38	−35.29	−12.12	523	376	−28.11	326	180	−44.79
5. Leather & textile	−50.32	−35.95	−37.77	−68.64	−66.21	−54.89	−42.09	386	262	−32.12	276	127	−53.99
6. Chemical industry	−8.08	3.05	13.91	−54.26	−70.69	−18.98	−1.50	768	606	−21.09	435	188	−56.78
7. Basic metal ind.	0.54	−5.30	13.83	−61.01	−70.00	−23.34	−6.87	1,003	782	−22.03	578	216	−62.63
8. Machinery/equipm.	−14.21	0.38	−0.38	−65.52	−75.86	−34.41	−7.24	2,821	2,074	−26.48	1,601	612	−61.77
9. Wood, paper, print.	3.38	−3.55	−23.93	−64.10	−65.64	−47.24	−10.19	641	458	−28.55	406	210	−48.38
10. Other manufact.	−14.50	−4.81	2.31	−57.76	−74.19	−31.41	−10.70	153	133	−13.07	112	49	−56.25
11. Transp. & communic.	−6.74	9.18	−29.83	−50.15	−54.90	−37.60	−1.04	1,226	908	−25.94	844	329	−61.02
12. Wholesale & retail	−17.10	1.65	−15.54	−54.81	−53.61	−39.24	−10.17	1,309	989	−24.45	918	493	−46.30
13. Business services	−14.74	48.48	34.20	−17.91	−35.83	−0.45	29.50	1,086	620	−42.91	357	330	−7.56
14. Personal services	7.92	13.68	−33.02	−42.66	−30.53	−35.60	2.65	410	288	−29.76	303	168	−44.55
15. Communal services	56.54	53.51	1.61	−29.44	−25.52	−14.57	38.48	939	882	−6.07	694	465	−33.00
16. Public administr.	18.41	28.74	−7.55	−48.53	−67.37	−25.35	16.63	1,541	1,433	−7.01	1,077	524	−51.35
Total employment	−2.40	2.94	−10.03	−54.99	−55.26	−34.16	−4.33	16,269	12,110	−25.56	9,832	4,864	−50.53
Total population	10.68	−6.51	−30.96				−9.07	16,344	14,861	−9.07	10,394	10,874	4.62

Netherlands

	1971–81							1971, 45–49	1981, 55–59	Change (%)	1971, 50–54	1981, 60–64	Change (%)
	<25	25–54	55–59	60–64	65+	55+	Total						
1. Agr., for. & fishing	−32.24	−19.11	−22.68	−44.73	−65.09	−40.16	−26.35	329	242	−26.44	310	152	−50.97
2. Mining & utilities	−35.25	−11.65	−13.92	−42.86	−100.00	−28.06	−16.82	132	68	−48.48	111	32	−71.17
3. Construction	−37.00	−1.13	−36.71	−64.03	−81.82	−51.55	−17.07	411	219	−46.72	348	100	−71.26
4. Food, drink, tobacco	−24.84	−5.72	−18.75	−56.44	−83.33	−38.87	−14.88	160	104	−35.00	140	44	−68.57
5. Leather & textile	−70.39	−51.23	−56.79	−75.44	−85.71	−66.45	−57.22	105	35	−66.67	86	14	−83.72
6. Chemical industry	−25.44	6.14	17.39	−57.78	−100.00	−17.36	−1.38	130	81	−37.69	97	19	−80.41
7. Basic metal ind.	−6.98	14.67	22.73	−46.15	–	−2.86	9.57	38	27	−28.95	26	7	−73.08
8. Machinery/equipm.	−33.10	−0.94	−2.42	−48.99	−86.49	−25.95	−11.37	473	282	−40.38	367	101	−72.48
9. Wood, paper, print.	−34.73	−2.76	−16.00	−55.00	−79.17	−38.73	−15.54	136	84	−38.24	118	36	−69.49
10. Other manufact.	0.00	43.11	0.00	−46.34	−75.00	−24.72	22.62	52	44	−15.38	46	22	−52.17
11. Transp. & communic.	−23.33	17.94	−2.19	−46.34	−73.91	−23.71	4.78	286	179	−37.41	228	66	−71.05
12. Wholesale & retail	−16.43	6.43	−21.82	−35.74	−68.59	−36.46	−5.33	421	258	−38.72	356	160	−55.06
13. Business services	−15.12	59.70	37.80	−17.76	−54.55	−4.18	33.67	192	175	−8.85	160	88	−45.00
14. Personal services	11.92	23.47	−37.08	−33.33	−65.38	−40.12	10.13	100	56	−44.00	88	38	−56.82
15. Communal services	29.39	82.26	22.87	−17.58	−58.21	−3.74	61.56	265	274	3.40	236	136	−42.37
16. Public administr.	13.09	35.16	5.35	−8.77	−50.00	−1.61	23.99	281	197	−29.89	257	104	−59.53
Total employment	−21.39	12.45	−10.92	−42.88	−68.60	−30.40	−1.08	3,511	2,325	−33.78	2,974	1,119	−62.37
Total population		20.00	13.02	7.86				3,670	3,419	−6.84	3,269	2,883	−11.81

Sweden

	<25	1970–81 (%)						1970, 45–49	1980, 55–59	Change (%)	1970, 50–54	1980, 60–64	Change (%)
		25–54	55–59	60–64	65+	55+	Total*						
1. Agr., for. & fishing	−8.11	−30.23	−36.06	−39.54	−36.35	−37.39	−31.00	266	199	−25.24	293	176	−39.85
2. Mining & utilities	−5.98	11.81	−4.08	−11.85	−68.86	−12.37	4.46	52	47	−9.96	52	32	−38.65
3. Construction	−26.68	−12.98	−37.27	−38.93	−79.73	−43.18	−21.41	316	205	−35.01	326	152	−53.44
4. Food, drink, tobacco	25.55	−4.06	−21.17	−32.65	−77.56	−33.72	−6.90	54	45	−16.10	53	35	−33.17
5. Leather & textile	−29.84	−40.18	−42.53	−48.35	−75.28	−50.04	−41.96	39	26	−34.15	42	22	−46.32
6. Chemical industry	3.39	5.50	−5.26	−11.16	−72.12	−15.39	0.84	52	47	−10.23	51	35	−32.30
7. Basic metal ind.	−14.62	−9.44	−23.36	−25.55	−85.49	−30.47	−14.96	67	54	−19.52	71	43	−40.25
8. Machinery/equipm.	−10.91	−2.33	7.24	1.20	−73.39	−5.12	−4.29	424	355	−16.38	392	248	−36.78
9. Wood, paper, print.	−7.25	−0.17	−15.14	−26.91	−74.61	−29.23	−8.43	183	159	−13.36	187	122	−34.53
10. Other manufact.	−23.22	−28.13	−37.52	−45.26	−82.24	−47.26	−32.20	46	31	−33.65	47	24	−49.09
11. Transp. & communic.	−5.66	2.02	8.46	10.73	−60.20	2.70	1.17	264	212	−19.68	256	111	−56.66
12. Wholesale & retail	4.41	11.72	2.33	−11.85	−53.58	−13.83	5.39	247	209	−15.33	224	149	−33.33
13. Business services	12.16	53.21	56.78	42.23	−43.38	29.58	44.26	100	122	21.95	90	90	−0.17
14. Personal services	8.18	14.79	−22.64	−30.34	−40.63	−28.50	4.58	32	23	−29.38	31	16	−48.21
15. Communal services	104.52	64.88	37.29	10.31	−39.44	14.91	58.05	181	203	12.00	158	140	−11.68
16. Public administr.	−17.83	7.20	12.83	8.13	−46.89	5.20	4.30	130	115	−11.76	126	74	−40.87
Total employment	−4.22	3.81	−8.16	−17.24	−56.85	−19.32	−2.30	2,453	2,049	−16.45	2,398	1,469	−38.75
Total population		4.81	−3.00	−0.04				2,657	2,454	−7.64	2,604	2,329	−10.56

The three countries are similar not only in their slight decline of total male employment, but also in the overall change of their employment structure by age: large declines of the group aged 65+, modest declines for 55 to 59. The main differences between Germany and the Netherlands as early-exit countries and Sweden as a (rather) late-exit country is for the group aged 60 to 64, which declines heavily in the former and considerably less in the latter.

In Germany, there is a decline in all of the 16 branches for the group aged 60 to 64. This is not very surprising, given the fact that the total male population of this age group also went down by more than 30 percent. But only in parts of the service sector – which are also those branches with the largest total growth – is the decline smaller than the population decline: considerably so in business services and slightly so in communal services. In all the other branches, the relative decrease of employment was larger. The relative change in total employment of the group aged 60 to 64 amounted to −55 percent just from 1970 to 1982.

Again, the picture is less clear for the group aged 55 to 59 because there is some employment growth in the generally growing sectors of business and communal services and also, somewhat surprisingly at first sight, in the shrinking sectors of the chemical and the basic metal industries. Recent development in these two sectors shows that special efforts have been made to shed this "burden" of older workers. Aside from these exceptions, however, there is a more or less uniform relative decline of employment in all the other sectors, resulting in an overall decline of 10 percent.

The Dutch findings are quite similar to the German regarding the relative changes in employment. In spite of a relative increase of the male population in the groups aged 55 to 59 and 60 to 64, there is a decrease of employment for the group aged 60 to 64 in all branches, while for the group aged 55 to 59, as in Germany, there is an increase only in business and communal services and in the chemical and basic metal industries.

The findings of Chapter 2 concerning the trends of male labor force participation as well as the results of the shift-share analysis in this chapter would lead us to expect that Sweden will show a somewhat different picture. The overall decrease in the employment of older men in Sweden (over 17 percent for the group aged 60 to 64 and more than 8 percent even for the group aged 55 to 59) is not reflected in a uniform decrease across all or at least most of the industrial branches. Not only the growing branches business services, communal services, and public administration but also a stagnant branch like transport and communication and a generally declining branch like manufacturing of machinery and equipment have positive employment changes for older age groups.

The general picture that emerges is as follows. Not surprisingly, the industrial branches with higher overall decreases in employment are also those with higher decreases among the older age groups. In all three countries, leather and textile has the highest overall decrease as well as the highest decrease in the 55+ age group (Table 3.8). When the branches are grouped according to their overall relative employment change (Table 3.9), the results go in the same direction, but the differences are much smaller than the troubled-industry hypothesis of early exit would predict. In Germany and the Netherlands, even the growing industries show a substantial decline in their number of older workers; only in Sweden is there a moderate increase. Thus, in the early-exit countries, the growing industries also contribute to the decrease of the older work force; early exit has not been restricted to industries that have had to reduce their work force.

Moreover, the difference between the total relative change and the relative change above age 55 is largest among the growing industries (Table 3.9, right side); in relation to their overall development, the latter thus have the highest decrease among older workers.[4] This might suggest that there is a practical limit to making older workers exit early and that the shrinking industries, by almost cutting in half the size of their older work force during the 10 years that we consider, have reached this limit of what is possible; but it is surprising to see that in the growing industries there is such a large difference between the growth rate of the young and middle groups and that of the older groups.[5]

The result is even more obvious in a sectoral grouping of industries (Table 3.10). In all three countries, the public part of the service sector – communal services and public administration – has the largest growth rate.[6] And in all three countries, this sector has the largest difference between the relative overall employment change and that of the elderly. In Germany this means a substantial relative decline and in the Netherlands a small relative decline; in Sweden there is a modest relative increase, but not nearly as high as the increase in total employment. Thus, the elderly do not participate proportionally in the growth of the

---

[4] At the other end of the work life, in the age group below 25, the relative changes in employment are more in line with the total relative change; in other words, the recruitment of young workers corresponds more closely to the general evolution of the industry.

[5] It should be remembered that the interpretation of shrinking numbers of older workers in terms of early exit is provisional; shrinking numbers could also reflect smaller cohorts entering the age bracket under question. For a more definitive analysis, we need a cohort framework, as discussed in the following paragraphs.

[6] The other service industries – especially transport and communication – are a mix between private and public parts in which it is impossible to assess the share of the latter.

Table 3.9. *Changes in employment by age in industries according to their overall employment change*[a]

Branches with a relative employment change of	Relative changes in employment (%)							Difference between relative changes by age and total relative changes					
	<25	25–54	55–59	60–64	65+	55+	Total	<25	25–54	55–59	60–64	65+	55+
					Germany, 1970 to 1982								
a. < −20%	−29.33	−32.31	−27.50	−59.42	−59.02	−49.65	−37.29	7.96	4.98	9.79	−22.13	−21.73	−12.36
b. −5% to −20%	−5.57	−4.57	−8.23	−61.60	−61.86	−36.50	−9.42	3.86	4.85	1.20	−52.18	−52.43	−27.08
c. +5% to −5%	−3.59	7.99	−20.12	−49.78	−44.29	−32.44	−0.47	−3.12	8.47	−19.65	−49.31	−43.81	−31.97
d. > +5%	15.97	41.17	1.91	−36.56	−34.46	−16.84	25.43	−9.46	15.74	−23.52	−61.99	−59.89	−42.27
Total	−2.40	2.94	−10.03	−54.99	−55.26	−34.16	−4.33	1.93	7.27	−5.70	−50.66	−50.93	−29.83
					Netherlands, 1971 to 1981								
a. < −20%	−40.90	−26.61	−29.70	−50.00	−66.67	−44.55	−33.07	−7.83	6.45	3.37	−16.93	−33.60	−11.49
b. −5% to −20%	−30.28	−0.42	−20.20	−50.83	−75.51	−38.29	−12.46	−17.82	12.03	−7.75	−38.38	−63.05	−25.84
c. +5% to −5%	−23.84	14.36	3.17	−49.40	−80.00	−22.00	3.00	−26.84	11.36	0.18	−52.40	−83.00	−25.00
d. > +5%	8.11	54.53	11.71	−20.52	−57.61	−9.25	35.35	−27.25	19.18	−23.65	−55.88	−92.96	−44.60
Total	−21.39	12.45	−10.92	−42.88	−68.60	−30.40	−1.08	−20.31	13.53	−9.84	−41.80	−67.51	−29.32
					Sweden, 1970 to 1980								
a. < −20%	−22.32	−21.18	−37.09	−40.30	−51.76	−41.08	−26.73	4.41	5.55	−10.36	−13.57	−25.02	−14.35
b. −5% to −20%	−2.85	−2.99	−18.08	−27.71	−76.71	−30.32	−9.58	6.74	6.60	−8.50	−18.13	−67.13	−20.73
c. +5% to −5%	−5.74	3.88	4.91	−2.42	−61.11	−6.55	0.55	−6.29	3.32	4.35	−2.97	−61.66	−7.11
d. > +5%	63.06	60.53	44.02	20.93	−41.19	20.16	52.85	10.21	7.68	−8.84	−31.92	−94.04	−32.69
Total	−4.22	3.81	−8.16	−17.24	−56.85	−19.32	−2.30	−1.92	6.11	−5.86	−14.95	−54.55	−17.02

[a]The branches at each level of change were as follows:
a. Branches 1 and 5 in Germany and the Netherlands and branches 1, 3, 5, and 10 in Sweden.
b. Branches 2, 3, 4, 7, 8, 9, 10, and 12 in Germany, branches 2, 3, 4, 8, 9, and 12 in the Netherlands, and branches 4, 7, and 9 in Sweden.
c. Branches 6, 11, and 14 in Germany, branches 6 and 11 in the Netherlands, and branches 2, 6, 8, 11, 12 (+5.39 percent), 14, and 16 in Sweden.
d. Branches 13, 15, and 16 in Germany, branches 7, 10, 13, 14, 15, and 16 in the Netherlands, and branches 13 and 15 in Sweden.

Table 3.10. Changes in employment by age in industrial sectors

Branches	Relative changes in employment (%)							Difference between relative changes by age and total relative changes					
	<25	25–54	55–59	60–64	65+	55+	Total	<25	25–54	55–59	60–64	65+	55+
							Germany, 1970 to 1982						
1, 2	0.16	−21.19	−16.45	−55.72	−59.07	−43.73	−24.81	24.97	3.61	8.35	−30.91	−34.26	−18.93
3	7.13	−11.73	−17.91	−67.69	−58.30	−42.33	−12.39	19.52	0.67	−5.52	−55.30	−45.91	−29.94
4–10	−10.38	−3.90	−4.50	−62.46	−68.70	−35.17	−9.63	−0.75	5.73	5.13	−52.83	−59.07	−25.54
11–14	−11.15	13.73	−16.44	−46.03	−46.83	−32.18	0.94	−12.09	12.79	−17.38	−46.97	−47.77	−33.12
15, 16	22.55	39.05	−4.26	−41.03	−33.75	−20.84	24.35	−1.80	14.70	−28.61	−65.37	−58.10	−45.19
Total	−2.40	2.94	−10.03	−54.99	−55.26	−34.16	−4.33	1.93	7.27	−5.70	−50.66	−50.93	−29.83
							Netherlands, 1971 to 1981						
1, 2	−32.81	−16.99	−20.92	−44.41	−65.90	−38.28	−24.05	−8.76	7.06	3.13	−20.36	−41.84	−14.23
3	−37.00	−1.13	−36.71	−64.03	−81.82	−51.55	−17.07	−19.93	15.95	−19.63	−46.96	−64.75	−34.47
4–10	−32.59	−2.88	−10.37	−54.58	−84.62	−33.24	−13.22	−19.38	10.33	2.85	−41.36	−71.40	−20.02
11–14	−15.28	21.45	−8.37	−34.33	−64.89	−27.67	6.43	−21.71	15.02	−14.80	−40.76	−71.33	−34.10
15, 16	17.83	76.99	14.88	−13.98	−57.14	−2.87	43.34	−25.51	33.65	−28.46	−57.32	−100.48	−46.21
Total	−21.39	12.45	−10.92	−42.88	−68.60	−30.40	−1.08	−20.31	13.53	−9.84	−41.80	−67.51	−29.32
							Sweden, 1970 to 1980						
1, 2	−7.69	−22.50	−31.72	−36.49	−37.49	−34.82	−25.44	17.75	2.94	−6.28	−11.06	−12.06	−9.38
3	−26.68	−12.98	−37.27	−38.93	−79.73	−43.18	−21.41	−5.27	8.43	−15.86	−17.52	−58.32	−21.78
4–10	−8.62	−4.89	−9.25	−18.36	−75.55	−21.79	−8.98	0.37	4.09	−0.27	−9.38	−66.57	−12.80
11–14	2.39	15.78	11.61	2.91	−51.60	−1.92	10.66	−8.27	5.12	0.95	−7.75	−62.26	−12.58
15, 16	51.06	42.54	27.32	9.54	−41.47	11.33	37.19	13.87	5.34	−9.88	−27.65	−78.66	−25.86
Total	−4.22	3.81	−8.16	−17.24	−56.85	−19.32	−2.30	−1.92	6.11	−5.86	−14.95	−54.55	−17.02

public sector, and this lack of participation must be due to a lack of demand because on the supply side a large pool of older workers is available. It should be noted that there is no forced premature exit from public employment (by dismissal or plant closings). Early exit is not simply a question of pressure by the employer but also of preferences of the workers; public-sector workers are privileged not only in job security but (partly) also in terms of availability of acceptable pathways into retirement. In future studies, these characteristics of public labor markets should be analyzed with more detailed data.

At this point it has to be noted that the method used here contains some problems. For instance, the impact of the demographic structure and its changes on the employment changes by age has already been pointed out on several occasions. More importantly, the age profile of industries may strongly differ from that of the total work force. For example, if an industry has had an especially high proportion of workers in the age groups below 55 at time 1, a small relative decline of those above 55 between times 1 and 2 may reflect the larger cohort size rather than a lower rate of early exit. One way to avoid this kind of possible distortions is to do a cohort analysis. For this, we need employment data for identical units (cohorts) over time, but data of this kind are available to only a limited degree.

Our employment data by industry and age allow a partial cohort analysis for the Netherlands and Sweden, using the fact that the two points in time are 10 years apart. Men aged 45 to 49 and 50 to 54 at the first time point are 55 to 59 and 60 to 64 years of age at the second. For Germany, the analysis is not quite correct because of the 12-year interval. The size of the German birth cohorts that were 50 to 54 years of age in 1970 (i.e., born during and immediately after World War I) is particularly small in comparison to the younger cohorts. In 1982 these people were 62 to 66 years old and not 60 to 64, which explains the otherwise astonishing positive growth rate of the male population.[7] This inadequacy will, however, not be critical for examining differences between industries.

The cohort results show that for the national economies as a whole, the decrease in the number of older workers has been even more pronounced than what is indicated by the comparison of the cross-sectional data for the two time points. (The only exception is the older Germany cohort, for the reasons just stated.) This is caused by the fact that the older cohorts of 1980 to 1982 are larger than the older cohorts of 1970 to 1971, so that in the cross-sectional comparison, the early exit from the

---

[7] An analogous problem has been noted for the German pension insurance data by Kaltenbach (1981:168); see also Conradi et al. (1987:183).

work force is partially masked by the growing size of the elderly population. During the 10 years, the number of workers in the older cohort has decreased by half in Germany and by more than three-fifths in the Netherlands. The decrease yielded by the cohort perspective is composed of two forms of early exit: retirement and death.

On the level of industries, the critical question is, of course, whether there is no entry into the cohorts between the two time points, in other words, no mobility between industries. For the age bracket with which we are concerned it seems plausible to assume that there is indeed no substantial mobility. But especially with growing industries, the assumption may not be completely justified. A definitive analysis would be possible only with longitudinal data for individuals.

Looking at the older one of the two five-year cohorts (see right side of Table 3.8), there is a decline of employment in all economic categories in Germany and the Netherlands that is clearly larger than the relative change of this cohort's total population. The unchanged male employment in the sector of business services in Sweden, in view of a decline in the population of this cohort by more than 10 percent, shows that the assumption of no inter-industry mobility is not completely covered by the empirical findings. There might be some absorption of older workers in other growing branches as well, such as communal services and public administration. In the younger cohort, both of these categories show a very low decrease in Germany, and in the Netherlands there is even a small growth in communal services.

As to single industries, the results are generally in line with those obtained from looking at relative changes. Leather and textile has the highest rate of early exit in the Netherlands – only one in three of the younger cohort ond one in six of the older cohort remain in work – and is among the highest in the other two countries as well. The practical limit to early exit thus seems to be considerably lower than we assumed on the basis of the cross-sectional data. For some industries – particularly for construction, and in Germany and the Netherlands also for mining and utilities – the cohort perspective yields relatively higher rates of decline, which means that at the earlier time point (1970 or 1971) these industries had especially small numbers in the older age groups (and/or especially high ones in the age group from 45 to 55); this might indicate that they had started the process of early exit earlier than the other industries.

In sum, the empirical findings of this partial cohort analysis correspond to the picture of early exit from the labor market that was drawn in the first parts of our analysis. Early exit can be observed in almost every branch. The rates, however, are different. Some parts of the service sector deviate in the same direction as found previously: They have comparatively less decline of employment or even some employment growth, especially for the younger cohort. There are also some differences between Germany and the Netherlands as early-exit countries and Sweden as a late-exit country.

3.3 CONCLUSIONS

One way of thinking about the dynamics of early exit from employment is that the expanding industries of the past decades brought in young skilled workers who developed long-term work attachment to their relatively highly paid jobs. Mobility occurred across firms and to a much lesser extent across industries. When these firms were forced to reduce their work force in response to technological change and/or declining market shares, they shed their older workers. This was especially true when these industries could "push out" the workers they no longer needed by using the available tools of public policy. Workers, in turn, could accept and even find attractive the incentive to exit, and the boundary between voluntary exit and expulsion became blurred. Thus institutional rules to facilitate cost reduction and the role of industrial relations in the process are important forces shaping the capacity of troubled industries to respond to their plight.

Our data show that countries do indeed have quite different industrial mixes and industry-specific age structures; yet these differences do not correspond strictly to differences in the rates of early exit. For example, Germany and the Netherlands represent two different labor-market structures in terms of the importance of services versus goods production, but are rather similar in the process of exit.

A better picture of the exit process is given by the data on changes in the age composition of industries between 1970 and 1980 (or 1971 and 1981 or 1970 and 1982). The highest rate of decline in the number of older workers can be found among troubled industries and, more generally, among those industries with the largest overall decline. But the growing industries have also contributed to early exit, and relative to their overall growth even more so than the declining industries. Early exit has thus been a prominent way of reducing the work force, but has not been restricted to this function.

The growing industries are mostly those of the service sector. At the beginning of the period that we consider, they had a higher proportion of older workers than the key manufacturing industries. The overproportional reduction of their elderly work force during this period means that they have approached the level of the manufacturing industries, so that the differences between sectors – and the variance across industries – have decreased.

The role of the state warrants some special comment. For the public services, the pattern identified for growing industries is particularly strong. On the one hand, they have only small declines in the size of their elderly work force, and in some cases even an increase. On the other hand, the gap between their total growth rate and that of their older workers is large, even larger than in the declining industries. Thus, the public sector acts as an offset to the erosion of employment occurring elsewhere in the economy. The lower rate of early exit from services in which the public sector plays a large role makes these services relatively more important for older men and slows down the overall exit process. But this buffer role is much too small to compensate for the declines in elderly employment in the other sectors.

This pattern of exit across industries suggests that the troubled-industry hypothesis holds to some degree, but does not offer a sufficient explanation of the whole process of early exit from the labor market. One reason for this is that some conditions of exit that prevail in given industries tend to even themselves out. For example, the pressures that troubled industries face are more ambiguous than appears at first sight. Since many schemes for early exit have to be partly financed by the firms, they constitute a financial burden that can only be carried by well-off industries. Also, industries may not be the most appropriate unit of analysis. If such data were available, it would be desirable to examine patterns of exit by categories of firms, for example, in terms of size; it is plausible to assume that large firms are more often part of the core segments of labor markets than small ones.

These findings are not limited to European countries. In a preliminary analysis of a new data base, we have undertaken a more detailed analysis covering the most recent time period in Britain, Germany, Japan, Sweden, and the United States. The total labor force in each country is disaggregated into 34 to 38 different industry groups. The data are based on National Employment Surveys of a population sample for Britain and the United States; census data, which are available every five years, in Sweden and Japan; and data from the Social Insurance Beneficiary Lists for Germany, which exclude the self-employed, life-time civil servants (*Beamte*) and workers with employment of less than 15 hours a week.

We find a clear decline in the employment shares of men aged 55 to 64 in Sweden, the United Kingdom, and the United States. The relative decline is over 20 percent in the United Kingdom, 11 percent in Sweden, and almost 8 percent in the United States. For these three countries, the pattern is unambiguous: The decline occurs in growing and declining industries. In Sweden the decline appears to be more or less uniform. In Britain the relative decline in employment shares of the elderly is higher in the rapidly declining industries and somewhat slower in the growing industries. In the United States the data show a small relative increase in employment shares in rapidly declining industries, but it is produced not by an increasing number of older workers but by the very rapid decrease in the share of young ones. Germany and Japan at first sight seem to be different, but this is largely a result of special demographic factors (unequal cohort size).

In general, these new data support the findings of the present study. The more recent time period and the addition of new countries where reentry and reemployment occur (Japan and the United States) do not substantially change the direction of our empirical finding that early exit of older men is taking place in almost every industry.

How will the industry mix of rates of exit evolve in the future? As noted earlier, the industries have become more alike, and as a consequence there is now less potential for different exit patterns. In other words, the differential process of early exit by industries has reduced the range for such differences. Nevertheless, the exit process is still far from being unified. For one thing, the transition to retirement may become more of a gradual process as formal partial retirement programs are implemented (e.g., Sweden, Denmark, Finland, and Germany) or as the boundary between work and retirement becomes blurred as a consequence of shorter working careers and increased longevity. Other lines of demarcation become obvious when we move from the timing of exit to aspects of quality. There remain large differences among industries in the availability of pathways to early exit (e.g., disability, unemployment, or preretirement), and these in turn vary as to cost distribution, control, social stratification, and cultural meaning. For example, in Germany there are conflicting views on whether future institutional exit regulations should be in the domain of the public pension system or – as the unions want it – in that of labor relations. To the extent that the unions' view will prevail, the differences between industries and sectors are likely to increase again.

APPENDIX

Formula for "Shift-Share" Analysis

$$A_1/N_1 - A_0/N_0 = \Sigma\, A_{i0}/N_{i0} * (N_{i1}/N_1 - N_{i0}/N_0)$$
$$+ \Sigma\, (A_{i1}/N_{i1} - A_{i0}/N_{i0}) * N_{i0}/N_0$$
$$+ \Sigma\, (A_{i1}/N_{i1} - A_{i0}/N_{i0}) * (N_{i1}/N_1 - N_{i0}/N_0)$$

where A = employment of certain age group (e.g., 60–64)

N = total employment

i = index for single branches

$0, 1$ = indexes for points in time (e.g., 1970, 1980)

REFERENCES

Conradi, Hartmut, Klaus Jacobs, and Winfried Schmähl. 1987. "Vorzeitiger Rentenbezug in der Bundesrepublik Deutschland." *Sozialer Fortschritt* 36:182–90.

Kaltenbach, Helmut. 1981. "Früher in Rente?" *Deutsche Angestelltenversicherung* 28:167–77.

CHAPTER 4

The Netherlands:
An extreme case

BERT DE VROOM AND MARTIN BLOMSMA

4.1 THE GENERAL TREND

DUTCH society is almost equally split into a "working" population
and a "nonworking" population. In 1985 only 52.3 percent of the Dutch
population (15 years and older) belonged to the working population,
which is very low compared with other Western industrialized countries.
If one were to construct a continuum, the Netherlands would be on the
very low end with Sweden (83.7 percent) at the opposite pole.[1]

The low labor force participation rate in the Netherlands is the result
of two special features of the Dutch labor market. The first is the historical low participation of women. Until the 1960s female participation
rates always were less than 20 percent, whereas the average participation of men ranged from 60 to 75 percent. This low participation of
women is frequently explained by pointing to the dominant family ide-
ology in the Netherlands (Morée 1986; Becker and Koper-Sluijter 1987).[2]
In terms of "exit/entry," female workers have to cope with entry, not
with exit. This has been true ever since the early 1970s: The participation
of Dutch women rose from 27.7 percent in 1973 to 35.9 percent in 1985,
which is still very low compared with other countries.

The second feature is the relatively higher exit rate for men aged 55
and over, compared with France, Germany, Great Britain, the United

---

[1] If the unemployed are excluded, the picture becomes even more extreme: In 1985 only
45.6 percent of the population was actually employed.

[2] The low female participation rate might, however, also be an effect of criteria used in the
data gathering. For instance, until 1971 employees working less than 15 hours a week
were excluded from the working population in the Dutch census. Also, until 1978 labor
exchange offices, responsible for the unemployment statistics, did not register persons as
unemployed if they were in search for work less than 30 hours a week. In that year the
criterion was changed to 25 hours, and nowadays it is 20 hours a week (among others,
Detmar and Dekker 1987). Because women frequently are involved in or are looking for
part-time jobs, it is reasonable to assume that these definitions have influenced the official
female participation rates.

States, and Sweden. In the period 1971–88 participation of males aged 55 to 59 and 60 to 64 declined, respectively, 31 percent and 80 percent. In Sweden – the extreme at the other end of the continuum – participation of males in these two age groups decreased only 6 percent and 18 percent (see Chapter 2, Table 2.2). The general entry trend for Dutch women partially offsets the decline of the average participation rate, but it hardly affects the exit trend of men.

Apart from sectoral characteristics and developments, exit of older workers in the Netherlands is especially stimulated by the existence of a whole range of "exit opportunities," which can be clustered into two types of exit pathways. Pathways are considered here as one or more institutional arrangements that (generally in combination) bridge the financial gap between the exit of older workers from the labor market and their retirement. We distinguish between exit through social security (welfare pathways), created as part of the postwar welfare state, and exit through private arrangements (private pathways), bargained between employers and trade unions. We will argue that the ongoing lowering of the actual age of retirement is not the product of a rational encompassing design, but the unintended outcome of different programs and activities that reinforce each other and initially were developed for other purposes. Paradoxically, a number of these programs – the social security regulations – were created to foster a "work society." These regulations were shaped in the 1950s and 1960s to fulfill demands of justice and recompense for injuries and loss of income, without the intention of producing exit. However, in the seventies these regulations became important instruments for obtaining the exit of older workers. This especially applied to the disability scheme because of a rather stern protection against dismissal through unemployment. These regulations partly shifted from social policy tools into labor-market tools. We will argue that this shift has not only been the result of the worsening state of the economy since the early 1970s but also is due to the strong involvement of employers and trade unions in the implementation of these social security regulations, or in other words the corporatist structure of the Dutch social security system.

The private pathways, the so-called preretirement schemes, introduced since the late 1970s were initially intended as instruments of social policy as well as labor-market policy. Trade unions in particular emphasized that some categories of older workers active in paid labor for many years under bad working conditions should be given the opportunity to leave work before the official age of retirement. In the 1980s these programs became very popular with employers, trade unions, and the state as a way of coping with unemployment and/or economic problems on the firm level. In the bargaining process between employers and the trade unions these schemes turned out to be very important means of exchange: A trade-off between wage demands and preretirement schemes for older workers took shape.

Another argument we develop is that the very existence of different compensatory programs (social security and preretirement schemes) has blocked a policy of integration and reintegration of older workers in the labor process. There was no need for firms, trade unions, and the state to design age-specific policies to deal – internally – with the problems of aging in the firms. Those problems could be externalized by shifting them to one of the many different exit pathways. The absence of (re-)integration policies in turn reinforced the use of exit routes. The ultimate outcome has been an overall, not explicitly intended exit trend, and a continuous lowering of the age of exit. This trend also resulted in a growing public awareness that exit before the normal age of retirement has become both a social right and an obligation for older workers – the latter in making jobs available for younger age groups. In this respect the process of exit in fact mirrors a "creeping age discrimination" in the Netherlands.

4.2 STAGE I: THE EXPANSION OF LABOR AND WELFARE (1945–70)

The postwar period 1945–70 was one of rapid expansion of both a labor society and a welfare state. In a sense the welfare state can be interpreted as a response to the key role of labor in the economic development after World War II.

The importance of labor in this period is reflected in an increasing labor force participation and a decreasing unemployment. The older age groups (50 to 64), in particular men, demonstrated an increasingly high labor force participation that went from 89.5 percent in 1947 to 91.1 percent in 1960 and then gradually went down to 83.6 percent in 1973. For women aged 50 to 64, as indicated earlier, the trend is different. Between 1947 and 1960 their labor force participation went down from 16.9 percent to 13.5 percent, but from then on participation increased to 17.2 percent in 1973 (CBS 1984a).

Parallel to the growing economic importance of wage labor the prewar tendency of trade unions to enter the area of national and sectoral economic and social policy was reinforced after World War II (Fernhout 1980:119–229). In the early 1950s a fairly developed corporatist system of Statutory Trade Associations and institutions charged with the implementation of social policy was established. Both national associations and sectoral interest associations of employers and workers became involved in a complex corporatist order.

In this period work gained its central social meaning and society was reframed with a newly introduced label: *arbeidsbestel,* which can roughly be translated as "labor order" or "labor system."[3] The *arbeidsbestel* is an encompassing "system," consisting of different regulations and corporatist bi- and tripartite institutions charged with the implementation of social and economic policy.

The development of the *arbeidsbestel,* the economic growth, the increased "general expectation of justice," and the "general expectation of recompense for injuries and loss"[4] culminated in the extension of a welfare state, strongly centered around labor. In exchange for labor force productivity and participation the general expectation of justice and recompense was tranformed into various regulations that would recompense workers for different risks.

In response to these demands the existing fragmented prewar social security regulations were replaced and/or extended into a comprehensive, integrated social security system with a key role for the state (Den Broeder 1986:57, 60). Apart from some interim acts and transitional arrangements, until 1987 the postwar social security related to labor was based on seven different types of insurance: one for the "risk" of aging (AOW), three for the risk of unemployment (WW, WWV, and RWW), two for the risk of disability (WAO and AAW), and one for the risk of sickness (ZW). In the same period, the state introduced specific disability and unemployment arrangements for its own employees.

Civil servants who become disabled do not enter the WAO scheme but the ABPW (1966), which roughly resembles it. Notwithstanding the fact that civil servants can hardly be dismissed, specific circumstances such as reorganization or overstaffing may expose them to the risk of "nonactivity." In that case the older civil servants generally do not enter the

---

[3] In fact the Dutch word *bestel* is hard to translate. Contrary to the terms "order" and "system," which suggest a certain logic or plan, *bestel* is more an unintended result of different historical developments and "incidents."

[4] Friedman (1985:5) argues that (in Western, industrialized countries) there has been a historical development of the mentioned "expectations" ("superprinciples"; p. 75), culminating in a "demand for 'total justice'" (p. 5). These expectations were stimulated through technological and industrial development that opened the eyes to the possibility of first physical and later social control. In the end "what people come to expect is a higher level of justice – social justice, life justice" (p. 51). These two superprinciples were translated into "a vastly greater level of demands on government" (p. 51) and created in the end the "welfare state" (p. 76).

unemployment schemes (WW, WWV), but the RWB or UR.[5] The latter guarantee them a slightly higher income replacement rate, and also an effort by the state to find them a new task. We consider the public-sector schemes as part of the social security system, since they share some central features.

When this system of social security regulations came into existence, the implementation of labor-related social security was delegated to corporatist institutions in which "recognized, representative" employers' associations and trade unions were strongly involved. Almost all aspects of implementation have been delegated to different corporatist institutions. In fact, the Dutch social security system can be characterized as a private system within a public frame. This private nature of the social-policy system has been rather important in the explanation of the exit of older workers in the 1970s and 1980s.

4.3 STAGE II: EXIT THROUGH SOCIAL POLICY (1970–88)

4.3.1 Welfare pathways

In the 1970s Dutch society was confronted with increasing economic and technological changes. As a result unemployment increased in certain industries. In particular, older blue-collar workers were pushed out of the labor process. Table 4.1 illustrates the increasing exit of older male workers. The high nonactivity rate of workers aged 65 and over is a direct effect of the normal retirement age of 65. The increasing exit of other age groups, however, was made possibly by combining various social security regulations into separate early-exit routes for older workers (pathways). Two types of pathways can be distinguished, according to the mode of entrance: unemployment (three different routes) and sickness/disability (two different routes). The options that make up the pathways were not designed for exit, nor for any specific age group. However, in creating a sequence of different social security options, exit routes for older workers took shape. The combination of different social security unemployment regulations in particular created a distinct pathway for the age group 57.5 and over. In the case of sickness and disability, exit

---

[5] RWB is for public servants with a permanent position, and UR is for public servants without a permanent position. Both regulations will probably cease to exist in the near future. Then the new unemployment act (NWW) will also be applicable to most older civil servants who are dismissed.

Table 4.1. *Exit rates^a for male age groups, 1973–85*

		Age groups		
Year	50–54	55–59	60–64	65+
1973	10.3	18.7	34.5	90.9
1975	12.8	22.7	41.3	92.0
1977	14.6	23.6	47.1	93.8
1979	17.0	28.0	54.2	94.6
1981	17.1	30.5	60.5	95.4
1983	20.9	35.7	67.1	95.7
1985	23.2	37.5	73.4	96.3

^aExit rate = number of persons not employed in the age group as a percentage of the total population in the age group.

from labor sometimes occurs at a very early age. Theoretically it is possible for anyone, regardless of age (between 17 and 65), to exit through sickness/disability. However, if we look at the current participants in the relevant schemes, the special significance in relation to the higher age groups is striking.

The most important pathway is the "sickness and disability route." It is composed of three different social insurance programs: the Sickness Benefits Act (ZW), the Disablement Insurance Act (WAO), and the General Disablement Act (AAW). The Sickness Benefits Act (ZW) grants a maximum benefit period of one year. At the end of this a person has to go back to work or apply for another source of income. When still sick after one year a person usually enters the disability schemes. In combining different legal arrangements in this way, an important exit route for the private sector has come into existence.

The importance of the different disability schemes in the exit of older male workers is illustrated in Table 4.2 for 1985. In that year 42.1 percent of the total population aged 60 to 64 participated in one of these schemes, which is extremely high compared with the other exit routes. The same conclusion can be drawn for the group aged 55 to 59 (32.7 percent).

The most frequently used unemployment pathway was constructed out of two social security regulations: the Unemployment Insurance Act (WW) and the Unemployment Provisions Act (WWV). The linking of these two options produces an exit opportunity at age 62.5. In 1975 an additional regulation was introduced, which guaranteed any person

Table 4.2. *Current participants (males aged 55 to 64) in social-policy and public-sector schemes, in absolute numbers and as a percentage of the total number in the age group, 1984–5*[a]

	55–59		60–64		55–64	
	1,000s	%	1,000s	%	1,000s	%
Disability						
WAO/AAW	85.4	25.6	102.4	31.8	187.8	25.9
ABPW[b]	12.0	3.6	17.3	5.4	29.3	4.0
Total disability	109.3	32.7	135.3	42.1	244.6	33.8
Unemployment						
WW	3.5	1.0	1.1	0.3	4.6	0.6
WWV	11.9	3.6	26.8	8.3	38.7	5.9
RWW	8.5	2.5	4.5	1.4	13.0	1.8
RWB/UR[b] (1981)	0.7		0.9		1.6	

[a] Current participants at the end of 1984; population at the beginning of 1985.
[b] Only civil servants.
Source: SVR, CBS, ABP, SVB.

aged 60 to 64 who was receiving a WWV benefit continued receipt of this benefit until the official retirement at age 65. This novelty created the possibility of dismissing workers aged 57.5 and over, in exchange for relatively attractive benefit conditions until the retirement age of 65. In terms of volume this exit route is far less important than the private-sector disability pathway (see Table 4.2).

The second unemployment pathway also consisted of WW and WWV, but here the "extended WWV option" was replaced by the Government Unemployment Benefit Act (RWW). This appears to be the "unlucky" pathway for older workers who have become unemployed before the age of 57.5. Because they do not meet the criterion of 60 years to enter the "extended WWV," they enter a specific – means-tested – program (RWW),[6] created as part of the National Social Assistance Act. The final benefits of this route are not particularly attractive, which may be one reason only a few older workers leave the labor market this way, as indicated in Table 7.2.

The third unemployment pathway is accessible only to civil servants and is slightly more attractive than the most generous unemployment

---

[6] Officially to guarantee an income for formerly employed and self-employed persons as well as school leavers who never had a job.

pathway for the private sector. Only very few civil servants aged 55 and over, however, are using this route. The most important exit route for civil servants is also the (public-sector) disability pathway.

4.3.2   *Social security: Legal and extralegal benefits*

The benefit structure of the Dutch social security system is set on a public and private footing. The state guarantees a benefit required by law. In addition, employers and trade unions may supplement social security benefits with so-called extralegal allowances. The "social partners" generally have used this possibility to supplement pension, sickness, unemployment, and/or disability benefits. These "private" benefits are the product of ad hoc agreements between employers and trade unions as part of a process of collective (or individual) bargaining. Consequently, in certain sectors there are no extralegal benefits, and in others the level and duration of this private benefit differ, depending upon specific sectoral circumstances. Sickness benefits and unemployment benefits are extreme cases in this respect. The official sickness benefit of 80 percent (before 1985) has in almost all sectors been supplemented to 100 percent of the net income, whereas the unemployment benefits were only incidentally supplemented. Disability benefits (WAO) are "privately" supplemented up to 90 to 100 per cent of the net income (only in the first year) in the larger part of the economy (more than 50 percent) (Grobbée 1986:81).

Also, the legal benefit levels may differ according to the scheme. A worker in the private sector can get a full disability benefit – 75 percent of the last earned wage (until 1985) – if he or she is declared at least 80 percent unfit for working. But until 1987 full benefits were also paid out to partially disabled persons if they could not find a proper job because of the nature of their handicap. This is one reason why the disability schemes became relatively attractive for older workers compared with the other schemes.

The unemployment benefit started with 80 per cent (until 1985) of the last earned wage, but after six months the benefit dropped to 70 percent, and after another two years it was reduced to the social minimum (RWW). Only upon entering the unemployment pathway for those aged 57.5 and over could the 70 percent benefit be kept until 65. The unemployment benefit is hardly "privately" supplemented, and the social minimum benefit (RWW) in fact blocks any additional benefit, because it is means tested.

In summary, exit through sickness and disability has been the more attractive route, followed by exit through the unemployment pathway

Table 4.3. *Current participants (males) in disability schemes, 1975–86*

Year	WAO/AAW (1,000s)		ABPW (1,000s)		Total disability (%)[a]	
	55–59	60–64	55–59	60–64	55–59	60–64
1975	57.6	64.6				
1977	67.0	81.6	1.4	2.2	25.5	35.6
1979	82.7	87.9	4.8	7.3	30.0	39.8
1981	84.4	94.1	8.8	12.7	31.3	42.6
1983	84.4	101.4	11.1	16.3	31.8	44.1
1985	87.5	100.5	12.6	17.8	33.6	41.5
1986	88.8	97.6	12.4	17.6		

[a] As a percentage of the total population in the age group.
Source: GMD, SVR, AOF, CBS.

that guarantees at least the so-called extended unemployment provisions benefit (WWV) until the age of 65. Exit through the unemployment route that ended in Social Assistance (RWW) has been a bad choice. In fact, it is an entry into "poverty," since in the end only a social minimum benefit is left.

4.3.3 Social security as instrument of labor-market regulation

The relative importance of the disability schemes for the exit of males aged 55 to 64 is illustrated in Table 4.2 for 1985. Table 4.3 illustrates the growing importance of the schemes since the mid-1970s in particular concerning the older age groups.

The WAO/AAW scheme is the most important one and has always had a disporportionate concentration of new entries and current participants in the higher age groups. For instance, in 1985, 40.9 percent of all WAO participants (male and female) belonged to the group aged 55 to 64, whereas the other age groups were represented with 3.6 percent (under 24), 10.8 percent (25 to 34), 17.6 percent (35 to 44), and 26.9 percent (45 to 54) (CBS 1986:86). Of the total male new entries in 1985, a disproportionate share (24 percent) were aged 55 to 64 (SVR statistics for 1980 to 1986).

The increased use of the sickness and disability pathway suggests a deterioration of the state of health. There is, however, an important labor-market (unemployment) component in the exit of older workers through disability (Einerhand 1986:17). Roodenburg (among others) concluded that in 1981, in a situation of rapidly rising unemployment, about 35 percent of all new disability benefit awards were given for labor-market reasons (Roodenburg et al. 1985). Van den Bosch and Petersen (1983) analyzed the growth of social security disability transfers on the sectoral level for the period 1968–79. They concluded that the increase of disability was not a result of a worsening state of health or a change in the legal or occupational structure. Their main explanations were a change in the "perception of health"[7] and, in particular, the economic development on the sectoral level. According to their analysis disability schemes seem to be partly turned into tools for exit of workers in troubled industries. However, one should not conclude that the overall process of exit can be found only in those industries. Almost all economic sectors – both troubled and growing industries – show a disproportionate decrease of males aged 60 to 64 between 1977 and 1985 (Blomsma and De Vroom 1987). In Chapter 3, this is documented for the Netherlands in more detail for 1971–81.

Not only disability schemes but also unemployment programs have been used for exit of older workers. As explained earlier, on the basis of a specific interpretation and implementation of unemployment benefit regulations industry was able to create a specific exit route for older workers. If employers wanted to lay off workers aged 57.5 and over they could "offer" them the "extended WWV" option as a better "choice" than the RWW-poverty pathway. This resulted in an age-specific tool for shedding older workers, which was not the original intention of this regulation.[8] Since 1987 the government has "closed" new entrance to this pathway and replaced it by four new, generally less attractive, unemployment pathways explicitly designed for older workers.

4.3.4   Strategy of firms and corporatism

There are two related circumstances in which industry would and could use non-age-specific social policy regulations for age-specific labor-market purposes. The first is as internal personnel policy. According to firm-level research by Kerkhoff (1981), firms in the Netherlands hardly recognize the specific problems of older workers. They do not develop strat-

---

[7] Bax (1984) has also pointed to this "subjective" explanation in relation to the declining societal importance of work and the impersonal character of the social security system that, he argues, removed existing social barriers to using social security to force the exit of older workers.

[8] Ganzevoort et al. (1984:38): This practice is "completely in defiance of the intention of the Legislator."

egies to integrate older workers. From the perspective of the firm, aging means problems, from both a social and an economic point of view. The only "social" strategy therefore is to replace older (i.e., problematic) workers with younger workers. This strategy has been stimulated by the different exit opportunities included in the social security regulations.

Second, the involvement of industry in the implementation of social security may help to explain why social security could be used to force the exit of older workers. Implementation of the schemes is delegated to private-sector corporatist institutions of employers and employees. This implementation system has evolved to a high level of organizational development with respect to specific technical know how, financial resources, personnel, and so forth. That is why, according to Ganzevoort et al. (1984:31), this system has the "capacity to handle the complex, obscure and diverse system of legal regulations" and why it can break away from the formal supervision of the Social Insurance Council (SVR).[9] The key role of these corporatist institutions concerning the process of exit has been illustrated by Ganzevoort et al. (1984:39) for the disability and unemployment pathways.[10] With respect to exit through disability it has been the "very broad interpretation" by the Industrial Insurance Boards of the relevant instruments that made disability regulation a tool of labor-market policy. This specific interpretation was based on a clause in the Disablement Insurance Act (WAO), which stated that in some cases the risk of unemployment as a result of partial disablement should be taken into account in determining the degree of disablement of a person.[11]

Also, with respect to the unemployment pathway ("extended WWV") the Industrial Boards used social security regulations as a tool to force older workers from the labor market (Ganzevoort 1984:38).

One may wonder why both employers and trade unions agreed on the use of social security benefits to force the exit of older workers. The most plausible explanation seems to be that exit is a phenomenon particularly linked to industrial sectors with severe economic problems or, putting it differently, industrial sectors with a structural threat of unemployment. By using the relevant social security regulations in a specific way the

---

[9] The SVR was established by the government in 1952 to perform a central coordinating and supervising role with respect to the complex system of social security regulations (Organisatiewet 1952). Recently, government has developed a plan to reorganize the system. In this plan the already important coordinating role of the FBV gets a legal status. In other words, the last private chain the social security organizational system will also get a "public government" character (SMA 1988).

[10] Ganzevoort et al. (1984:39).

[11] WAO, article 21.2; AAW article 12.2a.

firms could offer especially older workers a "better" way out than the other age groups. Generally speaking, this was more acceptable to the trade unions. On the other hand, employers could get "rid of" the problematic (more expensive and supposedly less productive) older workers and did not necessarily have to develop age-specific social policies on the firm level.

4.4   STAGE III: THE SHIFT FROM WELFARE TO PRIVATE PATHWAYS (1977–88)

4.4.1   Reconstruction of social policy

Starting in the late 1970s, unemployment increased exponentially from about 200,000 in 1976 to about 800,000 in 1984. The majority of the unemployed entered the social security system and caused a dramatic increase in costs for the welfare state. Government responded in 1987 with the reconstruction of the Dutch system of social security, which brought important changes in the pattern of unemployment and disability exit routes.

One change was the modification of the unemployment pathway into social assistance ("the poverty route"). More important, however, was the termination of the "extended-WWV" unemployment pathway. Instead, four new unemployment pathways came into existence. Three of them have been explicitly designed for older workers but do not generate very attractive levels of income replacement.[12]

The fourth new unemployment route was not meant to be age specific but turned out to be. We refer here to the New Unemployment Act. It offers a 70 percent income replacement until retirement to those aged 60.5 who have worked at least 40 years.[13]

A potentially very important consequence of the reconstruction of social security has been the transformation of the sickness and disability pathway. Since 1987, this is no longer an attractive pathway for the exit of partly disabled, unemployed older workers. For this category of workers (less than 80 percent incapable of work) a new pathway was created.

---

[12] The reconstruction was based on new regulation. The Unemployment Insurance Act 1952 (WW) was replaced by the New Unemployment Insurance Act 1987 (NWW). For older unemployed and partly disabled unemployed workers, a newly created "Aged and Partially Disabled Unemployed Workers Income Provision Act 1987" (IOAW) was introduced.

[13] Recent statistics (CBS) indicate that the NWW is becoming an exit route for older workers. At the end of 1988, 21 percent of its beneficiaries (i.e., 23,000) were in the group aged 60 to 64.

In the new pathway income is based on sickness benefits and a combination of disability and unemployment benefits. A person who is not able to find a suitable job for the part he or she is valid to work will enter for that part the unemployment schemes, which end up generally in less generous benefits. Also, the disability system for civil servants distinguishes more sharply between disability and unemployment since 1987.

There is no doubt that the new disability exit routes are less attractive to partly disabled unemployed workers than the original ones. Recent figures of the Central Bureau of Statistics indicate that until now most of the new pathways are not very important with respect to exit.

4.4.2 *Private preretirement schemes*

In the late 1970s it became more difficult for companies to achieve the exit of their older workers through social security. Finally, these routes even turned out to be rather unattractive for older workers because of the reconstruction of the system of social security (1987). In this context – since 1976 – industry itself started to introduce a new age-specific exit pathway for older workers: the preretirement scheme (VUT) (Table 4.4). This scheme was originally suggested by the trade unions, and contained both a "social" and an "employment" purpose. Preretirement as a social policy was intended to offer certain categories of older workers a financially sounder and socially more acceptable way out of paid labor than through disability or unemployment. Simultaneously, the preretirement program was meant to replace older workers by younger ones and thus serve as a tool in coping with the problem of unemployment. Once launched, the growing number of preretirement schemes attracted not only "troubled" blue-collar workers but also more highly educated and better paid employees. VUT does not seem to have been very successful as an instrument against unemployment of the younger age groups either. Actually, the preretirement scheme became the most important exit route for older male workers (60 to 64), without structural effects on entry of younger unemployed workers (Van Ginneken 1981; Bolhuis 1987). The ultimate effect was a less dramatic increase of the average official unemployment figure. The threat of massive redundancy since the late 1970s was (partly) offset by a policy aimed at encouraging the exit of older workers through VUT schemes. For different reasons – which we discuss later – preretirement options are rather attractive to both employers and workers compared with the existing social-policy pathways.

Since the introduction of the VUT in 1977 the "tacit" labor-market policy through social security has come under pressure from the labor-

Table 4.4. *Exit through preretirement (VUT), 1977–87*[a]

Year	Total current participants, males aged 60 to 64 (1,000s)	Total collective sector current participants, males aged 60 to 64 (1,000s)		
		ABPW-civil servants	PGGM-OBU	Total
1977	3.0			
1978	7.0			
1979	16.0			
1980	20.0			
1981	23.8			
1982	27.5	8.5	5.6	14.1
1983	43.0	15.3	6.5	21.8
1984	60.0	21.9	7.3	29.2
1985	75.0	27.7	8.1	35.8
1986	80.4	33.1	8.7	41.8
1987	93.5	37.6	9.3	46.9

[a] In the period 1977–87 almost all VUT schemes exclusively contained participants from the group aged 60 to 64. VUT statistics do not distinguish between male and female. Although female participation in the schemes is increasing, estimates for 1986 suggest that this component is no more than 5 percent. That is why we have interpreted "total current participants in VUT" as the "males aged 60 to 64."
Source: Koningsveld and Van 'T Hullenaar (1890); SoZaWe, Rapportage Arbeidsmarkt (1980–5); Ministry of Finance (1989); Bolhuis (1987).

market policy of the preretirement schemes (VUT). Table 4.5 clearly illustrates a shift in time. In 1977, 63.6 percent of men aged 60 to 64 who were not employed received a disability benefit, but this figure has shown a decline ever since. In 1985 it stood at 43.3 percent. Also, between 1977 and 1986 the new entrances per year in preretirement (60 to 64) gradually increased from 3,000 to 32,000, while the new entrances to WAO/AAW (60 to 64) gradually declined from 8,000 (1980) to about 2,500 (1986) per year (SVR, CBS). There is no reason to assume that an increasing state of health, better economic conditions, or a change in legislation in this period can explain the declining importance of the disability pathway. The only important change in this period was the introduction of the preretirement exit route. The public sector has also seen a clear shift. Between 1981 and 1986 the number of new ABPW disability benefits per year continuously declined (from 3,203 to 501), while simul-

Table 4.5. *Shift from social security to preretirement*
(males aged 60 to 64)

Year	VUT	WAO/AAW (%)[a]	ABPW (disability) (%)[a]	Unemployed (%)[b]
1975	–	56.4	–	7.9
1977	2.3	63.6	1.7	11.4
1979	10.9	59.9	5.0	8.7
1981	13.8	54.4	7.3	6.4
1983	21.2	50.1	8.0	11.3
1985	31.8	42.6	7.5	9.4
1987	37.9			

[a]Number of current participants (men aged 60 to 64) as a percentage of the number of not-employed men aged 60 to 64.
[b]Number of unemployed men aged 60 to 64 as a percentage of
the number of not-employed men aged 60 to 64.

taneously the yearly new entrances to ABPW-VUT rose (from 1,404 to
11,066).[14]

This enormous increase of VUT awards in the Netherlands is largely
the outcome of the downward pressure on the minimum age limit. At
the outset, the preretirement schemes were exclusively directed at persons 64 or 63 years of age. In 1988 entering a VUT scheme at the age of
61 or 60 was quite normal. Some schemes have even set the age limit at
about 55. This trend might be given further impetus by the reconstruction of the social security system.[15]

Exit on account of age (VUT) differs in many respects from exit
through unemployment or disability. The conditions and the level of
benefits, although they vary between different VUT schemes, are generally more attractive than the social security pathways or, until recently,
sometimes even work can offer. Exit through preretirement is also much
more accepted by workers themselves and society in general, whereas
exit through unemployment or disability has a much more negative con-
notation. One important difference in particular is the political process

[14] Ministerie van Financiën 1989:57.
[15] As yet, it is to soon to measure the quantitative effects of the reconstruction on the VUT
scheme.

and institutional structure. The initiation, norms, criteria, and conditions of exit through unemployment, sickness, and disability are produced in the national political arena: parliament, government, and the (corporatist) national advisory institutions like the Social Economic Council or Social Insurance Council. The outcome is a public (collective) commodity for the working population provided by government: No worker who meets the established criteria can be excluded from the consumption of this commodity and, in principle, the commodity is the same for everyone. This is one important characteristic of social security in the welfare state.

The preretirement schemes are embedded in a specific structure, which differs for the private and public (civil service) sector. In the private (industrial) sector, VUT regulations are a private affair, on either sectoral or firm level. Individual firms or employers' associations and trade unions may decide by collective agreement to introduce firm-level or sectoral preretirement schemes. The conditions of sectoral schemes are formulated by these actors, and the implementation is delegated to more than 100 different preretirement foundations (VUT-Stichtingen)[16] controlled by private interest organizations. Firm-level schemes, generally bargained between individual firms and trade unions, are usually implemented by the firms themselves. There is no state involvement in sectoral preretirement schemes, apart from confirmation. This implies that the state has the ability to "legalize" exit arrangements, as part of a collective agreement between the unions and employers' associations, by declaration.[17] As a result all firms – both members and nonmembers of the involved employers' associations – within the sector of a "legalized" VUT regulation are obliged to offer their employees the same access to preretirement and have to contribute on equal footing to the costs of the scheme. On the firm level there is no state involvement at all. Firms – instead of or alongside sectoral agreements – can introduce their own company preretirement schemes.

In contrast to the integrated pattern of social security institutions, the private preretirement institutions (VUT foundations and VUT funds) are not integrated in a coordinated and hierarchical system. All VUT foundations are formally autonomous institutions on the sectoral level. There is no "peak" organization, nor any private or public central institution with authoritative capacity.

---

[16] Already in 1980, 93 sectoral-level VUT schemes were in existence. In 1983 this number had grown to 113. In most cases single VUT regulations are implemented by separate VUT Foundations. (Blom 1983:98–9; SoZaWe 1985:10–11).

[17] Algemeen Verbindend Verklaring (AVV).

Preretirement in the collective/public sector is organized differently. Since 1984 civil servants have enjoyed a legally established opportunity[18] to exit before the age of retirement.

In the collective sector, in addition to the exit schemes for civil servants, there are various other schemes (in 1988, 14) for employees in the Health and Welfare Services. These are not embedded in a specific legal framework, but are part of general collective agreements between employers and trade unions in the collective sector. The most prominent preretirement scheme here is the transitional payment scheme (OBU[19]).

In the Netherlands VUT schemes are "produced" through sectoral bargaining processes, influenced by the current political and socioeconomic circumstances on the sectoral level. These have resulted in a fragmented and heterogeneous picture.[20] In 1988 there were 121 different sectoral and 335 firm preretirement schemes for the private sector and 16 different schemes for the public and nonpublic collective sector (SoZaWe 1989a). That year in the private sector 47 percent of all firms offered a preretirement opportunity to their employees. In 1988, 99 percent of the institutions in the collective sector were covered by a preretirement scheme. Still, a fairly large segment of the working population – especially in small firms (fewer than nine workers) – had no access to this exit pathway, because their employers did not run a scheme (in 1988 about 33 percent). Accessibility is also influenced by specific conditions in the schemes. In most cases (about 80 percent in 1988) employees need to have worked at least 10 years in the sector/firm and have to be at least 60 years of age before they are entitled to a benefit. All other employees are excluded. A number of schemes also exclude employees who do not live in the Netherlands or who are older than 64.5. In 1988 about 23 schemes of the private sector employees were excluded from entering the preretirement pathway if they had worked less than 50 or 70 percent part-time. In these cases employees have to pay for preretirment schemes but are not granted the benefits.

The effects of sectoral bargaining are reflected in the differences between schemes. Table 4.6 registers differences with respect to the age of entry, the required number of years in service, and the level of benefits of 66 sectoral and 8 large firms' VUT schemes. Together they covered about 70 percent of all workers under collective agreements in 1988.

In particular, the age of entry to preretirement and the level and distribution of costs/benefits are subject to the exchange process. For

---

[18] "Wet uitkering wegens vrijwillig vervroegd uittreden" (Staatsblad 1984:273).
[19] Overbruggingsuitkeringsregeling.
[20] Van Voorden (1987), in line with our argument, has characterized collective agreements as the mirror image of labor relations.

Table 4.6. *Differences in VUT schemes (December 1988)*

Age of entry	No. of schemes	Years in service	No. of schemes	Benefit	No. of schemes
				% of gross wage:	
59	20	0	1	71	1
59.5	1	5	12	75	5
60	34	7	2	80	26
60.5	1	8	1	85	4
61	7	10	58	90	1
				% of net wage:	
61.5	0			85	4
62	9			87.5	17
62.5	1			90	9
63	1			92	1
				95	1
				100	2
Total	74		74		71

Source: SoZaWe (1989a).

instance, the actual exit age is created through a double bargaining process. On the one hand, employers and unions may agree on a certain age
of exit, which is formulated in the regulation. This is the so-called regular
age of exit, which exists for the duration of the regulation and varies from
one to five years. On the other hand, employers and unions may reach
an agreement on "temporary changes" in the age of exit. This transitory
alteration of the age of entry has become an important ("structural") element of the bargaining process. Between 1984 and 1988 the number of
agreements on lowering the age of entry on a temporary basis increased.
In exchange for the introduction of VUT schemes and/or the lowering
of the age of entry, the trade unions felt inclined to reduce wage
demands and/or to accept a reduction of the benefit level as a contribution to the costs of these schemes.[21]

---

[21] The reduction of wage demands might go in three different directions: giving up
demands for wage increases, reducing the existing wage level, or giving up price index-
ation. The choice and also the level of wage reduction differs by sector.

4.5 INTEGRATION AND REINTEGRATION OF OLDER WORKERS

So far we have discussed different regulations and pathways that basically compensate older workers for leaving the labor market. Our argument is that the very existence of these different compensatory programs has blocked the development of effective integration and reintegration programs by individual firms, trade unions, and the state.

From the perspective of the individual firm, there is no need to feel responsible for lifetime employment of their workers or to elaborate specific management strategies to cope with "aging problems," since these problems can easily be shifted to the external "safety net." According to Kerkhoff (1981), the existence of the different compensatory programs (WAO, VUT, etc.) stimulates the firms to use an exit strategy instead of developing a new age-specific social policy.

But trade union policy also failed to stimulate firms to develop integrative policies. On the one hand, since the early 1970s the trade unions bargained for special "integrative" provisions for older workers, such as relief from shift work and overtime, compensation for the loss of shift premiums and the guarantee of basic wages for older workers downgraded to lower-paid jobs (Casey and Bruche 1983). But on the other hand, they undermined the real significance of these integrative policies by simultaneously encouraging the above-mentioned compensatory policies. This practice elevated provisions for older workers to mere symbolic issues, as immediately becomes clear if we look at the declining activity rates of older workers. A particularly important factor has been the trade unions' growing emphasis on preretirement schemes (VUT) in their collective bargaining, which has distracted attention from age-specific solutions on the firm level.

To a certain extent the state did develop some reintegration programs for unemployed and disabled workers. Notwithstanding the non-age-specific character of these measures – higher age groups are just one element among others[22] – most of these programs are oriented toward the younger age groups. The institutions charged with the implementation of reintegration activities – which are the same ones charged with the implementation of disability and unemployment schemes – exclude older age groups almost explicitly from reintegration. For instance, between 1975 and 1981 on average only 2 to 3 percent of the 55- to 64-

---

[22] Memorie van Toelichting (1962).

year old participants in the disability scheme were involved in the integration activities of the Industrial Medical Services (GMD). In 1984 this percentage had decreased to 1.7 percent. Instead of reintegration of disabled older workers the implementation institutions used the social security regulations to bring about the exit of older workers (among others, Besseling and Bruinsma 1987; Herweyer 1981). Since the mid-1980s, however, (re)integrative policies for the (partly) disabled have been more forcefully promoted by the government. For instance, the introduction in 1986 of the Disabled Workers Employment Act (WAGW) now offered an instrument to force employers to utilize the existing labor capacity of the partly disabled. There is an indication that this may have influenced the return to employment of a slightly growing number of older disabled persons (GMD, 1989a).

As for the older unemployed, there is still hardly any reintegration policy. On the contrary, since 1983 unemployed workers aged 57.5 and older no longer even have to register, which means that reintegration of this group is officially defined as "unrealistic."

This lack of reintegration policies toward older workers confirms the general picture that early exit is more or less accepted in society.

4.6   EXIT AND SOCIOECONOMIC STRATIFICATION

Is exit from the labor force an overall trend or are some groups more involved than others? From different sources we can draw the conclusion that among the group aged 50 to 64 those who exit differ in various respects from those still employed. First, the average age of those who exit is higher, though, since 1980, more "younger older" are entering the exit routes. Second, their average level of education is lower. Since 1980 the "educational gap" has widened. Third, the economic position (income, luxury goods) of those who exit as compared with those who continue to work is lower and has grown worse in the 1980s.

These socioeconomic differences are (partly) due to the fact that the various exit routes have been mainly used by or for (unskilled) blue-collar workers and white-collar workers (employees) from the middle levels, whereas the top-level employees have stayed at work and have become relatively overrepresented among those aged 50 to 64 who are still employed.

In addition, the exit group itself has become more and more internally differentiated. The initial description of the average worker who left the labor market before age 65 through unemployment, disability, or preretirement was the older blue-collar worker who worked under bad labor conditions. This profile is still correct as far as exit through social security – in particular the disability scheme – is concerned. These pathways have become obligatory exit routes for older, low paid, unskilled blue-collar workers in the old and troubled industries. At the same time the VUT route has become the main exit route for the middle-level civil servants and white-collar workers from the noncommercial service sector.

In the public opinion the VUT-participant profile is the "healthy, creative sexagenarian with a relatively good income and a positive prospect on the third phase of his life-cycle" (Van Seumeren 1987).

The general picture of both types of exit participants is confirmed in various studies. From a comparison between WAO participants and the working population it became clear that 67 percent of all WAO participants belonged to the blue-collar category (SVR 1987). In addition to their blue-collar status, this group was also characterized by a number of "underclass" features. They worked under bad labor conditions, their income and educational level was low, they had hardly any career perspectives, and they were frequently confronted with the threat of unemployment. This research also clarified that the majority of WAO participants came from the old and troubled economic sectors: construction, textile industry, and agriculture. The analysis by Einerhand (1986) confirms the socioeconomic distinction between different exit groups, and empirical research concerning the well-being of exit groups by pathway also found psychological differences between groups. The well-being of those who left paid labor because of sickness, disability, or unemployment clearly decreased more (in the period 1976–82) than the well-being of preretired and retired persons (Thijssen 1985:146).

Preretirement schemes are applied in all economic sectors, but since the early 1980s exit through VUT has increased disproportionately in the civil service sector. From 1982 to 1987 the share of the civil service among current VUT participants in the total preretirement scheme increased from 30.9 percent to 40.2 percent (Table 4.4), which represents almost 15 percent of the total employment (CBS 1987b). Between 1983 and 1985 the old industrial sectors, like the metal industry and construction, "supplied" only about 25 percent of all current VUT participants, and this decreased to 14 percent in 1986 (SoZaWe 1984–6). One might argue that these differences are probably the result of an older age structure in the civil service sector. However, the opposite is true. In this period the construction and metal industries were characterized by a relatively higher proportion of older workers (RvA 1983:50). The fact is that, compared with the private sector, a higher percentage of the eligible civil servants actually utilize the preretirement pathway: 65 percent versus 40 percent (Bolhuis 1987). The civil servants' interest in preretirement is concentrated with the middle-level employees. Top-level and low-level civil servants show less interest. The argument of the "top" is that preretirement will "take away important status aspects of their function"; the low-level civil servants say they have "problems with the possible financial consequences" of preretirement (RPD 1982–6).

In other words, the process of exit may be a general trend as far as the decreasing participation rate is concerned. But with respect to stratification, different exit routes have evolved for separate groups, implying diversity in socioeconomic and psychological effects on the individual level. The stratification "break" coincides more or less with the interval between social security and private pathways. The first pathways have become routes for the underclass, whereas the preretirement schemes have developed into exit routes for the better paid, middle-level, white-collar workers.

4.7 PUBLIC DISCOURSE: FROM CONVERGENCE TO CONFLICT

4.7.1 *Changing opinions of actors*

Until the early 1980s there was hardly any critical public debate with respect to the overall decline of the age of exit. This consensus was, however, misleading in the sense that there was not a comprehensive long-term plan regarding this structural change in the labor society. In fact, the different actors involved – government, political parties, trade unions, employers, organizations of the elderly, and also science (gerontology) – used different arguments concerning the position of older workers, which in the end all converged in the process of exit. These arguments clustered around three issues: social justice, employment, and economic productiveness.

Until the 1970s exit of older workers was primarily motivated on the basis of social justice and ideas of welfare. Trade unions and political parties argued that older workers – in particular those who have worked for years under bad conditions – should be given the opportunity to leave the labor market before the age of 65. This opinion, which was not debated, led to the described creeping transformation of different compensatory welfare-state programs. In the 1970s, when the economy had to cope with severe problems, exit also became a tool to restructure firms and/or to create employment for younger age groups. Trade unions in particular supported the latter idea, and the state adopted it in the early 1980s. From the perspective of the employers, early exit of older workers became a tool that could be used to increase economic productivity. On the one hand, they needed to contract their labor force as a consequence of the economic problems. On the other hand, by relieving older workers they could get rid of the "less productive" and "most expensive" ones. Because of dismissal protection in the Netherlands it was rather difficult for them to get rid of these workers through unemployment, so they reached an implicit understanding with the unions to utilize the "easier" disability route for this purpose. In the 1980s, with respect to the promotion of preretirement, the motives of employers hardly changed.[23]

In the 1970s social, youth employment, and economic arguments all supported in the increasing exodus of older workers. The social and youth employment arguments, but also the "disengagement theory" in gerontology, legitimated the idea that the exclusion of older workers from the labor process was the right policy. Exit of older workers, originally an ad hoc solution to "marginal" problems, developed into an encompassing trend – an "iron law" – from which actors hardly could escape. In the public opinion the decreasing age of retirement became normal and in fact led to a social redefinition of the retirement age. Workers considered preretirement a vested right. Working after 50 has even become a social taboo; work is seen as almost an exclusive right for the younger age groups.

There are various examples of the (implicit) redefinition of "old age." In the 1950s and 1960s old age started at about 65, with eligibility for the old-age pension (AOW). In the 1970s the definition of old age changed. In governmental reports the elderly were defined as the groups aged 55 and older (CBS 1976, 1984b). The associations of the elderly have also redefined their domain. Until the late 1970s only people aged 65 and over could become members, but nowadays many associations of the elderly use 55, or even 50, as the age of entry (Egas 1986).

The increasing trend toward early exit also stimulated a creeping age discrimination by employers, workers, and (quasi)state institutions. As discussed before, older age groups are excluded by (quasi)state institutions from (re)integration policies such as occupational training or support in finding work. We have also mentioned the lack of age-specific personnel policies of firms. In addition, there seems to be a tendency for firms to define an age ceiling for personnel recruitment. An analysis of personnel advertisements in 1986 indicated that 29.1 percent explicitly used maximum age limits (NFB 1987).

Recently, the public discourse has changed. The different actors are revising their opinions and positions with respect to exit. Exit from the

---

[23] In 1986 only 7 percent of 130 firms interrogated considered preretirement an instrument to create jobs (Koningsveld 1988:17).

labor market is an issue of conflict, confusion, and contradictory activities. It is too well established to reverse directions easily.

The changing public debate started more or less midway through 1987, with a critique of the expanding preretirement schemes (Bolhuis 1987) based on a cost/benefit evaluation: The benefits in terms of employment have been too low, whereas the costs of the schemes have become too high. In the end, it was argued, the increasing costs will have a negative impact on the position of Dutch firms in international competition, which in its turn will have negative effects on employment. In other words, exit along the preretirement pathway should be reduced. The cost argument has dominated public debate ever since and has set the stage for the bargaining process on conditions of employment between employers and trade unions.[24]

The employers, however, seem to have fallen into disarray. The small and middle-sized firms (craft and trade) do not reject the preretirement schemes. On the contrary, the employers' associations of this sector (like KNOV)[25] disagree publicly with the most powerful associations of the industrial sectors (large firms) on the issue. The KNOV holds the view that the preretirement schemes worked very well and should be continued. This positive attitude toward preretirement is also reflected in a collective agreement in the small trade metal sector (late 1987). Trade unions and employers agreed on the continuation of preretirement until at least 1989. The age of entrance was set at 59.

On the other hand, employers in the construction and industrial sectors (in particular the large firms), but also in sectors like banking and insurance, want to curtail the possibilities for preretirement and for reduction of work time in general. With costs as their main argument, these employers want to reduce the number of preretirement schemes and would like to see them less generous. Occasionally, the more principle-related and structural aspects of exit have also been put on the agenda. The employers' association FME,[26] representing one of the largest industrial sectors (metal and electronic industry), and some large (multinational) companies, declared that "the growing misconception of exit as a new social right must be stamped out" (AKZO) and that the possibilities of "paid nonwork" must be reduced (Philips). Instead of reducing the work time and the work life, the FME promoted the extension of the work week and of the work life.[27] One main concern of these firms

---

[24] The bargaining process in the Netherlands always starts in the end of the year and may continue several months, depending upon the positions and stakes of the actors involved.

[25] Koninklijk Nederlands Ondernemers Verbond.

[26] Vereniging voor de Metaal – en Electrotechnische Industrie.

and employers' associations was the threatening lack of (qualified) workers in the coming years. In the background of this concern was a growing uneasiness among employers about the fact that they cannot control the process of exit through the preretirement pathway. In contrast to the social security pathways, they cannot select employees for entering the preretirement schemes. Both the cost and the structural arguments were reflected in various suggestions for change brought forward by the employers. The increasing costs prompted them to get rid of existing preretirement schemes, raise the age of entry, lower the level of benefits, and/or adopt exclusively short-term VUT contracts (only one year, for instance).

To deal with the structural problems, they wanted "selective VUT schemes,[28] which can be applied for only by selected employees, or "flexible VUT schemes," which could offer the possibility of lengthening the work life, or "part-time VUT schemes," which could keep "indispensable" older employees at least on a part-time basis.

Trade unions in these sectors, however, were against the abolition of the existing voluntary preretirement schemes. They wanted to keep these opportunities and even to enlarge them.

So the bargaining process in 1987–8 became the first public conflict between employers and trade unions concerning the process of exit. Trade unions of the banking sector claimed the preretirement schemes as a "vested right" and demanded contracts for three to five instead of one year and a lowering of the age of entry from 62 to 60. In the dairy sector the trade unions required the lowering of the age of entry in the scheme from 60 to 58. The trade unions in the industrial sector protested against the proposals of the employers' association FME. They wanted a permanent lowering the of age of entry to preretirement in order to create work for younger age groups, for women, and for the long-term unemployed.[29] Employers were pressed to accept their requirements; otherwise they would shift their strategy to wage demands. The conflict between employers and trade unions in the metal industry became the most serious one. The bargaining process started in November 1987. In April 1988 there was still no collective agreement. Most of the bargaining partners have agreed to postpone dealing with the issues of early exit

---

[27] The FME stated that VUT should stand for "later retirement" *(Verlate UitTreding)* instead of preretirement *(Vervroegde UitTreding),* and ADV should stand for work time lengthening *(ArbeidsDuurVerlenging)* instead of work time reduction *(ArbeidsDuurVerkorting).*

[28] A specific example of "selection" was the proposal of the employers in the dredging sector during the 1987–8 collective bargaining. It contained the abolishment of the VUT for technical and administrative personnel (but not for blue-collar workers).

[29] Volkskrant, November 20, 1987.

until 1994. Illustrative for the seriousness of the conflict was the threat made by one of the trade unions (IB-FNV) at a certain point to mobilize its members on this particular issue.[30]

Although the discourse has changed, the average age of entry to the preretirement schemes continued to recede until the end of 1988. It now stands at 60. In 1988 only one relatively small subsector in retail and trade introduced an increase.

The game was completely different in the civil service sector. While employers in the private sector tried to make the preretirement schemes less attractive, government in its role of employer even tried to stimulate the use of preretirement schemes by older civil servants. However, the argument for stimulating early exit had changed. In the early 1980s government introduced exit as a tool to create employment for the younger age groups. In 1987–8 the employment argument was replaced by the economic argument. In order to reduce costs, government wanted to get rid of older (higher paid) civil servants. In other words, government had shifted to the strategy the private sector used in the late 1970s and early 1980s.

4.7.2   *Potential conflicts between the "established" and the "outsiders"*

The process of exit has also raised another issue in the public discourse: the role of the elderly in society. One of the conflicting issues is whether exit from the labor force simultaneously means exit from society. A leading figure in the Dutch "gray movement" labeled the elderly in this respect the "eliminated part of the population" (Egas 1986). The increase of the "younger-older" age groups (50 and over) outside the labor force and the growing political consciousness and activities of these groups explain why the organizations of the elderly are now undergoing structural changes. Initially set up as "clubs" producing "social goods" for their members, many of these organizations are now moving in the direction of interest associations, which try to influence political decision making in favor of the elderly.[31]

Traditionally, the orientation of the organizations of the elderly was based on a concept of social care. For that reason they were imbedded in the institutions and "culture" of social welfare. In the 1980s this orien-

---

[30] The trade union (IB-FNV) had selected one large firm (Fokker), but at the time the members did not (yet) want political action (which, then, was partly due to the economic problems of Fokker).

[31] This trend and also the inherent problems of the change are described in Duipmans (1986).

tation shifted from social care to emancipation and from welfare state to the labor society. This shift was attended by a gradually increasing conflict with the established institutions of the labor society. First, there is a (potentially growing) overlap between the membership structure of trade unions and organizations of the elderly. Nowadays the organizations of the elderly try to represent the interests not only of older age groups outside the labor force but also of those inside the labor process. They are already targeting workers aged 40 and over, because by then "age discrimination starts."[32] Second, there is a growing overlap/conflict with trade unions with respect to the process of exit, in particular the preretirement schemes. The organizations of the elderly are against age-specific exit routes. In their view the voluntary preretirement schemes are in fact compulsory exit routes based only on age. Nevertheless, these organizations are in favor of flexible retirement schemes, based not on age but on specific individual (social, physical and psychological) circumstances. Third, since the income[33] of the elderly outside the labor force is largely based on (changing) agreements reached in the bargaining process between employers and trade unions, the organizations of the elderly also want to be involved in this institutional framework.

The established organizations within the *arbeidsbestel* and also those in the sphere of welfare (the professionals of social care), however, want to keep the organizations of the elderly outside "their" domain.

In the near future it is expected that the organizations of the elderly will get "their" institutionalized entry to government, the advisory council on the policy for the elderly (WVC 1987).

4.8   CONCLUSION

Participation in the labor force always has been very low in the Netherlands, compared with other industrialized countries. This extreme position seems to be consolidated by a relatively stronger exit trend since the 1970s. This trend is explained by the existence of a complicated system of exit possibilities. We have argued that the increasing exodus of older workers is the result of unrelated actions and logics that reinforced one another and unintentionally produced an ever-growing exit of the "younger-older" age groups.

In the 1970s exit was channeled through combinations of social security programs, which were implemented by corporatist institutions on

---

[32] Information on the internal changes and external conflicts of the organizations of the elderly is largely based on interviews with key persons of the organizations.
[33] VUT, pensions, extra-legal benefits in the social security system, and so forth.

the sectoral level. In the 1980s this "system" was extended and partly replaced by private exit routes, bargained between employers and trade unions (the so called preretirement schemes, VUT). But this change did not disturb the exit trend. On the contrary, while exit through social security could (partly) be used by firms for a selective exit strategy (mainly of blue-collar older workers), exit through preretirement schemes completely escaped from control by employers. The ultimate outcome was that almost all employees aged 55 and over disappeared from the labor force.

Another effect of the existence of a whole range of exit opportunities has been the neglect of (re)integration policies by firms, government, and trade unions, for which there was no rationale. This fact, as we have argued, has in its turn reinforced the "logic of exit."

In the public discourse, exit has almost become accepted as a natural fact, a new social right. At the same time, labor force participation by older workers has become a taboo and exit has also stimulated a creeping age discrimination.

Only very recently are we entering a new phase in the public discourse: Convergence is (slowly) shifting to conflict. There is a growing debate about costs and the threat of a shortage of labor in the future. At the moment there is no consensus at all. Employers in the industrial and commercial service sectors differ from employers in small and medium-sized firms. Trade unions still want to expand the process of exit, although they have become more sensitive to the trade-offs involved. And also government in its role of employer is still encouraging the exit of its older employees.

One may wonder which direction the public discourse will take in the future and whether the trend toward early exit can be reversed. At the moment there is no consensus with respect to the direction the labor society should go. If nothing happens, the early exit trend will most likely continue. Reversing this trend seems possible only if responsibility for "lifetime employment" is (re)introduced on the firm level. In the existing system no one feels the need to be responsible, since various programs compensate older workers who have left the labor market.

REFERENCES

Bax, E. H. 1984. *Maatschappelijke verandering en arbeidsongeschiktheid.* The Hague: Ministerie van Sociale Zaken en Werkgelegenheid.

Becker, U., and M. Koper-Sluijter. 1987. "Vrouwen op de arbeidsmarkt. Een internationale vergelijking." *Economisch-Statistische Berichten* 72(August):756–9.

Besseling, J. J. M., and H. B. Bruinsma. 1987. "De WAO 1977–1983, cijfers en interpretatie." *Sociaal Maandblad Arbeid* 42(May):321–37.

Blom, L. H. 1983. "Vut; de analyse van een verschijnsel in ontwikkeling." *Sociaal Maandblad Arbeid* 38(February):95–103.

Blomsma, M., and B. de Vroom. 1987. *Pathways into Early Retirement. Early Exit of Older Workers in the Netherlands.* Leyden Institute for Law and Public Policy (Working Paper 14).

Bolhuis, E. 1987. "De VUT met pensioen?" *Economisch-Staatische Berichten* 72(August):726–8.

Casey, B., and G. Bruche. 1983. *Work or Retirement? Labour Market and Social Policy for Older Workers in France, Great Britain, the Netherlands, Sweden and the USA.* Aldershot/Brookfield: Gower.

CBS. 1973–85. *Arbeidskrachtentelligen.* The Hague: CBS.

1984a. *Vijfentachtig jaren statistiek in tijdreeksen, 1899–1984.* The Hague: Staatsuitgeverÿ.

1984b. *De leefsituatie van de Nederlandse bevolking van 55 jaar en ouder 1982,* deel 1b. The Hague: Staatsuitgeverÿ.

1985a. *Statistisch Bulletin, 1985/1986.* The Hague, CBS.

1985b. *Onderzoek huishoudens met eenmalige uitkering 1984.* The Hague: CBS.

1985c *Sociaal Economische Maand statistiek,* no. 9. The Hague: CBS.

1986. *Statistisch Zakboek 1986.* The Hague: Staatsuitgeverÿ.

1987a. *Statistisch Zakboek 1987.* The Hague: Staatsuitgeverÿ.

1987b. *Sociaal-economische maandstatistiek,* no. 11. The Hague: CBS.

1989a. *Statistisch Bulletin,* no. 17. The Hague: CBS.

1989b. *Sociaal-economische maandstatistiek,* nos. 7 and 11. The Hague: CBS.

den Broeder, A. L. *Bestuurbaarheid van de sociale zekerheid.* Deventer: Kluwar.

Detmar, H., and B. Dekker. 1987. *Het werkloosheidscijfer nader onderzocht.* The Hague: Social Zaken en Werkgelegenheid.

Duipmans, D., J. Naafs, and G. P. A. Braam. 1986. *Tussen Bingo en Belang. Het funktioneren van afdelingen ouderenbonden als organisaties voor belangenbehartiging.* Enschede: Universiteit Twente.

Egas, C. 1986. "Ouderen als uitgeschakeld volksdeel." *Namens* 1(December):435–40.

Einerhand, M. G. K. 1986. "Uittreded uit het arbeidsproces." *Statistisch Magazine,* no. 4, CBS.

Fernhout, R. 1980. "Incorporatie van belangengroepen in de sociale en economische wetgeving." In H. J. G. Verhallen et al. (red.), *Corporatisme in Nederland. Belangengroepen en democratie.* Alphen a/d Rijn: Sansom, pp. 119–229.

Friedman, L. M. 1985. *Total Justice.* New York: Russell Sage Foundation.

Ganzevoort, J. W., R. J. A. Gent, T. J. Nathans, and R. J. L. Noordhoek. 1984. "Het sociale zekerheidsnetwerk, voor wiens zekerheid?" In R. J. L. Noordhoek, F. G. van den Heuvel, J. W. Ganzevoort, J. Kooiman, and W. A. Sinninghe Damsté. *Haalbaarheid van veranderingen in de sociale zekerheid.* The Hague: Vuga, pp. 24–62.

Grobbée, J. J. J. 1986. In J. A. H. Bron et al. (red.), *Privatisering van de sociale ze-kerheid.* The Hague: Vuga, pp. 79–87.

GMD. 1989a. *WAO-toetreders 1987, een beschrijving.* GMD-cahier no. 16. Amsterdam: GMD.

1989b. *Reintegratie van WAO'ers.* GMD-cahier no. 17. Amsterdam: GMD.

Herweyer, M. 1981. "Arbeidsongeschiktheid als een vorm van vervroegde uittreding." *Gerontologie* 12(2).

Kerkhoff, W. H. C. (1981), *Ouder worden, Verouderen en het Personeelsbeleid.* Amsterdam: Universiteit van Amsterdam.

Koningsveld, D. B. J. 1988. *VUT, nu en straks.* Assen/Maastricht: van Gorcum.

Koningsveld, D. B. J., and Van 't Hullenaar. 1980. *Policies for Older Workers in the Netherlands.* Berg en dal: GITP.

Memorie van Toelichting. 1962. op Wetsontwerp WAO, Tweede Kamer 62/63.

Ministerie van Financiën. 1989. Rapport van de heroverwegingswerkgroep, *VUT in de collectieve sector,* Begrotingsvoorbereiding 1990, deelrapport no. 3.

Morée, M. 1986. "Vrouwen en Arbeidsmarktbeleid 1950–1985." In K. Schuyt and R. van der Veen (Red.), *De verdeelde samenleving.* Leiden: Stentert Kroese, pp. 73–97.

NFB. 1987. *Vijtfig jaar en uitgerangeerd?* The Hague (NFB Verkenningen no. 5).

Pensioenkamer. 1987. *Witte vlekken op pensioengebied.* The Hague: Pensioenkamer.

Roodenburg, H. J., and W. J. M. L. Wong Meeuw Hing. 1985. *De arbeids-marktcomponent in de WAO.* CPB occasional papers no. 34.

RPD (Rijks Psychologische Dienst). 1982–6. *VUT-enquetes.*

RvA (Raad v.d. Arbeidsmarkt). 1983. *Arbeidsmarktverkenning.*

SMA (Sociaal Maandblad Arbeid). 1988. Themanummer, no. 6.

SoZaWe (Ministerie van Sociale Zaken en Werkgelegenheid). 1984–6/1989. *Rapportage Arbeidsmarkt.* The Hague: SoZaWe.

1985. Dienst Collectieve Arbeidsvoorwaarden (DCA). *Vervroegde Uittreding in CAO's.* The Hague: SoZaWe.

1989a. *Vervroegde uittreding in CAO's.* The Hague: SoZaWe.

1989b. *DCA-bevindingen 1988.* The Hague: SoZaWe.

1989c. *CAO-afspraken 1988.* The Hague: SoZaWe.

SVR (Sociale Verzekerings Raad). 1987. Eindrapport Determinantenonderzoek.

Thijssen, L. 1985. "Uittreding uit het arbeidsproces; gevolgen voor het welbe-vinden." *Tijdschrift voor Gerontologie en Geriatrie* 16:141–8.

Van den Bosch, F. A. J. and C. Petersen. 1983. "An Explanation of the Growth of Social Security Disability Transfers." *De Economist* 131(1):65–79.

Van Ginneken, P. J. 1981. *VUT. Vervroegde uittreding in ontwikkeling.* The Hague: Ministerie van Sociale Zaken en Werkgelegenheid.

Van Seumeren, H. 1987. *Volkskrant,* Dec. 24, 1987.

Van Voorden, H. 1987. "De CAO als spiegel der arbeidsverhoudingen." *Sociaal Maandblad Arbeid* 42(November):673–81.

WVC. 1987. *Naar een Raad voor het Ouderenbeleid.* The Hague: WVC.

CHAPTER 5

France: Massive exit through unemployment compensation

ANNE-MARIE GUILLEMARD

5.1 INTRODUCTION

FRANCE is an extreme example of the international trend toward early withdrawal from the labor force in two respects. First of all, the employment activity rate of persons aged 55 to 64 is lower there, and in the Netherlands, than in any other industrialized country (see Chapter 2). Since 1984 less than half of this age group still hold jobs. Furthermore, France is the only country that lowered the age of retirement with a full pension, reducing the age from 65 to 60 in 1983. Second, this early-exit trend has been abetted, above all, by various arrangements managed by the Unemployment Compensation Fund. As a result, the transition from work to retirement in France is much simpler than those of other countries where several public and private welfare subsystems (disability insurance, retirement, or long-term coverage under health insurance) have been used to foster early exit.

A description of the French early-exit trend (section 5.2) is followed by an analysis of the various institutional arrangements that enable workers to leave the labor force early (section 5.3) and an examination of the social dynamics that have shaped and reshaped new pathways out of the labor market (section 5.4), with attention paid to various actors and their strategies. Finally, on the basis of an assessment of early exit's financial, economic, and social consequences (section 5.5), the chapter concludes with a discussion of both current debate about early exit and this trend's prospects in France (section 5.6).

The research reported in this article was supported by a grant from the Mission Interministérielle de Recherche-Expérimentation (MIRE) within the French Ministries of Labor and Solidarity. This article was translated from French by Noal Mellott, CNRS, Paris.

5.2 DEFINITIVE EXIT IN FRANCE: EARLIER AND EARLIER FOR MORE AND MORE PEOPLE

The tables presented in Chapter 2 enable us to compare, for the age group most directly affected by early exit, the employment situation in France with that in other major industrial countries. In France, as in the Netherlands, the sharpest drop in the labor force participation and employment activity rates of 55- to 64-year-olds has occurred since 1970. Looking at the latter, which indicates the proportion of persons actually working (i.e., those left after subtracting the unemployed, most of whom are definitively jobless since at this age they have no hope of finding work), we notice that, since 1984 in France, a minority of men aged 55 to 64 still hold jobs whereas in the early 1970s more than 70 percent did so. By 1988, only 44 percent of these men were working in France (and 35 percent in the Netherlands). For these two countries, the age threshold of definitive exit has lowered considerably. The early-exit trend has taken on greater proportions here than in other affected countries, such as West Germany, the United Kingdom, and the United States. By comparing labor force participation and unemployment rates, we discover a degree of covariation, after the age of 55, between the decline in employment and the rise of unemployment.

By using the results of French annual employment surveys (Table 5.1), labor force participation rates by age group can be analyzed over the past 20 years, and several conclusions can be drawn. First, the decline in labor force participation has definitely affected older people most. The participation rate has barely changed for men aged 25 to 54 and has even increased for women. The rate for 15- to 24-year-olds has, it is true, decreased as the period of education has stretched out; but this decrease is moderate compared with that of the oldest groups. Second, Table 5.1 reveals that the labor force participation rate of 60- to 64-year-olds dropped first, as early as 1975; then, after 1981, that of 55- to 59-year-olds began falling too. The rates for women in these age groups are less telling for reasons explained in Chapter 2. A cross-sectional analysis of women's participation rate involves two contrary phenomena: the massive entry of especially younger, but also older, women into the labor market versus the rising early-exit trend.

Given that so many early-exit arrangements in France have been managed by the Unemployment Compensation Fund, we are led to scrutinize employment activity rates too, as depicted in Table 5.2. In fact, less than a quarter of men aged 60 to 64, and less than two-thirds of those aged 55 to 59 were still working in 1988. It should also be pointed out that 50- to 54-year-olds are now caught up in this trend; their employment rate fell by seven percentage points from 1975 to 1988.

Table 5.1. *Labor force participation rates by age group, 1968–89*[a]

	Men					Women				
Year	15–24	25–49	50–54	55–59	60–64	15–24	25–49	50–54	55–59	60–64
1968	55.7	97.5	93.2	83.9	65.9	46.1	47.5	48.4	45.7	35.3
1969	52.9	97.3	93.4	84.2	66.8	47.1	48.7	48.8	47.2	33.5
1970	52.5	97.3	93.4	82.5	65.3	46.2	49.3	49.1	45.8	33.7
1971	51.7	97.3	94.4	82.0	64.7	44.7	50.4	48.6	44.5	32.7
1972	50.9	97.6	93.8	82.0	63.4	44.3	51.9	50.1	45.0	32.7
1973	49.1	97.5	93.7	82.8	61.8	43.7	53.7	51.2	42.9	32.5
1974	48.5	97.4	93.6	82.0	60.4	43.7	55.7	50.9	43.6	31.2
1975	50.1	96.7	93.1	83.3	56.7	45.6	58.3	52.2	43.5	29.8
1976	48.9	96.8	93.6	82.7	51.6	45.7	59.8	51.8	44.9	27.7
1977	48.5	96.6	93.4	83.9	48.8	45.4	61.4	52.5	46.4	27.2
1978	46.9	96.5	92.2	82.6	45.0	44.1	62.0	52.0	45.7	24.1
1979	47.6	96.8	92.3	82.3	45.1	44.4	63.8	53.1	45.9	24.0
1980	47.1	97.0	92.9	80.9	47.6	43.2	64.5	54.7	47.3	27.3
1981	45.5	96.8	92.4	79.5	42.5	42.5	65.5	56.8	46.6	25.3
1982	51.5	96.9	91.4	75.6	40.0	42.5	67.6	57.6	46.1	23.3
1983	50.8	96.9	91.7	71.0	33.6	41.5	68.8	56.7	43.7	20.6
1984	49.3	96.6	91.4	68.1	31.1	41.1	70.0	58.1	42.9	19.0
1985	49.0	96.6	91.2	67.8	30.8	40.3	70.8	57.8	42.8	18.9
1986	47.7	96.7	90.8	69.4	27.4	39.7	72.4	59.1	43.1	18.4
1987	46.3	96.6	90.4	67.3	25.7	38.7	72.3	59.8	44.6	18.0
1988	43.5	96.4	90.2	67.3	25.4	36.1	72.9	60.4	45.3	17.9
1989	42.3	96.3	90.1	68.1	24.0	35.2	73.0	62.2	44.7	17.7

[a] The ratio of the number of members of an age group in the labor force to its total number of members.
Source: INSEE, *Enquête d'Emploi, Collection D* (INSEE, Paris, 1968–89).

By studying the labor force participation for single ages from 55 to 64 (Figure 2.9 in Chapter 2), we observe how definitive exit has been rescheduled. The age by which more than half of Frenchmen were inactive has not stopped decreasing: It stood at 63 in 1976, 62 in 1977, 61 in 1978, and 60 in 1983. Although a majority of men under 60 are still working, 59 is now the median age when nearly half the men no longer work. The participation rates of men aged 57 or 58 have decreased noticeably since 1982. Only men aged 55 have maintained a relatively stable rate.

New institutional arrangements have laid the groundwork for this decrease in French labor force participation after the age of 55. Let us see how they have developed.

Table 5.2. *Employment activity rates by age group, 1975–88*[a]

	Men					Women				
Year	15–24	25–49	50–54	55–59	60–64	15–24	25–49	50–54	55–59	60–64
1975	46.7	94.8	91.8	81.2	55.1	41.0	55.6	52.2	43.5	29.1
1976	45.3	94.6	91.6	80.7	49.2	39.3	56.7	51.8	44.9	27.7
1977	44.3	94.5	91.1	81.4	46.3	38.5	58.0	50.3	44.1	25.8
1978	42.9	94.4	90.6	79.4	42.6	37.5	58.7	52.0	45.7	24.1
1979	42.8	93.9	89.7	79.1	43.1	36.3	60.1	50.7	43.1	22.9
1980	42.1	94.3	90.4	77.4	45.0	33.8	60.4	51.7	44.3	25.7
1981	39.6	93.4	89.2	75.5	40.6	30.2	60.7	53.4	43.6	23.8
1982	38.3	92.8	87.6	71.2	38.3	31.8	62.3	54.1	42.9	22.1
1983	37.2	92.6	87.9	66.3	32.2	30.9	63.5	53.1	40.2	19.7
1984	34.0	91.2	87.1	63.2	29.9	28.7	63.8	54.1	39.2	18.0
1985	32.6	90.6	86.1	62.2	29.4	28.0	63.9	53.1	39.3	17.6
1986	32.3	90.2	85.2	63.2	26.4	28.7	65.0	54.8	39.6	17.4
1987	32.5	89.8	84.8	61.2	24.8	27.7	63.9	55.1	40.2	17.0
1988	30.0	90.0	84.5	61.6	24.2	26.5	64.8	55.6	40.5	17.1

[a] The ratio of all employed persons (including the self-employed) in an age group to the total number of persons in the age group.
Source: INSEE, *Enquête d'Emploi, Collection D* (INSEE, Paris, 1975–88).

5.3   INSTITUTIONAL ARRANGEMENTS PROVIDING FOR EARLY EXIT

In France, unlike the United States, Great Britain, and The Netherlands, early-exit arrangements have been mostly public; private ones, whether under industry-wide agreements or company-level programs, have been the exception. These new arrangements have been added onto existing public welfare programs (see Figures 5.1 and 5.2).

The main early-exit pathways in France have run through unemployment insurance. To understand why, we must first look at the public retirement system, in particular at the principles underlying the creation in 1945 of the Old-Age Fund under Social Security.

Because the old-age pension system was set up after World War II when workers were scarce, incentives were offered to keep people working beyond the legal age for retirement with a full pension, 65 at that time. This system's provisions reflected the values of a work-oriented society: One could retire at 60 but with a pension cut in half, in other words, equal to 20 percent instead of 40 percent of average gross wages during the last ten years worked (in 1971 these percentages rose to, respectively, 25 percent and 50 percent of average gross wages during the ten years of highest earnings). Exceptions were subject to very tight conditions. Nonetheless, persons who were seriously disabled or unfit for work and former prisoners of war could receive full pensions at 60. In 1975 this possibility was extended to manual workers who had contributed to the Old-Age Fund for 40 years and to working-class mothers, and in 1977 it was extended to all women who had contributed for 37.5 years. Significantly, however, wage earners were encouraged to work beyond the age of 65, since there was then a pension increment of 5 percent a year.

Things stood thus until the March 26, 1982, reform lowering the legal age of retirement with a full pension from 65 to 60 for wage earners who had contributed to the Old-Age Fund for at least 37.5 years. This same reform did away with the aforementioned pension increments.

Another grand principle of the French retirement system also calls for attention: The receipt of a pension does not entail giving up gainful employment. Under French Social Law, the right to an old-age pension does not suspend the right to employment. By the way, the supplementary retirement funds, which provide additional benefits to all wage earners, operate on much the same basis as Social Security.

The very strong incentives offered by the retirement system to people who continued working – incentives that were maintained even when jobs became scarcer than in 1945 – account for the Unemployment Compensation Fund's leading role in the early-exit trend. Oriented as it was toward encouraging people to keep working, the public retirement system was unable, in effect, to assume this role.

Another characteristic of the French retirement system is the high replacement rate of pensions to wages. As Table 5.3 shows, France, Sweden, Italy, and Austria have the highest wage/pension ratios. In order to make early exit worthwhile to wage earners, it was, therefore, necessary to offer them the opportunity to stop working early with a rate of compensation at least equal to that of retirement. Furthermore, this opportunity had to be set up so as not to reduce the rate of old-age pension they could expect to receive later on, had they worked normally until retirement.

For these reasons, unemployment insurance has, in France, opened the major early-exit pathway; but the institutional arrangements used to bridge the period from gainful employment to regular retirement have been worked over, and over, during the past 20 years. Let us examine how.

France has had no active employment policy. There have been a few measures for young people but none for helping aging workers keep or possible coverage under unemployment — GRL — Retirement

Guaranteed-Income Dismissal Scheme (1972–83) managed by the Unemployment Fund

GRD — Retirement

Guaranteed-Income Resignation Scheme (1977–83) managed by the Unemployment Fund

AS-FNE (excep-tional) — GRL — Retirement

Since 1981, AS-FNE benefits for dismissed wage earners under contracts between the National Employment Fund and companies

AS-FNE — GRL benefits and then retirement as soon as the beneficiary has contributed to the Old-Age Fund for 37.5 years or reaches the age of 65 — Retirement

AC-FNE special benefits + half-time job — Retirement

Half-time preretirement for wage earners threatened by dismissal (since 1983)

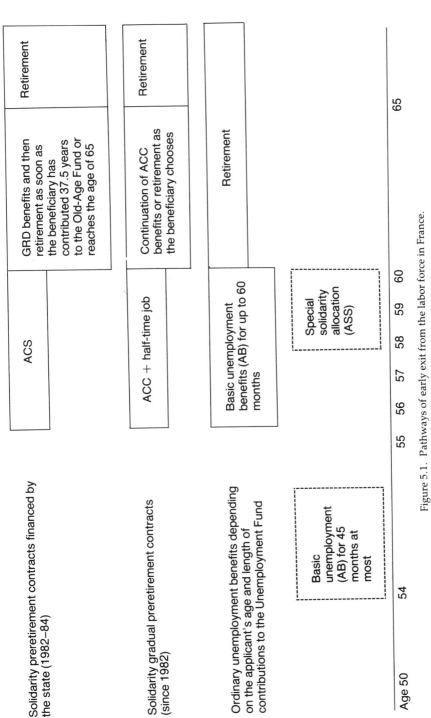

Solidarity preretirement contracts financed by the state (1982–84)

| ACS | GRD benefits and then retirement as soon as the beneficiary has contributed 37.5 years to the Old-Age Fund or reaches the age of 65 | Retirement |

Solidarity gradual preretirement contracts (since 1982)

| ACC + half-time job | Continuation of ACC benefits or retirement as the beneficiary chooses | Retirement |

Ordinary unemployment benefits depending on the applicant's age and length of contributions to the Unemployment Fund

| Basic unemployment benefits (AB) for up to 60 months | Retirement |

Basic unemployment (AB) for 45 months at most

Special solidarity allocation (ASS)

Age 50   54   55   56   57   58   59   60   65

Figure 5.1. Pathways of early exit from the labor force in France.

Under a December 18, 1963, act, the FNE was set up to help "restructure" the economy. Since personnel turnover had to be increased to help firms modernize, the FNE provided, under agreements signed with companies and tightly controlled by public authorities, special allocations to dismissed wage earners over 60 years old.

Under a March 1972 national labor agreement, persons over 60 years old in the private sector who had contributed to the Unemployment Fund for at least 10 years could, in case of dismissal, draw guaranteed-income dismissal benefits (GRL) from UNEDIC till retirement at 65. These benefits amounted to 70 percent of former gross wages. As of June 1977, UNEDIC adopted a guaranteed-income resignation measure (GRD) that extended, in the private sector, to "voluntary" resignees of the same age group what had previously been limited to those who had lost their jobs through dismissal. Both these guaranteed-income schemes were terminated in 1983.

In late 1980 the National Employment Fund offered a "special" allocation (AS-FNE) for preretirement at the age of 56 years and 2 months, or exceptionally 55, of any employee dismissed by a firm that had signed an agreement with the state. Benefits amounted to 70 percent of gross wages (reduced to less than 65 percent after 1983). This program, which is still in effect, was broadened in 1983 with the possibility for half-time preretirement.

In early 1982 the government adopted a new early-exit program, valid for two years, for 55- to 59-year-olds. Under solidarity contracts signed with companies, the state would cover a large part of preretirement costs. Significantly, these contracts stipulated that new hirings were to replace preretirees. Under one type of contract, employees who voluntarily resigned received, until age 60, a solidarity contract allocation (ACS) equal to 70 percent of average gross wages; but no more such contracts have been signed since early 1984. Under a second sort of solidarity contract still in effect, employees at least 55 years old who agree to work half-time until, at the latest, the age of 65 years and 3 months receive their half-time income plus a solidarity contract complementary allocation (ACC) equal to 30 percent of gross wages.

As of April 1983 the normal age of retirement with a full pension was lowered from 65 to 60 for persons who had contributed to the Old-Age Fund for at least 37.5 years.

In 1986, an authorization from the Work Inspection Office was no longer necessary before making dismissals.

Figure 5.2. The variety of early-exit measures. (Compare with the data in Table 5.4.)

Table 5.3. *Ratio of old-age pensions to average wages in industry: An international comparison (1969–80)[a]*

	Single person						Aged couple					
Country	1969	1975	1977	1978	1979	1980	1969	1975	1977	1978	1979	1980
Austria	67	63	64	65	67	68	67	63	64	65	67	68
Canada	24	33	33	32	33	34	41	47	47	47	48	49
Denmark	31	29	27	28	30	29	45	44	44	48	54	52
France	41	60	64	67	67	66	56	74	78	79	77	75
West Germany	55	51	54	54	50	49	55	51	54	54	50	49
Italy	62	61	64	66	66	69	62	61	64	66	66	69
Japan	26	37	53	54	54	54	27	39	57	57	57	61
Netherlands	43	43	45	44	44	44	61	61	65	65	65	63
Sweden	42	57	59	63	68	68	56	73	73	79	79	83
Switzerland	28	40	39	38	37	37	45	60	59	58	56	55
United Kingdom	27	31	28	29	29	31	43	47	43	45	45	47
United States	30	38	40	41	41	44	44	58	60	61	62	66

[a] Average wages during the last year worked.
Source: B. Aldrich. "The Earnings Replacement Rate of Old-Age Benefits in 12 Countries, 1969–1980." *Social Security Bulletin*, November 1982, pp. 3–11.

find jobs. Nor are older wage earners specially protected against dismissal. Programs for adapting jobs to age have been scarce, hardly amounting to more than very general ministerial guidelines. From 1967 to 1971 a few firms did try to adjust the pace of work for older employees and proposed a system of gradual retirement,[1] but they rapidly gave up – soon after public authorities approved of using unemployment compensation to guarantee the incomes of dismissed aging workers. This public policy "socialized" the costs that firms had, until then, borne.

The French early-exit trend has been grounded in the offer of compensation for lost jobs. However, such compensation tends to turn back against the group from which the beneficiaries come. In effect, the provision of better unemployment compensation coverage for the aging makes it possible to do away with all restrictions against cutting them from the work force. Whenever the job market slumps, employees who are thus better "protected" are the first to be deemed redundant and to lose their jobs.

[1] Company gradual retirement programs were put into effect at Turboméca (1968), Gillette-France (1971), SNECMA (1971), and Merlin Gérin (1970). For the history of these agreements and an analysis of their impact, see Audras (1973).

Indeed, as the employment situation worsened in France, special arrangements for older workers under unemployment compensation were expanded, and more and more of them were thrown out of the labor market. At first, these arrangements concerned those aged 60 to 64, but starting in the early 1980s, the group aged 50 to 59 came to swell the ranks of an inactive population awaiting retirement. Variations in the labor force participation rates of these age groups (shown in Table 5.1) provide clear evidence of the successive expansions of arrangements under unemployment compensation.

5.3.1   *1972–81: The creation and sudden expansion of guaranteed income schemes for the aging unemployed*

On March 27, 1972, a guaranteed income agreement was worked out within UNEDIC (Union Nationale pour l'Emploi dans l'Industrie et le Commerce [National Union for Employment in Industry and Commerce] called hereafter the Unemployment Compensation Fund) for persons aged 60 or older who were dismissed from their jobs. This scheme was worked out by the "social partners" – labor unions and the national employer's organization – who founded in 1958, and still run, UNEDIC. Accordingly, private-sector wage earners over 60 who had contributed to the Unemployment Fund for at least 10 years could, if dismissed, draw guaranteed-income dismissal benefits (*guarantie de ressources licenciement,* henceforth GRL) until age 65 when they would receive regular retirement pensions. These benefits amounted to 70 percent of former gross wages or salary during the last three months worked. It is noteworthy that the GRL's ratio to wages was higher than retirement's: 80 percent versus 60 percent of net wages. This ratio, of course, takes no account of severance pay or special bonuses for dismissal, nor of provisions that, under collective agreements in certain companies or industries, endowed beneficiaries with 100 percent of former wages. Moreover, this arrangement did not penalize beneficiaries when they went on retirement, since their old-age pensions would equal what they would have received had they continued working normally.

UNEDIC, funded by contributions from employers and employees, bore the costs of this new scheme, whereas the state's part in the guaranteed-income scheme dwindled from 1973 to 1978 (Ragot 1985):

1973	12.7 percent
1974	8.6 percent
1975	5.5 percent
1976	4.5 percent
1977	3.3 percent
1978	2.6 percent

Since 1979, following a reform of UNEDIC's finances, the state's part has increased, as we shall see.

Management and labor had followed a prototype in working out the GRL scheme. Under an act passed on December 18, 1963, the FNE (Fond National pour l'Emploi [National Employment Fund]) provided, under agreements signed between companies and public authorities, special allocations with the aim of facilitating employee mobility and, therefore, the "preretirement" of dismissed wage earners over 60 years old. This act was intended to help restructure the French economy by favoring personnel turnover. The FNE's program was tightly controlled by the administration: There were barely 10,000 beneficiaries at any point in time (Table 5.4). The impact on definitive exit was slight. In contrast, the guaranteed-income scheme had opened a pathway out of the labor force that would be increasingly taken as the employment situation worsened.

A decisive step was made in June 1977 when clauses were added onto the GRL agreement offering the same benefits to resignees. This guaranteed-income resignation measure (*guarantie de ressources démission*, henceforth GRD) was valid for two years, but would be renewed biennially until March 1983.

From this moment on, any private-sector wage earner between 60 and 64 years old could be compensated if he or she stopped working before retirement age. This expanded guaranteed-income scheme generalized a new way of leaving the labor force, and the number of such "preretirees" did not take long to swell. Whereas this scheme had, during its first five years, served a moderately increasing number of beneficiaries (fewer than 100,000 in 1977, column 2 in Table 5.4), it would, during the next five, expand at a breathtaking pace to cover nearly 300,000 beneficiaries in 1981 (column 2 plus column 3). Given a base of 100 in 1972, the total of these two columns rose to 400 in 1977 and 1,300 in 1981! This cannot be linked to the size of the group aged 60 to 64, which was decreasing because of the small birth cohorts from 1915 to 1919. Taking a base of 100 in 1972, this age group represented 61 in 1980 but 71 in 1981.

Besides offering 60 to 64 year-old private-sector employees the opportunity of a guaranteed income in return for their jobs, this scheme also had advantages for the jobless aged less than 60. Employees dismissed at the age of 56 years and 3 months or thereafter could, starting in 1975, combine various arrangements (all managed by the Unemployment Compensation Fund) until regular retirement, for example, ordinary unemployment benefits until the age of 60 and then GRL benefits until 65 when full old-age pensions could be drawn. Because of this possibility, 55- to 59-year-olds became the favorite target when firms had to cut personnel even further. In 1981, 68 percent of admissions under the GRL scheme were persons who had been on ordinary unemployment and

Table 5.4. *Beneficiaries under various preretirement arrangements, 1968–88 (as of December 31 each year)*

Year	1963 FNE Act (1)	Guaranteed-income dismissal (GRL) (2)	Guaranteed-income resignation (GRD) (3)	Subtotal 1+2+3: programs covering 60- to 64-year-olds (4)	National Employment Fund (AS-FNE) (5)	Solidarity contracts preretirement (ACS) (6)	Solidarity contracts gradual preretirement (ACC) (7)	Subtotal 4+5+6: programs covering 55- to 59-year-olds (8)	Grand total (9)
1968	11,333			11,333					11,333
1969	13,868			13,868					13,868
1970	13,105			13,405					13,405
1971	13,992			13,992					13,992
1972	14,151	23,186		37,337					37,337
1973	11,921	40,984		52,905					52,905
1974	9,423	54,924		64,347					64,347
1975	7,393	76,827		84,220					84,220
1976	5,942	97,470		91,412					97,412
1977	4,753	99,571	9,598	113,922					113,922
1978	3,629	99,983	43,441	147,563					147,053
1979	1,975	93,754	62,891	158,610					158,610
1980	1,221	118,029	95,538	214,788					214,788
1981	642	154,893	138,027	293,562	23,792			23,792	317,354
1982	53	201,831	197,472	399,356	53,207	61,701	146	115,054	514,410
1983	2	204,531	229,551	434,084	86,456	183,448	1,199	271,103	705,187
1984	1	188,849	220,790	409,640	121,750	150,545	1,432	273,903	683,543
1985		159,800	190,582	350,382	155,493	107,622	2,805	265,920	616,302
1986		126,840	162,254	289,094	175,000	62,680	5,370	243,050	532,144
1987		88,920	137,980	226,900	184,670	21,740	8,080	214,490	441,390
1988		84,800	135,100	219,900	186,230	18,510	8,510	213,250	433,150

Source: UNEDIC, *Bulletin de liaison*, appendix VIII, no. 92-206, 1987.

had, therefore, definitively stopped working before 60. In fact, wage earners who stopped working at 60 to be directly covered by this scheme were a minority – 32 percent!

The exploding number of guaranteed-income beneficiaries signaled a revolution. This scheme, soon the major early-exit pathway, was reshaping the process of definitive exit. A new phase of life, called preretirement *(préretraite)*, was now occurring for most wage earners in the private sector between the time they stopped working and the time they started receiving an old-age pension. The Unemployment Compensation Fund, whose duty is to compensate wage earners for short periods of joblessness, was assuming responsibility for covering jobless aging workers for as long as five years or more. It was being changed into a sort of old-age fund.

To glimpse the guaranteed-income scheme's impact on definitive exit, we need but notice that, by 1981, a minority of 60- to 64-year-olds in the private sector still had jobs: Adding together guaranteed-income beneficiaries plus job seekers in the same age group yields a total of 337,227 aging persons who, in one way or another, depended on unemployment compensation – compare this with the 287,496 age mates still working in the private sector. The Unemployment Compensation Fund had grown so much that it was taking the place of the Old-Age Fund in providing the means of definitive exit. According to a 1981 Ministry of Labor survey about definitive exit in the private sector (see Table 5.5), a minority – less than 18 percent – of departures from the labor force involved going on retirement normally at 65. Moreover, going on early retirement (at that time possible at 60) with full or reduced pensions accounted for only 14.5 percent of departures. In contrast, nearly two-thirds (60.2 percent) of these definitive exit cases were "preretirees" managed by Unemployment Compensation. A small percentage (7.6 percent) had given up their jobs under company-sponsored programs.

I might add that the most important of these company- or industry-wide programs (which have nothing to do with the Unemployment Fund) is the 1977 iron and steel agreement, part of a plan for "restructuring" this industry in France. This agreement, renewed since then, provides that workers doing hard labor can stop working as early as 50, and the others as early as 55, while receiving 75 percent of former wages. To give an idea of its impact, it covered nearly 30,000 wage earners from mid-1979 until the end of 1981, half of whom stopped working before 55.

The full impact of preretirement via unemployment compensation as a means of regulating definitive exit cannot be assessed without counting the mass of jobless 55- to 59-year-olds who, in fact, form a "precate-

Table 5.5. *Definitive exit by pathway, 1981*[a]

Pathway	Men (%)	Women (%)	Total (%)
1. Retirees at 65 with full pensions	17.3	18.4	17.7
2. Early retirees			
With full pensions:			
a. Disabled	8.8	6.8	8.1
b. World War II prisoners and veterans	2.2	0.3	1.5
c. Working mothers manual workers, and women who had worked for 37.5 years	1.9	2.7	2.2
With reduced pensions	2.7	2.6	2.7
3. Preretirees under:			
a. The special National Employment Fund program (AS-FNE)	15.6	12.8	14.7
b. The 1972 guaranteed-income dismissal sheme (GRL)	17.1	16.9	17.1
c. The 1977 guaranteed-income resignation scheme (GRD)	26.7	32.1	28.4
d. Company-sponsored gradual retirement programs	7.7	7.4	7.6
Total	100.0	100.0	100.0

[a]These statistics cover wage earners in the private sector who, at the age of 55 or over, went on retirement, early retirement, or preretirement between January 1, 1981, and October 31, 1981.
Source: Ministry of Labor Survey (cited in G. Magnier. "Les sorties de la vie active en 1981," *Bulletin mensuel du travail,* no. 95, October 1982).

gory" of preretirees. These long-term jobless, with no hope of working again, were awaiting eligibility for preretirement or retirement. In 1981, 170,000 of them were drawing ordinary unemployment benefits. Their ranks swelled as preretirement measures expanded. Table 5.6 depicts the worsening situation with regard to the unemployment rates of older age groups. Although 55- to 59-year-olds had previously run little risk of joblessness, their unemployment rate nearly doubled from 1975 to 1981, increasing even faster than that of 15- to 24-year-olds, the group most exposed to joblessness.

This new precariousness of 55- to 59-year-olds can also be seen in UNEDIC's statistics. From 1980 to 1981, the number of such persons

Table 5.6. *Unemployment rate by age group, 1975–88*

	Men					Women				
Year	15–24	25–49	50–54	55–59	60–64	15–24	25–49	50–54	55–59	60–64
1975	6.7	2.0	1.8	2.5	2.8	10.1	4.5	3.2	3.6	2.9
1976	7.5	2.3	2.2	2.4	4.5	14.1	5.1	3.5	4.4	4.3
1977	8.7	2.2	2.5	3.0	5.0	15.1	5.5	4.3	4.8	5.0
1978	8.7	2.5	2.5	3.9	5.3	15.0	5.5	3.9	4.1	4.2
1979	10.1	3.0	3.5	3.9	4.3	18.3	5.8	4.6	5.0	4.4
1980	10.6	2.8	2.7	4.3	5.6	21.7	6.5	5.5	6.2	6.0
1981	12.9	3.5	3.4	5.0	4.4	23.5	7.3	5.9	6.5	5.7
1982	15.6	4.2	4.2	5.8	4.2	25.1	7.8	6.0	6.8	5.4
1983	16.9	4.3	4.1	6.8	4.2	25.4	7.8	6.3	7.9	4.5
1984	22.1	5.5	4.7	7.0	4.1	30.2	8.9	6.9	8.6	5.5
1985	24.5	6.2	5.6	7.6	4.5	30.5	9.7	7.3	8.0	6.5
1986	22.8	6.6	6.1	9.0	3.7	27.5	10.1	7.2	8.0	5.5
1987	20.7	7.0	6.2	9.2	3.6	28.5	11.5	7.9	9.9	5.3
1988	16.9	6.1	6.4	8.4	4.7	24.2	11.6	7.9	10.7	4.3

Source: INSEE, *Enquêtes d'Emploi,* Collection D, Paris 1975–88.

receiving ordinary unemployment benefits rose 54 percent – at a faster rate than the average (35 percent) (Lenormand and Magnier 1983). This age group was not very "vulnerable" to unemployment, but this is no longer so. Likewise, its normally low "employability" has diminished even more. Table 5.7 shows the dramatic increase in the "unemployability" index of workers 50 and over. A first shock hit in 1976; a second, in 1980. As a result, the percentage of long-term unemployed men over age 50 rose more than 50 percent!

Legislation went along with the deteriorating employment situation of 55- to 59-year-olds. In late 1980 the National Employment Fund created a "special" allocation (*allocation spéciale,* henceforth AS-FNE) for pre-retirement at the age of 56 years and 2 months, or exceptionally at 55, of any wage earner dismissed by a firm that had signed an agreement with the state. Preretirement thus began reaching down into the group aged 55 to 59. This would set off a groundswell (Table 5.4, column 5).

5.3.2 1982–4: Lowering the age of definitive exit

With the coming to power of the Socialists in May 1981, two sorts of measures were adopted to lower the definitive exit age. For one thing, the normal retirement age was lowered from 65 to 60, a decision that

Table 5.7. *Vulnerability and unemployability indexes by sex and age group, 1968–87*[a]

	Men				Women				Men and women			
Year	15–24	25–49	>49	Total	15–24	25–49	>49 yrs	Total	15–24	25–49	>49 yrs	Total
						Vulnerability (%)						
1968	0.6	0.2	0.1	0.2	0.7	0.2	0.1	0.3	0.6	0.2	0.1	0.2
1969	0.8	0.2	0.1	0.2	0.6	0.2	0.1	0.3	0.7	0.2	0.1	0.3
1970	0.8	0.2	0.2	0.3	0.6	0.2	0.1	0.3	0.7	0.2	0.1	0.3
1971	0.7	0.2	0.1	0.3	0.9	0.2	0.1	0.3	0.8	0.2	0.1	0.3
1972	0.9	0.2	0.2	0.3	0.9	0.2	0.2	0.4	0.9	0.2	0.2	0.3
1973	0.7	0.2	0.1	0.3	0.7	0.2	0.1	0.3	0.7	0.2	0.1	0.3
1974	0.9	0.2	0.1	0.3	1.2	0.3	0.1	0.5	1.0	0.2	0.1	0.3
1975	1.3	0.3	0.2	0.4	1.2	0.5	0.2	0.5	1.3	0.4	0.2	0.5
1976	1.0	0.2	0.1	0.3	1.5	0.4	0.2	0.6	1.2	0.3	0.1	0.4
1977	1.3	0.2	0.2	0.3	1.4	0.4	0.2	0.5	1.3	0.3	0.2	0.4
1978	1.0	0.3	0.2	0.4	1.5	0.4	0.2	0.5	1.2	0.3	0.2	0.4
1979	1.3	0.2	0.1	0.3	1.8	0.3	0.2	0.5	1.5	0.2	0.2	0.4
1980	1.3	0.3	0.1	0.4	1.8	0.3	0.1	0.5	1.5	0.3	0.1	0.4
1981	1.3	0.3	0.2	0.4	1.8	0.4	0.2	0.6	1.5	0.3	0.2	0.5
1982	1.6	0.3	0.2	0.4	1.9	0.5	0.2	0.6	1.7	0.4	0.2	0.5
1983	1.6	0.2	0.1	0.4	1.5	0.4	0.2	0.5	1.5	0.3	0.1	0.4
1984	1.8	0.3	0.2	0.5	1.8	0.5	0.1	0.6	1.8	0.4	0.1	0.5
1985	1.8	0.3	0.2	0.4	2.0	0.5	0.1	0.6	1.9	0.4	0.2	0.5
1986	2.0	0.4	0.2	0.5	1.7	0.5	0.2	0.6	1.9	0.4	0.2	0.6
1987	1.6	0.4	0.2	0.5	2.0	0.4	0.3	0.6	1.8	0.4	0.2	0.5
						Unemployability (%)						
1968	13.5	18.6	42.8	23.1	16.9	27.1	33.9	23.7	15.2	22.0	39.7	23.4
1969	7.6	25.4	45.1	25.7	16.3	26.1	38.7	24.8	12.2	25.7	42.6	25.3
1970	6.5	19.5	40.0	20.3	13.2	24.4	40.9	22.8	9.9	21.6	40.4	21.4
1971	6.3	15.3	40.6	19.7	13.3	26.1	37.8	22.7	10.5	20.4	39.6	21.2
1972	9.1	15.5	43.7	21.3	11.1	24.3	43.3	22.4	10.2	19.8	43.5	21.8
1973	7.8	17.3	48.6	21.6	8.6	23.3	42.3	19.6	8.3	20.1	46.1	20.6
1974	7.4	17.8	49.9	20.6	11.5	18.7	39.8	18.4	9.9	18.3	45.2	19.4
1975	8.8	11.3	49.7	13.8	12.9	20.3	37.1	19.2	11.2	16.6	33.0	16.9
1976	14.4	20.2	43.7	22.8	18.4	26.5	48.0	25.3	17.0	23.8	45.7	24.3
1977	13.1	21.4	44.8	23.2	17.7	30.3	43.7	26.5	16.0	26.8	44.3	25.1
1978	15.6	19.0	44.8	23.3	24.9	34.0	46.5	31.4	21.3	27.8	45.5	28.0
1979	15.2	25.3	46.4	26.2	24.4	36.5	54.8	33.1	21.0	31.6	50.0	30.1
1980	15.0	30.7	55.8	30.2	24.2	36.6	58.0	33.8	21.0	34.3	56.9	32.4
1981	16.8	23.6	51.7	26.5	25.9	39.0	46.2	36.4	22.6	32.7	57.7	32.3
1982	19.1	32.3	54.3	31.8	31.7	40.8	62.6	39.6	26.9	37.1	58.1	36.2
1983	23.3	35.3	65.5	36.4	33.7	43.3	64.6	61.9	29.5	39.8	65.1	39.5
1984	24.6	33.1	59.5	33.9	34.5	46.0	74.3	44.2	30.5	40.0	66.3	39.4
1985	28.6	41.2	62.3	39.8	38.0	50.4	70.2	47.4	33.8	46.2	65.8	43.9
1986	27.0	43.8	66.9	42.1	34.6	49.2	70.5	46.3	31.1	46.7	68.4	44.3
1987	24.5	45.8	65.2	42.9	34.8	50.5	69.6	47.6	30.4	48.4	67.2	45.5

[a] The vulnerability index measures the risk of unemployment by the ratio of the number of persons unemployed for less than one month to the actively working population in the age group. The unemployability index measures the difficulty of being reclassified or reintegrated in the labor force in terms of the number of persons unemployed for more than a year to the total unemployed for the age group. The ages indicated are those persons reached during the given year.
Source: UNEDIC.

somewhat restored the Old-Age Fund its power to regulate definitive exit, at least of 60- to 64-year-olds. For another, preretirement was shifted toward 55- to 59-year-olds, increasing numbers of whom would now go, first, on preretirement under unemployment compensation and then, at age 60, on retirement.

Lowering the retirement age. Following a March 26, 1982, decree and a concomitant February 4, 1983, agreement (which made adjustments in the supplementary pension funds), wage earners could receive a full pension at the age of 60 if they had contributed to the Social Security Old-Age Fund for at least 37.5 years. This decree, which went into effect on April 1, 1983, covered both the private and public sectors. This decision to lower the retirement age affected the prevailing definitive exit arrangements.

As a result of increasing competition since 1972 from the guaranteed-income schemes managed by the Unemployment Compensation Fund, the retirement system had been losing its power to regulate definitive exit. The total of new retirees (Table 5.8) gives an idea of the impact of these schemes, before 1983, on Social Security's own early-retirement arrangements. Several points in these tables merit attention.

First, new admissions under the guaranteed-income schemes increased so rapidly that they were, in 1981 and 1982, reaching toward the total of new early retirees (column 17 versus column 10). Even though, in the early 1970s, new measures had been adopted to extend early retirement with a full pension to some new categories, the total of new early retirees decreased between 1975 and 1979, a period when ever more 60- to 64-year-olds were entering the guaranteed-income schemes.

Second, although the eligibility requirements of "inaptitude" for work were loosened in 1971, the number of new admissions for this reason (column 4) reached a relative maximum in 1976 (which it would not attain again until 1981) because the principal recipients, namely, manual workers, were leaving their jobs under the better-paying guaranteed-income schemes. It should be pointed out that, under inaptitude, full old-age pensions were offered at 60 to wage earners who were, on the basis of medical declarations, deemed to be 50 percent unfit for continuing in their current job or occupation without seriously impairing their health.

Third, the pathway out of the labor force through disability insurance is not well trodden. It led the beneficiary at 60 straight into coverage by the Old-Age Fund. In contrast with inaptitude, disability is proven when a wage earner is unable to do any kind of work whatsoever. New admissions from disability insurance into the retirement system barely exceeded 13 percent of all new retirees during the period in question (col-

Table 5.8. *New admissions (men and women) to the public retirement system and guaranteed-income schemes 1970–88*[a]

					Less than 65 years old					
Year	With reduced pensions (1)	With full pensions (2)	Disabled (3)	"Inapt" (4)	Veterans, prisoners of war (5)	Manual workers (6)	Working mothers (7)	Women having contributed for 37.5 years to the Old-Age Fund (8)	With full pensions, total of columns 2 to 8 (9)	Less than age 65, total of columns 1 to 9 (10)
1970	31,898		29,440	46,425					75,865	107,763
	(11.75)		(10.85)	(17.10)					(27.95)	(39.70)
1971	31,953		28,127	48,527					76,654	108,607
	(11.78)		(10.37)	(17.89)					(28.26)	(40.04)
1972	25,422		28,434	57,641					86,075	111,497
	(9.38)		(10.49)	(21.26)					(31.75)	(41.13)
1973	22,694		24,337	65,290					89.627	112,321
	(8.53)		(9.14)	(24.53)					(33.67)	(42.20)
1974	25,682		25,575	62,752	21,427				109,754	135,436
	(8.85)		(8.81)	(21.62)	(7.38)				(37.82)	(46.67)
1975	21,065		22,676	77,850	80,009				180,535	201,600
	(5.77)		(6.62)	(21.34)	(21.93)				(49.49)	(55.27)
1976	22,834		16,555	80,377	48,181	997	416		146,526	169,360
	(6.50)		(4.72)	(22.90)	(13.73)	(0.28)	(0.12)		(41.74)	(48.25)
1977	19,928		15,743	66,857	37,294	4,151	1,629		125,674	145,602
	(6.36)		(5.02)	(21.33)	(11.90)	(1.32)	(0.52)		(40.09)	(46.44)
1978	17,450		17,717	54,516	37,500	2,435	760	8,274	121,202	138,652
	(5.87)		(5.96)	(18.34)	(12.62)	(0.82)	(0.26)	(2.78)	(40.77)	(46.64)
1979	17,312		19,710	48,356	28,682	2,992	366	10,952	111,058	128,370
	(6.16)		(7.01)	(17.20)	(10.20)	(1.06)	(0.13)	(3.90)	(39.51)	(45.67)
1980	25,011		34,129	67,772	18,831	2,943	521	9,880	134,076	159,087
	(8.47)		(11.56)	(22.96)	(6.38)	(1.00)	(0.18)	(3.35)	(45.41)	(53.89)
1981	30,505		37.067	80,242	14,246	4,610	603	10,914	147,682	178,187
	(10.84)		(13.18)	(28.53)	(5.06)	(1.64)	(0.21)	(3.88)	(52.50)	(63.35)
1982	32,014		35,049	82,383	11,138	5,107	552	9,027	143,256	175,270
	(11.66)		(12.76)	(30.00)	(4.06)	(1.86)	(0.20)	(3.29)	(52.16)	(63.82)
1983	42,983	113,755	36,555	82,338	8,136	2,340	637	4,042	247,803	290,786
	(10.84)	(28.69)	(9.22)	(20.76)	(2.05)	(0.59)	(0.16)	(1.02)	(62.49)	(73.33)
1984	39,644	155,645	35,251	82,559	4,667	63	725	182	279,092	318,736
	(8.93)	(35.05)	(7.94)	(18.59)	(1.05)	(0.01)	(0.16)	(0.04)	(62.84)	(71.77)
1985	33,088	155,388	36,770	73,266	3,252	4	675	90	269,445	302,533
	(6.90)	(32.42)	(7.67)	(15.29)	(0.68)	(0.00)	(0.14)	(0.02)	(56.22)	(63.12)
1986	33,468	162,962	37,041	71,940	2,740	2	701	60	275,446	308,914
	(6.89)	(33.53)	(7.62)	(14.80)	(0.56)	(0.00)	(0.14)	(0.01)	(56.67)	(63.55)
1987	34,913	186,444	34,346	68,294	2,184	0	667	14	291,949	326,862
	(7.02)	(37.49)	(6.91)	(13.73)	(0.44)	(0.00)	(0.13)	(0.00)	(58.70)	(65.72)
1988	39,621	208,707	36,184	64,838	1,925	0	605	3	312,262	351,883
	(8.12)	(42.78)	(7.42)	(13.29)	(0.39)	(0.00)	(0.12)	(0.00)	(64.01)	(72.13)

[a] Absolute numbers are given for each year, with the percentages in parentheses below them.
Source: Caisse Nationale Vieillesse des Travailleurs Salariés.

	65 and older						
Year	Given full pensions at age 65 (11)	Given full pensions over age 65 (12)	Given increased pensions over age 65 (13)	Age 65 or older, total of columns 11 to 13 (14)	Pensions under special retirement funds (15)	Total of columns 10, 14, and 15 (16)	Guaranteed-income schemes, 60–64 age group (17)
1970	108,905 (40.12)		30.583 (11.27)	139,488 (51.39)	24,164 (8.90)	271,415 (100)	
1971	107,714 (39.71)		32,035 (11.81)	139.749 (51.52)	22,876 (8.43)	271,232 (100)	
1973	107,017 (39.48)		30,236 (11.15)	137,253 (50.63)	22,314 (8.23)	271,064 (100)	23,250
1973	103,221 (38.78)		30,136 (11.32)	133,357 (50.10)	20,482 (7.70)	266,160 (100)	28,029
1974	102,516 (35.32)		32,435 (11.18)	134,951 (46.50)	19,825 (6.83)	290,212 (100)	27,255
1975	110,658 (30.34)		47,979 (13.15)	158,637 (43.49)	4,542 (1.25)	364,779 (100)	39,411
1976	120,714 (34.39)		59,654 (16.99)	180,368 (51.38)	1,303 (0.37)	351,031 (100)	36,289
1977	113,442 (36.19)		52,711 (16.81)	166,153 (53.00)	1,746 (0.56)	313,501 (100)	44,624
1978	104,751 (35.24)		53,253 (17.92)	158,004 (53.15)	597 (0.20)	297,253 (100)	69,401
1979	101,225 (36.01)		50,989 (18.14)	152,214 (54.15)	513 (0.18)	281,097 (100)	53,446
1980	85,224 (28.87)		50,482 (17.10)	135,706 (45.97)	440 (0.15)	295,233 (100)	87,671
1981	62,517 (22.22)		40,318 (14.33)	102,835 (36.56)	272 (0.10)	281,294 (100)	117,049
1982	63,341 (23.06)		35,432 (12.90)	98,773 (35.96)	606 (0.22)	274,649 (100)	134,235
1983	75,621 (19.07)	18,045 (4.55)	11,962 (3.02)	105,628 (26.64)	129 (0.03)	396,543 (100)	110,678
1984	90,654 (20.42)	31,726 (7.14)	2,908 (0.65)	125,288 (28.21)	93 (0.02)	444,117 (100)	59,186
1985	139,410 (29.09)	36,066 (7.53)	1,164 (0.24)	176,640 (36.86)	109 (0.02)	479,282 (100)	64,057
1986	137,311 (28.25)	39,631 (8.15)	132 (0.03)	177,074 (36.43)	70 (0.01)	486,058 (100)	62,861
1987	129,594 (26.06)	40,077 (8.06)	747 (0.15)	170,418 (34.27)	65 (0.01)	497,345 (100)	52,391
1988	98,000 (20.09)	37,341 (7.65)	602 (0.12)	135,943 (27.86)	45 (0.01)	487,871 (100)	23,892

umn 3 percentages). In France, unlike West Germany or the Netherlands, disability insurance has not much abetted the early-exit trend.

A fourth and final point: Lowering the retirement age somewhat
restored lost power to the Old-Age Fund, at least with regard to the
group aged 60 to 64, as can be seen in the number of new retirees before
the age of 65 with full pensions (column 9). In 1983 this total shot up and
has stayed high since; it amounts to about 60 percent of all new admissions into retirement.

It should be kept in mind, however, that many wage earners taking
retirement before age 65 had already stopped working because of the
guaranteed-income schemes. Lowering the retirement age did not,
therefore, fully restore the Old-Age Fund as the regulator of definitive
exit. What it did do, above all, was replace one arrangement with
another; and it did this, initially, in order to limit early-exit costs. Thanks
to this reform, wage earners who have contributed for 37.5 years to the
Old-Age Fund are no longer covered by preretirement arrangements
under Unemployment Compensation. Instead, they now depend on the
Old-Age Fund, which provides pensions at a lesser percentage of former
wages than the guaranteed-income schemes. Consequently, these now
useless schemes have been left to run out. Nonetheless, doing away with
them has not put an end to preretirement, for it has been shifted forward
in the life span, under arrangements covering 55- to 59-year-olds, as we
shall see.

As a result of the retirement age reform, the Old-Age Fund has been
able to take up from the Unemployment Compensation Fund responsibility for the age 60 to 64 stretch of the life span. Although this reform
especially helped the Unemployment Compensation Fund solve its
financial problems caused by the guaranteed-income schemes, public
opinion took it to be a sign that the government had finally yielded to
labor unions, which had, for a long time, been demanding a lower full-
pension retirement age. This popular reform brought about a new legal
situation that differed from the contractual agreements underlying the
guaranteed-income schemes, which, tied to the business cycle, were of
limited validity. Moreover, previously ineligible categories, such as public-sector employees, could now retire earlier.

Extending preretirement to 55- to 59-year-olds: Solidarity contracts. In order
to halt unemployment, the government, besides lowering the retirement
age, set up in early 1982 a new preretirement program valid for two
years. These so-called solidarity contracts *(contrats de solidarité)* were an
attempt to regain control over definitive exit. During former President
Giscard d'Estaing's term, early withdrawal had been more or less left up

to employer and union organizations, and arrangements had come out of labor–management compromises. Now the state would systematically cover a large part of preretirement costs under solidarity contracts to be signed between it and firms. Public authorities thus became a full party to preretirement agreements with the objective of stimulating hirings. To this end, three sorts of measures were proposed, only one of which would have a significant impact.

1. *Government aid for shortening the workweek.* The state would pay all employer contributions owed to Social Security by any company with a net increase in its work force as a result of its significantly shortening the workweek and, therefore, needing to hire more persons.
2. *Solidarity preretirement resignation contracts.* As part of a solidarity contract signed with the state, a firm could promise to hire one job seeker for each employee over age 55 who voluntarily resigned before December 31, 1983. These resignees would, until age 60, receive solidarity contract allocations (ACS, *allocation conventionnelle de solidarité,* column 6 in Table 5.4) equal to 70 percent of average gross wages (i.e., about 80 percent of net wages) corrected for inflation and financed as follows: 50 percent from the Unemployment Compensation Fund and 20 percent from the state. As part of this contract, the employer was committed to maintaining, for at least a year beyond the date set for departures on preretirement, the overall size of his work force as measured in multiples of full-time wage earners. It should be pointed out that resignees under these contracts would receive, upon retirement, the same pensions they would have received had they continued working.
3. *Solidarity gradual preretirement.* Under another solidarity contract formula still in effect, a firm can commit iteslf to hiring job seekers as a counterpart for reducing from full- to half-time the jobs of voluntary candidates over 55. The employer promises to maintain for two years the overall size of the work force in multiples of full-time jobs. Candidates who thus agree to work half-time until, at the latest, the age of 65 years and 3 months receive about 80 percent of their full-time wages. This amount, periodically adjusted for inflation, is broken down as follows: 50 percent in current wages for the half-time work and 30 percent as a solidarity contract complementary allocation (ACC, *allocation conventionnelle complémentaire,* column 7 in Table 5.4) equal to 30 percent of average gross wages during the past 12 months. Two-thirds of this allocation (20 percent) come from UNEDIC; and the other third (10 percent), from the state.

Formally, solidarity contracts were negotiated case by case. The proposal for such an agreement was closely examined by the Ministry of Labor's local offices. This office and the employer worked out all clauses after taking into account collective bargaining in the firm and hearing personnel representatives. The contract was signed if it was expected to affect the employment situation and if the firm offered guarantees that it would hold to its obligations.

Significantly, solidarity contracts opened a broad early-exit pathway for the age group just below the one previously covered by the guaranteed-income

Table 5.9. *New admissions to the guaranteed-income schemes and public preretirement arrangements, 1972–88[a]*

	Guaranteed-income schemes				Public preretirement arrangements				
Year	GR 72 (1)	GRL (2)	GRD (3)	1+2+3 (4)	AS-FNE (5)	ACS (6)	ACC (7)	5+6+7 (8)	Total (9)
1972	23,250			23,250					23,250
1973	28,029			28,029					28,029
1974	27,255			27,255					27,255
1975	39,411			39,411					39,411
1976	36,289			36,289					36,289
1977	24,037	11,151	9,436	44,624					44,624
1978	4,408	28,200	36,793	69,401					69,401
1979	2,569	23,553	27,324	53,446					53,446
1980		44,001	43,670	87,671					87,671
1981		53,615	63,434	117,049	24,984			24,986	142,033
1982		61,599	72,636	134,235	30,241	47,683	170	125,947	260,182
1983		42,505	68,173	110,678	47,276	143,307	1,168	191,751	302,429
1984		30,800	28,386	59,186	55,122	8,951	306	73,632	132,818
1985		27,855	36,198	64,057	60,838	9,836	1,666	72,370	136,423
1986				62,861	50,517		3,363	54,478	117,339
1987				52,391	40,257		3,319	44,253	97,584
1988				23,892	48,551		4,305	53,674	77,566

[a]For definitions of the abbreviations, see Table 5.4.
Source: UNEDIC.

schemes. Since the late 1970s, increasing numbers of 55- to 59-year-olds were being forced to enroll on unemployment until they reached the age of coverage under the guaranteed-income schemes. Now there was a chance that they could draw solidarity preretirement benefits instead.

Of these three formulas, only the preretirement resignation one was widely successful. The number of beneficiaries exceeded all expectations. During the first two years, nearly 200,000 older workers took this pathway out of the labor force (column 6, Table 5.9), whereas its potential had been estimated at 50,000 a year! The gradual preretirement formula (column 7) was not much of a success, having 1,338 new admissions during the same period. Its conditions were not attractive because the beneficiary, by working half-time, received only 10 percent more than the full-time "preretiree" and accumulated half as many Social Security retirement points. Gradual preretirement was not very attractive to employers either because it forced them to reorganize work.

In late 1984 the total number of 55- to 59-year-old preretirees reached 273,903 (Table 5.4). Afterward, it decreased as solidarity preretirement resignation contracts ran out. In late 1984, there were also about 150,000 ordinary jobless persons in this age group, whose employment rate had fallen to 63 percent for men and 39 percent for women (Table 5.2). From 1982 to 1984, a period when solidarity contracts were being signed, the employment rate for men in this age group dropped from 76 percent to 62 percent (Table 5.2).

5.3.3 *Since 1985: With preretirement blocked, more and more older wage earners on unemployment*

Given the preretirement groundswell, which starting in 1981, thanks to solidarity contracts and the new AS-FNE allocations, swept over wage earners from the age of 55 on, it would not take long for its financial brunt to be felt. Since 1979, the state had been paying a larger part of preretirement costs (Ragot, 1985):

1979	13.1 percent
1980	23.5 percent
1981	26.3 percent
1982	32.8 percent
1983	36.4 percent

Despite this increasing share, the Unemployment Compensation Fund was running deeper in the red. Expenditures on unemployment compensation for persons over 55 went on rising – even though the decision to lower the retirement age had shifted the costs of the guaranteed-income schemes, which, moreover, were allowed to run out after 1983.

Along with the number of beneficiaries, the costs of these various programs were soaring. Table 5.10 reveals a major change. During 1983 and 1984 more was paid out in preretirement than in total unemployment benefits. Nevertheless, on December 31, 1983, there were 705,000 preretirees but more than a million persons on unemployment. Preretirement costs had risen to 23-fold from 1973 to 1984, whereas the costs of unemployment had increased eightfold.

Managed by five labor unions (CFDT, CFTC, CGC, CGT, and FO) and by the national employers' organization (CNPF), and financed through contributions from both employers and employees, UNEDIC had deviated from its objective of providing an income to the jobless who met certain requirements. It was, in fact, bearing the burden of providing benefits to hundreds of thousands of persons who were no longer working but were not really either job seekers or jobless. Recall that, in 1984,

Table 5.10. *Costs of preretirement and unemployment compensation benefits (in millions of current French francs), 1973–84*[a]

	Costs under:						Total unemploy-ment benefits	Index
Year	Guaranteed-income schemes	AS-FNE pre-retirement programs	Solidarity contracts	Iron and steel agreement	Total	Index		
1973	445.2	186	–	10.7	651.9	100	1,627.9	100
1974	836.9	183.5	–	14.3	1034.7	139.7	2,316.4	125.2
1975	1,427.2	186.5	–	5.5	1,619.2	195.7	6,398.7	309.6
1976	2,084.7	182.5	–	21.6	2,218.5	244.6	8,843.1	390.4
1977	2,581.8	172.7	–	15.9	2,770.4	278.9	11,526.5	464.6
1978	4,330.1	159.1	–	49.6	4,538.8	418.2	15,983.9	589.6
1979	6,073.3	132.4	–	439.6	6,645.3	553.5	20,980.8	699.8
1980	8,851.8	76.5	–	690.4	9,618.7	705.8	24,345.4	715.4
1981	14,528.4	741.7	–	1,206.7	16,476.8	1,066.8	36,521.6	946.9
1982	22,093.2	2,264	772.2	1,468.4	26,597.8	1,537.9	44,950.9	1,040.8
1983	28,041.6	3,926.5	10,375.2	1,912.5	44,255.8	2,337.8	41,901.2	886.4
1984	25,299	6,307.8	11,248.1	1,905.4	44,760.3	2,346.4	40,835.9	802.3

[a]This table provides a view of the major, but not of all, benefits paid to the jobless and preretired.
Source: Comptes de l'Emploi, 1973–80, and UNEDIC, *Bilan 1980–2.*

more than a third of private-sector wage earners aged 55 to 59 were on preretirement.

Since the organizations that manage UNEDIC became aware that the Unemployment Fund's financial difficulties could be blamed on the new early-exit pathways, preretirement arrangements were curtailed, and decisions were made about sharing costs with the state. This was the intent of a February 24, 1984, agreement about reforming the unemployment compensation system. This reform took the incentive out of certain preretirement arrangements (for example, to calculate benefits, wages would be averaged over a longer reference period). But more importantly, it set up a dualism between "insurance" and "solidarity," and the costs of the latter – preretirement – were shifted onto the state. Preretirement benefits could no longer be paid through employer and employee contributions but would come out of the government's general tax revenues. Hence, the Unemployment Fund was restored to its duty by providing coverage to job seekers for a relatively short time.

Since April 1, 1984, only two of the aforementioned preretirement programs remain in effect: AS-FNE and solidarity gradual preretirement. The other solidarity contracts have been terminated. Under both existing programs, the state pays part of the benefits previously due from the

Unemployment Fund. For instance, it pays most AS-FNE costs, even though the company also makes a contribution unless exempted because of financial difficulties. Furthermore, lower benefits are now provided; this special allocation now amounts to less than 65 percent of gross wages averaged over the past 12 months (instead of 70 percent). As a consequence, the total number of preretirees started declining in 1985 despite the rising number of AS-FNE and ACC beneficiaries (Table 5.4). Furthermore, the number of newly admitted beneficiaries under the more important of these two current programs, which covers dismissed preretirees, dropped in 1986 and 1987 (Table 5.9).

However, this drop did not in any reflect fewer dismissals of wage earners over age 55. In fact, the employment rate of 55- to 59-year-olds has continued waning. Likewise, the unemployability index of workers over 50 has worsened considerably (Table 5.7). In brief, restricting preretirement has not halted the eviction of older wage earners from the labor force. Ever more often, such persons depend on unemployment benefits for a living.

The declining number of preretirees can be set down to tightening of conditions under the AS-FNE program: on the one hand, increasing the minimal period that applicants have to have contributed to the Unemployment Fund as well as requiring that they have twice as much seniority in the company, and on the other hand, increasing the company's share in the program's costs as well as exempting fewer firms from paying it. These measures have definitely taken the incentive out of the FNE agreements.

This drop in the number of newly admitted preretirees has set off a countercurrent to the trend from the 1984 reform, which was intended to restore the Unemployment Fund to its original calling by putting an end to its duties as a pseudo-old-age fund, these duties being shifted onto the state. But what is acutally taking place? Responsibility for early exit is being shifted from the state-run preretirement program, because of its tighter eligibility requirements, back onto the Unemployment Fund.

Since conditions under state-run preretirement programs have been tightened, more and more of the aging jobless have been forced back into the unemployment system. Since 1986 a new pathway has been cleared for definitive exit. It starts at dismissal, passes through a long period of unemployment compensation, and leads on to retirement.

This new path has become well beaten since the government abolished the requirement that firms submit dismissals for approval. Until 1986 public authorities, through the Work Inspection Office, had a right to review dismissals made for "economic reasons" (notably redun-

Table 5.11. *Newly admitted beneficiaries (over age 55) drawing basic unemployment and AS-FNE preretirement benefits, 1985–88*

Year	Basic unemployment (AB)	AS-FNE	Total	AB (%)	AS-FNE (%)	Annual variations of AS-FNE (%)
1985	51,798	60,868	112,666	46.0	54.0	—
1986	67,790	50,717	113,307	55.4	44.6	−12
1987	80,497	40,257	120,754	66.7	33.3	−24
1988:						
1st quarter	21,710	13,040	34,750	62.5	37.5	
2nd quarter	16,484	11,680	28,164	58.5	41.5	
3rd quarter	10,080	11,600	21,680	46.5	53.5	+14

Source: UNEDIC, November 1988.

dancy). A company could not dismiss employees on its own authority. It had to obtain an authorization from the Ministry of Labor's administration, which both checked out the serious, real cause of dismissal and, whenever more than 10 persons were targeted, examined the company's "social plan." This authorization was a means the administration could use to goad companies to enter into agreements with the FNE and thus negotiate arrangements so as to avoid the sudden dismissal of persons over age 50. Abolishing this authorization deprived the administration of its powers to review and negotiate cases at the very time that the FNE preretirement program was being restricted and the employer's share of its costs increased.

The impact was soon to be felt. The ranks of beneficiaries over 50 drawing various sorts of unemployment benefits have swollen while companies have been shunning the FNE program. As can be seen in Table 5.9 (column 5 versus column 7), there have been too few admissions under solidarity gradual retirement to make up for the overall decrease in the FNE's preretirement program. Like companies, workers have not shown much interest in this program, since many of them are eligible for higher basic unemployment benefits, which average out to 64 percent of gross wages and can be received for up to 50 months. Until early 1986 wage earners over 55 were dismissed mainly under the coverage of FNE agreements. Out of a monthly average of nearly 10,000 new beneficiaries in 1985, 5,400 were admitted for AS-FNE benefits and 4,600 were admitted for basic unemployment benefits (AB, *allocations de base*). In Table 5.11 we can observe the shift from the National Employment Fund toward the Unemployment Compensation Fund in the second quarter of 1986 and throughout 1987.

Starting in 1986, as Table 5.11 shows, more people over 55 were being admitted to receive basic unemployment than AS-FNE benefits. Clearly, the definitive exit pathway through ordinary unemployment compensation is now being more frequently trodden. Abolishing the requirement of administrative approval of 55- to 59-year-olds for dismissals brought about a 30 percent increase in new enrollments on unemployment from 1986 to 1987, an increase that reached 66 percent for men (UNEDIC, 1981, p. 102).

As aging workers turn back toward unemployment compensation, costs are shifting from the state back onto the Unemployment Fund. The latter's financial situation is, once again, shaky. New measures have been taken to deal with this transfer of costs. For example, employers now have to pay a special contribution to the fund for every employee 55 or over dismissed for economic reasons without coverage under an AS-FNE agreement. In turn, the Unemployment Fund pays to the state a fixed amount for each beneficiary admitted under this FNE program. Other measures have made it more appealing for companies to sign agreements with the FNE, in particular the creation in 1983 of a half-time preretirement program for wage earners threatened by dismissal. Although the effects of these recent measures cannot yet be clearly discerned, the pendulum seems to be swinging back from basic unemployment toward AS-FNE since the third quarter of 1988 (Table 5.11).

There are still, however, masses of aging workers drawing unemployment compensation, whether basic under insurance or assistance (the new solidarity requirement). In 1987, the group aged 55 to 59 represented 22 percent of the beneficiaries (twice as many as the group aged 25 to 29) of the special solidarity allocations (ASS, *allocation spécifique de solidarité*) provided to jobless wage earners who have reached the term of basic unemployment benefits; and the group aged 50 to 59 represented nearly 40 percent (Table 5.12). Not only does the group aged 55 to 59 stand in the front line of beneficiaries receiving these low long-term benefits, but also it has drawn unemployment longer than any other age group – 797 days.

A major definitive exit pathway now runs through basic unemployment compensation, followed by a special minimal solidarity allocation during a waiting period for retirement. Wage earners aged 50 to 54 are also being forced to look in this new direction out of the labor force, even though fewer of them than older fellow workers have yet had to head that way.

The opening of this pathway can be explained by new retirement measures in effect since 1983. Persons at least 60 who have contributed to the Old-Age Fund for at least 37.5 years can now go on retirement with a full pension. In some cases, long-term unemployment has taken the

Table 5.12. *Recipients of special long-term unemployment benefits (ASS) and length of unemployment by age group as of December 31, 1987*

Age group	No. of recipients	Days of joblessness	Percentage of total recipients
<20	20	109	—
20–24	1,566	195	0.6
25–29	27,660	396	10.1
30–34	41,834	551	15.3
35–39	36,831	591	13.4
40–44	28,286	591	10.3
45–49	27,461	621	10.0
50–54	41,151	716	15.0
55–59	60,279	797	22.0
60–64	9,075	1,071	3.3
Totals	274,163	646	100.0

Source: UNEDIC, *Bulletin de liaison,* 110, September–October 1988, p. 170.

place of preretirement as the bridge spanning the time between the last job and retirement, but this pathway is much more perilous than the preretirement one, since basic unemployment benefits are drawn for a length of time that depends on how long the beneficiary held his or her last job and how long he or she has contributed to the Unemployment Fund. Hence, there are many people who will stop drawing basic unemployment before they reach 60, in particular those who, as early as the age of 50, have trouble keeping their jobs. They will become "solidarity" cases to whom a very moderate special allocation, subject to conditions about total household income, will be paid for renewable periods of six months (ASS).

5.4 THE SOCIAL DYNAMICS OF EARLY-EXIT ARRANGEMENTS

The foregoing chronological analysis has shown the fluctuations of early-exit arrangements. What strategies have guided the actors who have worked these arrangements out and modified them during the past 15 years?

Three main actors have confronted one another over this issue, namely, labor unions, employers (represented, in particular, by the Conseil National du Patronat Français, CNPF), and the government. By analyzing their arguments, clashes, and negotiations, we can discern four periods, each corresponding to a particular rationale for reworking early-exit arrangements. (For a more thorough analysis, see Guillemard 1985, 1986a, 1986b).

During the first period, when the guaranteed-income scheme was invented for dismissed aging wage earners, these three actors were at odds, each attempting to impose its own rationale and definition of the issues. Debate was splintered. To limit the exploitation of workers, the unions were fighting for an expansion of the right to retirement. In 1970 and 1971 they launched major campaigns for a lower retirement age and a raise in pensions. The government responded to this offensive by trying to focus debate on its version of the issues, namely, the implementation of a policy of social integration of the elderly through the provision of facilities and services that would help them lead autonomous lives. In 1971 a program for helping old people remain living at home was adopted, and legislation was passed for raising pensions while keeping the age for retirement with a full pension at 65. To counter the union campaign, the CNPF tried to shift the terms of debate toward the issues of personnel management and the employment of older workers. It tried to impose its version of the issues, namely, that retirement policy should be adjusted so as to regulate and manage the work force. The March 27, 1972, agreement on the guaranteed-income dismissal scheme was proof that this counteroffensive had, ironically, paid off. The demand for the right to a full old-age pension at 60 was warped into an agreement about compensating aging workers for lost jobs. This scheme provided companies with the means of freely – as needed and at least cost – getting rid of older wage earners over 60. It did so by increasing the employer's power to dismiss them without paying additional costs, since the guaranteed-income scheme was financed through the Unemployment Fund. As a consequence, companies that had set up preretirement programs put an end to them, because such costs could now be borne by the unemployment system.

During the second period starting in 1975, the three actors began having a like preoccupation on their minds. For all parties and not just the CNPF, issues were clarified as a matter of jobs. As economic growth slowed down and the labor market slumped, the actors modified their objectives and strategies. The unions gradually gave up their offensive for lowering the retirement age and made a defensive stand on jobs. "Better retired than unemployed," their slogan first voiced in 1975, echoed this new thinking. From then on, lowering the retirement age would be a palliative for the labor market. Choosing the lesser of two evils, the unions decided to defend jobs for young people while agreeing to sacrifice the right of older workers to employment.

Meanwhile, under President Giscard d'Estaing, state interventionism in the social and economic spheres was being lessened. Programs for the social integration of the elderly lost impetus. The government tended to leave early exit up to management–labor negotiations without intervening in negotiations as it had in 1972. In other words, it was no longer a brake on the early-exit trend. And the CNPF and unions more or less agreed about using preretirement as part of a jobs policy.

This new social dynamics led to the June 13, 1977, agreement for extending the guaranteed-income scheme to resignees, an extension in line with all parties' intention to improve conditions in the labor market. This new agreement, initially valid for two years, was not at all meant to be a flexible retirement plan; it was a jobs measure linked to the business cycle. According to a CNPF spokesman, it was "anti-retirement at 60." It gave companies the greater flexibility they wanted in matters of personnel policy, especially with regard to older workers. Under its clauses, employers could "negotiate" so as to offer incentives, such as bonuses, to workers who resigned. Consider yet another example: Since the amount of guaranteed-income benefits was, in compliance with the principles of the Unemployment Fund, based on wages averaged over the last three months worked, it was easy for an employer to get rid of aging workers by negotiating a wage increase for the three months preceding resignation. Attractive financial conditions were thus offered to employees at a moderate cost to the employer.

From then on, nothing would keep the early-exit trend from accelerating. Only budgetary limitations, as of 1981, would slow it down somewhat. In the meantime, the guaranteed-income schemes had become the principal early-exit pathway.

The third period began in 1981 when the Socialists came to power. The new government founded its legitimacy on the redistribution not only of wealth following the logic of social democracy but also of jobs at a time when the problem of unemployment, particularly of young people, was preoccupying public opinion. The government's intervention was twofold: an active jobs policy based on intergenerational solidarity and the decision to lower the retirement age. In pursuit of the former, solidarity contracts were, as already mentioned, signed with companies in order to allow workers aged 55 to 59 to quit. Far from remaining uninvolved (as previously) in preretirement, public authorities were a full party to these contracts. The decision to lower the retirement age had two objectives. On the one hand, the government, during this period of Socialist rule under the Fifth Republic, thus activated the welfare state's system of social transfers. The decision was symbolically important for this reason. But it was also symbolic because, initially at least, most private-sector wage earners aged 60 or older were already no longer working – owing to the guaranteed-income schemes. On the other hand, this decision was meant to help control exploding early-exit costs by replacing these schemes with the less expensive coverage provided by the Old-Age Fund.

One of the main factors underlying the social dynamics of early exit can be clearly observed during this third period: the replacement of one fund with another and the subsequent shifting of costs with this instrument's substitution (Casey 1987). Several factors motivated the government to replace the guaranteed-income schemes with retirement. These schemes' exploding costs were not just the result of their generous benefits and consequent success. They also had a demographic origin. From 1975 to 1980, there were, in all, only 1,600,000 persons aged 60 to 64 because of the trough in age cohorts born between 1915 and 1919, during World War I. But starting in 1985, full age cohorts would be reaching this age and the group aged 60 to 64 would be 2,800,000 strong. According to the Minister of Finance, the Unemployment Fund would no longer be able to bear the costs of the guaranteed-income schemes as of 1985.

Meanwhile, the positive effects of guaranteed-income schemes on the labor market were tailing off, since most 60- to 64-year-olds had already stopped working. The objective of improving the employment situation implied shifting preretirement foward in the life span – toward the next lower age group, those 55 to 59. As can be clearly seen, preretirement was essentially a jobs measure.

The fourth, and most recent, period started in 1984. The logic underlying it, too, has been one of shifting costs about. Expenditures on preretirement were absorbing more and more of the Unemployment Fund's budget. In 1984 preretirements (under the guaranteed-income schemes, solidarity contracts, and FNE agreements) amounted to 55 percent of its outlay (Table 5.10). This Fund has been becoming a pseudo-old-age fund. The 1984 reform of the unemployment system was an attempt to transfer these costs onto the state.

As already pointed out, the state's attempts to manage, and contain, preretirement have, given the abolition of the administrative approval of dismissals, consequently shifted early-exit costs back onto the Unemployment Fund, as more and more older jobless persons take the pathway through long-term unemployment toward retirement. In November 1989 the government announced that, as of April 1990 and in compliance with a 1983 agreement with employer and labor organizations, it would like to cease paying part of the extra costs (to the supplementary retirement funds) of its 1983 decision to lower the retirement age. If this happens, these extra costs will have to be fully made up through employer and employee contributions.

The rationale of cost shifting is important for understanding the social dynamics of the early-exit trend at present. The issues have been continually narrowed down and focused on the short-term question of who should pay the costs. Rationing jobs for aging workers is still a reality that neither the government, nor the CNPF, nor the unions have faced or tried to change.

As conditions in the labor market improve, we might expect the government to begin supporting the integration of aging workers, a policy that would somewhat alleviate the difficulties of retirement funds by encouraging people to prolong their working lives. But instead of this, it seems as though each of the three actors is seeking to get rid of the burden of these workers by shifting it onto the others. Meanwhile, aging workers, still excluded from the labor market, shift about from one set of arrangements to another as they try to "grab" the best opportunities and highest benefits offered for early exit.

5.5   THE SOCIAL IMPACT OF EXPANDING EARLY-EXIT PROGRAMS

Let us now look at the social implications of early withdrawal. This calls for turning our attention to the consequences for aging wage earners themselves, the effects on the organization of the life course, and the impact on the labor market as well as the welfare system.

5.5.1   *Consequences for aging definitive withdrawees*

The social stratification of early exit. Even though a large number of older wage earners withdraw early from the labor force, not all of them do so; and not all of those who do leave by the same pathway. Have certain occupational categories been more affected by the early-exit trend? Have they taken specific pathways, different from those followed by other categories?

A supplement to the 1985 annual employment survey helps answer this question (see Heller 1986, 1987). According to its findings about a sample of 30,000 persons aged 55 to 64 who had stopped working between 1981 and 1984, preretirement arrangements had opened the principal pathway out of the labor force. Depending on the criteria used, there were, in 1985, 512,000 "preretirees" under public programs and

41,000 under private or company programs, in contrast to 138,000 job-less persons and 373,000 retired former wage earners. Preretirees mostly came from big industry. About two-thirds of them (65 percent) had worked in industry, compared with less than 30 percent in the tertiary sector. However, the latter was better represented among preretirees who had withdrawn under resignation rather than dismissal schemes: 41 percent of GRD and 35 percent of preretirement solidarity contract ben-eficiaries came from the service sector.

It was mainly big companies that used preretirement to manage the work force: 40 percent of preretirees came from firms with more than 500 employees, whereas only 30 percent of 55- to 64-year-olds still working were employed by large firms. This trend was even clearer with the AS-FNE program: 57 percent of beneficiaries were from big companies.

Heller's analysis (1986) by socioeconomic category shows that prere-tirement principally affected the working class: 54 percent of all prere-tirees had blue-collar jobs, whereas 34 percent of wage earners who had gone on retirement at the normal age were blue-collar workers. Table 5.13, which is extracted from this survey, reveals differences in the ways socioeconomic categories definitively stopped working. Blue-collar workers represented more than 60 percent of preretirees for both sexes. This overrepresentation was especially noticeable among those who lost their jobs under dismissal programs (GRL and AS-FNE). Also notewor-thy, male blue-collar workers were overrepresented among the unem-ployed 55- to 64-year-olds. In contrast, white-collar workers were more frequently covered by resignation schemes (GRD and ACS). Notice too that a larger proportion of them continued working. This was also the principal socioeconomic category that profited from the lowering of the retirement age in 1983. This could be expected since there were more potential retirees from 60 to 64 years old in this category whereas, as we have seen, most blue-collar workers had already exited through prere-tirement or unemployment.

A characteristic of early withdrawees under preretirement arrange-ments was that they had worked for a long time in their companies. When all arrangements are taken together, 55 percent of preretirees under public programs had more than 20 years of seniority with their last employer (Table 5.14). In this respect, they were like retirees of the same age. In contrast, seniority sets the jobless aged over 55 apart from pre-retirees and retirees, since 39 percent of the unemployed had stayed for less than five years at their last company.

Let us dwell awhile on the uses to which the 1983 retirement age reform has been put. According to surveys carried out in 1983, 1984, and 1987 by the National Old-Age Fund (Caisse Nationale de Vieillesse),

Table 5.13. *Definitive exit by socioeconomic category and sex (percentages)*[a]

| | Preretirees | | | | | | | | | | | | | Retired wage earners | | Unemployed | | Still working | |
| | Guaranteed-income dismissal (GRL) | | Guaranteed-income resignation (GRD) | | National Employment Fund (AS-FNE) | | Solidarity contracts (ACS) | | All public programs | | Private programs | | | | | | | |
Socioeconomic category	M	W	M	W	M	W	M	W	M	W	M	W	M	W	M	W	M	W
Blue-collar workers																		
Unskilled blue-collar workers	35	55	9	21	21	53	23	41	24	39	19	6	30	16	35	23	16	14
Skilled blue-collar workers	32	10	25	12	36	0	44	4	35	6	36	0	13	2	27	4	25	5
White-collar wage earners																		
Office employees																		
Low white-collar categories	6	25	7	47	10	30	5	47	7	38	8	80	16	44	8	63	15	58
Middle white-collar categories	18	7	38	11	22	17	20	9	22	12	26	7	25	29	21	8	24	16
Top-level executive white-collars	9	3	17	9	11	0	8	0	11	5	8	7	14	2	8	0	20	7
Others	—	—	4	—	—	—	—	—	1	—	3	—	2	2	1	2	—	—
Total	100	100	100	100	100	100	100	100	100	100	100	100	100	100	100	100	100	100

[a] This table presents statistics about 55 to 65-year-olds from 1981 to 1984. The data about such persons still working come from 1982 and 1983. Boxes have been drawn around the numbers that are much higher than the average of 55 to 64-year-olds still working. How to read this table: 35 percent of men who went on preretirement under the guaranteed-income dismissal scheme were unskilled workers.

Table 5.14. *Seniority with the last employer (percentages)*[a]

Status	30 years or more	20–30 years	10–20 years	5–10 years	Less than 5 years
Retired wage earners	44	26	20	5	5
Preretirees under all public programs	27 / 27	28	29	10	6
Preretirees under private programs	27	22	22	12	17
Unemployed	6	9	28	18	39

[a] How to read this table: 27 percent of beneficiaries from public preretirement programs had at least 30 years of seniority in the last company where they worked.
Source: Heller (1986).

Table 5.15. *The social stratification of the guaranteed-income schemes, July 1981*

Status	GRL (1)	GRD (2)	GRL + GRD (3)	Active wage earners 60–64 years old (4)	% en GR[a] (5)
Manual laborers	6,712	5,284	11,996	30,308	28.4
Unskilled blue-collar workers	23,015	17,917	40,932	46,636	46.8
Skilled blue-collar workers	40,405	36,535	76,940	47,350	61.9
Lower-level white-collar workers	40,180	46,057	86,237	89,089	49.2
Middle- and top-level white-collar workers	31,188	28,407	59,595	60,617	49.6
Total	141,500	134,200	275,700	274,000	50.2

[a]Column 5 equals column 3 divided by the total of columns 3 and 4.
Column 4 is the total of wage earners contributing to the Unemployment Fund.
Source: UNEDIC, "Garantie de ressources et emplois salariés du secteur privé." *Bulletin de Liaison UNEDIC,* December 1981, 83:21.

only about 40 percent of requests for retirement pensions following this reform came from wage earners who were still employed (in particular, white-collar workers), whereas 18 percent came from aging jobless persons who were, in fact, already out of the labor force. The remainder of requests were made by the "inactive," especially preretirees and women whose working lives were short or had already been interrupted. In effect, the possibility of retiring at 60 opened a "fake" early exit since most of those who took advantage of it were already definitively out of work. These surveys help us gauge how much definitive exit has been transformed during the past 15 years. Even in France, the only country that has so deliberately lowered the retirement age, the Old-Age Fund has not been restored as the regulator of definitive exit. Instead, preretirement arrangements have reshaped the transition toward the period of economic inactivity following the working life: A minority of persons now pass directly from the labor force onto retirement.

What conclusions can be drawn from this analysis of the social stratification of early exit? Apparently, preretirement has enabled unskilled or semiskilled blue-collar workers with long working lives behind them to exit sooner. We might, therefore, conclude that it represents significant social progress since these beneficiaries, who stop working earlier while receiving satisfactory compensatory benefits, belong to a generation that had hard jobs or performed repetitive tasks for nearly 40 years during a period when the workweek was almost 50 hours long. However, this conclusion has to be restricted for two reasons.

First of all, it is not necessarily worn out workers who have systematically taken advantage of preretirement. A close analysis of a 1981 UNEDIC study of the guaranteed-income schemes (Table 5.15) reveals that manual laborers – the least skilled blue-collar category – were definitely underrepresented among GRD and GRL beneficiaries (less that 30 percent) but overrepresented among 60- to 64-year-olds still working. In 1981 approximately half of unskilled workers and white-collar workers and more than 60 percent of skilled workers in the private sector had exited from the labor force under these schemes. These schemes have not, therefore, necessarily brought about more equitable conditions by granting the least privileged workers the right to stop working sooner.

Second, when looking more closely at how the right to rest and free time has been extended under various early-exit arrangements, we observe that this extension has not only advanced but also reshaped the definitive withdrawal schedule. The individual has lost much control over the scheduling of his or her transition toward economic inactivity.

The new transition out of the labor force. As preretirement has become the major definitive exit pathway, there have been at least two major effects on the transition toward economic inactivity. First of all, the timing of withdrawal is more often forced upon than chosen by the individual; and second, retirement becomes a cutting-off point, a definite definitive exit.

An imposed choice. The introduction of a preretirement period between work and retirement has fully changed the way more and more older wage earners quit working. When definitive exit took place through retirement, the transition was regulated, forseeable, and controllable. People knew at what age they would be entitled to a pension. In fact, one could even choose to go on retirement at 60 or later, and prepare for it much earlier.

Under the guaranteed-income dismissal scheme, aging workers were not entitled to rest like retirees. They no longer had the initiative in, nor control over, how their working lives would end. This power lay with the employer, whose decision to dismiss personnel set off the whole exit process. True, the preretirement arrangements based on resignation (the GRD from 1977 to 1981 and ACS from 1982 to 1984) were theoretically voluntary for wage earners. Not only do the major arrangements of this sort no longer exist, but these resignation schemes, too, turned out to be dependent on factors related to companies and their management of personnel.

My study (Guillemard 1986a:287ff.) of a sample of guaranteed income beneficiaries in 1980 has shown that even among those under the resignation scheme, only a quarter could be said to have, indeed, voluntarily resigned. For the others, resignations were mainly motivated by changes in working conditions or "economic restructuring" (24 percent) and health or fatigue (35 percent). These resignations were, therefore, given under pressure. They were not part of individuals' personal plans. Resignees had chosen the lesser evil: Given that their jobs were hard or tiresome, they no longer felt capable of keeping up on changes in their occupations; and a resignation, "negotiated" with the employer, seemed to provide an honorable and financially satisfactory settlement.

In fact, financial incentives for resignation were one of the first reasons cited by preretirees in another study (Heller 1986): 80 percent of resignees mentioned it, compared with 17 percent of dismissed preretirees. This author also points out that, as part of this negotiated resignation deal, 71 percent of preretirees had received from their firm a bonus or other compensation, which averaged to about 4.5 months of wages. When they deemed it necessary, employers added incentives onto public preretirement arrangements.

Wage earners' aspirations were not the main accelerator of the sudden, forced, massive movement of aging workers out of the labor force. This trend was sped up for economic reasons, in line with companies' personnel policies. Unlike under retirement, the individual did not have much say. True, preretirement offered some employees the opportunity to leave a job that, as they grew older, was tiresome or, as their health failed, became too hard. Nonetheless, such motivations were voiced less often than financial ones.

Preretirement has been imposed upon rather than freely chosen by individuals. Usually, preretirees have lost rather than quit their jobs. Evidence of this is that many of them would have liked to go on working. According to Heller's study (1986), nearly two-thirds of dismissed preretirees would have liked to continue working. To this percentage has to be added that of preretirees who would have liked to continue working part-time (see Table 5.16). These preretirees were more like the jobless of the same age (among whom 95 percent of men and 80 percent of women would have liked to continue working) than normal retirees (of whom barely more than 10 percent would have liked to continue working). Furthermore, nearly 30 percent of male preretirees covered by resignation arrangements (which no longer exist) would have liked to keep on working; they too lost rather than quit their jobs.

The close relationship between preretirement arrangements and the

Table 5.16. *Who would like to have continued working?*[a]

		Would like to continue working:		Part-time
Status		Full-time		
Beneficiaries of GRL and AS/FNE (dismissed)	Men	65		2
	Women	59		6
Beneficiaries of GRD and ACS programs (resignations)	Men	26		4
	Women	16		7
All preretirees regardless of the program	Men	46		3
	Women	29		6
Former wage-earners who retired normally	Men	10		3
	Women	13		6
Retirees who were not formerly wage earners	Men	25		10
	Women	24		11
The jobless aged 55 to 64	Men	95		1
	Women	80		14

[a] How to read this table: 46 percent of male preretirees would have liked to continue working full-time and 3 percent part-time.
Source: Heller (1986:101).

Unemployment Compensation Fund probably accounts for the similarity between the experiences of preretirees and of the jobless. For many wage earners, preretirement has been an ordeal similar to what is described for unemployment (Schnapper, 1981). According to my survey (Guillemard, 1986a) of preretirees in 1980, only 40 percent were satisfied or relieved to stop working; the rest strongly regretted having lost their jobs. The majority expressed feelings of obsolescence: "We were thrown out in the garbage after the best of our lives was used up." Heller's study (1986), too, has shed light on the similarity between the attitudes of the aging jobless and of preretirees, especially those dismissed from their jobs. Among beneficiaries under preretirement solidarity contracts, which stipulated that aging resignees were to be replaced by new hirings, feelings of relegation seem to be less strong. In effect, these preretirees most resemble retirees. Under these contracts, early withdrawal is not simply a matter of obsolescence; it also means freeing a job, "giving up your place to make room for young people." For this reason, these contracts are more acceptable than other arrangements.

The prevailing feeling among preretirees is uneasiness, even though some of them, like some of the jobless, manage to turn this traumatic experience into a positive one. The public's image of age groups is very telling. Since 1979, the relative position of 50- to 64-year-olds on a "moral scale," which COFREMCA drew up for polling French public opinion, has been steadily decreasing toward zero. This is the only age group to which this has happened; the others' positions have oscillated between 13 and 11 on this 20-point scale. This too provides evidence of the narrow choices offered to older persons and of the hovering menace of sudden obsolescence.

Definitive exit as a cutoff point. Not only has the scheduling of definitive exit changed, thus advancing the threshold of old age, but also the social content of this third stage of life has been altered – in line with preretirement arrangements – so as to exclude work. These arrangements were set up under the Unemployment Compensation Fund, whose logic has, in turn, been applied to definitive exit in general.

Accordingly, receiving benefits and holding a job have been made incompatible. This incompatibility breaks not only with the principles underlying the public pension system but also with the previously prevailing image of retirement. As stipulated in the 1945 French Social Security Act, retirement is the right to a pension, and entitlement depends on age and the length of one's working life. It does not entail giving up one's job. These principles were incorporated into the public's image of retirement, as various polls prove. Although these polls also provide evidence that people want to retire earlier,[2] the meaning of this should not be misinterpreted. For instance, out of SOFRES' June 1975 representative sample of the French population over age 15, 89 percent of men wanted to be able to retire at 60 or earlier, but 48 percent thought it better not to stop working completely upon retirement. The public did not associate retirement with economic inactivity. Instead, retirement meant, first of all, entitlement to a pension and, thereby, the possibility of receiving a substitute income when the decision was made to retire. However, the guaranteed-income schemes have, in line with the rules of

---

[2] See the public opinion polls carried out by SOFRES in 1972 for the CFTC and *Notre Temps* and in 1975 for *Notre Temps*, by IFOP in 1977 for *Le Nouvel Age*, and by CREP in 1978 for *La Vie Française*. Their results need to be refined since the desire to have the retirement age lowered varied according to socioeconomic category, age, and sex. See also Monnier (1979).

unemployment compensation, subordinated the right to a substitute income to the obligation to not hold a job. Holding a job has become unlawful for preretirees. The right to employment has been separated from entitlement to an old-age pension. The rest granted to aging workers carries a price: They have to give up their jobs. The benefits they receive are compensation for this loss.

The new logic of separating the rights to employment and to retirement tends to be brought over into the retirement system, too. For example, one measure in the 1983 retirement reform regulated the cases of holding wages and entitlement to retirement pensions by taxing severely retirees' wages and their employers. Concerned about the financial disequilibrium of public retirement funds, Prime Minister Chirac's government did away with this restriction in 1986.

This new work/retirement dichotomy can also be detected in behaviors. As pointed out, labor force participation rates flag starting at 55 and collapse after 60. There used to be more than a few persons who both worked and received an old-age pension during a transition lasting a few years. This flexibility was reflected in the broader dispersal of labor force participation rates by age. Now, the last stage of life has been specialized in economic inactivity, as though aging workers, often as young as 55, have been publicly declared to be useless. Indeed, the swollen ranks of jobless 55- to 59-year-olds, and now even 50- to 54-year-olds, are a straightforward declaration. Aging workers are targeted when the work force has to be trimmed. Their right to employment is no longer recognized. They are now penned up inside the category of dependent persons, who have to live on contributions of wage earners who are "competitive." They are swelling the ranks of those who, because they are a burden, are also social outcasts.

5.5.2   The consequences for the social organization of the life course

Early-exit programs have been based on a model whereby the life course is organized in three stages: education, work, and rest. They have pushed this model to its limits, as wage earners over age 50, about to leave the labor force, will soon have no other socially assigned function than imposed "economic inactivity" during a last stage of life definitively cut off from the world of work. Pushed to its limits, this threefold model seems, paradoxically, no longer reasonable. Let us focus on two ways this model is no longer capable of governing the experiences of current generations: On the one hand, the last stage of the life course is now unforseeable and uncertain; on the other, the boundary between work and nonwork is less clearly defined.

An uncertain life course. The age of entitlement to a pension used to be a clearly defined visible milestone erected between working life and old age. All generations thus had a definite image of the successive stages of life and of their chronological bounds. As early-exit arrangements have cropped up between the second and third stages, the life course's standardized, chronological order has come undone. Definitive exit now depends on the business cycle. It no longer occurs at a fixed age of entitlement to rest. Early withdrawal arrangements have, as shown, been continually reworked as a function of economic conditions and financial limitations. The last stage of life has become contingent and unforeseeable. No one working in the French private sector now knows at what age and under what conditions he or she will leave the work force. As we have seen, lowering the retirement age has not put an end to early definitive exits, which are still occurring along pathways running through public preretirement programs based on dismissal and long-term unemployment. Current proposals about reforming the retirement system (in particular, requiring more than 37.5 years of contributions to the Old-Age Fund for retirement at age 60, 42 years being currently mentioned today) are adding to the confusion.

The image these inactive persons have of their own situation is telling. For them, retirement is no longer a unifying principle bestowing a homogeneous, coherent meaning on the third stage of life. A minority of inactive 55- to 65-year-olds identify themselves with retirees. Instead, many of them declare that they are discouraged unemployed persons with no hope of finding work. Some of them fiercely deny that they are retirees. Persons in the third stage of life are losing their social identity, which used to be that of "retiree."

Definitive inactivity, old age, and retirement no longer happen together during an individual's life. Occupational old age starts with definitive exit, well before retirement. The threefold organization of the life course is no longer a uniform institution clarifying the future.

The blurred boundary between work and nonwork. Though based on the principle of radically separating work from retirement, early exit has, paradoxically, developed in a way that does away with the bounds between work and nonwork. Faced with arrangements that not only have taken little account of their social utility but have even publicly declared them to be useless, preretirees and young retireees have become a core group around whom new non-wage-earning activities have developed outside the business sector.

Traditionally, when people retired, they tended to give up their membership in organizations; but this is no longer so, at least not for preretirees. They are joining associations with businesslike as well as charitable objectives, while showing less interest in senior citizens' organizations and retirees' clubs devoted to leisure activities. Since the late 1970s, no fewer than three national retirees' groups (ECTI, EGEE, and AGIR) have been set up with the aim of providing consultancy services to companies in France and the Third World. Several regional or local associations, with similar aims, have also been set up. Preretirees and retirees are also increasingly involved in social and cultural activities. A report made at the prime minister's request (see Sueur 1985) made recommendations about how retirees can be socially useful in the nonbusiness service sector and charitable work. It mainly focused on doing away with certain administrative impediments to their involvement in nonprofit organizations. For example, UNEDIC may threaten to cut off benefits if they receive too many reimbursements for the expenses incurred in the course of their volunteer activities.

Through their new practices, preretirees and young retirees are helping create a new form of activity, voluntary or "free" work, alongside gainful employment. Even though a minority of them are involved in this trend, it is significant. Their involvement reflects the thoroughgoing reorganization under way in the life course, as the third stage of life is no longer devoted merely to leisure and associated with occupational inactivity. The traditional break between work and retirement is coming under review. Following gainful employment comes the time for free work, for voluntary activities. The distribution of social functions over the life course represented by the threefold model is being put in question.

5.5.3 The impact on unemployment and employment

The consensus underlying this massive early-exit trend mainly depended on the principle of transferring jobs from older to younger people. This principle was stipulated in solidarity preretirement contracts. However, departures on preretirement fell far short of reducing by a like number the ranks of unemployed young people. All assessments of preretirement have emphasized that the effects on employment were a far cry from the hopes placed in such measures (Magnier 1981; Franck et al. 1981; Pecher 1982; Galland, Gaudin, and Vrain 1984; Ragot 1985).

Impact on unemployment. The impact on unemployment turned out to be very moderate. Three major explanations have been advanced for this.

First of all, most departures on preretirement did not entail new hirings. The overall effect was to cut jobs during a recession: On the average, one person was hired for three who left on preretirement. Only the solidarity contract preretirement resignation measures had better results, as we shall see. Neary half (48 percent) of the jobs freed under all preretirement arrangements were either eliminated or left vacant, and 22 percent were filled through internal promotions, hence without recruitment from the outside (Magnier 1981).

Since firms could get rid of old wage earners as "preretirees" rather than having to dismiss or lay off younger workers who would be registered as unemployed, preretirement tended to slow down the rising jobless rate. However, this assertion needs to be toned down, for companies would very likely not have dismissed as many workers had preretirement not existed. These programs were an unexpected boon not only for resigning employees but also for employers, who could thus dump personnel at a relatively cheap cost both socially (owing to the consensus with other social actors) and economically (cheap, indeed, given the seniority of resignees who, had they been dismissed, would have filed costly dismissal claims). Even if hirings were then made, the pay would be less than what these older workers with long seniority had been receiving.

The solidarity preretirement resignation contracts carried clauses stipulating that the size of the work force should not decrease during the year following the deadline set for resignations. These clauses were usually fulfilled. According to controls by the Work Inspection Office, 95 percent of these preretirees were replaced. Still, these contracts had a positive impact on job openings for two years at most. Although there was reason to fear lest their termination lead firms, thus freed of contractual obligations, to try to catch up on dismissals, there is not much evidence that this has actually occurred.

Second, all preretirement arrangements taken together have had an ephemeral impact on unemployment. They made it possible to cut jobs sooner or to replace aging workers without having to wait for them to retire. This ephemeral positive impact even risked turning negative later on since, with preretirees laid off, there would be no more normal departures on retirement. Therefore, if an overall effect on unemployment was to be maintained once the stock of potential withdrawees was used up, one could not passively wait for younger workers to reach the preretirement age. Instead, it was necessary, once again, to lower the early-exit age; and this very process led to the extension, as of 1982, of preretirement to persons as young as 55.

A third reason that preretirement has but slightly affected unemployment is, ironically, that it has also made this very group ever more vulnerable to joblessness. Moreover, persons in the age group just below preretirees now risk being seen as having already reached the end of their career. Hence they are likely to be left out when decisions are made about promotions or job training. Given their short working-life expectancy, investing in job training for them will no longer be economically sound; and this, in turn, will worsen their risks of losing jobs as they grow older. The observed increase in the long-term unemployment of persons over 50 is evidence of their greater vulnerability to joblessness as a result of early-exit measures.

Impact on employment. The overall impact on employment is even more complicated to evaluate. Assessments have been made of short-term effects, but these are of little help for the long run. In particular, it is important to know whether the early-exit trend has made it possible for firms to reorganize their activities so as to increase productivity and thus, eventually, their chances of creating jobs.

According to assessments of solidarity contracts, which required new hirings to make up for departures on preretirement, companies did not always place the newly hired in the jobs left vacant by preretirees. Hence, these contracts helped speed up, or at least favored, reorganization within the firms concerned. These assessments indicate that preretirement arrangements directly affected the organization of work, firms' demographic structure, the grid of jobs and qualifications, and personnel mobility, as well as career profiles. Given available sources, it is hard to measure the precise impact. Firms did not think through the aforementioned changes, nor even control them; and nowadays, problems are cropping up as a result of blocked careers and "overqualification," problems ensuing from companies' massive recourse to early exit.

This lukewarm evaluation of the effects on employment leads us to inquire into the cost/benefit ratio of early-exit arrangements. The cost of "avoided unemployment" has been very high, and there is no certainty about its positive economic effects, which seem to have encouraged firms to adopt short-sighted policies and develop the habit of getting rid of aging workers first – without taking into account consequent distortions in the long run. Companies have thus felt free to do without long-term strategies for adjusting to the inevitable – in the coming decades – aging of the French labor force, a phenomenon calling for the foresightful management of human resources and in particular for policies of adjusting jobs to age and providing job training (Lion 1988).

5.5.4 Early exit's effects on the welfare system

The early-exit trend has two major, cumulative effects on the welfare system. First, it accounts for much of the overall increase in social service expenditures and has, consequently, run the welfare budget "into the gray," as the population over age 55 absorbs an ever larger share of these expenditures. Second, it has shaken the welfare system's architecture by making the Unemployment Fund into an old-age fund and thus jeopardizing the financial equilibria of both of these welfare subsystems. The whole welfare system is becoming less and less coherent.

A gray financial crisis. Retirement has, from 1960 to 1980, become the principal line in highly industrialized countries' welfare budgets. In France, it represented 44 percent of social expenditures in 1982, and the total cost of old age has steadily increased since then as a result of the massive early-exit trend, which consumed more than half the Unemployment Fund's budget from 1983 to 1985. Even though certain arrangements were left, in 1984, to run out, preretirement expenditures have been decreasing slowing, their inertia being due to the long-term obligations created under these arrangements. According to a 1984 estimate covering old-age pensions, health costs (one-third of which can be set down to the aged), and preretirement benefits, 55 percent of French social expenditures went to aging, definitively inactive persons (Chesnais, 1985). Given these statistics, the welfare state is, indeed, becoming a welfare state for the aged.

There is no doubt that early exit has caused social expenditures to plunge "into the gray." Besides the 7,500,000 persons over 65 who normally receive transfer payments in the form of old-age pensions, there is a further potential of 6,200,000 persons aged 55 to 64, half of whom are already living on transfer payments (pensions, preretirement, or unemployment). The early-exit trend has, therefore, nearly doubled the potential population of the definitively inactive. According to Babeau (1985), "the end of retirement pensions" may be in sight because of the emergence of this new way of forcing people into early withdrawal from the labor force.

The system's shaky architecture. The development of preretirement has been a major factor in UNEDIC's financial difficulties since 1979. The Unemployment Fund's payments to preretirees rose spectacularly and, in 1983, overshot unemployment benefits (Table 5.10). This Fund has thus become a pseudo-old-age fund. It has deviated toward insuring retirement-like pensions that have to be paid for a much longer time (five years or even longer) than unemployment benefits. However, unlike the Old-Age Fund, which pays out pensions depending on how long applicants have contributed to it, preretirement benefits have not been calculated on the basis of wage earners' contributions.

Table 5.17. *Average benefits to the unemployed and preretired as a percentage of former average wages in four countries (1980)*

Group	France	West Germany	Great Britain	Sweden
The real unemployed	51.5	35.9	27.0	50.2
Jobless persons in training programs	68.9	84.5	20.5	69.3
Preretirees	97.5	71.2	31.4	65.0
All three groups	57.7	42.8	26.4	58.9

Source: CERC, "L'indemnisation du chômage en France et à l'étranger" (Paris: Documentation Française), document no. 2, second quarter 1982, p. 42.

The relatively high ratio of preretirement benefits to net wages in France compared with other nations (Table 5.17) explains both the success of preretirement, which soon opened the main early-exit pathways out of the labor force, and the financial crisis of the welfare system that ensued. Nowadays, this difference between France and other European countries has probably lessened, since French preretirement benefits were reduced in 1982. As already mentioned, this reduction was one of a series of measures aimed at removing the Unemployment Fund from the financial straits into which it had been placed as a result of the massive early-exit trend. Another of these measures was to lower the retirement age from 65 to 60, and thus shift 60- to 65-year-olds from the better coverage of preretirement under the Unemployment Fund to the lesser coverage of retirement under the Old-Age Fund.

The Old-Age Fund was thus brought to the rescue of the Unemployment Fund and implicated in a jobs policy based on early definitive exit. This confusion about the way these funds were used and about the risks they were set up to cover soon had consequences. The new right to retirement with a full pension at age 60 soon became a legislative measure that led to rejection of aging workers (Mercereau 1982). Furthermore, the future of the social security and complementary old-age funds, already gloomy because of the French population's aging and the economy's slowdown, darkened even more as a result of this earlier retirement at 60. The Unemployment Fund – now running surpluses – is, in turn, helping finance the extra costs that, as a result of the lower retirement age, are borne by the supplementary old-age funds. This mixture, and confusion, of roles, duties, and finances has become the law.

The welfare system's architecture is now rickety, as a crisis of rationality is leading to a crisis of legitimacy. Repairs have not kept expenditures from growing, but they have made the problem of regulating costs inextricable because the logics of risks and their coverage have been all mixed up.

Now, it is the turn of retirement expenditures, partly because of the lowered retirement age, to explode. Until now, the active population has accepted having to pay more to public old-age funds in order to maintain its own protection for retirement. Payroll deductions for contributions to the old-age funds have more than doubled since 1974, but these funds' deficits have been deepening year after year. What is at stake in the coming years is how to slow down the increase in retirement costs. Solving this problem is all the harder since the habit has been formed of using retirement as part of an employment policy that rejects aging workers from the labor market.

5.6　THE PROSPECTS OF EARLY EXIT: THE CONSENSUS ENDS

As stated, the early-exit trend has advanced so fast since the 1970s because a relative consensus had emerged, in a context of economic recession and surplus labor, between "social partners" – labor unions, employers, and successive governments – who agreed, for varying reasons, on using preretirement to deal with the situation. Since the late 1980s, this consensus has been coming to an end, and new stands are being made on the issues. It is still difficult to foretell how political and social forces will line up around the problem of the employment, or unemployment, of aging workers, or to foresee the fate assigned to these persons.

5.6.1　*Employers: Eliminating aging workers no longer seems like a panacea*

Employers' unanimity about preretirement is coming undone. Some of them are beginning to glimpse the harmful effects of systematically cutting aging employees from the work force, even though this seemed to them, until recently, the least costly way, both socially and financially, to get rid of excess labor and "restructure" their firms. Since employees as young as 55 have been laid off, firms have had to face unforeseen problems, a few of which should be pointed out.

First, as the number of persons definitively inactive after 55 has increased, "semiold" employees from 45 to 50 no longer have very bright career prospects, since they have little hope for promotions or training. This problem is so acute that 16 alumni associations of France's prestigious *grandes écoles* wrote a report in 1985 entitled "45 Ans, un âge sans avenir? ou la viellesse à 45 ans" *(45 years old, an age without a future? Or old age at 45).* Uncertainty about how their working lives will end demotivates personnel and adversely affects firms.

Second, the massive early-exit trend has, in some companies, entailed a loss of experience and know-how. It has damaged the "company culture" so much that repairs will be hard to make.

Finally, although this trend has, in some firms, rejuvenated the age pyramid and even reduced labor costs, these apparent gains have been accompanied by serious problems. For one thing, the flow of careers has been obstructed. In some cases, most of the better-educated young people hired to replace aging employees do not have any career prospects at the workplace and lack motivation at the very time when their efforts are necessary to modernize the firm. In fact, one of the major industry-wide employers' associations (the one in mining and metallurgy) has just opened negotiations about the lack of career perspectives for young technicians (Lebaude 1989). In other branches, such as iron and steel where the work force has been reduced under collective agreements about preretirement at 50, the age pyramid has been flattened; the work force is now made up of persons from 30 to 50 years old. In 2000, if no measures are taken, more than half this work force will be between 50 and 60 years old. The continuous renewal of personnel by upcoming generations is endangered.

Employers' doubts about preretirement as a means of personnel management have deepened as the economy emerges from the recession and is expected to continue recovering in the 1990s. This prospect has made them see the harmful long-term effects of encouraging the exit of older wage earners. We can, therefore, assume that company policies with regard to aging employees are going to change. This is all the more likely inasmuch as, according to population predictions, it will be necessary to count on wage earners over 45 to help carry out technological transformations and face international competition. From now till 2040, the active French population of working age will not vary much in size, but it will be growing older: as of 2005, one working person out of two will be over 40, compared with 40 percent at present. The CNPF, which represents big companies, has recently agreed to help draw up measures for adapting jobs to age. This change of attitudes is also linked to the quest, as work is organized in a less Tayloristic way, for both new labor flexibility and the individualization of the wage-earning relationship.

In this new context, doubts are arising about the validity of age norms. Functional criteria based on competence are now preferred to the older chronological norms (such as seniority), which firms no longer deem fully compatible with the drive for efficiency. As Graebner (1980) has shown for the United States, the development of retirement pensions using chronological norms to fix the end of careers enabled companies to rationalize work and become more efficient. For wage earners, these pensions meant the right to a period of rest and the guarantee of a substitute income at a time when the rationalization of work was introducing age discrimination in the labor force. Nowadays, this solution no longer seems acceptable to firms, given the new challenges of technological and economic changes, the necessity of ongoing personnel training, and the need to propose regular occupational reorientation rather than life-time jobs. Nor does this solution any longer satisfy the need for security of wage earners who are precociously exposed to the obsolescence of their knowledge and the precariousness of employment.

The Institut de l'Entreprise (1985), a study group made up of some enlightened employers, has raised questions about the very concept of retirement, a concept that might have "reached its limits" and be "antiquated." This study does not call for making careers longer or for doing away with hard-won social rights (such as retirement). Instead, it suggests new fringe benefits that, compatible with "company efficiency," are to be negotiated with the personnel. It pleads for diversifying the ways people leave the labor force by individualizing employment and adopting a new pay policy based on efficiency.

Only a small minority of employers have, as yet, changed their attitudes. True, firms are turning toward career-management plans and are considering giving employees over 45 the training necessary to the firm's "restructuration." In the words of these employers, they are "using the old to make the new." However many companies will continue resorting to early exit. Age-based arrangements are still atttractive, since older employees both cost more, as long as careers advance as a function of seniority, and are the least adapted to a new organization of work, because their education and training are often inadequate.

Early exit remains a convenient means of managing the work force and, at the same time, compressing labor costs. There is no doubt that it will continue to be very frequently used.

5.6.2 *Public authorities: Containing the exploding costs of retirement*

After having endeavored to limit unemployment, the state is now trying to reduce the dangers hovering over the public retirement system. The relative calm on the employment front means that social programs, such as preretirement, for dealing with joblessness are now of secondary importance. Several recent reports and measures provide evidence that governmental interventions are being redefined in three ways (Commissariat General du Plan 1986; Malabouche 1987).

First, a reform of the public retirement system is being drawn as part of the Tenth Plan (1989–92). The objective is to make this system more dependent on contributions. One suggestion is to base pension rates on a wage earner's whole career, specifically to calculate benefits on the basis of the 25 (and no longer 10) years of highest wages. Another is to delay, by 2010, the normal retirement age by about two years – not by directly raising it but rather by lengthening the minimal period (from 37.5 to about 40 years) of required contributions to draw a full pension from the Old-Age Fund. Directly raising the retirement age would be risky in France, especially for a Socialist government, even though some observers do admit that maintaining retirement at 60 will not be as justified in the future when wage earners will be retiring who have not worked such long careers with long workweeks. Yet another suggestion is to offer incentives to persons who work beyond 60, for example, to increase pensions by 4 percent per year worked between 60 and 65.

Second, public authorities are well aware that retirement reforms aimed at prolonging careers will be ineffective unless the end of careers is better protected. Otherwise, older people will still be "marginalized" well before the age of retirement, especially those who, as discouraged job seekers, will be covered either by new preretirement arrangements or, if these are not renewed, by other, less costly arrangements that provide lower benefits under more precarious conditions.

The second employment plan adopted by the government in September 1989 contains measures for preventing the occupational exclusion of high-risk wage earners (i.e., young people and older persons who have been unemployed for a long time). In particular, measures are being applied for "returning to employment" long-term jobless persons over 50 years old: employers are being exonerated from their share of social security contributions until the wage earner reaches the age of retirement with a full pension. Furthermore, the company receives 10,000 francs from the state for each person hired under these conditions, and if it had to pay to retrain these wage earners, training costs are reimbursed. Meanwhile, the cost of dismissing older wage earners for redundancy has been increased for firms. These measures may seem lukewarm given the recommendations by the Haut Conseil de la Population et de la Famille, which advocated "reestablishing equal opportunity in employment and no longer basing the distribution of work on the exclusion of the oldest . . . since the use at present and in the future of the age criterion in employment policy has considerably affected the equilibrium of life in society" (Lion, 1988:76, 78). Although it is much too early to assess these measures, the state is – for the first time – adopting an employment policy encouraging companies to retain or hire the aging.

The third way public authorities are intervening is by trying to make unions and employers more responsible for retirement. Accordingly, the government has refused to continue assuming the third of extra costs for the supplementary old-age funds caused by the lowered retirement age (the other two-thirds being covered by the Unemployment Fund). The government argues that since this is a problem for society, the "social partners" have to settle it together. In this controversy, labor organizations are demanding that the state maintain its financial commitment; for they fear that, otherwise, the hard won right to retirement at 60 would be pared down. Employers are making the same demand but in order to be better able to undo this right if the state stops paying its share of the extra costs. As can be seen, the consensus formed in the early 1980s is coming to an end. What future is in store for early exit given these new positions?

The improvement in the labor market is not going to lead back to the situation prior to the early-exit trend. This much is certain. Early exit has thoroughly changed the practices and conditions having to do with definitive labor force withdrawal. Wage earners undeniably aspire to stop working sooner, all the more so since aging workers have in the long term lost their value in the labor market and increasingly experience job precariousness at the end of their career. The state is now refusing to make any additional financial commitments for preretirement and is restricting existing programs. As pointed out, it is encouraging companies to retain aging workers or even to rehire them.

Will an agreement be drawn up between those employers who want more job flexibility and the two other parties, unions and the state? This agreement could entail renegotiating welfare measures so as to improve the coverage of the new risks resulting from such flexibility: optional retirement with more flexible conditions, sabbatical leaves, ongoing job training linked to occupational mobility, and so forth. Firms would thus find the flexibility they are seeking, wage earners would thus acquire a new security, and the welfare state would thus clarify its social programs and improve its financial situation. If no such compromise is reached, wage earners risk the most. Companies will continue, as need be, cutting aged employees from the work force; but public authorities will refuse to pay for these cuts. The unions will be cornered and will have to fight to keep the hard-won rights of retirement, but retirement will be delayed and insured with less advantageous benefits. Many definitively inactive older people will have no other recourse than unemployment compensation and then, when this coverage ends, the recently passed national guaranteed-income program (RMI) or "small jobs."

REFERENCES

Audras, M. 1973. "Vers la retraite progressive." *Documents d'information et de gestion/gérontologie,* 23–24, July–October.

Babeau, A. 1985. *La fin des retraites?* Paris: Hachette.

Casey, B. 1987. "Early Retirement and Its Implications for Restructuring the Process of Retirement." *International Social Security Review* 4:343–60.

Chesnais, J. C. 1985. "Sécurité sociale et population." *Revue française des affaires sociales,* July–September, pp. 45–59.

Commissariat General du Plan. 1986. *Vieillir solidaires.* Paris: Documentation Française.

Franck, D., R. Hara, G. Magnier, and O. Villey. 1982. "Entreprises et contrats de solidarité préretraite démission." *Travail et emploi,* no. 13, July–September, pp. 75–89.

Galland, O., J. Gaudin, and P. Vrain. 1984. "Contrats de solidarité et stratégie des entreprises." *Travail et emploi,* no. 22, December, pp. 7–20.

Graebner, W. 1980. *A History of Retirement: The Meaning and Function of an American Institution (1885-1978).* New Haven: Yale University Press.

Guillemard, A. M. 1985. "The Social Dynamics of Early Withdrawal from the Labor Force in France." *Ageing and Society* 4:381–412.

1986a. *Le déclin du social: formation et crise des politiques de la vieillesse.* Paris: Presses Universitaires de France.

1986b. "Social Policy and Ageing in France." In C. Phillipson and A. Walker (eds.), *Ageing and Social Policy: A Critical Assessment.* London: Gower, pp. 263–79.

Heller, J. L. 1986. "La retraite anticipée: choix ou contrainte?" *Economie et statistique,* 193–4, November–December, pp. 97–109.

1987. "Les retraites anticipées." *Données sociales,* pp. 133–41.

Institut de l'Entreprise. 1985. *Sortir de la vie professionnelle, Application des concepts de la stratégie du temps rénuméré,* January.

Lebaude, A. 1989. "Emploi: La gestion prévisionnelle de l'après-crise." *Le Monde,* November 29, p. 49.

Lenormand, F., and G. Magnier. 1983. "Le développement des dispositifs de cessation anticipée d'activité: aspects sociaux et conséquences financières." *Travail et Emploi,* January–March, 15:47–62.

Lion, E. 1988. *Vieillissement et emploi. Vieillisement et travail.* A report of the Haut Conseil de la Population et de la Famille to the President's Office. Paris: Documentation Française.

Magnier, G. 1981. "Les sorties de la vie active." *Statistiques du Travail, supplément au bulletin mensuel,* no. 35., pp. 1–12.

Malabouche, G. 1987. "Retraites: les périls de l'an 2030." *Etudes et Recherches,* 5, April. Documentation Française.

Mercereau, F. 1982. "La retraite a 60 ans." *Droit Social,* June, pp. 452–64.

Monnier, A. 1979. "Les limites de la vie active et la retraite." *Population,* nos. 4–5, pp. 801–24.

Pecher, A. 1982. "Retraite et préretraite, faible impact sur le chômage en 1981." *Aspects economiques de l'Ile-de-France,* no. 5, September.

Ragot, Maurice. 1985. *La cessation anticipée d'activité salariée.* June 5 report to the Conseil Economique et Social, Paris.

Schnapper, D. 1981. *L'épreuve du chômage.* Paris: Gallimard.

Sueur, J. P. 1985. *Changer la retraite. Propositions pour le développement du volontariat des préretraitées et retraités.* Report to the Prime Minister's Office. Paris: Documentation Française.

UNEDIC. 1981. "Garantie de ressources et emplois salariés du secteur privé." *Bulletin de liaison,* 83, December, pp. 17–26.

1988. *Bulletin de liaison,* no. 110, September-October, p. 102.

CHAPTER 6

Germany: The diversity of pathways

KLAUS JACOBS, MARTIN KOHLI, AND MARTIN REIN

6.1 EARLY EXIT: LATE ATTENTION TO A FUNDAMENTAL TREND

ON November 9, 1989, the West German Parliament passed the Pension Reform '92 – one of the rare compromises between the ruling coalition and the Social Democrats, and hailed as a major step in retaining the financial viability of the public old-age insurance system. On the evening of the same day, the East Berliners started to flow over the wall – the event that triggered the collapse of the Communist regime, and of its state itself, at a pace that still seems unreal. The temporal coincidence should not suggest a direct causal link, but it is highly significant in two respects. It signals on the one hand the salience of social security, and especially of old-age security, for the "moral economy" of West German society – and thus for its triumph in the "system competition" with the East. And on the other hand, it marks the fragility of the basic assumptions on which social policy is built – assumptions (e.g., about the demographic and labor-market evolution) that have taken for granted the boundaries of the system, and have taken into account neither this dramatic boundary change nor the more foreseeable changes through mass migration and European unification.

In West Germany, the trend toward early exit from the labor force during the 1970s and early 1980s was not a major topic of social-political discourse. The latter was dominated by the many attempts and proposals to reduce mass unemployment; early exit was only one of many different measures in this context, and by far not the most noticed one.

Now, the picture has completely changed. Not that the unemployment problem has been solved in the meantime. On the contrary, a fairly constant number of above two million unemployed persons has still been predicted for West Germany until after the year 2000, and with the unification process, unemployment, at least in the short run, is likely to become even more dramatic. But early exit from the labor market has

181

become a pronounced topic of its own, especially with regard to the financing of old-age security.

Among the three different periods that can be distinguished in the process of early exit, the first two did not create any controversies.[1] When the state and the courts first set the stage by introducing possibilities of early retirement within the pension system, these reforms were designed to improve the conditions for special problem groups, and were not intended as a strategy to promote early retirement in general or as a response to labor-market shortcomings. The existence of this legislation, however, provided the social infrastructure that, in a later period of weak labor markets and high unemployment, was used by firms to forge a policy of early exit.

This second period was characterized by a broad social consensus of all actors involved. All were in favor of early exit: the state because it was an easy and "bloodless" way of reducing unemployment, the older workers because it offered favorable financial arrangements, the unions because it improved the chances for younger workers to get access to the labor force, and – above all – the firms. For some firms, early exit of older workers was an inexpensive way to reduce their work force in a time of economic troubles. For others – as the generalization of this trend across industries indicates (see Chapter 3) – early exit was a way of adapting their work force, in terms of its age/wage or age/skill mix, to the changing requirements of the production system in terms of rationalization and rapid technological shifts.

The increased attention that is now – in a third period – being paid to early exit results from the changing interest of the state. In the long term, as a result of changes in the demographic structure, there will be (all else being equal) critical financing problems in the pay-as-you-go system of old-age security, and also possibly a shortage in the labor supply. However, turning the trend around – that is, raising the age of exit from the labor force – will be much more difficult than it was to lower this age. The interests of older workers (to continue exiting early with acceptable benefit levels) and of many firms (to continue getting rid of older workers while passing the costs on to the state) have not changed.

6.2   INSTITUTIONAL MECHANISMS: DEVELOPMENT AND TAKE-UP

What different institutional mechanisms have been used to make early exit possible? And how have they developed – did they already exist

---

[1] For a more detailed analysis of this development, see Jacobs and Rein (1988).

before the process of early exit began in the early 1970s and simply begin to be used more, or were they introduced later to accommodate and accelerate this process? Before we discuss the new pathways of early exit and their structural meaning, it is necessary to know the institutional facts. In general, the major forms of exit from the labor market in Germany largely correspond to the entry into public social security programs, either directly into the pension system or via other institutions such as the unemployment insurance. In addition, there are possibilities of early exit outside the state programs, but they are usually also linked to the public pension scheme.

6.2.1 *Entry into the pension system before age 65*

The statutory pension insurance covers the majority (about 85 percent) of wage earners (who represent 89 percent of all workers) and is also accessible for the self-employed. There is a similar system for miners with some special early retirement opportunities, but with the decline of the coal-mining industry, its importance is decreasing. This is also true for the farmers, who have another special system of old-age assistance. Finally, there is an independent pension system for life-time civil servants (*Beamte*), who represent 9 percent of all workers.[2] This review is restricted to the first of these systems, the general statutory pension insurance.[3]

In administrative language, age 65 is still referred to as the "normal" retirement age. Empirically, however, there is no such standard retirement regime. In July 1989, 27 percent of a cross-section of all male old-age pensioners in the statutory pension scheme were below 65, the "normal" retirement age. (For women, this proportion was somewhat smaller because of their longer life expectancy: It amounted to almost 18 percent.) The average age of entry into the pension system has always been clearly below age 65 (see Table 6.1).

---

[2] For a detailed description of these regulations, see Zacher (1983). Significantly enough, they are not only highly complex but also not very well documented statistically. The system is noncontributory (the pensions are directly paid through the federal budget) and generous. It is thus part of the "structural patronage" by the state for its civil servants in return for the special loyalty that it requires from them (Kohli and von Kondratowitz 1987). This pattern of privilege is increasingly coming under attack, but so far, it has successfully resisted most attempts at "harmonization" with or even full integration into the normal forms of contributory social security.

[3] The evolution of the whole German social security system from 1881 to 1981 is described by Zöllner (1982; see also Kohli 1987). For a detailed description of the statutory pension scheme and a discussion of many of its actual and future problems, see Schmähl (1986). The structure of entries into the pension system and changes of this structure over the past 15 years are discussed in detail by Conradi et al. (1987).

Table 6.1. *Average age of entry into the statutory pension system*

Year	Men			Women		
	ArV[a]	AnV	All	ArV	AnV	All
1958	59.5	61.7	60.1	59.1	58.1	58.9
1959	58.7	61.6	59.5	58.7	58.1	58.5
1960	58.8	61.6	59.5	59.0	58.1	58.8
1961	59.1	61.9	59.7	59.4	58.5	59.2
1962	59.7	62.0	60.2	59.5	58.7	59.3
1963	60.2	62.5	60.8	60.3	59.5	60.1
1964	60.7	62.8	61.2	60.7	59.9	60.5
1965	60.9	62.8	61.4	61.0	59.9	60.7
1966	61.2	63.1	61.7	61.4	60.5	61.2
1967	61.1	63.1	61.6	61.3	60.5	61.1
1968	60.9	62.9	61.4	61.2	60.3	61.0
1969	61.0	62.8	61.5	61.4	60.5	61.2
1970	61.1	62.8	61.6	61.6	60.6	61.3
1971	61.0	62.9	61.5	61.6	60.5	61.3
1972	61.1	63.0	61.6	61.6	60.6	61.3
1973	61.7	63.3	62.2	61.8	61.0	61.6
1974	61.0	63.0	61.6	61.6	61.0	61.4
1975	60.6	62.5	61.2	61.6	60.5	61.2
1976	60.1	62.3	60.8	61.2	60.6	61.0
1977	59.5	61.8	60.3	60.8	60.0	60.5
1978	58.8	61.5	59.7	60.6	59.8	60.3
1979	58.2	61.0	59.1	60.4	59.8	60.2
1980	57.9	60.5	58.8	60.0	59.5	59.8
1981	57.5	60.3	58.4	59.6	59.3	59.5
1982	57.8	60.1	58.6	59.7	59.2	59.5
1983	57.9	60.4	58.7	59.7	59.4	59.6
1984	58.1	60.4	58.9	60.4	59.6	60.0
1985	58.0	60.6	58.9	60.8	59.9	60.4
1986	58.1	60.7	59.0	61.9	60.7	61.4
1987	58.3	60.8	59.1	62.3	60.8	61.7
1988	58.6	60.8	59.3	62.4	60.9	61.8

[a]ArV, pension scheme for wage earners; AnV, pension scheme for salaried employees.
Source: VDR-Statistik Rentenzugang (different years), Frankfurt, and our own calculations.

One can receive a pension before age 65 in a number of ways (see Figure 6.1 and Tables 6.2a and 6.2b for new entries into the pension system through different programs). They include age-free disability pensions, pensions after long-term unemployment at age 60, pensions for severely

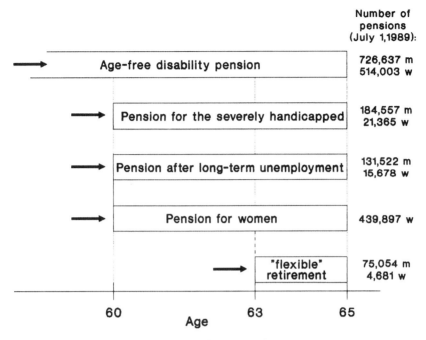

Figure 6.1. Types of pension before age 65.

handicapped persons at age 60, pensions for women at age 60, and the so-called flexible retirement at age 63. The main requirements for each of these pensions are briefly described in this section.

The benefit structure need not be discussed separately because the individual replacement rate is not dependent on the type of pension received. The age of entry into the pension system is important only in an indirect way: earlier entry reduces the number of insurance years, which is one of the two "personal factors" in the benefit formula.[4] But the reduction is far below the level that would result from an actuarial calculation taking into account both the shorter contribution span and

---

[4] The other is a composite value, cumulated over the whole period of contributions, of a person's salary position compared with the mean of all contributing salaried workers in each year. In addition, there is a "general factor" relating the pension level to the evolution of present salaries (by which the pension is, in other words, "dynamized" to account not only for inflation but also for economic growth).

Table 6.2a. *Entry into the statutory pension system by different types of pension:*
Men

Year	Total	Shares (in %)							
		BU	EU	60Al	60/2Gs	63flex	65norm	65+	Total
1958	288,014	22.65	35.58	2.07	—	—	39.69	—	100.00
1959	264,185	25.77	34.74	2.29	—	—	37.20	—	100.00
1960	225,124	27.44	33.35	2.38	—	—	36.82	—	100.00
1961	231,671	27.12	32.47	1.98	—	—	38.43	—	100.00
1962	244,408	26.36	30.55	1.67	—	—	41.42	—	100.00
1963	252,451	23.35	29.88	1.44	—	—	45.33	—	100.00
1964	269,144	19.97	29.83	1.36	—	—	48.84	—	100.00
1965	279,798	17.75	30.99	1.20	—	—	50.06	—	100.00
1966	295,013	15.57	31.45	0.81	—	—	52.18	–	100.00
1967	331,677	15.66	32.17	1.17	—	—	51.00	—	100.00
1968	327,012	15.55	32.67	5.84	—	—	45.94	—	100.00
1969	326,098	14.86	33.09	4.86	—	—	47.19	—	100.00
1970	316,231	12.61	35.58	2.83	—	—	48.98	—	100.00
1971	303,216	7.93	40.91	2.27	—	—	48.89	—	100.00
1972	304,212	6.49	41.04	3.51	—	—	48.96	—	100.00
1973	394,696	4.72	26.95	3.59	0.96	30.70	33.09	—	100.00
1974	383,600	5.29	29.89	2.59	1.69	30.33	29.98	0.22	100.00
1975	353,865	5.39	31.46	3.67	2.73	30.73	25.90	0.12	100.00
1976	356,179	5.30	32.06	6.34	3.66	29.00	23.27	0.36	100.00
1977	314,586	5.31	36.13	5.99	4.04	27.19	20.93	0.40	100.00
1978	277,931	5.79	40.03	5.79	3.74	23.55	20.30	0.80	100.00
1979	267,127	5.86	42.94	7.13	8.68	16.76	18.13	0.50	100.00
1980	283,910	6.00	42.21	7.63	16.24	13.03	14.58	0.30	100.00
1981	280,296	6.57	43.59	8.49	17.66	11.69	11.81	0.19	100.00
1982	291,802	7.14	41.03	10.45	17.10	14.35	9.78	0.15	100.00
1983	305,780	7.76	39.80	9.35	15.43	18.20	9.33	0.12	100.00
1984	317,846	7.66	39.61	10.75	12.82	16.67	12.36	0.12	100.00
1985	304,922	6.86	36.02	11.40	12.43	16.17	16.95	0.17	100.00
1986	291,565	6.39	34.27	10.96	13.01	16.38	18.83	0.18	100.00
1987	297,451	6.08	33.90	10.79	12.89	16.40	19.77	0.17	100.00
1988	326,598	5.95	32.14	12.59	12.45	18.42	18.29	0.16	100.00

Notes: Miners' pension scheme not included. BU, occupational disability pensions; EU, general disability pensions; 60Al, pension at age 60 after long-term employment; 60/2Gs, pension at age 60 (till 1979 at 62, 1980 at 61) for the severely handicapped; 63flex, "flexible" retirement at age 63; 65norm, "normal" old-age pension at age 65; 65+, deferred pension after age 65.

Source: VDR-Statistik, Rentenzugang (different years), Frankfurt, and our own calculations.

Table 6.2b. *Entry into the statutory pension system by different types of pension: Women*

Year	Total	Shares (in %)								
		BU	EU	60Fr	60Al	60/2Gs	63flex	65norm	65+	Total
1958	216,538	29.95	40.12	10.27	0.79	—	—	18.87	—	100.00
1959	180,714	31.61	37.46	11.80	0.67	—	—	18.46	—	100.00
1960	164,137	33.06	32.99	14.53	0.70	—	—	18.72	—	100.00
1961	174,575	33.39	29.08	16.37	0.65	—	—	20.51	—	100.00
1962	174,977	31.04	29.29	18.18	0.49	—	—	20.99	—	100.00
1963	171,995	24.94	28.39	19.59	0.42	—	—	26.66	—	100.00
1964	195,087	21.24	30.24	19.65	0.32	—	—	28.55	—	100.00
1965	201,898	18.46	31.69	20.50	0.27	—	—	29.08	—	100.00
1966	219,434	15.89	30.49	22.43	0.14	—	—	31.05	—	100.00
1967	245,353	15.20	30.12	23.62	0.15	—	—	30.90	—	100.00
1968	241,953	15.01	30.47	25.45	0.44	—	—	28.63	—	100.00
1969	255,436	13.47	30.64	26.13	0.38	—	—	29.38	—	100.00
1970	272,474	12.41	33.03	26.12	0.23	—	—	28.21	—	100.00
1971	278,474	10.30	36.23	26.19	0.20	—	—	27.08	—	100.00
1972	281,498	8.96	38.02	26.18	0.29	—	—	26.56	—	100.00
1973	299,385	7.47	35.94	27.48	0.34	0.01	1.51	27.24	—	100.00
1974	334,897	5.98	36.77	28.96	0.40	0.03	1.60	26.01	0.25	100.00
1975	321,364	4.82	41.23	27.09	0.73	0.05	1.71	24.28	0.11	100.00
1976	297,773	4.26	40.79	24.41	1.36	0.07	2.38	26.39	0.34	100.00
1977	273,979	2.55	45.92	22.96	1.47	0.07	2.17	24.52	0.34	100.00
1978	264,176	1.69	48.51	21.93	1.44	0.06	1.81	24.19	0.37	100.00
1979	282,902	1.40	47.64	26.41	1.46	0.19	1.11	21.52	0.27	100.00
1980	329,527	1.38	48.60	31.75	1.59	0.74	0.80	14.94	0.19	100.00
1981	321,830	1.45	50.88	32.85	1.76	1.09	0.70	11.12	0.15	100.00
1982	313,874	1.96	51.46	33.41	1.81	1.18	0.91	9.13	0.14	100.00
1983	319,670	2.22	49.87	34.62	1.30	1.23	1.34	9.32	0.10	100.00
1984	358,826	2.28	45.65	29.76	1.00	0.99	1.21	18.97	0.13	100.00
1985	282,763	1.85	28.36	34.30	1.02	1.09	1.33	31.83	0.22	100.00
1986	340,093	1.25	18.23	33.82	1.22	1.05	1.24	43.01	0.18	100.00
1987	346,106	1.10	17.45	30.15	1.14	0.98	1.24	47.78	0.16	100.00
1988	357,103	1.11	16.62	30.42	1.40	0.92	1.29	48.10	0.15	100.00

Notes: Same as Table 2a, with the addition: 60Fr, pension for women at age 60.
Source: VDR-Statistik, Rentenzugang (different years), Frankfurt, and our own calculations.

the longer pension span.[5] The absence of actuarially neutral deductions is often seen as an incentive for early retirement (i.e., before the "normal" age of 65).[6]

Disability pensions. Occupational and general disability pensions are not dependent on reaching a given age limit; the only requirement is a contribution period of five years.[7] As a result of two decisions of the Federal Social Court in 1969 and 1976 that changed their eligibility definition, their use has increased. Prior to these decisions, disability was defined strictly in medical terms. If a person, by medical judgement, could work a reduced number of hours (e.g., five or six hours per day), he or she was not eligible for a general disability pension even if no suitable part-time jobs were available. With the new court decisions, an older person – on the basis of the fact that there are practically no part-time jobs available – now receives a full disability pension even if he or she is only partially disabled and can work part-time. By this change, the disability pension has obtained the character of a "disability-unemployment pension" (Kaltenbach 1986, p. 357) and has strongly contributed to early exit. This is especially obvious for the group aged 55 to 59, for which no other public pension is accessible. In 1972 about 29,000 men and 22,500 women aged 55 to 59 entered the pension system via disability (i.e., 2.3 percent and 1.3 percent of the total male and female population of this age group), and in 1984 about 56,000 men and 64,000 women (3.4 percent and 3.3 percent of the total population aged 55 to 59) did so (Table 6.3).

In 1985 there was an important legislative change in the opposite direction: The requirements were considerably tightened to slow down early exit via this pathway. Eligibility now requires an employment history of at least three years within the last five years before applying for this pension. This rule change mainly affects housewives without recent work experience. Prior to 1985 disability was the only way for many women to enter the pension system because of the short contribution period that it required. The rule change (and the simultaneous shorten-

---

[5] Each insurance year counts as 1.5 percent (in the occupational disability pension, 1 percent of the personal and general level determined by the other factors. For example, a person with 40 contribution years accumulates 60 percent of that level; exiting one year earlier would thus amount to a pension loss of 2.5 percent, whereas an actuarily fair reduction at age 65 amounts to about 8 percent.

[6] Many of these regulations are subject to change under the pension reform of 1992. Most of the projected changes, however, will not become effective before the year 2001; see section 6.5.2 of this chapter for further details.

[7] "Contribution periods" are either periods in which contributions have been paid or substitute periods such as those of military service or captivity, or, since 1986, periods of child rearing (counted as one year per child).

Table 6.3. *New entries into disability pensions as a percentage of total population*

	Men			Women		
Year	50–54	55–59	60–64	50–54	55–59	60–64
1972	0.88	2.28	4.74	0.58	1.26	2.56
1973	0.85	2.28	3.96	0.57	1.33	2.70
1974	1.04	2.65	4.10	0.67	1.59	2.89
1975	1.08	2.58	4.02	0.74	1.63	3.05
1976	1.21	2.66	3.99	0.80	1.67	2.62
1977	1.25	2.77	3.79	0.87	1.91	2.48
1978	1.20	2.84	3.69	0.85	2.04	2.51
1979	1.23	3.07	3.60	0.85	2.21	2.75
1980	1.29	3.29	3.56	0.94	2.67	3.69
1981	1.40	3.23	3.29	0.97	2.73	3.78
1982	1.33	3.17	3.22	0.90	2.72	3.73
1983	1.35	3.21	3.06	0.87	2.70	3.55
1984	1.34	3.38	2.98	0.99	3.32	3.29
1985	1.31	2.98	1.92	0.75	1.86	0.93
1986	1.20	2.65	1.58	0.62	1.45	0.60
1987	1.30	2.91	1.66	0.64	1.43	0.46

Note: BU/EU, occupational and general disability pensions.
Source: VDR-Statistik Rentenzugang (different years), Frankfurt; Statistical Yearbook (different years); and our own calculations.

ing of the contribution period required for a "normal" old-age pension at age 65 from 15 to 5 years) now forces this group to wait until age 65. Whereas in 1984 disability still accounted for 48 percent of all new female entries into the pension system, this proportion dropped to 30 percent in 1985 and to 18 percent in 1988 (Table 6.2b). As a consequence, the average age of entry into the pension system for women increased from 60.0 in 1984 to 61.8 in 1988 (Table 6.1). For men, the decline was less steep, from 47 percent of all new entries in 1984 to 38 percent in 1988, and the average age of entry remained stable at 59.

For women, this is, however, only part of the story. The high number of women receiving a pension at age 65 reflects another rule change (in 1986) by which a woman is credited with one contribution year for each child. Since only five contribution years are now required for the receipt of the "normal" old-age pension, many women with a very short employment history or none at all – who otherwise would not have been entitled to a pension of their own – benefit from this new regulation. As a consequence, the absolute (and therefore also the relative) number of female pension entries at 65 has increased but early retirement has not stopped (as the cohort data in Table 6.4 demonstrate).

The pension at age 60 after long-term unemployment. The other ways of entering the pension system are contingent on reaching a given age limit in addition to fulfilling special requirements. The pension after long-term unemployment at age 60 requires a period of unemployment of at least 52 weeks within the last one and a half years (and a contribution period of at least 15 years). This kind of pension was introduced in 1957 as part of the major pension reform that created the present structure. Its utilization among men has closely mirrored the evolution of unemployment. It was of no great importance until 1968, with a share of all new entries of between 1 and 2 percent. This share increased to 4 to 5 percent in 1968–9 as a result of the first postwar recession in West Germany,[8] but dropped again to 2 to 3 percent until 1975. Since then, it has increased in two steps to 6 to 7 percent in the late 1970s and 10 to 12 percent in the 1980s. As it requires a period of unemployment, this way of entering the pension system is not equivalent to exit from the labor force; it is, however, the key element in the unemployment pathway of early exit (see section 6.3). The increased use of this pension has been entirely due to changed economic conditions; there have been no rule changes since 1957. For women, it is of no importance because of their general ability to retire at age 60.

The pension for women at age 60. This type of pension requires a contribution period of at least 15 years and an employment history of at least 10 within the last 20 years. Again, there have been no rule changes since 1957 (when its introduction was motivated by offering couples the possibility of retiring together, given the normal age difference between husband and wife). Its utilization, however, tripled from 10 percent (1958) to 30 percent (1988), certainly also a reflection of the growing labor force participation of women, which has enabled increasing numbers of them to fulfill its requirements (cf. Orsinger and Clausing 1982:265). Other factors such as early retirement of husbands and high unemployment may also have played a role.

---

[8] The recession showed the older workers to be particularly vulnerable. Unemployment remained minimal among those below 55, but increased strongly for those above. In 1968 the unemployment rate for men aged 55 to 59 was twice as high as the general male unemployment rate, and for those aged 60 to 64 more than five times as high.

Table 6.4. Entry into the statutory pension system of individual birth cohorts by age (in %)

Born in	Age												Total
	50–54	55–59	60	61	62	63	64	65	<60	60	61–63	64–65	
	Men												
1913	5.65	12.10	5.32	6.14	9.13	34.34	7.02	20.30	17.75	5.32	49.61	27.32	100.00
1914	5.83	12.42	6.23	6.92	11.88	32.05	5.80	18.86	18.25	6.23	50.85	24.66	99.99
1915	5.98	13.15	7.17	8.44	12.02	29.43	5.03	18.77	19.13	7.17	49.89	23.80	99.99
1916	6.37	14.37	9.01	8.46	11.95	26.37	4.94	18.54	20.74	9.01	46.78	23.48	100.01
1917	6.43	15.27	9.94	8.37	12.17	24.88	4.76	18.17	21.70	9.94	45.42	22.93	99.99
1918	6.26	16.38	10.12	14.55	8.89	21.54	5.24	17.01	22.64	10.12	44.98	22.25	99.99
1919	5.90	16.40	11.98	13.58	8.13	21.91	4.98	17.12	22.30	11.98	43.62	22.10	100.00
1920	6.02	17.38	21.62	11.72	8.46	23.67	4.34		23.40	21.62	43.85		88.87
1921	6.42	18.37	22.43	11.41	7.63	21.51			24.79	22.43	40.55		87.77
1922	7.01	18.92	23.94	10.71	7.61				25.93	23.94			49.87
1923	7.53	19.35	24.31	10.66					26.88	24.31			51.19
1924	7.86	20.09	24.45						27.95	24.45			52.40
	Women												
1913	4.45	9.84	24.76	12.08	7.96	8.76	4.58	27.56	14.29	24.76	28.80	32.14	99.99
1914	4.19	9.72	30.57	9.95	7.38	7.89	4.04	26.26	13.91	30.57	25.22	30.30	100.00
1915	4.25	10.59	32.70	9.45	7.03	7.29	3.85	24.85	14.84	32.70	23.77	28.70	100.01
1916	4.58	12.20	33.31	9.29	6.70	7.11	4.01	22.80	16.78	33.31	23.10	26.81	100.00
1917	4.76	13.39	33.91	9.04	6.89	7.29	4.13	20.60	18.15	33.91	23.22	24.73	100.01
1918	5.07	14.49	33.03	10.37	7.15	6.94	4.26	18.72	19.56	33.03	24.46	22.98	100.03
1919	4.63	14.15	33.68	10.22	6.54	6.39	3.48	20.91	18.78	33.68	23.15	24.39	100.00
1920	4.76	15.69	40.25	10.00	6.90	6.69	3.10		20.45	40.25	23.59		84.29
1921	5.03	17.26	38.67	9.67	6.89	6.32			22.29	38.67	22.88		83.84
1922	5.48	18.58	38.50	9.80	6.98				24.06	38.50			62.56
1923	5.91	19.28	40.41	9.51					25.19	40.41			65.60
1924	6.02	19.77	38.95						25.79	38.95			64.74

Source: Reimann (1985:408–9) and our own calculations.

The pension for the severely handicapped. This pension is a good example of the effects of legislative rule changes. It was set up in 1973, requiring a severely restricted state of health and at least 35 insurance years.[9] Its age limit, originally 62, was reduced to 61 in 1979 and to 60 in 1980. Whereas in 1978 it accounted for only 4 percent of all new male entrants, this proportion rapidly increased to 9 percent in 1979 and to 16 percent in 1980. For women, this pension has also never been important because of their general ability to retire at age 60.

Flexible retirement at age 63. This pension was introduced in 1973 as well, requiring 35 insurance years with a contribution period of at least 15 years. Immediately after its introduction, it became a very popular route for men: In 1973, 31 percent of the new entrants used it, resulting in a remarkable immediate downward shift in the labor force participation of those aged 63 and 64 (see Chapter 2). This proportion decreased, however, to 18 percent in 1988. This decline has been produced mainly by three factors that have already been mentioned: the reduction of the age limit of the pension for severely handicapped persons and the increased utilization of the pension after unemployment as well as the disability pension before age 60.

6.2.2   *Programs outside the pension system*

Although the pension system plays the key role in the exit from work, the transition is not always direct. In some cases, other institutional programs provide for interim periods. They are generated if persons exit before reaching the first accessible age limit of the pension scheme and if they are not eligible for (or not willing to take) a disability pension. The most important programs are those for unemployment and preretirement.

Unemployment of the elderly. Until 1980 workers over 55 had the highest unemployment rates of all age groups. In the early 1980s the youngest age groups took the lead in this deplorable contest, but in the last few years, the demographic squeeze[10] made their unemployment rates decline again so that the older workers – in spite of some statistical cos-

---

[9] For the number of insurance years, not only the contribution period but also periods of unemployment and, up to a certain limit, periods of education are counted.

[10] The postwar demographic history of West Germany is characterized by a comparatively late onset of the baby boom – the largest birth cohort is that of 1964 – and a particularly massive bust, with a decrease in the number of births of more than 40 percent in a period of 10 years.

metics directed at them (discussed later) are back in first place. Even more important than the unemployment rates is the fact that older workers have a longer mean duration of unemployment, with only a slim chance for getting back to work and a very likely prospect of a transition from long-term unemployment into definitive exit. In September 1986, out of 123,000 registered unemployed men aged 55 to 59, 38,400 (31 percent) had already been without employment for more than two years, 26,600 (22 percent) for between one and two years, and another 25,800 (21 percent) for between half a year and one year (Amtliche Nachrichten der Bundesanstalt für Arbeit [ANBA], No. 3/1987, p. 266).

Unemployed workers receive "unemployment money" (68 percent of the last net income for those with children and 63 percent for those without children) for a certain time span (originally one year at the most), which can be followed by means-tested "unemployment help" (with a replacement rate of 58 percent and 56 percent, respectively, of the last net income). With their long duration of unemployment, the majority of the unemployed elderly were no longer eligible for unemployment money. For this reason the maximum period of eligibility has been extended several times for older persons. First, it was lengthened from 12 to 18 months for the unemployed aged 49 and over in 1985. Only one year later, in 1986, it was set at 16 months for those aged 44 to 48, at 20 months for those aged 49 to 53, and at 24 months for those aged 54 and over. In July 1987 these regulations were changed again, by lowering the age for the first extension of the maximum period for receiving unemployment money from 44 to 42 and by extending this period gradually up to 32 months for those aged 54 and over. These quite turbulent legislative changes are presented by the federal government as substantial social achievements (see Sozialbericht 1986:17). They can, however, also be regarded as purely passive and resigned adaptations to labor-market shortcomings instead of an active employment policy.

Because of different definitions of unemployment used in the two main statistical sources (Mikrozensus and Federal Labor Office), data on unemployment by age differ considerably, especially for persons under 20 and over 55 (see Brinkmann 1980). The Mikrozensus counts as unemployed only persons who do not work a single hour per week (which corresponds to the OECD concept). Moreover, this information is given on a voluntary base, so the stigma of having no job may restrain some people from giving a correct statement. The Mikrozensus data are, therefore, likely to underestimate the real extent of unemployment. The Federal Labor Office statistics up to 1985 contained all registered unemployed. Registration is necessary for all those who want to receive unemployment benefits or to apply for the pension after unemployment at age 60. As a consequence of the availability of this pension, the official unemployment figures are especially high for those immediately below age 60 (see Figures 6.2a and 6.2b). Since 1986, however, the unemployed aged 58 and above no longer need to register for work; they retain their rights to unemployment compensation (and the following pension after long-term unemployment) but are no longer included in the official statistics. As a consequence, by the end of September 1986, there were 40 percent fewer registered unemployed 59-year-old men than in 1985.

Preretirement. Some institutional measures have been set up outside the social security system and negotiated between unions and employers. The latest and most popular of these has been the Preretirement Act of 1984 (see Casey 1985; Naegele 1987; Kohli et al. 1989). Introduced as temporally limited legislation to reduce unemployment, it became effective in May 1984 and expired at the end of 1988. The law set a frame in which a collective agreement between unions and employers or (in practice unlikely) an individual agreement between worker and employer was required. The minimum age of eligibility was 58. The preretirement span extended up to the first accessible retirement age of the statutory pension system, that is, until age 63 for most men and age 60 for severely handicapped persons and most women. The minimum benefit – which could be improved by agreement – was 65 percent of the last gross income, to be paid by the employer and partly subsidized (35 percent) by the unemployment insurance if the "preretiree" was replaced with an unemployed person. Up to a given limit (usually set at 5 percent of the total work force of a firm), all eligible workers had the right to claim preretirement, with the firm being obliged to let them go.

Preretirement was the focus of a bitter controversy among the unions themselves (cf. section 6.5.1); of the two largest unions, one (for the public workers) had no collective agreement with their employers, and the other (for the metal workers), only a very limited one. Thus, the program in fact was restricted to some industries only. At the end of 1988, about 107,000 persons were registered as preretirees (see Figure 6.5); since many had in the meantime left the program again to go into retirement proper, total use amounted to about 200,000 persons (IAB 1989). For almost half of them, the employers received subsidies for having replaced them. Of these preretirees, 38 percent were in construction, 13 percent in the chemical industry, 8 percent in manufacturing of machinery and vehicles, and 6 percent each in banking and insurance and in the food industry. As the basic motive for the Preretirement Act was to reduce unemployment, the job replacement rates are also of interest. The average job replacement rate was 47 percent, with a variation from

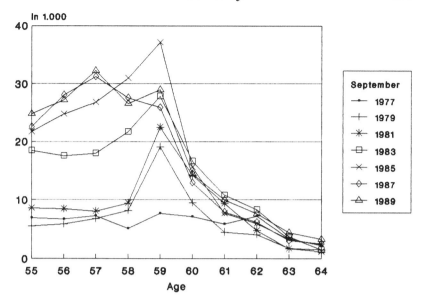

Figure 6.2a. Registered unemployed men by age. *Data source:* Federal Labor Office, ANBA.

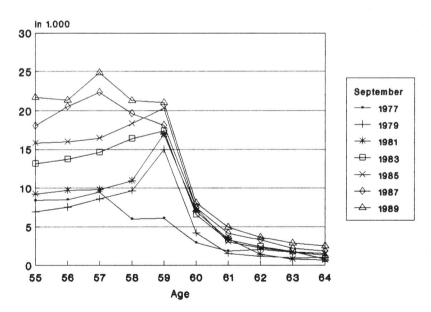

Figure 6.2b. Registered unemployed women by age. *Data source:* Federal Labor Office, ANBA.

almost 80 percent in the textile industry to only 28 percent in mining and 16 percent in banking and insurance. In addition, there have been indirect replacement chains, and some potential dismissals are likely to have been averted, so that the total replacement effect is estimated to be about 80 percent (IAB 1989).

Other programs of early exit. There exists a range of other collective agreements between unions and employers to make early exit possible on the branch or the firm level. One example is the practice in most breweries, where older workers are permitted to accumulate time that can be used to leave work before the formal retirement age. In the cigarette industry, workers can receive either a complete release from work two years before the normally accessible retirement age (in other words, at age 61 for men and 58 for women) or a reduction of working time by half with full income (see Wolf 1986). Data on this and other such programs are scarce, but they do show that the second (part-time or "gradual") transitional alternative is only minimally accepted.[11] It also has to be noted that in Germany, firm pension schemes are not as important as in many other countries[12] and that their role has been reduced even more over the last years.[13] Although almost 50 percent of the workers are covered by private schemes, the latter are insufficient to serve as the primary source of income. By themselves, they are thus not a major pathway into retirement; they are, however, often used to "top up" public unemployment programs (cf. section 6.3).

6.2.3   Phases of the exit process as reflected in participation rates

The effects of institutional changes to make early exit possible or of the changed utilization of existing mechanisms are visible in the decline of labor force participation (as described in Chapter 2), especially in the patterns for individual birth cohorts. The changes have been graphically described as a sequence of "landslides" advancing the transition to retirement, each "slide" displaying distinct features and comprising specific institutional redefinitions (see Orsinger and Clausing 1982). The first

---

[11] The same is true for all other arrangements of gradual exit on the firm or branch level. So far, none of these programs has had any success; see Deters et al. (1989) and Wolf and Kohli (1988).

[12] For private pension schemes in the general context of old age security, see Schmähl (1987).

[13] The importance of private pensions as pathways to early exit from the labor force might, however, grow in the future if the state is successful in closing down some public pathways; see Jacobs and Rein (1988).

slide began in 1973 with the introduction of flexible retirement at age 63; it resulted in an immediate loss of importance for "normal" retirement at age 65 for men. Of the men born in 1906 who did not enter the pension system via disability before age 60, more than 60 percent still received a "normal" pension at age 65; this proportion dropped to 40 percent for those born in 1910 and to 24 percent for those born in 1916.

The second slide consisted in the lowering of the age limit of the pension for severely handicapped persons from 62 to 61 in 1979 and to 60 in 1980. Its impact can be seen in the bulge between the participation rates for 1916 and 1920 birth cohorts after age 60, which is explained by cohort data on entry into the pension system (see Table 6.4): 9 percent of the men born in 1916 and 10 percent of those born in 1918 entered the pension system at age 60 (in 1976 and 1978, respectively), but more than 21 percent of those born in 1920 did so – this was in 1980 when the age limit had been lowered to 60.

A third slide occurred through lowering the age of entry into the pension system via disability, to be attributed mainly to the changed definition of eligibility for disability pensions by the Federal Social Court mentioned earlier. The labor force participation rates do not reflect this slide as clearly as the first two because juridical changes followed by administrative adjustments do not become effective immediately in the same way as legislative changes do. In addition, the process of getting classified as disabled involves different actors and takes some time (see section 6.3). But the effect is evident in the age structure of new recipients of disability pensions: In 1976, about 20 percent of new entrants were aged 55 to 59; in only four years, this share increased to about 35 percent.

Finally, a fourth slide can be distinguished that is directly based on work and unemployment (cf. Kohli and von Kondratowitz 1987). The first measure here was the intensified utilization of unemployment at (or before) age 59 and the pension after long-term unemployment at age 60; the second was the Preretirement Act. Both measures are inadequately reflected in the participation rates: The unemployed are still counted as part of the labor force, and the preretirees, in the absence of a specific category in the Mikrozensus questionnaire, are often misclassified as such.

Although the weak labor market since the mid-1970s was the driving force behind the process of early exit, many of the instruments that made this process possible were not intended to promote early exit generally but were designed for special problem groups. This is true for the introduction of the pension after long-term unemployment in 1957 and of flexible retirement and the pension for the severely handicapped in 1973, and partly valid as well for the Social Court's redefinition of disability – at least for its first decision in 1969. In contrast, the programs of the fourth slide were explicitly labor-market oriented.

6.3   PATHWAYS OF EARLY EXIT: ACTORS, COST, CONTROL, STRATIFICATION, AND CULTURAL MEANING

6.3.1   *The three major pathways*

In order to deal with how early exit has been institutionally facilitated, we have developed the concept of "pathways" of exit (see Chapter 1). A pathway is an institutional arrangement or – in most cases – a combination of different institutional arrangements that are sequentially linked to manage the process of transition to retirement, that is, the period between exit from work and entry into the normal old-age pension system. There are three major pathways (Figure 6.3).[14]

The unemployment pathway. This pathway consists of long-term unemployment of older workers (with unemployment benefits often being "topped up" by the firm) and the receipt of the pension after long-term unemployment (at least one year) at age 60. Unemployment can be a voluntary agreement between the firm and the worker (the "59er-rule," see section 6.3.2) or involuntary, as in the case of plant closings. As stated above, under present regulations a person can receive full unemployment benefits for up to 32 months before age 60.

The preretirement pathway. The preretirement program starting at age 58 was combined with entering a public pension at one of three different ages, depending on the personal situation and insurance or contribution years of the preretirees. Most women and the severely handicapped persons qualified at age 60, and thus benefited from preretirement for only two years. Most male preretirees retired at age 63 under the scheme of flexible retirement.

---

[14] We will not deal further with the ways of exit before age 65, discussed above, which consist of direct transitions from work into retirement as a consequence of reaching certain age limits of the pension scheme, namely, retirement for women and severely handicapped persons at age 60 and flexible retirement at age 63. The first two can be seen as single-program pathways, and in some cases they moreover function as part of a sequential pathway: when following a period of sick pay or a period of unemployment (taking the place of the disability pension or the pension after long-term unemployment, respectively), or a period of preretirement.

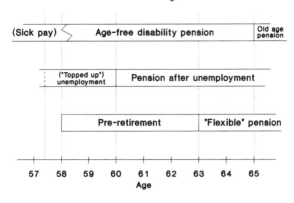

Figure 6.3. The three major pathways of early exit.

The health pathway. The first component of this pathway usually is the continued payment of full wages, mandatory for the employer during the first six weeks of the worker's inability to work as a result of sickness or the consequences of an accident. If the health restrictions still persist, the statutory health insurance takes over with sick pay of almost 90 percent of the previous net income. The general duration of sick pay is not limited, but it is restricted to one and a half years for a single health problem. After this period, the absence from work is assumed to be permanent, and the disability pension should take over from the health insurance.

The identification of older persons in this pathway is more difficult than for the other two pathways because continued wage payment by the employer and the ensuing sick pay from the health insurance cannot immediately be related to permanent exit from the labor force. It is only retrospectively, after a disability pension has been formally granted, that these periods can be identified as having been the first steps to permanent exit. Even this information is difficult to obtain, however, since data on sick pay by age are not generally available.

Pathways of early exit are thus financed directly and indirectly by a range of different institutions (Figure 6.4): by the unemployment insurance, the health insurance, the disability system, specific old-age pensions, or collective bargaining. In addition, there is the means-tested and age-free (locally administered) system of social assistance; it is not linked with former employment (and therefore with exit from work), but may play a role in the exit process either if the conditions of eligibility for

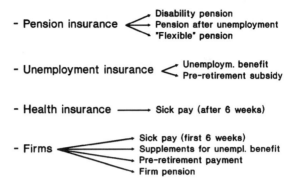

Figure 6.4. Institutions involved in pathways of early exit.

unemployment or pension benefits are not fulfilled or if benefit levels are below certain limits.

6.3.2 *Who are the actors, who is in control, and who bears the financial burden?*

The interests of the major actors. The logical starting point of a social policy analysis is with the state as actor.[15] It would, of course, be highly simplified to treat the state as a unified actor. At the least we need to distinguish the quasi-autonomous pension, unemployment, and health insurance bodies from the state administration and government; in Germany they are controlled by boards with representation by employers, unions, and/ or clients in addition to that by the state administration. The state makes up the deficits that these bodies might incur. This arrangement naturally leads the state to a politics of cost shifting among the insurance bodies as a way of rearranging the surpluses and deficits incurred by these institutions.[16] It also directly contributes a part of the total expenditures of the pension system, which, however, has declined over time and is now below 20 percent. (The state's contribution is much higher in special

---

[15] For a discussion of the different actors involved in the retirement process and their respective interests and preferences, see Jacobs and Schmähl (1989) and Kohli (forthcoming).

[16] This cost shifting (especially between the unemployment insurance and the statutory pension scheme) has been demonstrated for the period 1975–85 by Schmähl et al. (1986).

schemes for miners and other groups, and covers the totality of expenditures for the *Beamte*.) In a period of fiscal constraint, the state tries to reduce costs in other ways as well. Of special importance is how it seeks to redefine the rules of access to pensions, rather than going the cruder way of direct cutting of benefits. A good case in point is the recent rule change, described earlier, with regard to eligibility for disability pensions, which had an immediate effect on the pattern of entry of women. Thus the state's actions can block important pathways to early exit, but this does not necessarily mean a reduction in early exit if there is institutional substitution.

Not only is the state not a unified actor, it also does not have a unified interest structure. The problem has become one of managing three competing demands. The state not only has to keep the public finances viable; it also has to keep the private economy viable – by allowing the firms flexibility in the management of their elderly work force, and the possibility of externalizing (part of) the costs for early exit. And finally, the state has to keep the "social contract" viable, by finding ways out of the employment crisis that are socially legitimate and acceptable, and that make room for the integration of the young into the work force. The pressure of these competing demands has led to a "muddling through" in which competing measures have succeeded each other. Thus the measure to reduce access to disability pensions was accompanied by the extension of the maximum period of unemployment coverage for older workers to 32 months, which means that now the unemployment pathway can already be entered at the age of 57 years and 4 months.

The next key actors to consider are the firms and the unions. In the neoclassical model, the firm primarily acts through the wage structure, but in reality the picture is much more complex. To the extent that it operates with an internal labor market, the firm, for example, needs to reconcile its interests in opening the vacancy chains with its task of adjusting available labor to fluctuations in its output. The workers in turn make a moral claim for reciprocity for their life-time commitment to the firm, a claim that has to be honored, for example, by good exit arrangements. The social policy of the firm can be called "pro-active" (Jacobs and Rein 1988) in the sense that the firm makes extensive use of the social policy instruments set up by the state to realize its own economic aims, such as in promoting early exit.[17]

---

[17] As the other chapters on individual countries show, in the United States and the United Kingdom, but also in the Netherlands, the firms have to play a much more active role in the early-exit process in terms both of creating and of financing substantial pathway components.

Finally, one of the intriguing questions is why the individuals directly affected by retirement – the older workers and the retirees – do not organize into effective political movements to protect their interests. Surprisingly, there is no powerful pensioners' organization (apart from special ones such as the Association of War Victims). One might conclude that, as a consequence, the pension system would be rather minimal. But this is clearly not the case. The causal chain probably goes in the opposite direction: There is no powerful organization because the pensioners – at least those with a full work life (which would also be those who could most easily get organized) – are adequately provided for. Their interests are obviously well served by the existing set of actors: the unions and political parties plus the pension insurances (with their governing boards partly elected by the contributors and receivers themselves).[18]

The "59er rule": Actors in the unemployment pathway. As pointed out in section 6.2, the legislation introduced in 1957 was designed to aid older workers faced with unemployment and diminished prospects of returning to work but was not intended as a vehicle for firms to shed their unwanted workers and to externalize the costs of this operation. After the 1967 recession had shown the older workers to be particularly vulnerable, the unions successfully pressed for special protective agreements to prevent firms from dismissing older workers except in cases of plant closings or other severe economic troubles. The firms can therefore not simply force older workers to leave. They can, however, offer them a deal to make exit attractive to them. The difference between individual choice and imposed exit by the firms is not always clear. The workers cannot leave without the consent of the firm, but they can make their interest known. The firms, on the other hand, can initiate the process and exert some informal pressure. The "59er rule," then, is an example of early exit made sweet to the workers by "topping up" the state's unemployment benefit (until age 60) and pension (after age 60) so that workers pay no financial penalty or only a small one.

---

[18] As to social movements, there is a Grey Panthers organization, which has an advocacy contract with the Green Party and whose leader has been elected to the Bundestag on the Green ticket. Structurally, it seems to represent the deprived elderly (especially women) with a history of discontinuous and low-income work and therefore low pension incomes. Together with the Greens, the Grey Panthers thus represent an alliance of those at the margin of the "work society." Given this situation, it is logical that both groups have proposed to abolish the work-based social insurance system in favor of a general citizen's wage. The role of the Grey Panthers in this context is, however, rather small, both in terms of their number and of the political weight of their demands. Recently, they have tried to set up their own "Grey Party," but so far with minimal success.

With the increasing economic pressure of the 1970s, the firms started to make systematic use of this institutional pathway, either to reduce their labor force or to exchange their older workers for better qualified, healthier, and/or less costly younger ones. The state, not surprisingly, tried to pass the costs back to the firm. In 1982, a rule change was introduced, forcing the firms to reimburse the unemployment benefit paid to a formerly long-term employed worker who was dismissed at age 59. This rule change, however, was not effective because it was immediately challenged in the courts. Simultaneously with the Preretirement Act, the reimbursement clause was tightened, with the firm being forced to reimburse all social benefits of dismissed older workers until they reached the age for flexible retirement. Some branches (such as the steel industry) and firms were exempted from reimbursement because of their severe economic problems. This legislation again was challenged in the court, and until final ruling by the Federal Constitutional Court, the reimbursement clause was in practice suspended. The ruling finally came at the beginning of 1990, obliging the firms to make reimbursement in some but not all cases of dismissing workers. It remains to be seen to what extent this will deter the firms from using the 59er rule (which in the meantime, with the lengthening of unemployment compensation for older workers, has effectively become a "57er rule").

Actors in the preretirement pathway. The Preretirement Act introduced in May 1984 redefined the locus of control. Under the 59er rule, the firm formally decides both which workers are to be asked to exit and when the exit should occur. In preretirement, it was up to the eligible workers to decide whether and when to exit. Once the stage had been set by the negotiations among unions and employers, the firm had to accept the individual worker's decision. Moreover, the existence of a collective agreement made it possible even for those groups not covered by the agreement – such as managers and upper-level professional workers – to bargain for comparable terms.

Actors in the health pathway. The disability program introduces a different set of actors. As discussed above, the two court rulings in 1969 and 1976 transformed its character by connecting it more closely to labor-market conditions. In the abstract, a partially disabled person can work part-time, but in the concrete situation few suitable part-time work opportunities are available.

Disability thus constitutes a unique blend of medical and labor-market factors. The entrance into the disability pathway is via sickness and accidents. The physician is the key gatekeeper here.

Who initiates the request for sickness or disabilty? Obviously, the formal application must rest with the individual. But this is only part of the story; here again the boundary between individual choice and pressure by the firm can be fuzzy. A study (in the state of Baden-Württemberg) of all new disability pensioners in 1982 shows that the entry into the disability system of every sixth woman and almost every third man below age 60 was influenced by others (see Wasilewski et al. 1984). A 1988 survey of firms in the private sector demonstrates that the use of the disability system is very sensitive to whether the firms have stable, growing, or declining work forces: declining firms have higher rates of disability claims than growing ones (cf. Wagner et al. 1988, Table 5.1). If we assume that health is not influenced by the changing personnel requirements of the firm, we must conclude that at least some of the disability claims are not initiated directly by the individuals on the basis of health reasons.

6.3.3   Social stratification and cultural meaning

We have shown that the different pathways of early exit locate control over the exit decision in the hands of different actors: the state, the firm, the union, or the physician, in addition to the older workers themselves. It seems plausible to expect that individuals differentially located in the system of social stratification may not be equally able to protect themselves from external pressure and to expand the scope for personal choice.

The data on this point are extremely limited. There is some information on the basis of cross-classifying entry into pensions by blue- and white-collar occupations, suggesting that blue-collar workers are more likely to use disability (see Mörschel and Rehfeld 1981). For male blue-collar workers, the average age of entry into the pension system is two and a half years lower than for white-collar workers (see Table 6.1). In 1988 almost 80 percent of all new entries of men into the disability system were by blue-collar workers.

The pathways of early exit also differ in terms of their cultural meaning, and thus of their legitimacy or moral acceptability for the older workers (see Kohli and Wolf 1987). This is a consequence of the institutionalization of the life course and of the age boundary as part of it. The cultural patterns that define the "normal biography" also constitute a meaningful temporal relation between work life and retirement. The normal biography thus becomes the criterion for a "well-rounded" work life. This is particularly evident when comparing retirement with unemployment. One could assume them to be structurally identical, insofar as both consist of a socially enforced exclusion from gainful work. But in addition to the different income consequences of these two forms of "work deprivation," there are also moral differences. The relevant data here are obviously more difficult to assess as to their generalizability, but nonetheless conclusive at least for some cases. We have found in our case studies several versions of the moral significance of the age boundary. As an example, there are some men for whom the simple fact of having reached the point where – according to the criteria of the valid normal biography – their work life has come to its full term, and of having kept up their performance in spite of growing pains, is sufficient proof of having been a "good man." To them, the socially required and institutionalized work curriculum defines success in work and – as far as the work ethic is still valid – in the world itself. One could say that in these cases, the normal biography is a resource for transcendental meaning.[19]

In terms of this meaning, there is a clear difference between preretirement and early exit via disability. Although preretirement was at first met with some reluctance, stemming from insecurity not only about its financial implications but also about its moral status, it was soon overwhelmingly seen as a well-earned right of workers and as a part of a legitimate life course. Disability, on the other hand, carries the implication either of having failed personally or of having been confined to a degrading position that did not give room for bringing one's work life to a close. Given the fact that many more blue-collar than white-collar workers exit via disability, the aspects of social stratification and cultural meaning of early exit are linked.

6.4 EFFECTS ON ECONOMY AND SOCIETY

6.4.1 *Effects on the labor market and social policy*

It will not be possible here to go into a detailed analysis of the effects of early exit and to assess their magnitude. We will restrict ourselves instead to briefly mentioning the most likely types of effects. The main positive effect on the labor market is, of course, that it is unburdened. In addition

---

[19] To ward off a possible misreading, this does not mean that these men see themselves harmoniously integrated into a unified world. They feel that it is more difficult for them to achieve even this modest measure of success than for those higher up in the occupational hierarchy, for example, those "sitting in an office." Their producer's pride is based – for skilled workers (*Facharbeiter*) – on their competent participation in the production of the socially important goods, or – for unqualified workers – on having contributed their "bones" to it; in both cases, they set themselves off from those who "don't really work."

to the general quantitative effect, there may be structural advantages: To the firms, early exit offers the possibility of exchanging low-skilled workers for better educated ones, or sick ones for healthy ones, or costly ones (with respect to income and productivity) for cheaper ones – in short, of improving their work force so that, as the metaphor goes, it is turned into an "Olympic team."

The unburdening of the labor market is reduced to the extent that early exit leads to an increase in labor force activity in retirement, be it officially or in the form of shadow work. Up to now, the official activity rate of the elderly has been on the decline; gainful work among retirees is minimal, even though pensions after 65 demand no "work test" (i.e., inflict no financial penalties for income from work). With the decreasing age of transition to retirement (and the improving activity resources of successive cohorts, such as education and health), an increase may occur. However, as long as the pension level is satisfactory, financial needs will continue to play only a small role. It seems more likely that those activities will expand that are outside the sphere of gainful work but have some structural similarity to it, for example, voluntary work, organized consumption activities, and participation in institutionalized hobby cultures.

For the firms, those forms of early exit that leave the control to the elderly workers themselves (such as preretirement) may, however, present difficulties insofar as they threaten to "unburden" them of workers who are still needed, and thus lead to labor shortages. As mentioned above, this loss of control over the exit process was one of the main reasons for the firms' opposition to preretirement (and preference for the unemployment pathway). At present, many firms feel that there is already a shortage in several categories of skilled workers, although the general labor market is still heavily unbalanced.[20]

The increasing cost for the pension system is the most obvious negative effect of early exit and is its main limiting feature. With increasing dependency ratios (or "burden coefficients," as they are graphically called in German) due to smaller activity cohorts and increasing life expectancy, changes seem to be inevitable. However, if such changes are to increase the age of exit (and not simply shift the costs to the older individuals themselves), they need to be "ratified" by an increase in the demand for labor.

---

[20] Thus, one of the large chemical firms has turned to the unemployed, trying to requalify them, but they have – in the words of one of its personnel managers – proved to be worthless "scrap iron," so that now the firm wants to retain some of its elderly workers (until the next massive employment cut, it should be added).

6.4.2 *Effects on the "moral economy" and the organization of the life course*

Early exit is a highly popular and thus legitimate way of decreasing the supply of work. Its effect on the moral economy may be even more positive: To today's elderly cohorts, it offers a recompense for the particular hardships that they suffered during the war and the ensuing reconstruction period. Many of them view it in these terms not only of lifetime reciprocity in general, but of their specific generational life course.

This may, however, look different in terms of the intergenerational transfers, and of the present "generational contract" on which they are grounded. As mentioned before, early exit may create conflicts between younger and older workers over where to direct the available resources. Whether it be financed by the firms or by the state, the cost of early exit is ultimately borne by the gainfully active population, but its benefits go only to the elderly among them. (This might change if early exit turned into a well-entrenched "possession" and part of the normal life course on which the younger workers could count for themselves also.)

On the other hand, early exit also means a redistribution of work from the older to the younger age groups. For those who otherwise would remain outside or at the margin of the system of gainful work, early exit thus makes the "generational contract" more balanced again. It gives them a chance not only to earn a work income, but – given the construction of the welfare system around the work status – also to accumulate the claims for participation in social security. If this chance were not available, the pressure for transforming the present work-based welfare system into one based on a general citizen's wage would increase.

As long as early exit is a new phenomenon, not yet "normalized" as part of the standard life course, it is necessary for the individual to explicitly address and reflect on the process of transition to the new life phase ("biographization" of retirement), and to review and take stock of his or her work life. Moreover, early exit causes life after work to be less and less coextensive with "old age"; by the same token, it is becoming less a leftover and more a life phase of its own, giving rise to new projects.

Finally, as has been noted, early exit may lead to increasing participation in activities that are similar to formal work. As such participation increases, the boundary between formal work and other forms of activity may become blurred. We would thus have the paradox that early exit, which is aimed at keeping up the tripartition of the life course and the existing boundaries of the formal sector of work even in the face of a diminishing demand for work, would also contribute to eroding these boundaries.

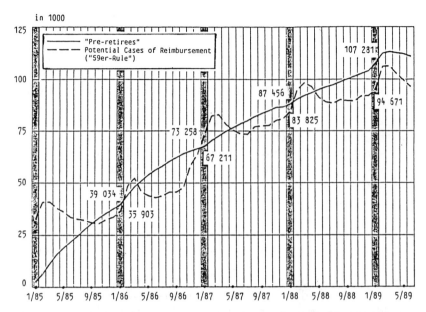

Figure 6.5. Take-up of preretirement and "59er rule." *Source:* IAB (1989).

6.5 THE POLITICAL DISCOURSE

6.5.1 *The past: Preretirement as an example*

As implied in the preceding sections, early exit has become the focus of political conflict and negotiation on several levels. It obviously concerns labor-market and social policy, but it also extends into basic questions of industrial relations and of the moral economy. For a short overview of the lines of conflict, the preretirement pathway is a particularly apt example. It has involved all of the relevant actors over the past few years and has been part of the politics of work time more generally.

When the Preretirement Act was planned prior to 1984 – at first still under the Schmidt government – its aim was twofold: to ease the labor-market pressure and to meet the long-standing demands of the unions for a reduction of the retirement age limit. In addition, such a measure could be expected to be broadly popular with the workers themselves. Surveys in the early 1980s had shown that among the possible ways to effect a reduction of work time, shortening the work life was the most popular (even among the younger workers, surprisingly enough).

Among the unions, however, a split developed: the "moderate" unions (e.g., those for construction and for chemical workers) agreed to concentrate on early exit via preretirement, while the more "radical" ones (especially the largest one, the Metal Workers' Union) opted for a reduction of the weekly work hours (without pay deduction) and went on strike for it. Thus, the unions had decided to "use" a large part of the productivity gains available for income raises for work-time reduction instead, but in two different forms, one of which was clearly more acceptable to the employers. The strike for the 35-hour week was one of the most bitter and costly in the postwar German economy, the more so as it became the first testing ground between the unions and the new conservative government over the latter's attempts to curb the unions' power. In this situation, the employers of the other branches were willing to top the benefits provided by the Preretirement Act by contracts that were rather favorable to their unions, even though they could be expected to be quite costly for the firms.

The evolution of preretirement has followed these lines of conflict. The workers' reluctance at first to make use of the preretirement option was regretted by those who had committed themselves to it and was gloatingly commented upon by the other side. In the meantime, it has become clear that there is little reason for regret or gloating. After a slow start, take-up has increased regularly (Figure 6.5).[21] A study in the chemical industry (Kohli et al. 1989) shows that the initial reluctance of the workers was due to insecurity about its (mostly financial) consequences and that preretirement was later massively taken advantage of, in some firms even to the extent that the 5 percent limit of total personnel was reached, creating a waiting list. The pattern of acceptance over time closely follows that expected on the basis of other processes of diffusion of innovation.

The Preretirement Act as well as the contracts had been set up as a temporary provision, expiring at the end of 1988. For some time, there was a heated debate over a possible prolongation. The terms of this debate are highly instructive with regard to the interests of the various actors.

The direct evaluation. For the employers, preretirement turned out to be even costlier than expected. In addition, they strongly disliked the shift of control over the exit process to the workers themselves. Another reason for preferring to terminate preretirement was that with a prolongation, the workers and unions might increasingly have come to regard it

---

[21] It should be repeated that Figure 6.5 shows only those presently on preretirement; including those who have already moved from preretirement into retirement, total incidence is estimated at about 200,000 persons.

as a well-entrenched "possession" not to be given up easily. This was disliked by the employers because of the possibility that the oversupply of labor might, for demographic reasons, turn into a shortage. According to all economic predictions (even before the recent unification prospects), the time for such a possible turn of the labor market is moving to the more distant future – not 1990, as envisaged some years ago, but rather 2000 or later. In this context the labor-market rationale would clearly have been to continue with preretirement. But the fear that it could then never be retracted made the employers reluctant.

The unions that had opted for preretirement saw no reason to discontinue it. Among the older workers in the respective branches, it had become enormously popular. In the chemical industry, although there were desires for higher financial benefits, four-fifths of those who would be eligible in the next few years wanted to take it even without improvements (Kohli et al. 1989). There were many indications that they indeed started to see preretirement as a well-deserved right and as something to count on in their biographical planning. On the other hand, there were also some signs of uneasiness among younger workers. They resented the fact that all efforts were going into preretirement, and there was thus some prospect of intergenerational conflict along these lines.

On the issue of cost shifting, employers and unions agreed that the state should assume a larger part of the burden. In the chemical industry, the two parties issued a common statement to that effect. The political actors, however, quickly agreed that this was not possible. Even the Social Democrats signaled that they saw no room for higher state contributions, so that the only possibility would have been to extend the Preretirement Act as it stood. Within the government, the left wing of the Christian Democrats opted for prolongation, while the right wing and the Free Democrats opposed it, in correspondence with the majority of the employers.

The relation to other pathways of early exit. As mentioned earlier, the attempt of the state to shift the cost of the "59er rule" back to the firms had been suspended in view of the pending court case. Because it was generally assumed that the Constitutional Court would eventually rule in favor of the employers, the latter could easily satisfy their needs for making older workers exit early by the "59er" (unemployment) pathway. In addition to the lower financial burden, this pathway also gave them control over the exit process. The workers had contrary interests: Even though the unemployment pathway was often as attractive financially as preretirement – in some cases, the firms were even prepared to make it more attractive in order to counter preretirement – only preretirement offered them the right to leave by their own will. For the unions, however, it became less pressing to fight for the continuation of preretirement (and pay a price for it) as many of those leaving early did so via the unemployment pathway. The latter indeed did not lose its importance; its use increased at about the same rate as preretirement (see Figure 6.5).

The relation to other forms of work-time reduction. The threat of pressing for other demands, especially the 35-hour week, had been a prime asset of the "moderate" unions in the fight for preretirement, and it made the employers more inclined to agree to a prolongation of the act and the contracts. However, in the metal industry, the results of the strike over the 35-hour week had been less disruptive than the employers had feared; the schedule of weekly work-time reduction was fairly slow, and the firms were able to cope with this reduction better than originally expected. The threat therefore became less menacing to them. To the extent that the weekly work-time reduction was effectively – even if slowly – implemented, it raised a problem for those unions opting for preretirement: It increased the discontent of their own younger workers about what their unions got for them.

Corporate power and coalitions. In the Unions' Confederation, the conflict between the "radicals" and the "moderates" was very heated for some time. For the latter, it meant that they could get more out of their employers (who were glad to contribute to strengthening the moderate side), but they had to balance this against the interest of keeping the Confederation intact. Thus, the leadership of the Chemical Workers' Union did not support the Metal Workers' Union in its strike (and was accused at least implicitly of being "on the other side"), but took care not to let the conflict escalate by declaring preretirement and the 35-hour week "separate ways towards the common goal." It was interested in weakening the radicals' position within the Confederation, but not to the extent that the union movement as a whole would have been jeopardized. As for the employers, those complying to the demands of the moderate unions by agreeing to favorable contracts were similarly under attack by the hard liners who wanted to seize the occasion to deal a blow to the union movement as such. In the political domain, the interests were defined accordingly. The issue evidently turned into one of symbolic politics also: The actors who had committed themselves to a given course of action were interested in making it a success not only for the sake of the goal itself but also simply for the sake of being successful.

In this battlefield of interests, the fate of preretirement remained undecided for some time. The scale tipped when the largest of the moderate unions, the Chemical Workers' Union, which had long rallied strongly for preretirement, abandoned it in summer 1987. The reason was that it had to negotiate a new long-term wage contract, in a situation in which it was still unclear whether the government would finally get around to extending the Preretirement Act (which is a precondition for corresponding collective agreements not in principle but in practice). The wage contract aimed at abolishing the official distinction between blue-collar and white-collar workers by incorporating the latter into a unified salary system – a question of secular importance in terms of the structure of the workers' movement and of the organizational power of the union itself, given the rapidly increasing share of white-collar work in the chemical industry. To obtain such a contract from the employers, the union was prepared to give up everything that was not strictly necessary, including preretirement with its insecure prospects. The course of events also highlights the links between the corporate and the political system. In the final decisive round of negotiation, the head of the union – one of the leaders of the traditional workers' wing of the Social Democratic Party, which is now clearly its right wing – was called personally by the Minister of Work – who is the uncontested leader of the left wing of the Christian Democrats and was at that time one of the most prominent candidates for succeeding the present chancellor – imploring him to stick to preretirement. The signals from the chancellor's office however were mixed, so that it seemed unreasonable to pay the price given its uncertain returns.

As the governing coalition (and the employers backing it) deemed it too risky to simply drop the Preretirement Act, it was "replaced" by a law providing for partial exit (described later). However, since none of the partial-exit options had ever been accepted by the workers, and since the unions took no interest in the new law, it was obvious from the outset that the law was nothing more than a measure of political cosmetics without any empirical effect in terms of take-up – and this has indeed turned out to be so. Among those whose plans for early exit through preretirement were thwarted, there was massive disappointment, and the unions were confronted with heavy criticism from their older constituency.

The broader consequences of the abolishment of the Preretirement Act are not yet clear, but it will be a good case for examining the process of instrument substitution. As the labor market imbalance is likely to continue for the next few years at the least, we expect that early exit will not decrease but will take place through other pathways, albeit with different financial and moral costs for those directly involved.

6.5.2 The future: Raising the age of retirement – and privatization of early exit?

Problems of unification. In the political discourse about the long-term future of early exit and retirement, the reform of the statutory pension system has for some years now occupied center stage. The broad consensus between the major political parties (with the exception of the Greens), the Employer's Association, and the Unions' Confederation reached in November 1989 over the pension reform legislation was an exceptional event in German politics, but because of the more prominent events of the unification process it went almost unnoticed.

Since then, the unification of the two Germanies has become the most important topic in all fields of public policy. The situation in East Germany had been characterized by very rigid retirement rules offering no exit possibilities below the uniform retirement age (65 for men and 60 for women), coupled with the obligation on the part of the firms to employ all persons. Firms had no interest in getting rid of workers; in fact, in many cases it was in their interest to hoard workers to be able to comply with changing output requirements. There was officially no unemployment, with low productivity expressing itself in an undersupply of work, so that even workers past retirement age were still in demand. The "right to work" was guaranteed for old age as well, and motivation to work was increased by a rather low pension level. Data on labor force participation by age are not generally available, but it seems that there was practically no early exit.[22]

Since July 1990, all pieces of West German legislation are being "imported" to the East, including the statutory pension system with its provisions for early exit. A "preretirement" program had already been introduced in February 1990 as one of the last important legislative steps of the Socialist-led transitional government, providing for a claim to exit five years before retirement age for reasons of health or unemployment, with benefits (to be paid by the state) set at 70 percent of the last net income.

The main reason for this program was the expectation of high unemployment during the transition period to a Western-style market system. In the meantime, this expectation has skyrocketed, being set by some

---

[22] The only data that exist concern the participation rates of those in retirement, that is, men above 65 and women above 60 (Winkler 1990:324). As in the West, they had decreased drastically, from 29.2 percent for men and 15.3 percent for women in 1972 to 11.0 percent and 9.5 percent in 1988, but were still higher than in most Western countries.

analysts at up to four million workers, or almost half of the total work force. In this period, an extensive use of early exit is likely to occur in order to remove some of the burden from a collapsing labor market – at least in the completely obsolete manufacturing sector with productivity rates about one-third of those of the West German economy, but also in large sectors of the enormously overstaffed public bureaucracies. In addition to reducing the aggregate oversupply of labor, early exit will also aid in coping with workers who are poorly qualified for the new requirements of the market economy, and/or politically "incriminated." With this aim, the preretirement threshold in East Germany has been further reduced to age 55 in July 1991.

It is difficult to estimate the duration of this transitional process. The relatively small size of the East German population (about 16 million) in comparison to West Germany (over 61 million) and the expected positive effects of the unification process for the already prospering West German economy could be factors for a rather quick integration of East Germany into the labor market and the social security system of the new Federal Republic. On the other hand, some observers predict an "Italian pattern" of internal colonization, with persisting regional disparities and corresponding mass migration.

The demographic outlook. The West German pension reform had been conceived without any anticipation of these dramatic developments in the East. Its most important motif was the demographic change predicted for the next decades. The projection that served as its main demographic basis was that of 1985 (Table 6.5), with an assumption of no migration.[23] It documents the considerable shift in the West German age structure that occurred between 1970 and 1985; while the total population remained roughly constant, the number of persons under age 20 declined from 18.2 to 14.4 million, and the number of persons over 60 increased from 11.6 to 12.4 million. The projection to the year 2030 shows a massively declining and aging population.[24] The total population would decline by 15 million, and the age dependency ratio would

---

[23] In 1987 this projection was slightly revised on the basis of a larger increase in life expectancy, resulting in an even somewhat more dramatic picture as to future population aging and decline. Even though this projection also took into account some positive net migration, it by and large still took the boundary of the West German system for granted. There has been no official updating since the beginning of the massive immigration from the East and of the unification process.

[24] In international comparison, while all OECD countries face the prospect of population aging, West Germany is projected to reach the highest proportion of the elderly (together with Switzerland) and the most massive population decline (OECD 1988).

Table 6.5. *Development of the West German population and dependency ratios*

	No. of persons (millions)				Dependency ratio (%)		
Year	<20 (a)	20–<60 (b)	60+ (c)	Total (d)	Youth (a/b)	Old age (c/b)	Total [(a + c)/b]
1960	16.0	30.3	9.0	55.3	52.6	29.6	82.2
1965	16.7	31.4	10.5	58.6	53.2	33.3	86.5
1970	18.2	31.3	11.6	61.2	58.2	37.2	95.4
1975	17.9	31.6	12.4	62.0	56.8	39.3	96.0
1980	16.5	33.1	11.8	61.4	49.9	35.7	85.5
1985	14.4	34.3	12.4	61.1	41.9	36.1	77.9
1990	12.7	35.4	12.8	60.9	35.8	36.1	71.9
1995	12.3	34.9	13.1	60.3	35.4	37.4	72.8
2000	12.2	32.9	14.1	59.2	37.0	43.0	80.0
2005	11.4	31.4	14.8	57.6	36.3	47.0	83.4
2010	10.3	30.8	14.7	55.8	33.4	47.7	81.1
2020	8.5	27.7	15.1	51.3	30.8	54.6	85.4
2030	7.7	22.1	16.4	46.2	34.9	74.2	109.1

Note: From 1960 to 1985: statistical results. From 1990 onwards: prognosis under the assumptions made by the 1985 *Rentenanpassungsbericht* (no migration, rise in life expectancy of more than 0.5 year for men and 0.75 year for women until 1989 compared with mortality charts of 1981–3, fertility ratios based on average 1981–3); incongruent sums due to rounding off.
Source: Sozialbeirat (1986).

double: In 1985 there were 36 persons aged 60 and over for every 100 persons between the ages of 20 and 60, and this is projected to rise to 74 per 100 in 2030. With the present pay-as-you-go pension system, this would imply (all other things remaining equal) a doubling of the contribution rate. Given its present level of 18.7 percent of gross income (shared equally between employer and worker), such an increase is unrealistic. In this situation, extending the age of entry into retirement seems to offer an easy (even if only partial) remedy.[25]

The first signs of how questionable the West German demographic projections were came with the growing immigration of German nationals – or people who successfully applied to be recognized as such – from Eastern Europe, especially Poland and Russia, beginning in 1987. In

[25] For the pension and survival situation of 2030, it is estimated that raising the mean age of entry into the pension system by one year would allow for a reduction of the contribution rate by 2.25 percentage points (Eckerle et al. 1987:88).

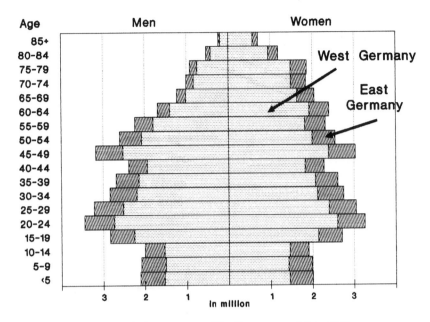

Figure 6.6. Age structure of the German population, 1987.

1989 there were 344,000 such immigrants plus another 377,000 from East Germany. Both groups were considerably "younger" than the resident West German population. The number of Germans living in Eastern Europe and interested in migrating to Germany is now estimated at around three million. The completely unanticipated immigration process has generally raised the level of consciousness about future possibilities of mass migration (whether politically desired or not) and has fueled the debate over whether Germany should become an "immigration country" with a "multicultural" society.

Of course, the gain in population "youthfulness" caused by the migrants from East Germany has in the meantime revealed itself to be only temporary. It is now clear that the German unification process will not substantially change the demographic picture. Mainly because of a lower average life expectancy (by three years at birth for women and two years for men), East Germany has a somewhat lower age dependency ratio. But the very low birth rates are not restricted to the West. And given the much larger size of the West German population, the age structure of unified Germany will not significantly change (Figures 6.6 and 6.7).

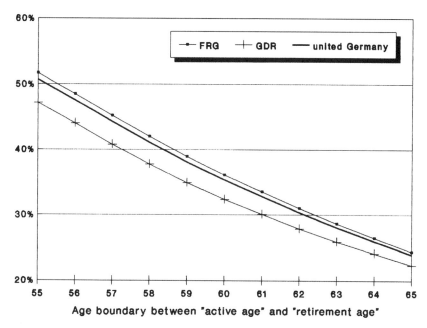

Figure 6.7. Old-age dependency ratio as a function of the age limit, 1987.

To the extent that there will be demographic changes, they are likely to have an impact on the labor market. A declining population of working age could, however, be offset in a number of ways other than by reversing the trend to early exit: by increased labor productivity, growing female labor force participation, a higher proportion of foreign workers, or earlier entry of the young into the labor force.

Partial pensions: A realistic option? As stated earlier, when the Preretirement Act was discontinued at the end of 1988, an "Old Age Part-Time Act" was implemented as a substitute. Under this program, older workers of age 58 or above can cut their weekly work time half. The employer pays them about 70 percent of their last net income and receives a subsidy from the Federal Labor Office if the newly created part-time job is filled by a formerly unemployed person. There was no doubt among observers that the take-up of this program would be next to zero.[26] The

---

[26] The first available data confirm this view. In the second half of 1989, fully 168 persons entered this program (ANBA No. 2/1990, p. 188).

major reasons for this skepticism were that there are practically no part-time jobs available,[27] especially for older workers, that the older workers themselves as well as the unions have so far shown no interest at all in part-time programs, and that there are other pathways for complete early exit (some of which start at an even earlier age). The very same reasons have already been responsible for the complete failure of combinations between part-time work and the receipt of a partial pension in other European countries (see Jacobs 1988), with the exception of Sweden where this exit pathway seems to be attractive for both workers and employers (see Chapter 9).

Not only economic aspects but also gerontological arguments are put forth in support of partial or gradual retirement as an alternative to the abrupt termination of the work life, but so far these arguments have not been convincing (see Kohli 1990). Many institutional decisions have to be made in this context (see Jacobs and Schmähl 1989), for example, whether gradual retirement programs should be integrated into the statutory pension system or be the subject of negotiations between unions and employers, or what age limits to choose. But again the most important questions are whether suitable part-time jobs are available for the elderly and whether more attractive alternative pathways of complete exit exist. At present, a failure of partial pension programs seems much more likely than a success.

The pension reform of 1992. The agreement reached in November 1989 was on a complex reform package that will become effective starting in 1992. Among its many elements, there are financial changes such as raising the contribution rates and increasing the state's contribution out of general taxation, but the most important and most controversial change is a gradual raising of the age limit for most types of pensions, to take place starting in 2001. With the sole exception of the pension for the severely handicapped at age 60, all other age limits will be gradually raised to 65. This concerns the pension for women, the pension after long-term unemployment (both in several steps until the year 2012), and the "flexible" retirement (until 2006). There will still be the possibility of early retirement up to three years before age 65, but each year prior to age 65 will be penalized by a 3.6 percent reduction of the pension amount. In order to stimulate late retirement, each year of postponing entry into the pension system beyond age 65 will lead to a 6 percent pension increase.

---

[27] Exactly this was the main reason for the changed definition of disability by the Federal Social Court; see section 6.2.

These rule changes have been explicitly motivated not only by financial but also by labor-market reasons – their goal is to extend the individual work life. The Social Democrats and, most of all, the unions tried to avoid a concrete schedule for raising the retirement ages, arguing that only substantial improvements in the labor market with significantly lower unemployment would establish the preconditions necessary for any extension of the work life; they were, however, only successful in somewhat postponing the schedule for this measure that, in the long run, they see as inevitable as well. Public protest against this worsening of the terms of trade for future retirement cohorts has been minimal so far, as the issue has been submerged by the dramatic events of unification. In addition, the long time lag until the measures become effective may have contributed to the low profile of the debate. But the issue may be forced back onto the public agenda as the "hour of truth" draws nearer, especially if the labor market remains favorable to early exit.

Continued early exit outside public programs? The state thus tried to reverse the trend to early exit. But the interests of the other actors – the older workers, the unions, and even the firms – may still point in the opposite direction. It is therefore not implausible to expect a new period of social policy, one dominated by a contest between the firm and the state. If firms continue to reduce their personnel, shedding the older workers is still the most socially acceptable way. Early exit is also attractive to them in terms of altering the skill mix and the age–wage profile of their work force. Given this divergence of interests, we may be entering an era of discussion about cost sharing and cost shifting. If no successful accommodation can be reached between these key actors, one likely outcome is a shift of the costs of early exit to the individual workers themselves in the form of lower benefit levels – as already anticipated with the introduction of actuarial deductions for pension take-up prior to age 65. In view of the salience of old-age security to the "implicit contract" between labor and capital in Germany, and to the social fabric more generally, this would create a high potential for conflict.

REFERENCES

Brinkmann, C. 1980. "Zum Unterschied in der Erfassung von Arbeitslosen durch die Bundesanstalt für Arbeit und von Erwerbslosen im Mikrozensus." *Beiträge zur Arbeitsmarkt- und Berufsforschung* 44:172–80.
Casey, B. 1985. *Early Retirement Schemes with a Replacement Condition: Programmes and Experiences in Belgium, France, Great Britain and the Federal Republic of Germany.* Discussion paper IIM/LMP 85-6a, Wissenschaftszentrum, Berlin.

Conradi, H., K. Jacobs, and W. Schmähl. 1987. "Vorzeitiger Rentenbezug in der Bundesrepublik Deutschland." *Sozialer Fortschritt* 36:182–9.

Deters, J., W. H. Staehle, and U. Stirn. 1989. *Die Praxis des gleitenden Übergangs in den Ruhestand. Geht eine sozialpolitische Idee in Rente?* Berlin: edition sigma.

Eckerle, K., et al. 1987. *Gesamtwirtschaftliche Entwicklungen und gesetzliche Rentenversicherung vor dem Hintergrund einer schrumpfenden Bevölkerung.* Basel: Prognos.

IAB. 1989. "Der Vorruhestand läuft aus," *IAB-Kurzbericht* (intern) vom 9. Aug. 1989.

Jacobs, K. 1988. "Teilrentenmodelle: Erfahrungen im In- und Ausland." *Internationale Chronik zur Arbeitsmarktpolitik*, no. 32, pp. 1–9 (also published in French: "Les retraites partielles: une comparaison européenne." In: P. Auer, M. Maruani, and E. Reynaud (eds.), *Chroniques internationales du marché du travail et des politiques d'emploi 1986–1989.* Paris: La Documentation Française, 1990, pp. 109–19).

Jacobs, K., and M. Rein. 1988. *The Future of Early Retirement.* Discussion paper FS II-202, Wissenschaftszentrum, Berlin.

Jacobs, K., and W. Schmähl. 1989. "The Process of Retirement in Germany: Trends, Public Discussion and Options for its Redefinition." In: W. Schmähl (ed.), *Redefining the Process of Retirement. An International Perspective.* Berlin: Springer, pp. 13–38.

Kaltenbach, H. 1986. "Probleme der Rentenversicherung bei den BU/EU-Renten einschließlich der Zukunftsperspektiven." *Die Angestellenversicherung* 33:357–61.

Kohli, M. 1987. "Retirement and the Moral Economy: An Historical Interpretation of the German Case." *Journal of Aging Studies* 1:125–44.

Forthcoming. "Labor Market Perspectives and Activity Patterns of the Elderly in an Aging Society." In: W. van den Heuvel et al. (eds.), *Opportunities and Challenges in an Aging Society.* Amsterdam: Elsevier.

Kohli, M., and H.-J. von Kondratowitz. 1987. "Retirement in Germany: Toward the Construction of the 'Citizen of the Work Society.'" In: K. S. Markides and C. L. Cooper (eds.), *Retirement in Industrialized Societies.* London: John Wiley & Sons, pp. 131–66.

Kohli, M., and J. Wolf. 1987. "Altergrenzen im Schnittpunkt von betrieblichen Interessen und individueller Lebensplanung. Das Beispiel des Vorruhestandes." *Soziale Welt* 38:92–109.

Kohli, M., et al. 1989. *Je früher – desto besser? Die Verkürzung des Erwerbslebens am Beispiel des Vorruhestands in der chemischen Industrie.* Berlin: Edition Sigma.

Mörschel, R., and U. Rehfeld. 1981. "Untersuchungen der Rentenzugänge im Zeitablauf. Teil I: Der Zugang an Berufs- und Erwerbsunfähigkeitsrenten in der Rentenversicherung der Arbeiter und der Angestellten – ein Maß für Umfang und Entwicklung der Invalidität?" *Deutsche Rentenversicherung* 4:234–53.

Naegele, G. (ed.). 1987. *Theorie und Praxis des Vorruhestandsgesetzes.* Augsburg: Maro.

OECD. 1988. *Ageing Populations: The Social Policy Implications.* Paris.

Orsinger, C. and P. Clausing. 1982. "Verkürzung der Lebensarbeitszeit im Spiegel der Rentenversicherung." *Die Angestelltenversicherung* 29:261–8.

Reimann, A. 1985. "Trend zur Frühverrentung noch ungebrochen." *Die Angestelltenversicherung* 32:406–13.

Schmähl, W. 1986. *Economic Problems of Social Retirement.* Studies and Documents No. 6 of the European Centre for Work and Society, Maastricht.

——— 1987. "Public and Private Pensions for Various Population Groups in the Federal Republic of Germany: Past Experience and Tasks for the Future." In: Internationl Social Security Association (ed.), *Conjugating Public and Private: The Case of Pensions.* Geneva: ISSA, pp. 57–79.

Schmähl, W., H. Conradi, K. Jacobs, R. Meierjürgen, and A. Prinz. 1986. *Soziale Sicherung 1975 1985. Verteilungswirkungen sozialpolitischer Maßnahmen in der Bundesrepublik Deutschland.* Frankfurt/Bern/New York: Lang.

Sozialbeirat. 1986. *Gutachten über eine Strukturreform zur längerfristigen Konsolidierung und systematischen Fortentwicklung der gesetzlichen Rentenversicherung im Rahmen der gesetzlichen Alterssicherung.* Bundestags-Drucksache 10/5332 vom 16. Apr. 1986.

Sozialbericht. 1986. Edited by Der Bundesminister für Arbeit und Sozialordnung, Bonn.

Wagner, G., E. Kirner, and J. Schupp. 1988. *Verteilungs-, sozial- und arbeitsmarktpolitische Bedeutung eines Teilrentensystems.* DIW-Gutachten im Auftrage des Ministers für Arbeit, Gesundheit and Soziales des Landes Nordrhein-Westfalen ("Stufenweise in den Ruhestand?"), Berlin.

Wasilewski, R., et al. 1984. *Frühinvalidisierung: Ergebnisse einer Untersuchung in Baden-Württemberg.* Stuttgart.

Winkler, G. (ed.). 1990. *Sozialreport 1990.* Berlin: Institut für Soziologie und Sozialpolitik der AdW der DDR.

Wolf, J. 1986. "Wie flexibel ist der flexible Ruhestand? Der 'Vorruhestand' als berufsbiographische Phase bei Beschäftigten der deutschen Zigarettenindustrie." In: H.-G. Brose (ed.), *Berufsbiographien im Wandel?* Opladen: Westdeutscher Verlag, pp. 194–219.

Wolf, J., and M. Kohli. 1988. "Neue Altersgrenzen des Arbeitslebens: Betriebliche Interessen und biographische Perspektiven." In: L. Rosenmayr and F. Kolland (eds.), *Arbeit – Freizeit – Lebenszeit.* Opladen: Westdeutscher Verlag, pp. 183–206.

Zacher, H. F. 1983. "Versorgung der Beamten, Richter und Soldaten." In: Sachverständigenkommission Alterssicherungssysteme, *Darstellung der Alterssicherungssysteme und der Besteuerung von Alterseinkommen.* Gutachten der Kommission, Berichtsband 2, Bonn, pp. 127–206.

Zöllner, D. 1982. "Germany." In: P. A. Köhler and H. F. Zacher (eds.), *The Evolution of Social Insurance 1881–1981. Studies of Germany, France, Great Britain, Austria and Switzerland.* London: Frances Pinter, pp. 1–92.

CHAPTER 7

Great Britain: The contradictions of early exit

FRANK LACZKO AND CHRIS PHILLIPSON

7.1 INTRODUCTION

IN the 1980s the British economy saw the establishment of a new phase in the development of retirement. This was reflected in the reduced proportion of older workers employed during the years preceding their eligibility for a state pension. Retirement emerged as a period that may commence before the receipt of a state pension, during which individuals are reliant upon a combination of private income and state benefits. Although this development meant that more older workers could be considered to be retired in terms of the accepted commonsense meaning of "giving up work" (Parker 1982), they reached this state through different types of retirement and different routes out of the labor market.

For many older men and women, especially those from manual occupations, the period spent out of the labor force, but not necessarily the period spent in retirement (in terms of drawing an old-age pension), is increasing. Thus the life span is being socially redefined in a more complex fashion, with a variety of routes being constructed to assist the individual's transition from full-time work to retirement. In this chapter we outline the relative importance of each of the various pathways out of the labor market. We call these pathways "exit" rather than "retirement" pathways to make clear that we are talking about people who in many cases have left the labor force because of sickness or unemployment and who do not necessarily regard themselves – in a subjective sense – as "retired" until they become eligible for a state old-age pension (Laczko 1988).

Our interest is in identifying the various ways both labor-market and social policies have shaped the pattern of early exit from the labor force. The questions we seek to answer are these: How is it that the age of exit from the labor force has fallen substantially in recent years even though the institutional arrangements that permit exit have not been substantially modified? Does the situation in the United Kingdom support the

222

view that early exit takes place regardless of what institutional routes are available? What has been the impact of social policy on the distribution of the costs of exit? How has government policy in the United Kingdom affected the access of older workers to early retirement and their incomes prior to the age of eligibility for a state pension? Who are the most important actors influencing the extent and pattern of early exit in the United Kingdom?

To advance our understanding of these questions, we need to gain a better understanding of the role played by different actors in the process of early exit. It is therefore useful to develop an institutional framework that describes the different exit pathways. For this purpose, the chapter is divided into five main parts. First, we review the historical background of early exit from work (section 7.2); second, we describe the different pathways to early exit (section 7.3); third, we review the incomes of those leaving work before the age of eligibility for a state pension (section 7.4); fourth, we consider whether those following the pathways described define themselves as retired (section 7.5); and finally, we consider some of the political debates surrounding early exit and the conflicting positions taken by different social actors (section 7.6).

7.2 THE HISTORICAL BACKGROUND OF EARLY EXIT

The position of older workers has been the subject of considerable debate in the postwar period (Phillipson 1982; Fennell, Phillipson, and Evers 1989). Each decade has seen, in different ways, vigorous debates on issues such as how to employ older men and (less commonly) older women in greater numbers, how best to utilize the skills and accumulated knowledge of older workers, how to combat age discrimination in the labor market, and how to increase the productivity of older workers and improve their performance in the workplace (National Advisory Committee on the Employment of Older Men and Women 1955; Fogarty 1975; Bosanquet 1987).

Other concerns have, at different times, influenced this debate on the older worker. In particular, the level of supply and demand for labor, the ratio of the economically dependent to economically active, and, last but not least, the overall state of the British economy (Phillipson 1982, 1991; Johnson, Conrad, and Thompson 1989).

In the late 1940s and 1950s there was an extensive debate on how the employment of older workers might be encouraged (Phillipson 1982). This interest in employing older people arose at that time for a number of reasons. First, Britain had an acute shortage of workers in the early

1950s, and older people were targeted as an important source of additional workers (Ministry of Labour and National Service 1953). Second, there was pessimism in the late 1940s and early 1950s about long-term demographic trends, with alarm being voiced about the economic implications of an aging population (Royal Commission on Population 1949). Third, forecasts of economic growth suggested a lengthy period of stagnation, a factor that increased the concern about the social demands likely to be made on the British economy (e.g., by people in retirement). One outcome of this concern about population and economic growth was a research and policy interest in retaining older people in the work force. Indicative of this was the funding of a number of research projects, from the late 1940s onward, focusing on issues such as retraining older workers, the adaptability of workers in middle and later life, and the performance of older workers in comparison with younger workers (Welford 1958, 1976; Dex and Phillipson 1986).

In general terms, the various projects found that chronological age was a poor guide to understanding work capacity and ability, and that individuals could adjust to and offset many of the changes affecting them in later life (Welford 1958). They also found that older workers who did experience a job change invariably experienced a loss of status and earnings, and were working well below their full potential (Heron and Chown 1967).

In policy terms, the implications of this research strengthened the case for keeping workers in their *existing* jobs (rather than moving them to new employment) but, at the same time, redesigning and modifying their work when necessary (Griew 1964).

7.2.1   The growth of early exit

As the economic need for older workers was reduced, so research pointed to their increasing difficulties in retaining a secure hold in the labor market. By the 1960s and early 1970s numerous studies documented the employment difficulties of older workers in settings as diverse as mining (Department of Employment 1970) and car assembly (MacKay 1973). MacKay's work suggested that redundant car workers beyond their mid-forties stood a much lower chance than younger workers even of being reengaged by their previous firm. Daniel's (1972) study of redundant workers indicated that the older the worker was the greater the likelihood of lower earnings in any subsequent employment. Fogarty's study *40 to 60: How We Waste the Middle Aged,* found a widespread tendency to bar middle-aged applicants from recruitment to professional and managerial jobs "[a] tendency [that] probably increased from the 1950s to the early 1970s" (Fogarty 1975:83).

The problems facing older workers were, however, largely ignored in the 1960s in the context of what was seen as a more fundamental issue affecting British industry – the problem of overstaffing. Low productivity came to be seen as a major influence on Britain's poor (by international standards) economic performance, and the government was searching for ways of rationalizing inefficient and unprofitable sections of industry (Glyn and Sutcliffe 1972). Britain's economic problems were deepened by the oil crisis in the winter of 1973–4, which was a contributory factor in the international recession of 1974 (Armstrong, Glyn, and Harrison 1984). These elements combined to consolidate the rising levels of unemployment that had begun to affect Britain by the late 1960s and early 1970s (Allen et al. 1986).

Against this background, the focus in labor policy was on the need for redundancies, "shake-outs," and early retirements. Britain's economic position (and the condition of its industry) demanded, it was argued, a smaller and more efficient work force. Given also that the postwar baby boom was producing a surfeit of young workers, it was the replacement of the old with the young that emerged as a significant element in labor policy. One aspect of this was the launch of the Job Release Scheme (JRS) in 1977 (see section 7.3.1), a measure that was introduced "with a view to creating job vacancies and otherwise mitigating the effects of high unemployment" (Department of Employment 1978). The scheme was set up to encourage older workers to leave their jobs on condition that their employer agreed to recruit a person registered as unemployed.

Another important means of influencing the age and occupational profile of industry was through the system of redundancy payments, which had been established by the Redundancy Payments Act of 1965. The act requires employers to make lump-sum payments to workers who lose their jobs because of reductions in the need for their labor. The thinking behind the legislation was that overstaffing was a major barrier to economic expansion and that the payments would, first, secure greater acceptance of the need for technological change and, second, help to redeploy workers to new jobs. In fact, the effects of the act were felt most keenly by older workers, with age becoming an important criterion for determining who was redundant (Parker et al. 1971; Martin and Fryer 1973; House of Commons 1989). A study by the Department of Employment concluded that "[redundancy acts] as a social mechanism [removing] from the labour force older people who are nearing retirement after long service, by means of comparatively generous compensation" (Jolly,

Creigh, and Mingay 1980). And, of course, once having been made redundant, older workers (particularly those aged 60 to 64) either remained unemployed or entered early retirement (McGoldrick and Cooper 1989).

In fact, given the pressures facing British industry from the late 1960s onward, older workers were always likely to be the most directly affected. This was the case because, in the period under discussion, Britain had an aging work force, particularly in industries such as agriculture, mining, and vehicles (for men), and metal goods, textiles, food, gas, electricity, and water (for women). The implications of this for the workers involved were spelled out in a study by the Department of Employment:

In terms of the changing age profiles of industries it may be noted that the decline in the older male employment is consistent with older men working in slow-growing industries with lower earnings, and that older females (whose employment has increased) are associated with undynamic labour-intensive industries. Neither in terms of the number employed nor of the work situation does the employment position of the older worker appear to be entirely satisfactory. (Jolly et al. 1980:80)

7.2.2   The institutionalization of early exit

The exit of older men and women from the labor force accelerated throughout the 1970s and 1980s (see Chapter 2). Early retirement, as Laczko and Walker (1985) comment, emerged as the only policy measure to combat unemployment that was supported by both Left and Right of the political spectrum.

The growth of early retirement was, of course, closely linked to the emergence of mass unemployment. Indeed, as Jackson (1984) observes, its acceleration from the mid-1970s onward must be seen "as a response to unemployment rather than as the response to a demand for change on its own merits from any section of industry." The key factors that consolidated the drift of older workers from employment were (1) the decline in semiskilled and unskilled jobs (Bosanquet 1983), (2) the entry or reentry into the labor market of women workers and the willingness of employers to accommodate them at lower wages (Townsend 1979), (3) the growth – through occupational pension schemes – of financial provision for early retirement on the grounds of ill health, and (4) the growing number (albeit a minority) who chose early retirement as a positive and valued alternative to full-time work (McGoldrick and Cooper 1989).

The development of high levels of unemployment is crucial for understanding the dynamics of early exit. Thus, as many commentators have pointed out, present conditions may lead some workers to accept early exit not because they really want to do so, but because of workplace pressure or their own view that retirement may lead to a younger person getting a job (Bytheway 1986; Walker 1989). Such pressures may be felt most keenly by unskilled and semiskilled workers, who are more likely than white-collar workers to suffer from ill health and to work in industries experiencing long-term decline and/or technological change.

In conclusion, our argument suggests that from the 1970s onward, older workers were increasingly marginalized in the labor force. This arose through: (1) their concentration, in many cases, in contracting industries; (2) the operation of particular schemes to promote worker redeployment (e.g., the Redundancy Payments Act) or replacement (the Job Release Scheme); (3) the pressure of mass unemployment; and (4) changing attitudes among government, business, trade unions, and older people themselves with regard to the older workers' right to employment in relation to other, younger age groups. The impact of these changes on economic activity rates were analyzed in Chapter 2. In the next section of this chapter we review the pathways out of the labor market taken by older workers.

7.3 PATHWAYS TO EARLY EXIT

In the United Kingdom, unlike in many other European countries, public measures in favor of early retirement have been, until recently, highly selective and limited in scope. Nevertheless, in the United Kingdom as elsewhere, the trend toward early exit from the labor force has been marked in recent years. As we saw in Chapter 2, the fall in the employment rate of British men aged 55 to 64 since 1970 is comparable to the fall that has occurred in other "high-exit" countries (e.g., France and Germany) where public provision for early exit has been greater.

The figures for 1985 in Chapter 2 (Table 2.1) show that although the United Kingdom tends to have a somewhat higher participation rate and employment rate for older men than countries such as France and Germany, this difference exists mainly because the United Kingdom began the 1970s with a higher participation and employment rate among this age group. The decrease in the employment rate between 1970 and 1985 has actually been quite similar in the United Kingdom, France, and Germany. In all three countries there has been a 27 to 30 percent fall since 1970. In 1970 the employment activity rates for men aged 55 to 64 in

France, Germany, and the United Kingdom were 74 percent, 81.5 percent and 86.7 percent, respectively. By 1985 the figures for the three countries were 46.7 percent for France, 51.6 percent for Germany, and 57.5 percent for the United Kingdom. These figures suggest that perhaps rule changes explain less of the decline in the employment rates of older men in recent years for the United Kingdom than for other high-exit countries. We shall next examine what institutional mechanisms exist in the United Kingdom that facilitate exit and how they became pathways of early exit that could be taken before the ages at which the state retirement pension was available (60 for women and 65 for men.).[1]

In the United Kingdom we can identify four main pathways of early exit:

1. Public preretirement (until 1988 the Job Release Scheme)
2. Unemployment/long-term social assistance
3. Sickness
4. Occupational pensions/enterprise route

7.3.1   *The Job Release Scheme: The public preretirement pathway*

The social security system in the United Kingdom does not allow for the early receipt of a state pension, but between 1977 and 1988 the government enabled some older workers to retire early via the Job Release Scheme (JRS). JRS was a special temporary employment measure that allowed specific categories of full-time older workers to retire early, on the condition that their jobs were filled by job seekers who were unemployed.

No individual had the right to choose to join the scheme. Acceptance depended on whether the employer would provide a new job for someone who was unemployed. Eligibility criteria for the scheme were altered on a number of occasions (see Table 7.1) in response to changes in employment and unemployment, and government public expenditure requirements.

Between 1977 and 1988 more than 250,000 individuals took advantage of JRS, 80 percent of whom were males. Coverage of JRS was at a peak of 95,000 on April 1, 1984, but declined substantially later in the 1980s. By June 1987 only 22,000 people were receiving JRS allowances

---

[1] The retirement pension is paid to men at age 65 and women at age 60 provided that they have left the work force. Both men and women can opt to delay their pension for up to five years. Those who defer receiving their pension receive a small additional pension. The pension is paid at two rates, one for a single pension and one for a married couple (in 1991 the rates were £52.00 for a single person and £83.25 for a married couple). A small supplement is paid to those aged 80 and over.

Table 7.1. *Main policy changes in the Job Release Scheme*

Date	Change
Full-time JRS	
January 3, 1977	Scheme introduced. Applied to employed and unemployed people within one year of the National Insurance (NI) retirement pension age (59 for women, 64 for men) in the Assisted Areas.
July 1, 1977	Scheme restricted to persons in *full-time employment* in Assisted Areas.
April 1, 1978	Extended to cover persons in full-time employment within one year of NI retirement age in Great Britain.
May 1, 1979–March 31, 1980	Scheme extended to men aged 62 and 63 and disabled men aged 60 and over.
April 6, 1980	Scheme open to the following groups of workers in full-time employment in Great Britain: Men aged 64 Women aged 59 Disabled men aged 60 to 63.
November 1, 1981–March 31, 1984	Scheme also open to men aged 63.
February 1, 1982–March 31, 1984	Scheme also open to men aged 62.
January 31, 1988	Scheme closes for applications.
Part-time JRS	
August 8, 1983	Part-time scheme opens for application. (Allowances paid from October 3, 1983.) Open to: Women aged 59 Men aged 62 to 63 Disabled men aged 60 to 61.
March 31, 1986	Closure of part-time scheme.

Source: House of Commons (1989).

(see Table 7.2). This seems to be because JRS was restricted after April 1, 1984, to able-bodied men aged 64.

However, even during the period when the age span of the scheme was greatest (in 1979–80), take-up by eligible males was only 12 percent (Makeham and Morgan 1980). For the years 1983–4, when similar conditions of entry were applicable, a take-up rate of 6 percent for females and 11 percent for males was calculated (Bushell 1984). The EC Labour Force Survey 1981 suggests that about 56,000 economically active males aged 60 to 64 entered early retirement during 1980–1. It also suggests

Table 7.2. *Coverage of full-time Job Release Scheme*

Year supported	Numbers supported[a]
1977	11,700
1978	13,100
1979	37,600
1980	63,800
1981	54,900
1982	68,400
1983	81,700
1984	88,200
1985	60,600
1986	36,200
1987	22,000

[a] Numbers supported are an average of monthly observations.
Source: House of Commons (1989).

Table 7.3. *JRS new entrants by financial years and by scheme type (thousands)*

Financial year	Women	Men, 62–64	Disabled men, 60–61	Total
1980–1	7	10	8	25
1981–2	6	27	9	42
1982–3	5	36	5	46
1983–4	5	39	5	49

Source: Bushell (1984:11).

that about 24,000 females entered early retirement during the same period. Of these new entrants probably a third were JRS recipients, as there were 25,000 new entrants to the JRS scheme in 1980–1 (Bushell 1984). In later years the importance of JRS was probably even greater as the number of new entrants to JRS rose to 49,000 in 1983–4 (Table 7.3). As Table 7.3 shows, the bulk of this increase was due to a rise in the number of able-bodied men aged 62 to 64 taking early retirement. The numbers of women and disabled men entering the scheme actually declined in the period up to 1984.

Unlike preretirement benefits in a number of other countries, the Job Release Allowance was not earnings related, but paid at a flat rate. This explains in part why take-up of the scheme was low and why the overwhelming majority of recipients were low-paid semiskilled and

Table 7.4. *JRS successful applicants by social class (percentages of total entrants)*

Class[a]	All adults in full-time work, 1982	JRS applicants 1984	JRS applicants 1978
Higher or intermediate managerial, administrative, or professional	18	7	4
Supervisory, clerical, junior managerial, administrative, or professional	25	22	20
Skilled manual	37	29	25
Semiskilled and unskilled manual	21	42	51

[a]Class of applicants based on last job.
Source: Bushell (1984:16).

Table 7.5. *JRS successful applicants by industry, 1983–4*

Division/class	Industry	JRS applicants (%)	All workers (%)
Div. 0	Agriculture, forestry, fishing	0.9	1.8
Div. 1	Energy and water supply	1.9	3.1
Div. 2	Mining/metal, mineral, chemical manufacture	3.1	3.9
Div. 3	Metal goods, engineering vehicles	19.8	12.5
Div. 4	Other manufacturing	11.5	10.4
Div. 5	Construction	3.9	4.9
Div. 6	Distribution, hotels, catering, repairs	14.3	19.6
Div. 7	Transport and communication	11.2	6.4
Div. 8	Banking, finance, insurance business services, leasing	2.1	8.6
Div. 9			
Class 91	Public administration, national defense, social security	20.6	7.6
Class 93	Education	3.4	7.2
Class 95	Medical, health, veterinary services	4.6	6.2
Rest of Div. 9	Other services	2.5	7.8

Source: Bushell (1984:14).

unskilled workers (Table 7.4) (Bushell 1984). JRS was financially unattractive to people who were receiving above average or average wages and who would not be able to supplement JRS with a pension from their employer (Makeham and Morgan 1980:34). In 1983–4, 64 percent of successful applicants held occupational pensions; this perhaps explains why JRS applicants are overrepresented in the public sector because manual workers in this sector are more likely to have an occupational pension than those in the private sector (Table 7.5).

7.3.2   *The unemployment pathway*

In the absence of alternative preretirement options to JRS, high numbers of older workers, mainly those from manual occupations (Laczko et al. 1988), have had to rely on unemployment benefits and social assistance paid as a result of unemployment in the years approaching the age of eligibility for a state pension. Since November 1981 all unemployed men aged 60 and over who have been out of work for over a year and who are entitled to supplementary benefit (now called income support) have been able to claim the long-term rate of supplementary benefit and no longer have to register as unemployed. This measure was extended in 1983 to all unemployed men aged 60 and over irrespective of their duration of unemployment. By comparison, there remains no special assistance for unemployed older women.

Another important change that came into effect in 1983 was the removal of the requirement for men aged 60 and over to register as unemployed in order to obtain contribution credits for the purpose of safeguarding their entitlement to a retirement pension when they reach 65. Retirement pension credits are now automatically awarded to fill any gaps in the contribution of men between the ages of 60 and 65, whether the gaps were due to low earnings or to unemployment. To some extent the unemployment rate of men aged 60 to 64 had been inflated because of this factor up until 1983. Between April and August 1983, 162,000 older men were no longer included in the unemployment count. In July 1982 the unemployment rate of men aged 60 and over was 19.7 percent. By July 1983 the rate had been halved to 9.6 percent. Of those who were removed from the unemployment figures, the Department of Employment estimated that about 85,000 persons had registered as unemployed to safeguard their contribution record. However, it cannot automatically be assumed that these people would not have taken a job if suitable employment had been available. Earlier surveys of unemployed men in the group aged 60 to 64 show that a high proportion were "keen" to work (Donaldson 1979).

As unemployment has become increasingly prolonged, more and more unemployed older workers have ceased looking for work, or at least have become less active job seekers, but do not have formal retirement status, although many may regard themselves as being retired. In 1983, 42 percent of unemployed women aged 50 to 59 who were receiving unemployment benefit were not actively looking for work (Laczko 1987).

Given their poor reemployment prospects, it is not surprising that many unemployed workers stop looking for work. For example, in 1985

Table 7.6. *Older male claimants by reason not seeking work (percentages)*[a]

Reasons not seeking work	Aged 50–59		Aged 60–64	
	1981	1983	1981	1983
In paid job	11	11	5	7
Discouraged worker	29	28	27	24
Retired	8	10	33	33
Sick/disabled	22	23	15	16
Others[b]	26	23	9	13
Total	100	100	100	100
	(131)	(566)	(143)	(545)

[a] Percentages rounded.
[b] Includes those temporarily sick or waiting to start a new job and those on holiday.
Source: Labour Force Surveys 1981, 1983; our own calculations.

a quarter of unemployed men aged 45 and over had not worked for three years or more. Of the latter, nearly half had not worked for five years (LMQR 1986). A significant proportion of older unemployed workers fall into the "discouraged worker" category; that is, they have given up looking for work because they believe there are no jobs. In Table 7.6 we examine the main reasons given by older unemployed workers in 1981 and 1983 for not seeking work. The most important reason given by over a quarter of men aged 50 to 59 was that "they believed no jobs were available." Roughly a quarter of men aged 60 to 64 also gave this reason, but a somewhat higher proportion, around a third, said they were not looking for work because they considered themselves to be retired. A significant proportion of men aged 50 to 59 and 60 to 64 said they were not looking for work because they were too sick to work (23 percent and 16 percent, respectively).

Thus, although these older men appear in the official U.K. unemployment figures, which are based on the numbers of persons receiving unemployment-related benefits, their views suggest that they have left the labor force. Despite the fact that many may not be receiving occupational pensions and few will be receiving invalidity benefit, a substantial proportion seem to regard themselves as being sick/disabled or retired rather than unemployed or falling into the "discouraged worker" category. In short, a high percentage of unemployed older workers have effectively exited from the labor force in the United Kingdom, with unemployment benefits themselves becoming a key measure facilitating early exit.

7.3.3   The health pathway

In the United Kingdom labor market "chances" are not explicitly taken into consideration when invalidity benefit is awarded to older workers, in contrast to some other European countries (see, in particular, the discussion of the relevant policy changes in Germany, Chapter 6). However, although this is not official policy, an increasing number of older workers on invalidity benefit have been leaving the labor market early in recent years and a substantial part of the decrease in older men's activity rates is accounted for by a rise in the proportion of older men defining themselves as disabled. In contrast to many other countries, an individual in the United Kingdom does not have to have a fixed level of disability before he or she can receive invalidity benefit. It is usually left to a doctor to judge whether they are incapable of working and to provide the relevant medical certificate. No doubt such judgments vary according to the labor-market situation. Some research suggests that part of the increase in disability is attributable to the general rise in unemployment.

Piachaud (1986), for example, examined data drawn from the Censuses of England for 1971 and 1981. The Census return provides self-reported information about self-defined economic positions, and therefore categories such as retired and disabled are not directly comparable with social security categories (e.g., a man who says he is retired could be receiving unemployment benefit). Piachaud found that in 1981, 6 percent of men aged 55 to 59 and 11 percent of men aged 60 to 64 fell into the disabled category: These were roughly doubly the proportions in 1971. Why has there been an increase in disability? Using Census data for the 46 counties of England, Piachaud related changes in disability, retirement, and economic activity to chang s in unemployment. He found that a substantial proportion of the overall increase in disability and the decline in economic activity is attributable to the increase in unemployment.

The evidence suggests that unemployment itself is not the direct cause of the increase in disability. If the experience of unemployment did lead to future disability, then it might be expected that disability would rise among younger men and women as well as among older men; this has not been the case. Piachaud shows that while the proportions of disabled have risen for all these age groups, the increases have been very much smaller than for older men. Therefore it appears that as labor-market conditions have deteriorated more older men have been seeking and have settled for the status of "disabled." In terms of the class background of these men, data from the General Household Surveys 1980–2 confirm that by far the majority (79 percent) of men aged 60 to 64 who define themselves as sick or disabled were employed in manual occupations (Laczko et al. 1988). We also know that nearly all the men aged 60 to 64 who defined themselves as sick or disabled were receiving sickness or invalidity benefits (Laczko et al. 1988).

For the older individual, "disabled" status has a number of advantages. First, social security benefits for the disabled are higher than those received by the unemployed. In 1971 the unemployment benefit was paid at the same rate as the invalidity benefits, but by 1981 disabled people received about one-third more (Laczko 1988:159). Second, the unemployment benefit is only paid for a year whereas the invalidity benefit can be paid until age 70. Third, there may be less stigma associated with being classified as disabled rather than unemployed.

7.3.4 *Occupational pensions/enterprise route*

The other option available to some workers wishing to leave work ahead of normal retirement age was to draw an occupational pension. Over half (51 percent) of the work force in the United Kingdom were covered by occupational pension schemes in 1985 (European Commission 1987). Coverage is much greater in the public sector than in the private sector. Three-quarters of public-sector workers have an occupational pension compared with just over a third of private-sector workers (Miller 1982). There are also important class and gender divisions. A survey by the Equal Opportunities Commission in 1983 found only 52 percent of male manual workers and 18 percent of female manual workers to be members of occupational pension schemes; in the case of nonmanual workers the figures were 72 percent for men and 40 percent for women (see also Groves 1991). In some schemes the normal retirement age is below the age required for a state pension (65 for men and 60 for women), but in most occupational pension schemes this is not the case and if employees retire earlier at their own request they receive reduced benefits, unless their employer supplements their income. Women also lose out if they do part-time work for lengthy periods (as the majority do). The result of this may be a reduced pension from the various options that may be available (e.g., the state earnings-related pension scheme, a pension from an employer, or a "personal pension").

In the private sector, although it is less common to find schemes with lower retirement ages, virtually all occupational pension schemes provide members with the right to an early retirement pension in cases of ill health and inability to continue working (Government Actuary 1979). It is also possible for an individual to opt to take early retirement for his or her own reasons, but this usually means a substantial loss of potential pension income. However, when it is also in the interests of the firm for an individual to take early retirement, either for staff-cutting purposes or because a reorganization is taking place, a company may use discretionary clauses in the occupational pension scheme to pay a full pension (Brown and Small 1985:191).

During the 1960s most British companies did not have a standard policy in their treatment of early retirement (McGoldrick 1982). From the mid-1970s onward, however, surveys of the National Association of Pension Funds show the increasing prevalence of early-retirement arrangements, on an established basis. By the 1980s nearly all (95 percent) schemes made specific provisions for employees to retire early voluntarily. A survey of manufacturing establishments conducted in 1978–9 found that the use of early retirement by employers to manage reductions in their work force was widespread and the numbers retiring early were considerably increased when occupational pension schemes provided early retirement options. Indeed, it was found that early-retirement policy at the level of the firm or establishment is possible only when there has been the prior development of occupational pension schemes (White 1980).

Later studies have shown that early retirement continues to be used on a substantial scale by employers to effect reductions in head count (IMS 1983, 1987). However, a study of 40 large organizations with well-established occupational pension schemes suggests that managers are becoming more sophisticated in their use of early-retirement packages (IMS 1987). There is a trend away from open-access early-retirement schemes, toward targeted, closed-access schemes. The latter are particularly found in the service sector. Closed-access packages are aimed at a target population, usually defined by the type of job or specific individuals. They are associated with work-force pruning rather than wholesale rapid shutdown. Such arrangements are frequently used by employing organizations as a tool for managing careers and aiding organizational and technological change.

Figures for 1983 for men aged 60 to 64 show that 17 percent of those not in employment were inactive occupational pensioners who were not receiving Invalidity Benefit, Supplementary Benefit, or the Job Release Allowance and were not unemployed (Table 7.7). The relative importance of this route compared with others can be seen in Table 7.7. The

Table 7.7. *Benefit status of men aged 60–64 not in employment in 1983*

Status	Percent of all men[a]	Percent of whom had an occupational pension
Unemployed	32	(53)
Invalidity Benefit	28	(54)
Job Release Allowance	11.7	(50)
Long-term Supplementary Benefit and not registered as unemployed	5.7	—
Inactive Occupational Pensioners not included above	17	(100)
Other (includes other supplementary benefit and unregistered unemployed)	5.6	—
Total	100	

[a]Total population: 700,000.
Source: Adapted from unpublished table supplied to authors from DHSS 1983.

most important benefits in 1983 were the unemployment benefit, received by 32 percent of men, and the invalidity benefit, received by 28 percent. Since 1983 the importance of long-term supplementary benefit as a source of income for men who leave work early has increased substantially, while the importance of the Job Release Allowance has gradually declined.

For the period in the 1970s and 1980s when early exit increased rapidly, the occupational pension route showed a marked degree of stratification, both in terms of the likelihood of certain groups receiving an occupational pension and the amount of pension received. This is illustrated by data from the General Household Survey (GHS), a continuous survey of the adult population in Great Britain. Victor (1989) has undertaken a secondary analysis of the 1980 GHS, focusing on income inequality among those 65 and over. Tables 7.8 and 7.9 confirm the extent of class, age, and gender differentiation in occupational pension provision. The data also support the view that, on its own, this route of exit from the labor force was of significance only to nonmanual groups. A near majority of male manual workers aged 65 to 69 were not in receipt of an occupational pension; for those who were, and taking social classes 4 and 5, the median weekly payment was just £19. For manual workers, therefore, these data confirm the importance of the unemployment benefit and the invalidity benefit pathways (findings confirmed in the survey by McGoldrick and Cooper [1989]).

Table 7.8. *Percentages of elderly persons receiving occupational pensions by social class, age, and sex*

| Social class | Age and sex | | | | | | | | | |
| | 65–69 | | 70–74 | | 75–79 | | 80+ | | All ages | |
	M	F	M	F	M	F	M	F	M	F
1 and 2	76	28	68	17	53	41	68	36	64	24
3n	64	23	60	25	53	33	40	25	52	25
3m	55	17	44	17	47	11	56	25	48	17
4 and 5	55	11	46	16	39	16	34	15	46	14
All classes	57	16	48	17	44	21	43	18	51	18
N	698	809	507	611	298	476	195	367	1,698	2,263

Source: Cited in Victor 1989.

Table 7.9. *Median weekly payment of occupational pension by social class, age, and sex (to the nearest pound)*

| Age | Sex | Social class | | | | | | | |
| | | 1 and 2 | | 3n | | 3m | | 4 and 5 | |
		£	N	£	N	£	N	£	N
65–69	M	140	69	65	96	26	141	19	94
	F	132	11	40	63	19	15	19	46
70–74	M	130	51	29	52	26	79	21	60
	F	93	9	20	40	19	12	19	44
75–79	M	125	35	47	23	29	48	14	26
	F	103	11	50	42	11	6	19	40
80+	M	135	12	45	20	17	38	14	20
	F	48	4	20	32	19	13	19	27

Source: Cited in Victor 1989.

7.3.5   Reasons for leaving work early

We have already noted the importance of the health pathway in the United Kingdom and that part of the increase in disability that has occurred is attributable to the rise in unemployment. It is also the case that a substantial and rising proportion of older workers enter retirement after long-term unemployment, and after receiving social assistance (supplementary benefit or income support). These facts cast some doubt on the voluntary nature of early exit. Recent research, from the British Labour Force Survey, on those defining themselves as "early retired" provides further evidence of the current pressure on older workers to leave the labor force early (Laczko et al. 1988).

Among men aged 60 to 64 who had retired early, the main reason given for leaving their last job among those who had left work in the three years before the survey was that their employer had introduced an early-retirement scheme in order to reduce the work force. Men from manual occupations were more likely than men from nonmanual occupations to give this reason (62 percent compared with 47 percent). Men who retired early from manual occupations were also more likely than those from nonmanual occupations to have left their last job because of redundancy or dismissal (14 percent compared with 3 percent). Unlike earlier investigators (see, for example, Parker 1982), Laczko et al. (1988) did not find that ill health was a major reason for early retirement. Thus it is clear that older manual workers are the ones who have been excluded from the labor market most often. They are more vulnerable to unemployment, and even the minority who consider themselves to have retired early are more likely to have retired because their employer was cutting back on personnel.

7.4 POVERTY, EARLY EXIT, AND OLD AGE

Unlike those in many other European countries, state preretirement benefits in the United Kingdom are not earnings related. Moreover, as we have seen, the "social assistance" pathway to early exit is particularly important in the United Kingdom, probably more important than in any other European country. There is also a higher incidence of poverty among the elderly in the United Kingdom than in a number of other OECD countries (Hedstrom and Ringen 1987). It is therefore perhaps not surprising to find that men who leave the labor force early in the United Kingdom have a high risk of living in, or on the margins of, poverty (Laczko et al. 1988).

A study of the incomes of married men aged 60 to 64 who defined themselves as retired, sick, or unemployed found that 25 percent of the nonmanual "nonemployed" and 51 percent of the manual "nonemployed" had incomes in or on the margins of poverty during the years 1980–2 (Laczko et al. 1988). The poverty line used in the study was the long-term rate of supplementary benefit (social assistance) that is payable to the elderly, which is the definition of poverty most often used in U.K. studies concerned with assessing pensioner poverty. Those with incomes up to 140 percent of this level are conventionally considered to be on the margin of poverty. Current levels of poverty among older men who have left the labor force early are likely to be even higher given that the research refers to years prior to 1983 when all unemployed men aged 60 and over were unable to withdraw from the labor force on social assistance. Within the early-exit population, men describing themselves as early retired tend to have higher incomes than the sick or the unemployed. For example, whereas over half of those who retired early from manual occupations had incomes above the 140 percent of supplementary benefit level, only slightly over a third of the unemployed manual workers and just under half of the sick manual workers had incomes above this level.

The low incomes of the early-exit population and in particular of men from manual occupations can be attributed to their overwhelming reliance on state benefits and the low level of these benefits. For example, two-thirds of the average gross income per week of "poor" early-retired couples, that is, couples with incomes below 140 percent of the supplementary benefit level, is from state benefits, mainly long-term benefits, whereas the corresponding figure for "non-poor" early-retired couples is less than a quarter (23 percent). Avoiding poverty in early retirement entails having other sources of income and in particular a good occupational pension, which, as we noted earlier, manual workers are less likely to have. Even those older manual workers who are members of occupational pension schemes are often at a disadvantage because schemes often base their calculation of the pension on the final year's salary of the individual. This results in a lower level of benefit for manual workers, whose earnings tend to decline past middle age.

Even if early exit does not force older workers into poverty, in the short-term they are still likely to have lost some income given that their contribution record will be shorter, and the fact that they will have to live for a longer period on a lower income may increase the likelihood of relative poverty in later years. Research across a number of countries has documented the fact that length of time since last employment is an important factor in the incidence and depth of poverty among the very elderly (see especially Shanas et al. 1968).

What is not yet clear is what the effect of the rise in numbers of older men and to a lesser extent older women leaving the labor force early will be on poverty and inequality among the elderly in the United Kingdom. Recent evidence suggests that because the dispersion of incomes among nonemployed men aged 60 to 64 is substantially greater than among retired men aged 65 to 69 it is likely that the extent of inequality in income within the elderly population will increase (see Laczko 1988).

However, this may not necessarily lead to an increase in relative poverty among the elderly, if the modest improvement in the incomes of the elderly as a whole in the United Kingdom continues (Laczko 1988). Instead what might happen is a widening of inequalities among older people (Victor 1989).

7.5 DO THOSE WHO LEAVE EMPLOYMENT EARLY SEE THEMSELVES AS RETIRED?

We have outlined the early-exit options that exist according to the benefits available to people who leave work early. Another way of examining the pattern of early exit that has emerged is to consider the way in which people who have left the labor force early define themselves in large government surveys such as the Labour Force Survey and the General Household Survey. The Labour Force Survey, for example, allows nonworkers to classify themselves into six groups: the unemployed (those without jobs but actively seeking work), the "discouraged" (those who are not looking for work because they believe no jobs are available), the long-term sick, the retired, those not wanting jobs, and "others."

Before presenting our findings it is important to point out that these categories are not completely arbitrary subjective headings. There is a fairly close correlation between the type of benefits people receive and the way in which they define their status (Laczko et al. 1988). For example, nearly all those who define themselves as long-term sick receive invalidity benefit, and the majority of those who see themselves as unemployed receive unemployment benefit.

Tables 7.10 and 7.11 provide an indication of the relative importance of different routes out of the labor force for men and women between 1979 and 1986, according to how they define their status. Even though the absolute number of older men and women defining themselves as retired has increased in recent years in Britain, the increase in those citing other reasons for not being in employment has been even greater. The inappropriateness of the "early-retirement" label with respect to older nonworkers is apparent from Table 7.10, which shows that in 1986 only one in eight men aged 55 to 59 and only just over a third of men aged 60 to 64 categorize themselves as "retired" (Casey and Laczko 1989).

A similar trend is apparent among women. The proportion of older women not in employment who describe themselves as retired has declined since 1979 and was only 11 percent in 1986. It is particularly striking that the proportion of women aged 60 to 64 who say they are retired has dropped significantly from 64 percent to 50.2 percent. Given that the absolute number of women outside of the labor force rose during

Table 7.10. *Older nonworking men by age and current status, 1979 and 1986*

	55–59		60–64	
Status	1979 (%)	1986 (%)	1979 (%)	1986 (%)
Unemployed	26.8	27.6	13.5	9.4
Discouraged	1.6	10.6	1.8	10.1
Long-term sick	53.8	36.7	30.1	34.2
Retired	11.7	13.1	49.6	36.4
Does not want job	0.9	4.8	1.1	5.7
Other	5.2	7.4	3.0	4.3
All not employed	100.0	100.0	100.0	100.0
	(199,644)	(383,342)	(376,798)	(725,510)

Source: 1979 and 1986 Labour Force Surveys; Casey and Laczko (1989).

Table 7.11. *Older nonworking women by age and current status, 1979 and 1986*

	55–59		60–64	
Status	1979 (%)	1986 (%)	1979 (%)	1986 (%)
Unemployed	4.6	5.8	0.7	0.9
Discouraged	0.2	4.9	0.04	1.6
Long-term sick	9.3	16.8	2.2	7.0
Retired	13.3	10.9	64.0	50.2
Does not want job	0.6	20.5	0.1	15.1
Other, looking after home	72.1	41.0	32.9	24.7
All not employed	100.0	100.0	100.0	100.0
	(852,112)	(772,112)	(1,105,943)	(1,267,363)

Source: Our own calculations of 1979 and 1986 Labour Force Survey data.

this period, much of this decline was relative. Nonetheless, Table 7.11 does reveal the growing importance of other exit routes for older women. In particular, there has been a significant rise in the proportion of older women leaving the labor force early who describe themselves as long-term sick or disabled. In 1979, 9.3 percent of women aged 55 to 59 fell into this category compared with 16.8 percent in 1986. As we saw at the beginning of this chapter, most of the early-exit options that exist are primarily for men. Older women are less likely to have a good occupational pension, they are not able to claim the long-term rate of supplementary benefit, and the Job Release Scheme was only open to women aged 59. Invalidity benefit therefore provides an especially important means by which older women can leave the labor force early.

However, as expected, by far the majority of women fall into the "looking after home and other" category. This category has substantially declined in importance since 1979. A large proportion of this category will be women who have never been employed, but among this group there are also women who have left the labor market early to care for a sick relative. One in six women aged 55 to 59 who leave employment early do so in order to care for a relative in poor health. It is perhaps not surprising therefore that these women do not define themselves as retired. They may have retired from employment, but they have not retired from work (Ungerson 1990).

There is a general difficulty in applying the concept of retirement to women (Dex and Phillipson 1986). Retirement most accurately describes what happens to men who leave paid employment in later life, but it is less useful in describing the experience of older women. Even at age 60 (the pensionable age for women), two-thirds of women who are not employed do not describe themselves as retired.

Equally apparent, however, is the inappropriateness of the character-ization of older nonworkers as unemployed. Only a quarter of men aged 55 to 59 and a tenth of men aged 60 to 64 described themselves as "unemployed." Despite the deterioration of the labor market, this pro-portion actually fell slightly for 60- to 64-year-olds between 1979 and 1986. However, among women aged 55 to 59 the proportion of unem-ployed rose somewhat, from 4 to 6 percent in 1979 to 5.8 percent in 1986. Indicative of the growing number in the age range from 55 to 64 with an indeterminate status is the rapid growth of the discouraged-worker cat-egory, which accounted for 10 percent of all older male nonworkers in 1986 compared with well under 2 percent in 1979. Among women aged 55 to 59, the proportion of discouraged workers was insignificant in 1979, but was almost 5 percent in 1986. Also growing fast was the cat-egory of those claiming not to want a job, an insignificant proportion in 1979 but 1 in 20 of the older nonemployed in 1986 (Casey and Laczko 1989). Among women aged 55 to 59 the growth in this category has been even greater, rising from less than 1 percent to over 20 percent.

7.6 THE POLITICS OF EARLY EXIT

In the section 7.2 we discussed the growth of early exit in Britain from the 1950s onward. Section 7.3 provided a detailed commentary on the pattern on withdrawal and the pathways followed by different groups of workers. In this final section we explore the attitudes of key political actors toward early exit, focusing in particular on government, the trade unions, business organizations, and the voluntary sector.

Chapter 2 suggested that early exit had been facilitated because of its popularity with most of the actors involved. According to this argument, early exit is the product of a cooperative effort on the part of management, trade unions, and older workers themselves, with the state intervening either to create new routes or to allow the use of existing routes out of the labor market. However, in the case of Britain this observation is only partially accurate. Indeed, the approach to early exit, through the 1970s and 1980s, has functioned at two levels. On the one hand, the majority of political actors have advocated a flexible system of retirement, with the possibility of individuals working beyond normal retirement age as well as retiring before it. On the other hand, within the context of high levels of unemployment, there has been a tendency to accelerate the pace of early exit, through, for example, the modification of pension schemes, the use of redundancy payments, and the development of special programs such as the Job Release Scheme (see section 7.3.1). In fact, developments in the 1980s confirm the validity of the view that the state has used older workers as a reserve army of labor to be ejected or encouraged to stay at work, according to perceptions of demographic change and the likely supply of younger workers (Phillipson 1982). Although this has been criticized as a "conspiratorial interpretion of the process of early retirement" (Johnson et al. 1989), it appears to have strong empirical support from the experience of older workers over the past 10 years.

7.6.1 *Perspectives on retirement*

The case for a flexible retirement system has been made by a range of organizations and actors. Evidence for this can be found in submissions to the House of Commons Social Services Committee when it investigated the age of retirement. Here we find a virtual consensus among the organizations and individuals called to give evidence that a flexible system of retirement was both a realistic and a desirable goal of social policy. The Confederation of British Industry (CBI) argued that there should "as a matter of urgency" be flexibility for people to retire early on a reduced pension. At the same time, increased pensions should also be given to those who defer "retirement," thus creating a "valuable incentive to persuade key workers to continue in employment" (House of Commons 1982:275).

Age Concern England, one of the major voluntary organizations campaigning on behalf of older people, put forward the following proposal: "A flexible retirement system should be introduced with legislation to ensure that there is no compulsory retirement, on age related grounds, before the age of 70. Any minimum pension age should not, in effect, become a compulsory retirement age and legislation would be essential if the minimum pension age is lowered" (House of Commons 1982:241).

At the same time, it would be misleading to suggest that there has been total consensus regarding the adoption of a flexible retirement age. The two major exceptions, in Britain at least, have been the trade unions and pressure groups representing working-class pensioners. For these organizations, the main demand has been for a retirement age – for men in addition to women – of 60 years coupled with a substantial increase in the state pension. Two factors have influenced this approach: The first, as regards the trade unions, is the impact of mass unemployment: the second is the reduced life expectancy of working-class men and women. There has been a tendency to see a common retirement age as a means of creating job opportunities for the young. As Ray Buckton put it, in presenting the Trades Union Congresses submission to the House of Commons Social Services Committee:

Now we have millions of people who are not working, and we are having to pay them to sit at home doing nothing at the present time. Perhaps we could shift that to people over sixty, and let them retire gracefully with an adequate pension, thereby letting these younger people come into industry and start producing the wealth that we are looking for. (House of Commons 1982:216)

This view was echoed by evidence from the National Pensioners' Convention Steering Committee, a group closely linked to the trade union movement. Their statement to the House of Commons committee argued:

Earlier retirement is desirable to provide more job opportunities, to achieve equality between men and women and, particularly, to permit people who have given, perhaps forty years services to the British economy to enjoy their last years of life in relative ease. . . . Our Declaration of Intent spells out that people should as of right be eligible for an adequate retirement pension on ceasing work, at any time of their choice after the age of 60 years, without being subject to an earnings rule. In our view an "adequate" income is a pension level of not less than half average gross earnings, for a married couple, not less than one-third of average gross earnings for a single person, uprated at six-monthly intervals. We would oppose any general move to early retirement which does not guarantee a proper income to the pensioner. (House of Commons 1982:373)

Earlier retirement is also seen to be justified because of the harsh working environment for those in manual occupations. The view of the General and Municipal Workers' Union (GMWU) is representative of this argument:

The GMWU's policy on Pensions and Retirement is influenced by the experience of our members. Thousands of GMWU members work in dangerous and hazardous jobs, for example as gypsum miners, in the chemical industry, and with asbestos. Many do not survive to collect their pension at 65. Among our thermal insulation engineering members, for example, the average age of death from occupational causes is 54. Thermal insulation engineering workers constitute half per cent of our membership but by 1980 accounted for 30 per cent of claims for union's occupational death benefit. About 50 per cent of our thermal insulation engineering membership directly exposed to asbestos for say 20 years can expect to die prematurely from industrial disease. The hazardous nature of many occupations is one of the principal motivations for the repeated and urgent call for progress towards reduction of the retirement age for men. (House of Commons 1982:337)

Despite such arguments, the trade union case for retirement at 60 has been firmly rejected by successive governments; neither, on the other hand, has there been progress toward flexible retirement. Flexibility may have been popular as a statement of intent and goodwill to older workers; as a realistic policy, in a period of high unemployment, it has been seen as having little to commend it. The key political actor here has been government, with both Labour and Conservative administrations in the 1970s and 1980s encouraging discussions on the viability of flexible retirement, while carefully avoiding any firm commitment as regards implementation.

7.6.2   State policies toward retirement age

For governments, the problem has been that neither flexibility nor a common retirement age (at 60 years) on a full state pension has been viewed as realistic in a context of budgetary constraints and competing social priorities. Thus, creating greater flexibility in the age of retirement is seen as administratively complex as well as entailing a substantial financial cost to industry and the taxpayer. A common retirement age of 60 years is viewed as even more expensive and likely to place an unacceptable burden on economic resources.

At the same time, Labour and Conservative governments have shared the view that flexibility is at least preferable to equalizing the age of retirement, and they have recognized, in addition, the political support behind such a change in policy. While accepting the case for flexibility, however, they have expressed uncertainty about the process of implementation. The Labour government's 1978 discussion paper *A Happier Old Age* reviewed the various arguments regarding a common and a flexible retirement age, and invited the general public to join the debate. The White Paper *Growing Older,* a product of the first Thatcher administration, identified the issues relating to a flexible retirement age between 60 and 70 in the following terms:

At whatever "normal" point was chosen, men and women would have the choice of taking their full pension and continuing to work full-time or part-time with no earnings rule; deferring their pension to earn a higher one when they wished to retire or of giving work up altogether. Men and women who wish to retire before that age could do so on a reduced pension (DHSS 1981:18).

The White Paper concluded that although spending constraints prevented short-term consideration of such a proposal, it should be kept in view as a "long-term objective." However, the proposals for the reform of social security, which emerged in the second Thatcher government, still held back from taking the debate any further. Indeed, after rehearsing the now familiar arguments, the government returned to a formula similar to that devised by the Labour government in 1978: "The government would welcome more flexibility in the State Pension Scheme. We recognize the attractions and increased choice which a retirement decade, in particular, would offer. The Government would therefore welcome views now on how the State Pension Scheme might be changed to meet this aim, without imposing unacceptably high costs" (DHSS 1985:10).

This proposal did, in effect, kill the idea of flexibility as a medium-term objective of government policy. In its place, as we have seen, came a range of measures to promote early exit – particularly for those on low incomes, in poor health, and/or in contracting industries. The phenomenon of early exit thus emerges within the context of political inertia over flexible retirement and outright opposition to the equalization of retirement ages at 60. Compared with the numerous political groups demanding action on unemployment, the forces pressing for a coherent policy on retirement were neither as united nor as unambiguous in their demands. The trade unions' demand for retirement at 60 (with higher state pensions) could be dismissed by a Conservative administration as being unacceptably expensive. Response to the calls for flexibility could be delayed because of technical and financial problems (Would sufficient part-time jobs be created? What would be the long-term problems faced by those opting for early retirement on a reduced pension?). In addition, we might also argue that flexible retirement was rejected because it raised difficult structural issues about the organization of work and pensions. Inertia on this issue fits in with a view of policy-making as the science of "muddling through." According to this conception: "Policy-makers do not consider a wide range but a narrow range of alternatives. In comparing the limited number of alternatives open to them, those making policy do not waste time on broader goals and values, but start with the problem and consider a manageable range of alternatives for dealing with it" (Ham and Hill 1984).

We can see, therefore, the ad hoc creation of different pathways from the labor force as the preferred solution to coping with structural change in the economy. Instead of creating a limited number of distinctive pathways (each with a high social status and favorable economic support), the state has encouraged numerous points of exit, many poorly financed and of low social status. The consequence is periods of insecurity for some (in Britain a majority) and relative freedom before and after retirement for others. It has, further, created a major change in work practices, without an equivalent shift in the economic and social support for exit and retirement itself.

Indeed, what is more likely in the next two decades is a questioning of retirement at fixed ages and attempts to persuade people to delay leaving work in their fifties and sixties. One example of this is the proposal for a retirement decade between the ages of 60 and 70. Thus in 1985 the Government proposed, in the Green Paper *Reform of Social Security: Programme for Change,* that people might be able "to pick the point in the decade at which to retire, knowing what they would expect by way of state pension at each point. There would be no set pension age as such: people would get permanently higher or lower pensions according to whether they retired early or late in the decade" (DHSS 1985:10; House of Commons 1989).

The argument for a retirement decade may, in fact, be used in both positive and negative ways. It may be used to allow choice, thus enabling some to withdraw earlier or go on working later in line with their own preferences. Conversely, it may be used to encourage some workers to delay retirement, on the grounds of the alleged burden associated with population aging and the crisis provoked by the shortage of younger workers (see Johnson 1989 and Johnson et al. 1989 for arguments along these lines). The effect of this debate may be to maintain the financial and social insecurity that many older workers experienced in the 1970s and 1980s. On the one hand, few governments are likely to be interested in making retirement attractive: the economic "costs" will be viewed as too great. On the other hand, very few initiatives are being developed – in Britain at least – to give older people greater security in the labor market. In the context of a 30 percent drop (by 1995) in the number of young people entering work, it is married women who are targeted as a key group for meeting shortages in labor supply (women are projected to take 80 percent of the 900,000 new jobs on offer in the seven years preceding 1995). Older workers are more likely to be used for low-paid part-time jobs, particularly in the new service industries.

Yet an increase in part-time working may not greatly reduce the degree of insecurity experienced by older workers. They may still face above-average unemployment; at the same time, financial support from the state may become more limited and targeted at particular groups. In short, in Britain at least, early exit is likely to continue in the 1990s and to be characterized by many of the tensions and difficulties present in the 1970s and 1980s.

REFERENCES

Allen, S., A. Waton, K. Purcell, and S. Wood. 1986. *The Experience of Unemployment.* London: Macmillan.

Armstrong, P., A. Glyn, and J. Harrison. 1984. *Capitalism Since World War II.* London: Fontana Books.

Bosanquet, N. 1983. *After the New Right.* London: Heinemann.

1987. *A Generation in Limbo.* London: Public Policy Centre.

Brown, C. J., and S. Small. 1985. *Occupational Benefits as Social Security.* London: Policy Studies Institute.

Bushell, R. 1984. "Great Britain, the Job Release Schemes. Paper produced for OECD panel, *Measures to Assist Early Retirement.* OECD, Paris (mimeo).

Bytheway, B. 1986. "Making Way: The Disengagement of Older Workers." In: C. Phillipson, M. Bernard, and P. Strang (eds.), *Dependency and Interdependency in Old Age – Theoretical Perspectives and Policy Alternatives.* London: Croom Helm, pp. 315–26.

Casey, B., and F. Laczko. 1989. "Early retired or long-term unemployed? The changing situation of non-working men from 1979 to 1986." *Work, Employment, and Society.* 3(4):509–26.

Daniel, W. W. 1982. *Whatever Happened to the Workers of Woolwich?* London: PEP.

Department of Employment. 1970. *Ryhope: A Pit Closes.* London: HMSO.

1978. "Measures to Alleviate Unemployment in the Medium Term: Early Retirement." *Department of Employment Gazette,* March, pp. 283–5.

Dex, S., and C. Phillipson. 1986. "Social Policy and the Older Worker." In: C. Phillipson and A. Walker (eds.), *Ageing and Social Policy: A Critical Assessment.* Aldershot: Gower Books.

DHSS. 1981. *Growing Older.* Cmnd. 8173. London: HMSO.

1985. *Reform of Social Security: Programme for Change,* vol. 2. Cmnd. 9518. London: HMSO.

Donaldson, A. 1979. *The British Unemployment Figures in Context.* Berlin: International Institute of Management.

European Commission. 1987. *Old Age Pensions. Net Benefits Compared to Previous Net Earnings,* vol. A. Overall Report. Brussels: Commission of the European Communities.

Fennell, G., C. Phillipson, and H. Evers. 1989. *The Sociology of Old Age.* Milton Keynes: Open University Press.

Fogarty, M. 1975. *40 to 60: How We Waste the Middle Aged.* London: Centre for Studies in Social Policy/Bedford Square Press.

Glyn, A., and B. Sutcliffe. 1972. *British Capitalism, Workers and the Profits Squeeze.* London: Penguin Books.

Government Actuary. 1979. *Occupational Pension Schemes.* Government Actuary, Fifth Survey. London: HMSO.

Griew, S. 1964. *Job Re-design.* Paris: OECD.

Groves, D. 1991. "Women and Financial Provision for Old Age." In: M. MacLean and D. Groves, *Women's Issues in Social Policy.* London: Routledge.

Ham, C., and M. Hill. 1984. *The Policy Process in the Modern Capitalist State.* London: Wheatsheaf Books.

Hedstrom, P., and S. Ringen. 1987. "Age and Income in Contemporary Society: A Research Note." *Journal of Social Policy* 16(2):227–39.

Heron, A., and S. M. Chown. 1967. *Age and Function.* London: Churchill.

House of Commons. 1982. Third Report from the Social Services Committee, Session 1981–2, *Age of Retirement.* London: House of Commons.

——— 1989. Employment Committee (Second Report), *The Employment Patterns of the Over-50s,* vol. 11. London: House of Commons.

IMS. 1983. *Early Retirement.* Brighton: Institute of Manpower Studies.

——— 1987. *Patterns of Retirement.* Brighton: Institute of Manpower Studies.

Jackson, M. 1984. "Early Retirement: Recent Trends and Implications." *Industrial Relations Journal* 15(3):21–8.

Johnson, P. 1989. "Old Age Creeps Up." *Marxism Today,* January, pp. 34–9.

Johnson, P., C. Conrad, and D. Thompson (eds.). 1989. *Workers Versus Pensioners.* Manchester: Manchester University Press.

Jolly, J., S. Creigh, and A. Mingay. 1980. *Age as a Factor in Employment,* Research Paper No. 11. London: Department of Employment.

Laczko, F. 1987. "Older Workers, Unemployment and the Discouraged Worker Effect." In: S. Di Gregorio (ed.), *Social Gerontology: New Directions.* London: Croom Helm.

——— 1988. "Between Work and Retirement: Becoming 'Old' in the 1980s." In: B. Bytheway, T. Keil, P. Allatt, and A. Bryman (eds.), *Becoming and Being Old: Sociological Approaches to Later Life.* London: Sage Books.

Laczko, F., A. Dale, S. Arber, and N. Gilbert. 1988. "Early Retirement in a Period of High Unemployment." *Journal of Social Policy* 17(2):313–34.

Laczko, F., and A. Walker. 1985. "Excluding Older Workers from the Labour Market: Early Retirement Policies in Britain, France and Sweden." In: C. Jones and M. Brenton (eds.), *The Year Book of Social Policy in Britain 1984–85.* London: Routledge and Kegan Paul.

LMQR. 1986. *Labour Market Quarterly Report.* Manpower Services Commission, Sheffield, July.

MacKay, D. I. 1973. "Redundancy and Re-engagement: A Study of Car Workers." *Manchester School,* September.

Makeham, P., and S. Morgan. 1980. *Evaluation of the Job Release Scheme,* Research Paper no. 14. London: Department of Employment.

Martin, J., and R. H. Fryer. 1973. *Redundancy and Paternalist Capitalism.* London: Allen and Unwin.

McGoldrick, A. 1982. "Early Retirement and Double-Edged Strategy." Paper presented to British Society of Gerontology Conference, *Old Age in a Changing Society,* September 1982, Exeter (mimeo).

McGoldrick, A., and C. Cooper. 1989. *Early Retirement.* Aldershot: Gower.

Miller, M. 1982. *The Development of Occupational Pension Schemes in Britain between 1936 and 1979.* Unpublished typescript, University of Bath, October.

Ministry of Labour and National Service. 1953. *Annual Report, 1952.* Cmnd. 8893. London: HMSO.

National Advisory Committee on the Employment of Older Men and Women. 1955. *Second Report.* Cmnd. 9262. London: HMSO.

Parker, S. 1982. *Work and Retirement.* London: George Allen and Unwin.

Parker, S., et al. 1971. *Effects of the Redundancy Payments Act.* London: HMSO.

Phillipson, C. 1982. *Capitalism and the Construction of Old Age.* London: Macmillan.

Phillipson, C. 1991. "Inter-Generational Relations: Conflict or Consensus in the Twenty-First Century." *Policy and Politics* 19(1):27–36.

Piachaud, D. 1986. "Disability, Retirement and Unemployment of Older Men." *Journal of Social Policy* 15(2):145–62.

Royal Commission on Population. 1949. *Report.* London: HMSO.

Shanas, E., et al. 1968. *Old People in Three Industrial Societies.* London: Routledge and Kegan Paul.

Townsend, P. 1979. *Poverty in the United Kingdom.* Harmondsworth: Pelican Books.

Ungerson, C. (ed.). *Gender and Caring.* London: Harvester Wheatsheaf.

Victor, C. 1989. "Income Inequality in Late Life." In: M. Jeffries (ed.), *Growing Old in the Twentieth Century,* London: Routledge.

Walker, A. 1989. "The Social Division of Early Retirement." In: M. Jefferys (ed.), *Growing Old in the Twentieth Century,* London.

Welford, A. T. 1958. *Ageing and Human Skills.* London: Oxford University Press for the Nuffield Foundation.

   1976. "Thirty Years of Psychological Research on Age and Work." *Journal of Occupational Psychology* 49:129–38.

White, M. 1980. *Shorter Working Time.* London: Policy Studies Institute.

CHAPTER 8

The United States:
The privatization of exit

HAROLD L. SHEPPARD

8.1 INTRODUCTION AND HISTORICAL
BACKGROUND

THE historical aspect of this chapter could begin as far back as the mid-nineteenth century to identify examples of the first prototypes of private and public employer retirement policies and programs – more specifically, pension-age policies and programs. At that time there were a small number of voluntary philanthropic aids of various types for "superannuated" employees. Graebner (1980) in his historically oriented study, *A History of Retirement: The Meaning and Function of An American Institution, 1885–1978,* cites – in agreement with the conventional wisdom of historical gerontologists – the American Express Company as the first U.S. corporation to introduce a pension system. To discuss "retirement" is really to discuss "pensionable age," but Graebner does not inform his readers on the issue critical to us: the age at which employer pensions were available to employees.

The late nineteenth century and the first decade of the twentieth century witnessed the growth of private-sector pensions in the railroads, public utilities, banks, and metal industries. "The year 1910 was a benchmark, for in the decade that followed, new plans were established at a rate of at least 21 per year" (Graebner 1980:133).

The persistent theme in Graebner's perspective is the overwhelming motivation of efficiency and/or labor force control – goals or values of employing organizations – not the more generally popular theme of rewarding men and women for their many years of toil in the workplace, or as some form of social justice. A more balanced approach might recognize an interactive perspective, which would include the desires or demands of employees themselves. But early retirement (retirement in general, for that matter) cannot be explained adequately as an act derived from an individual's own characteristics. Social policy is one of the primary factors in this ever-changing process.

252

The passage by the U.S. Congress in 1935 of the Social Security Act included a major provision for benefits for workers who ceased work upon reaching age 65. In subsequent years, this was reduced to 62, first for women and later for men. This legislation was designed to tackle the unemployment crisis of the Great Depression in two different forms: (1) Unemployment Insurance, and not merely (2) Old Age or "Retired Workers" Insurance. The dominating drive for the second provision of the Social Security provision was the need to alleviate the high jobless rate, and one way out was to remove "older" men and women from the labor force by transferring them into another social category, namely, the retired population. This does not mean that other reasons and social forces were not at play in this social legislation.

The early decades after World War II were characterized by a high demand for labor, partly met by the beginnings of an expanded female supply source, but also by keeping and hiring older workers (primarily men). The literature of industrial relations and of industrial sociology and psychology, during the period of 1945–65 or so, was replete with emphasis on retraining, job redesign, and so forth, as techniques and measures to assist older adult workers in coping with changing technologies and product markets.

But in the early 1970s, and certainly by the midpoint of that decade, possibly influenced by the entry of larger numbers from the post–World War II "baby boom" and the rapid rate of entry of women, especially married ones (and not just baby boom females), the secular trend of a decline in the labor force participation rates of males was accelerated. What Standing (1986) has called the "progressive marginalization of older workers" began to emerge as a pattern.

For New Deal liberals, writes Graebner, retirement was a way of achieving "certain economic and social goals, rather than a time in a person's life when work would cease in favor of some state of security. There was a good deal of cold-blooded calculation in the process.[1] The benefits of retirement were expected to rebound to the larger society and the young through unemployment relief and job creation, rather than to the aged. Older railroad workers, organized in a powerful national association, might force the society to act; but it was action in the form of retirement, to social security. If this was the welfare state, it was built along lines descended from the limited vision of retirement generated in the progressive era" (Graebner 1980:180).

---

[1] One might claim that Grabner's image of "New Deal liberals" is the opposite of the conventional image of them as soft-hearted sentimentalists not concerned about rationality and efficiency.

For a rather long period of time, a core of American workers was assured of relative job security based on seniority and/or a low level of disjunctures in the stability of enterprises and industries. The United States in the 1980s, however, underwent "de-industrialization," international competition for world and domestic markets, and sharp technological shifts. "Restructuring" especially hit older workers, possibly because the industries most affected were old ones, and older industries ipso facto mean an older work force. Older workers thus affected face greater difficulties in finding reemployment, or reemployment acceptable to them.

8.2   RECENT DEVELOPMENTS

Recent years (since the early 1980s) have witnessed the visible surfacing of special early-exit incentives – the "golden handshake." This relatively new phenomenon (at least in terms of magnitude) is a symptom or a leading indicator of the economic and industrial "restructuring" of the Untied States. Given a systematic decision to reduce the work force in various industries, it is understandable why early exit from work has become easier than in past decades. *The Employee Benefit Plan Review* of October, 1986, cites a Wyatt Company (pension consultants) study showing, for example, that among the 50 largest industrial companies there has been a substantial increase in firms that offer early pension provisions without any actuarial reductions. Very often, other attractions are offered the employee, such as lump sum payments, continued fringe benefits, and so forth.[2]

8.2.1   Indirect public-policy influence on the private sector

The General Accounting Office (GAO), an evaluation and inspection agency for the United States Congress, has pointed out that the "federal government has no consistent policy regarding retirement age" (General Accounting Office 1986:10). The popular versions of this lack of consistency typically point to the poor coordination of pension-age policy, if any, between government and the private sector. But it is very important to recognize that the early-exit trends and practices of the private sector

---

[2] In 1984, according to the Bureau of Labor Statistics, more than three-fifths of all workers in companies with pension plans could retire before 65 with full pension benefits compared with only one-half in 1980; however for many of these employees years of service are a further requirement for such benefits. In a survey of roughly 350 companies in 1984–5, Rhine (1984) found that nearly 40 percent of them had early retirement ages as young as 55. Three-fifths of that group provided less than actuarially reduced pension – in other words, pension benefits higher than an actuarial formula would allow.

(in contrast to recent legislation concerning age discrimination and Social Security retirement age) are made into policy by previous and long-standing government legislation and policy that offer favorable tax provisions to employers whose pension programs *"allow and encourage retirement at ages 62 and younger"* (italics not in original). Even individual retirement income plans allow a person to withdraw the funds without any tax penalty as early as age 59½.

In essence, all of the pension programs in the U.S. retirement "system" are subsidized (and/or influenced) in one way or another by the government. The GAO report, in this connection, may be one of the first signs of official recognition of the role of the state in the determination of private-sector policy on retirement age. The private-sector system does not operate outside of rules, norms, and laws set by the state, but this does not necessarily mean that the state has consciously and deliberately selected a given pension age for the private sector. It is instead the recognition – at least by this arm of Congress – that there are some unanticipated consequences of policies and legislation that are not explicitly or directly designed to determine retirement age but nevertheless do have an impact on age at exit.

The GAO cites 1986 estimates that preferential tax exemptions and privileges amount to about $88 billion. Thus, it is not completely correct to claim that the exit-age practices of the private sector are unrelated to policies and practices belonging to the sphere of government. Such an estimate of lost tax revenues is but one measure of the costs of retirement at a public macro-level.

Early exit on the part of greater and greater proportions of a population of "working age" (a term that is itself subject to sociocultural definitions) is made possible by, and is dependent upon, the resources of a society's economy. This raises the issue of the capacity of that economy to support a given population of nonworking adults at a given level of retirement income or its equivalent, or an even larger population of such adults at a lower level of retirement income. The significance of this point about resources and capacity lies in the fact that these two elements (along with societal willingness) set major parameters or conditions within which workers have the "freedom" to exit from work at a certain age or at the earliest pensionable age.

In addition to government, there are organizational "actors" whose views and interests impinge on decisions by the state, for example, labor and management, nonprofit welfare-related organizations, and so forth.[3]

---

[3] As a result of the influence of various church and private welfare groups, incidentally, the original Social Security Act did not cover their employees under any of its provisions (unemployment insurance, old-age insurance, etc.).

8.3 LABOR FORCE PARTICIPATION TRENDS

The following observations characterize the progress of early exit in the United States:

In the 1950s, the labor force participation rate of men aged 60 to 64 began to decline.

In the 1960s, the participation rate for men aged 55 to 59 started its decline.

In the late 1980s, there were some signs of the decline starting as early as 50 to 54.

Whether we use the measure of labor force participation (number of employed *and* unemployed as a percentage of the population) or employment activity rate (number of employed as percentage of the population) of different age groups, we cannot ignore the long-term downward trends in both measures for all men, but especially older ones (starting at about age 45), and the downward trends of women, too, but starting only at about age 60 in the United States. The male–female discrepancy is so great that it is misleading to talk about the decline of older Americans in general when discussing attachment to the work force.[4]

Using age 55 as an arbitrary, potential "early-exit" cutoff point, we should note that the 1970–86 decline in labor force participation rates of men and women vary by age group (Table 8.1)

In general, the older the age, the greater the rate of decline over the 16-year period covered in Table 8.1. The large change in the decline rates of both men and women between age 61 and age 62 is a reflection of the availability of "early retirement" Social Security retired-worker benefits for both sexes at age 62. The average or mean age of retired-worker awards between 1960 and 1985 went down from 66.8 to 63.7 for men (a figure that has remained virtually unchanged since 1982) and from 65.2 to 63.4 for women (also unchanged since 1982). No longer should it be said that 65 is the typical or "normal" retirement age in the United States, and the same generalization applies to other countries of the "more developed," industrialized world (see Chapter 2).

It should be noted that, especially among men, the shift in labor force participation rate between age 61 and age 62 is only partly a function of the latter age being the earliest retirement age under Social Security. This shift also points not only to the possible influence of the unemployment

---

[4] This caveat is applicable as long as lower proportions of women have long-term attachment to jobs, especially full-time jobs, and (2) lower proportions have pension coverage, and so forth. In a later section of this chapter, we concentrate in some detail on information that distinguishes men and women and also takes into consideration marital status.

Table 8.1. *Rates of change in labor force participation rates, by single age for men and women, 1970–86*

	% Decline 1970–86	
Selected ages	Men	Women
55	−6.6	+6.1[a]
57	−8.9	−0.2
59	−13.6	−1.7
61	−16.6	−0.5
62	−25.5	−12.7
63	−32.9	−6.3
65	−37.9	−26.7
66	−39.4	−22.8
67	−34.5	−21.6

[a]Rates of increase are based on the "Stouffer" method, i.e., % in time 2 − % in time 1/(100% − % in time 1).
Source: Bureau of Labor Statistics unpublished data.

experience but also to the growing coverage of workers by private-employer (and by public-employer) pension plans. Many workers defer exit from work until they are eligible for retirement income from both sources – Social Security and private pensions. But there are also many workers who exit from the labor force before age 62 – with and without retirement pensions from sources other than Social Security.

For women in the middle-age group of 40 to 54, during the 20 years from 1965 to 1985, labor force participation showed relatively high rates of increase: It grew from 49 percent to 72 percent for those aged 40 to 44, from 52 percent to 68 percent for those aged 45 to 49, and from 50 percent to 61 percent for those aged 50 to 54. These patterns are clearly different from those for men. The labor force participation rate for women aged 55 to 59 showed only a slight increase in the same 20-year period (from 47 percent to 50 percent), and the rate has remained virtually at a plateau for the group aged 60 to 64 – the so-called preretirement age group (a label that may need to be transferred soon to the younger age group of 55 to 59, given the contemporary early-exit trends).

It should be pointed out that, on a longitudinal basis, the decline in the participation rate for women aged 55 to 59 in any given time period has increased since the 1965–70 period. The sharp drops between 1970 and 1975 may partially reflect the severe recession that occurred during that five-year period. The decline rate between ages 55 to 59 and 60 to 64 during that earlier (1965–70) time frame was 23 percent, compared with at least 30 percent in each of the three five-year periods following 1965–70.

8.3.1   Unemployment and labor force participation

The relationship of the unemployment experience to early exit has been shown in several studies.[5] Take, for example, the finding that during the period 1970–5, which encompassed several years of relatively high unemployment, the labor force participation rates of men 50 to 54, 55 to 59, and 60 to 64 years old dropped more steeply than in any of the three five-year periods surrounding the years from 1970 to 1975. Table 8.3 shows a sharp increase from the 1965–70 period to the 1970–5 period in the decline of participation rates. Although the participation rates of women in the same age groups have ordinarily been increasing, this certainly was not the case during the period under discussion. When the general jobless rate for women increased from 3.2 percent to 5.8 percent (at a rate of 2.7 percent),[6] the labor force participation rates of women in the three pertinent age groups declined (Table 8.2). But during the periods 1965–70, 1975–80, and 1980–5, when the female jobless rate either plummeted sharply or increased only imperceptibly, the participation rates of these three "preretirement" age groups actually ascended. It should be noted that during the latest period covered in this analysis, 1980–5, the labor force participation rates of women in the group aged 60 to 64, however, barely rose (by only 0.1 percent). This period, too, included some years with very high overall unemployment.

From 1970 to 1975, unemployment among men 16 and older rose from 4.4 percent to 7.9 percent (at a rate of 3.6 percent over the five years). Over the same period, the participation rates of "younger older" male workers declined at rates well beyond those for the previous and subsequent five-year periods. (Table 8.3)

Even though the pattern of an above-average reduction in participation rates accompanying above-average increases in jobless rates prevails among both women and men, it is also important to note that the participation declines for women are substantially below those for men. This difference may be attributable to differences in the industry-occupation mix between men and women, and also to the possibility that in times of high husband joblessness, wives might enter the job market.

---

[5] See section 8.4.4 for a detailed discussion of the role of job loss in early, and very early (before age 62), exit from the labor force.

[6] This rate is calculated by using the Stouffer method for measuring rates of increase in proportions. See Table 8.1 for explanation.

Table 8.2. *Changes in labor force participation rate relative to general female jobless rate for four different five-year periods*

Period	Rate of change in jobless rate of females aged 16+[a]	% Change in labor force participation		
		50–54	55–59	60–64
1965–70	+0.4	+7.4	+3.6	+3.2
1970–75	+2.7	−0.9	−2.2	−4.4
1975–80	−25.2	+9.6	+1.3	0
1980–85	+0.2	+7.1	+3.3	+0.1

Table 8.3. *Changes in labor force participation rate relative to general male jobless rate for four different five-year periods*

Period	Rate of change in jobless rate of men aged 16+[a]	% Change in labor force participation		
		50–54	55–59	60–64
1965–70	+0.4	−2.0	−0.8	−3.8
1970–75	+3.6	−3.2	−5.7	−12.4
1975–80	−12.7	−0.9	−3.0	−7.2
1980–85	+0.3	−0.8	−2.1	−8.9

[a]Stouffer's method of measuring rates of increase in proportions.

8.3.2   Employment activity rate

The employment activity rate[7] of older men shows no great drop between ages until the 61- to 62-year-old shift, for obvious reasons (especially the eligibility at age 62 for retired-worker benefits). In 1970 this rate was 81 percent for men aged 61 and 74 percent for men aged 62, an 8.6 percent rate of difference. By 1980 the rates had declined to 70 and 57 percent, respectively, showing a difference rate of 18.6 per-

---

[7] This measure refers to the number actually employed as a percentage of the total number of persons in a given age category – not to be confused with the labor force participation rate, which includes in the numerator persons without employment but seeking it. Neither of these measures, incidentally, refers to work experience data.

Table 8.4. *Rate of difference between the employment activity rates of 61- and 62-year-olds in 1970, 1980, and 1986[a]*

	Rate of difference (%)	
Year	Men	Women
1970	−8.6	−6.7
1980	−18.6	−16.3
1986	−18.2	−15.9

[a]Rate of difference is calculated as follows: (employment rate for 61-year-olds minus rate for 62-year-olds)/(rate for 61-year-olds) × 100.

cent. By 1986 the figures were 66 and 54 percent, an 18.3 percent rate of decline.

Over this 16-year period, accordingly, the employment activity rate of 61-year-olds dropped by 18.5 percent, but for 62-year-olds the rate slumped much more, by 27.6 percent.

Women so far show a different picture. To begin with, both their employment activity and participation rates show no discernible decrease (indeed, show an increase) over this 16-year period for certain single ages until age 62. But to return to a comparison with the data in the previous paragraphs about men, Table 8.4 provides the pertinent information.

8.4 PATHWAYS OF EARLY EXIT

Dealing coherently and simply with the U.S. retirement "system" is not an easy task, at least when attempting comparisons with other modern, industrialized nations. It has about 800,000 private-sector employer pension plans, not to mention 6,500 state and local government plans, the federal civil service retirement program (including some small special employee ones), and the military pension system, as well as the 16 million individual pension accounts (consisting mostly of employees' Individual Retirement Accounts, and Keogh – self-employed – plans). Many labor force participants and retirees receive benefits from more than one of these retirement income sources.

Table 8.5. *Non–Social Security pension sources, by age and sex of recipient*

Sex	Pension source	% of age group who are recipients			
		50–54	55–61	62–64	65+
M	Private	28.2	48.4	59.5	69.9
	Military	54.4	19.3	8.9	4.0
	Federal govt.	6.1	17.1	15.5	9.7
	State or local govt.	10.0	12.6	10.9	12.5
	Combinations of above	1.3	2.6	5.2	3.9
	Total	100.0	100.0	100.0	100.0
F	Private	54.3	59.2	55.0	56.2
	Military	6.5	2.2	2.9	1.6
	Federal govt.	24.5	17.0	14.9	10.7
	State or local govt.	14.7	18.3	23.8	28.1
	Combinations of above	0	3.3	3.3	3.4
	Total	100.0	100.0	100.0	100.0

Source: General Accounting Office (1986:28–9), Tables 2.4 and 2.5).

Table 8.6. *Pension sources for men by age of recipient*

Pension source	% of age group who are recipients			
	50–54	55–61	62–64	65+
Private	61.8	60.0	63.3	72.8
Federal govt.	13.4	21.2	17.0	10.1
State or local govt.	21.9	15.6	12.0	13.0
Combinations of above	2.9	3.2	100.2	4.1
Total	100.0	100.0	100.0	100.0

The private-pension world, over the past 15 years or so, has been characterized by increases in plans with provisions providing for pre-62 "retirement" (but not necessarily labor force exit). It is difficult, however, to capture systematic information on the numbers of workers exiting with such pre-62 pensions. The pathways of early exit can nevertheless be clarified somewhat by examining the information on sources of men's non–Social Security pensions by age of recipients, as shown in Table 8.5. In Table 8.6, we exclude military pensions for men (because many young recipients are still in the labor force).

Male recipients as young as 50 to 54 (and 55 to 61) are disproportionately made up of persons receiving pensions from state and local governments, and the proportions receiving private pensions increases in parallel with the age of the recipient. But to repeat, these data only *suggest* the age at exit from the labor force. They do not tell us whether, for example, 55- to 61-year-old recipients of state or local government pensions are in or out of the labor force, or when they exited.

A significant finding cited in the GAO report concerns the accelerated downward trend of labor force participation by male pension recipients 55 to 61 years old, from 1974 to 1984. Starting in 1974 the rate was about 50 percent but decreased by 1984 to only 42 percent. The greatest drop occurred, however, in the first half of this period, 1974 to 1979; thereafter, it changed only slightly, from 43 percent to 42 percent. During the same period, it should be noted, the participation rate of nonrecipients declined at a far slower rate (from 88 percent to 83 percent).[8]

8.4.1   The employer-pension pathway

The primary exit pathway in the United States, is, of course, through the retired-worker benefits program under Social Security. More than 95 percent of U.S. workers are covered by it. Actuarially reduced retirement benefits can be awarded as early as age 62. The 1982 New Beneficiary Survey found that during 1980–1, 37 percent of all such new beneficiaries, however, had left the labor force *before* that age; another 23 percent exited at age 62, and the remainder, 40 percent, exited when 63 or older (nearly all before age 65).

More than one-half of these retirees exiting before age 62 were married women, a finding that goes a long way toward explaining how such a large proportion of U.S. workers (37 percent) can leave the labor force before they are eligible to receive a retiree benefit under Social Security. In most cases, these wives are able to exit so early because their husbands still receive income, through either earnings or retirement benefits. Indeed, 70 percent of women who left the labor force before age 62 existed before their husbands did. Furthermore, women exiting before age 62 had the highest proportion of husbands receiving a private pension.

As for non–Social Security early-exit pathways, the Packard and Reno (1988) report using the New Beneficiary Survey shows that among all

---

[8] It should also be noted that for women of the same age group (55 to 61) during the same period participation actually increased for nonrecipients, while it essentially declined for pension recipients.

Table 8.7. *Percent receiving private and public employer pensions, by age at exit, sex, and marital status*

	Men		Women		
Exit age	Married	Not married	Married	Not married	Total
Under 55	44	—[a]	7	20	14
55–61	64	45	32	48	48

[a]Based on fewer than 50 cases.
Source: Table 9.5 of Packard and Reno (1988).

Table 8.8. *Percent receiving private pensions, by early-exit age, gender, and marital status*

	Men		Women		
Exit age	Married	Not married	Married	Not married	Total
Under 55	12	NA	4	13	6
55–61	39	27	18	29	29
Total under 62	36	21	12	24	22

Source: Analysis of New Beneficiary data prepared for this chapter by John Henretta, University of Florida.

workers exiting before age 55, only 14 percent received any kind of employer pension (including private-sector, government, or military pension); for those exiting between 55 and 62, the proportion rises to 48 percent.[9] These proportions vary widely according to sex and marital status – for example, 44 percent of married men exiting before 55 received an employer pension compared with only 7 percent of married women. Among those exiting between 55 and 62, 64 percent of married men, but only 32 percent of married women, were pension recipients (Table 8.7).

In Table 8.8 we report our own analysis of the New Beneficiary Survey data concerning proportions of early exiters receiving private (i.e., exclusive of military, local government, and federal government) pensions.

[9] For those exiting at 62 or later, the proportion is approximately 56 percent.

The overall generalization is that for roughly one-fifth of all beneficiaries exiting before age 62, private-sector pensions were a pathway for their early exit.

State and local government pensions constituted the second significant non–Social Security pathway for early exit for the later beneficiaries of Social Security retired-worker benefits. Among all the New Beneficiary Survey respondents exiting before age 62, slightly more than 7 percent reported receipt of state and local government pensions, according to our preliminary analysis.

8.4.2 Early-exit incentive programs

Because of economic difficulties, corporate mergers, "downsizing," and restructuring, along with product and technological changes, many private companies have introduced early-exit incentive programs, over and above traditional pension-plan liberalization aimed at encouraging older workers to leave.

A major characteristic of all such incentive programs is cited by Meier (1986): They "are in reality termination programs," not programs designed for workers in poor health or wanting more leisure. They are introduced as economy and profit-making measures.

Another important characteristic, one more relevant to the early-exit issue, is that they are typically targeted at relatively young employees, in their early or mid-50s. Accordingly, many early exit incentive programs offering benefits without full actuarial reductions are quite expensive, at least in the short run.

Unfortunately, there is no systematic and comprehensive information about how many companies actually have introduced early-exit incentives or how many older employees have accepted them. Thus we have no way of knowing how many of the 22 percent reported as exiting before age 62 by the New Beneficiary Survey were participants in such programs.

What we do have are occasional surveys of selected corporations, by pension consultant firms, for example. From such surveys we find that some employers offer "carrots," such as the liberalization of exit benefits and temporary pension supplements; others offer "sticks," involving a deadline for acceptance of increased pensions after which pensions will be reduced (a "window") or the elimination of lump-sum payments (Mutschler, no date). Some of the special features of such plans include pension benefits without any actuarial reduction and salary continuity for limited periods (or until age 62 or eligibility for regular company retirement). Table 8.9 shows a comparison of 10 early-exit plans com-

Table 8.9. *Comparison of 10 early-retirement incentive programs*[a]

Company	Eligible employees	Percent accepting	Pension reduced	Cash subsidy	How paid	Continued medical coverage
Ameritrust Co., Cleveland, Ohio	176	72	No	$24,000	Over two years	Full
B. F. Goodrich, Akron, Ohio	768	22[b]	Yes	$52,500	Over three years	Full
Caterpillar Tractor, Peoria, Ill.	845	41	Yes	$19,200	Over four years	Full
Consumers Power, Jackson, Mich.	1,360	54	No	$17,300	Lump Sum	Full
Eaton Corp. Cleveland, Ohio	126	67	Yes	$20,000	Varies	Full
National-Standard Co., Niles, Mich.	108	52	No	Social Security–bridging pay	Varies	Reduced
Polaroid Corp., Cambridge, Mass.	6,328	14	Yes	$75,000	Varies	Full
Portland General Electric, Portland, Ore.	114	36	No	Social Security–bridging pay	Varies	Reduced
Public Service, Electric & Gas, Newark, N.J.	2,120	62	No	$42,000	Over seven years	Full
Sears, Chicago, Ill.	2,300	60	Yes	$45,000	Over three years	Full

[a] Assumes early retirement at age 58 with 30 years' company service and annual salary of $30,000.

[b] Maximum allowed.

Source: Data based on a survey by the management consultant firm of Towers, Perin, Forster & Crosby and reported by Shuman (1983). Reproduced from Mutschler (no date).

piled by Shuman (1983) from data based on a survey by a prominent consultant company.

In a later study, Mutschler (1986) concentrates on the experience of a major corporation (in the Fortune 500) with more than 700 employees exiting in different years under different incentive plans or remaining in their jobs. She finds that, unlike the results of most previous research on factors in the exit decision, "in the absence of formal incentive plans, health status was not a major determinant . . . when incentives are offered." Instead, the financial attractions of the pension plans were dominant. It must be noted, however, that this study did not focus on age at exit, nor did it provide any information as to whether the employees left the labor force or merely left the employer covered in the study for another employer. Indeed, this is one of the major shortcomings of the research on this topic.

8.4.3 The disability pathway

A major government-based exit pathway for U.S. workers under the age of 62 is, of course, the Social Security program of disability benefits. (Unlike practices in some European countries, this program is not used deliberately to alleviate problems of older long-term unemployed workers or those in distressed industries.) From 1965 to 1987, the average age for awardees under this program declined from 53.0 to 49.0 for men and from 53.2 to 49.5 for women. The total awardee numbers are shown in Table 8.10.

The more rapid increase of women in this pathway is partly a result of the growth in the total numbers of women entering the labor force before and during this two-decade period. How do these statistics compare with those concerning the "normal" early retirement (at age 62 to 64) under the retired-worker program of the U.S. Social Security program? This question, in part, has to do with which of these programs has become the one more frequently used as an exit pathway.

The first thing to note is that over the 1965–87 period, total retired-worker awards increased by 40 percent, a lower rate of growth than total disability awards (62 percent). If we use this comparison, we would have to conclude that the early-exit pathway of disability pensions is moving in the direction of overtaking the overall retired-worker exit pathway. But further examination shows that the number of persons being awarded retired-worker benefits at age 62 – the earliest age for such benefits in the U.S. Social Security program – has grown at a remarkably greater rate than the number receiving all disability awards and the total retired-worker awards (Table 8.11).

Table 8.10. *Disability awards, 1965 and 1987*

	1965	1987	% Increase
Both sexes	253,500	409,600	62
Men	186,800	265,900	42
Women	66,700	143,700	115

Table 8.11. *Percent increase in Social Security awards for disability, to all retired workers, and to workers retiring at age 62, 1965–87*

Type of award	Total	Men	Women
Disability	62	42	116
All retired workers	40	31	55
Retired workers at age 62 only	252	323	195

The comparison shown in Table 8.11 is but one way in which to high-light, once again, the accelerated pace of early, perhaps very early, exits from the U.S. labor force. Both pathways – disability and retirement at age 62 – have tremendously outpaced the overall "regular" retired-worker benefit program. These two routes may indeed resemble the European pattern referred to previously, wherein "invalidity" pensions are partly an early-exit route.

Two of the major factors in this changing pattern have to do with (1) the growing availability of private pensions, especially at early ages, and (2) high unemployment levels at various times during this 20-year period.

It should be obvious by now that there is a need to single out the 62-year-olds and not to combine information about that single-year age category with data for those aged 63 and 64. The convention among ger-ontologists and labor force analysts – even this author – has been to use the "early-retirements" category of 62 to 64. One reason for the need to treat 62-year-olds separately is related to results of several research projects showing that some people "retiring" at 62 (or receiving retired-worker benefits for the first time at this age) had been unemployed or jobless prior to receiving such benefits, or had been receiving private and employer pensions before reaching age 62.

Disability is one pathway, then, that can be measured, at least in terms of the number of workers exiting before age 62. (Some disabled workers do exit, however, without receiving such disability benefits.) Joblessness is another pathway, but unlike several European countries, the United States has no formal government-sponsored program explicitly designed to provide early-exit pensions for unemployed older workers. When coupled with data on Social Security awards for disability and with our insights into the separate and joint roles of unemployment and non–Social Security sources of early-exit income, the trends in awards at age 62 suggest that we may well be witnessing a substantial overlap of pathways of early exit from the labor force.

8.4.4   Job loss

Whereas even in recent decades attention was focused on the sharp drops in the labor force participation rate of male workers 65 and older, or at best those 60 to 64, the declines among men as young as 55 to 59, and perhaps as young as 50 to 54, are impressive. In 1965 over 90 percent of men aged 55 to 59 were still in the labor force, but in a space of 20 years this proportion plummeted to less than 80 percent – a decline rate of nearly 12 percent. Nearly one-half of this decline took place in only one five-year period, from 1970 to 1975. This was a period in which U.S. unemployment was at one of its highest rates. As for the group aged 50 to 54, the labor force participation rate dropped from 95.0 percent in 1965 to only 88.6 percent in 1985 – a rate of decline of 6.7 percent. Thus, about 12 out of every 100 men as young as 50 to 54 years old were not working in 1985, compared with only 5 out of every 100 in this age group 20 years earlier.

The 1982 New Beneficiary Survey of the Social Security Administration also deals with the issue of the influence of early unemployment experience. That study's data indicate that 36 percent of all the new retirees who were no longer working had stopped working before they were eligible for retired-worker benefits. (Not all stopped because of job loss, however.) This measure varies considerably by sex and marital status: 26 percent of married men and 33 percent of unmarried men stopped working before age 61½, whereas 55 percent of married women and 30 percent of unmarried women did so. The pattern for married women who had stopped working before reaching the Social Security pension age is attributable to their leaving when their husbands did, or to the possibility that income from their husband's earnings (for those still working) reduced the incentive for the wife to continue working.

The more critical question here is to what extent joblessness is associated with age of exit. Data reported by Packard and Reno (1988) show that the issue is especially pertinent in early exits of men. As Table 8.12

Table 8.12. *Percent exiting because of job loss, by age at exit*

	Total	Under 55	55–61.5	61.6–62	63 or older
Both sexes[a]	12	15	15	11	9
Men	11	24	13	11	8

[a]Separate data for women are not provided by Packard and Reno (1988). "Exit" is defined here as leaving the labor force completely. It excludes part-time employment, or any work accompanied by earnings.

indicates clearly, the younger the age at which men exit from the labor force, the greater the proportion citing joblessness as the reason – from only 8 percent of those exiting at 63 or older to nearly one-fourth of those exiting before the age of 55.[10]

Several sensitive and controversial policy issues are raised by Kingson (1981) in his report on early retirement for the U.S. House of Representatives' Select Committee on Aging:

Is early retirement primarily a cost problem for pension systems – including private and Social Security systems?
Will demographic developments increase these cost pressures?
Is the problem of early retirement essentially a matter of worker responses to "pension incentives"?
In contrast, what is the role of health problems and unemployment experience?

In regard to this last issue, it is Kingson's opinion that "pension incentives that encourage many able workers to retire early are, in large part, a symptom of an economy unable to provide employment for all who are willing and able to work" (p. 95). Whether early retirement is a matter of conscious and deliberate policy on the part of major actors in this domain, as was largely the case for the origins of the Social Security Act or, instead, the response of individual workers, there can be no question about the role of joblessness – especially prolonged joblessness – in the trend of very early exit from the labor force.

---

[10] Other studies, such as the 1981 NCOA Survey (at about the same time as the New Beneficiary Survey) confirm the greater impact of joblessness on younger than on older retirees, regarding age at retirement and employment status. Sheppard's (1977) analysis of the 1966–73 data tapes for the National Longitudinal Survey also reveals a relationship between previous employment and early – or very early – withdrawal from the labor force.

The Government Accounting Office report *Retirement Before Age 65* points to the increase in the proportion of all men 55 to 61 years old receiving a pension, from only 8 percent in 1973 to 17 percent 10 years later, in 1983. For women in the same age group, the corresponding proportions are 4 percent and 7 percent. These figures refer to the current age of these individuals, not the age at which they first started receiving such pensions, which makes the upward trend even more impressive.[11]

8.4.5 Findings of the New Beneficiary Survey

Much of the previous discussion and the empirical data presented have been based on all persons who were pension recipients, without regard to their age at complete exit from the labor force. The New Beneficiary Survey of the Social Security Administration, based on 1982 interviews with men and women first receiving their retired-worker benefits from mid-1980 to mid-1981, is unique in this regard and provides certain insights not possible through studies – whether longitudinal or cross-sectional – based on retirees regardless of when they first received their benefits.

The previously cited report on retirement based on the New Beneficiary Survey by Packard and Reno (1988) found that 35 percent of men exiting before age 55 were receiving an employer pension, compared with only 9 percent of women; for persons exiting at age 55 to 61.5 (before drawing retired-worker benefits), the corresponding proportions with employer pensions were 61 percent of men and 35 percent of women (Table 8.13).

Using the the New Beneficiary Survey's data on the respondents' assertions as to the most important reason for their exiting – especially exiting before age 62 – we may be able to gain a more detailed understanding of the major pathways through which American workers move completely out of the labor force.[12] This approach may be one of the few methods that can approximate the use of explicit, formal institutional pathways that better characterize the European situation.

As stated earlier, in the United States the situation is much more complex and has much less of a coherent structure. The "formal" pathway

---

[11] The GAO suggests that the 1973–83 increase in pension receipts "may be due to economic conditions." The 1983 unemployment rate was about double that in 1973. Workers laid off at these "young old" ages could then begin to take advantage of any pension opportunities.

[12] This survey, conducted in 1982, included 9,100 retired-worker beneficiaries first receiving their benefits in 1980–1.

Table 8.13. *Percentage of new beneficiaries receiving an employer pension, by age when they left their last job*

	Total	Age left last job				
		Under 55	55–61.5	61.5–62	63 or older	Still working
Total	47	14	48	55	57	22
Men	58	35	61	61	59	28
Women	34	9	35	44	53	13

Source: Adapted Packard and Reno (1988), Table 5.

for very early (under age 62) exit that does exist is the disability route under the Social Security system. It has already been pointed out that the number of persons exiting via this pathway has increased at a much greater rate than the "normal" retired-worker awards. Furthermore, the retired-worker awardees at age 62, it appears, experience job disloca-tions such as shutdowns and layoffs before that age, but cannot receive retired-worker benefits until they are 62. Many of these workers may have experienced disabling conditions as well. Others include working wives exiting before 62 but having to wait until that age for benefits.

Our analysis of the factors identified by the New Beneficiary Survey respondents exiting before age 62 as the most important reason for com-plete exit yielded a finding that reinforces the disability pathway, that is, "bad health" as a reason for exiting. Bad health ranked number one among early exiters in the list of their most important reasons for com-plete exit, regardless of sex. Among those exiting at 62 or older, its rank was second, way below the first-ranking "tired of working" (Table 8.14).

As discussed earlier, job loss is clearly another pathway for exiting fol-lowed more frequently by the early exiters than by the late ones. This is true of women as well as men in the New Beneficiary Survey. These two pathways (bad health and job loss), it needs to be emphasized, account for roughly two-fifths of all early exiters, compared with only one-third of those exiting at 62 or later. They are especially critical in the early exit of men. In accounting for the pattern among women, we cannot ignore their unique status in society as presently structured – not just in the labor market. As Table 8.14 shows, caring for others and/or the retire-ment of their husbands may also be conceptualized as special routes of early exit. More than one-fifth of the women exiting before age 62, but

Table 8.14. *"Most important" reason for retiring, by age at exit (in percent)*

Reason	Under 62			62 or later		
	Total	Men only	Women only	Total	Men only	Women only
Bad health	24.8	30.5	21.4	23.6	22.7	24.4
Tired of working	20.5	28.2	15.9	40.0	43.0	33.5
Job loss	14.4	14.3	14.6	9.8	9.2	10.7
Mandatory retirement age	2.2	4.7		7.2	8.2	
Care for others			14.2			7.7
Spouse retired			6.2			4.8

Note: Columns include percentages only for the most frequently cited reasons and hence total less than 100 percent.

only one-eighth of those leaving after that age, left work primarily because of these factors.

These findings evoke another crucial question, the role of pensions (other than Social Security retired-worker benefits) in facilitating exit by the major pathways cited here, as well as the exits related to caring for others and spouse's retirement reported by women in the New Beneficiary Survey.

8.4.6 Pensions as facilitators of "very early" exit (before age 62)

Until recently, and even today, references to "early retirement" in the U.S. Social Security literature typically defined it as receipt of a retired-worker benefit from ages 62 to 64, that is, before age 65. But the New Beneficiary Survey findings point very definitely to large numbers and proportions leaving the labor force completely even before age 62: 37 percent at the time of the 1982 survey. For married women alone, the proportion was 60 percent! There is a widespread belief that age-at-exit decisions are heavily influenced by the availability of non–Social Security pensions (i.e., private and public employer pensions exclusive of Social Security retired-worker benefits). Is it possible that exit before age 62 is facilitated by a pension "opportunity"? More especially, how, if at all, does a pension facilitate exit before age 62 when the worker's primary reason for exiting from the labor force is taken into account? Finally, how does sex/marital status relate to these critical questions?

If we examine the New Beneficiary Survey sample as a whole, we would have to conclude that as far as exit before age 62 is concerned,

Table 8.15. *Percent exiting before 62, by pension receipt, sex, and marital status*

	Total Sample	Men		Women	
		Married	Unmarried	Married	Unmarried
With pension	36	31	35	59	23
Without pension	40	22	31	62	39

pensions do not facilitate such behavior, at least not at the present time. Future developments in pension-age policy could change this for new generations of employees. But do pensions facilitate exit before 62 under selected conditions? We refer here to the reasons given by the New Beneficiary Survey respondents as the most important, or primary, reason for complete exit. Only job loss constitutes a distinct exception to the general conclusion that pensions do not facilitate exit before 62: Among workers exiting primarily through loss of employment, 51 percent of the ones with a pension, but only 43 percent of those without a pension, exited before age 62.

In addition to job loss, there is the possibility that spouse's retirement is another pathway for exit before age 62 facilitated by pension receipt: 53 percent of workers citing this factor as the primary exit reason and receiving a pension exited before 62, compared with only 47 percent of those without a pension (but leaving the labor force for the same reason).

To a very slight extent, bad health may be another pathway facilitated by pension receipt: Among workers citing bad health as their primary reason for exit, 39 percent of pension recipients and 37 percent of non-recipients exited before age 62. But it appears that with or without a pension, younger workers in poor health are forced to exit from the labor force.

These comparative statistics refer to primary reasons for exit and whether exit is facilitated by pension receipt. How do sex and marital status relate to the influence of pensions on "decisions" to exit before age 62? Analysis by sex/marital status shows that pensions do play a role in exit before 62, but only among men – regardless of marital status (Table 8.15). Pension influence is clearly at play in the case of the married men: 31 percent of them with a pension exited before age 62, compared with only 22 percent of those without a pension.

The more subtle (and precise) question, however, is how, if at all, pensions influence the "very early" exit phenomenon when we simultaneously take into account the primary exit reason and sex/marital status.

Table 8.16. *Percent exiting before 62, with and without a pension, by primary reason for exiting, sex, and marital status*

Most important exit reason and sex/marital status	With pension	No pension
Job loss, total	51	43
Married men	42	29
Unmarried men	31	37
Married women	71	61
Unmarried women	34	45
Bad health, total	39	37
Married men	34	25
Unmarried men	37	32
Married women	58	58
Unmarried women	22	37
Care for others, total	55	66
Married men	39	17
Unmarried men	24	84
Married women	69	80
Unmarried women	43	58
Spouse retired, total	53	47
Married men	0	0
Unmarried men	0	0
Married women	57	53
Unmarried women	64	51
Tired of working, total	23	24
Married men	18	12
Unmarried men	33	6
Married women	39	48
Unmarried women	16	13

The basic source for our narrative here is the data in Table 8.16. It refers to proportions exiting before age 62, holding constant the following variables: (1) pension receipt, (2) sex, (3) marital status, and (4) selected (most frequently cited) "most important" reasons for exiting. The "most important" (or primary) exit reasons included in Table 8.16 are the five most frequently cited ones and encompass more than three-fourths of all the respondents.

Pension receipt facilitates exit before age 62 only for a few reasons and only for selected sex/marital status groups. The most crucial finding from this type of analysis is that for four or five primary exit reasons, pension receipt facilitates the exit of married men before age 62. For no other sex/marital status group are there so many primary reasons or conditions in which pensions facilitate "very-early" exit. Pensions make a difference for married men who exit because of job loss, bad health, having to care for others, and being tired of work.

One paradox in this case lies in the fact that married men as a whole have the lowest "very-early" exit rate: Only 26 percent exit before age 62.[13] In the event of job loss, bad health, and having to care for others, pension receipt facilitates "very early" exit for these married men at levels greater than their overall average rate.[14]

8.4.7 Myopia in retirement policy research

It is pertinent at this point to comment on the general tendency in the economics of aging and related fields to draw major conclusions about retirement issues derived only from the study of men, and essentially to ignore the significance of women in the labor force and their own retirement patterns – or to assume that generalizations derived from analyses of data based on males apply, across the board, to women.

The "revolution" in sustained labor force participation of women (including wives) must be permanently recognized in policy research – including research directed at the retirement phenomenon. In addition, marital status is too often neglected or minimized. It should be clear from the approach used in our analysis of the New Beneficiary Survey data that both sex and marital status must be essential units of policy research scrutiny.

A dramatic and telling demonstration of this principle pertains to married women, judging from the New Beneficiary Survey data and our focus here on pensions as a potential facilitator of "very early" exit (exit before age 62), and taking into account primary reasons for exit. We

---

[13] The comparable rates are 31 percent for unmarried women, 35 percent for unmarried men, and 60 percent for married women.

[14] Another interesting sidelight is that while job tiredness is a factor *not* associated with early exit, pension receipt among married men citing this factor as a primary exit reason appears to make for "very early" exit: 18 percent of the pensioners citing work tiredness, but only 12 percent of nonpensioners exited before age 62. Pension receipt as a facilitator of "very-early" exit among workers claiming work-tiredness as their most important exit reason is indeed confirmed for all of the New Beneficiary Survey respondents except married women (Table 8.16).

stated earlier that pensions apparently do not facilitate "very-early" exit among married women. Among those with a pension (including their own and their husband's), 59 percent exited before age 62. But this proportion is actually slightly less than the one for married women exiting without any pension – 62 percent. These two percentages point once again to the conclusion that, generally speaking, in the case of married women pensions make no difference as far as exit before 62 is concerned. Attention to a more fundamental dimension is called for, however. That is the issue of *who* is the pension recipient, both husband and wife or wife only?[15]

If we isolate the married respondent herself as the only pension recipient, the results show – perhaps paradoxically – that only 43 percent of these wives exited before age 62 – far lower than the 62 percent of wives reporting no pension at all (neither for themselves nor their husbands)! Even when we include cases in which both wife and husband are pension recipients, the proportion remains at 43 percent. Obviously, something other than pensions is at play among the factors and conditions influencing the exit of wives before age 62. More telling is the finding that when only the husband is the pension recipient, the proportion of wives exiting before age 62 is 73 percent – far higher than the 59 percent of all wives with access to a pension and the 61 percent of nonrecipients.

Returning to a principal topic of this section – the degree to which (if at all) pensions facilitate "very-early" exit via such routes as job loss, bad health, and so forth – how does this interaction work itself out among married women? Without regard to *who* is the pension recipient, it is clear that pension receipt facilitates "very-early" exit by wives. For example, among those giving job loss as the primary reason for exit, 71 percent of pensioners, but only 61 percent of nonpensioners, exited before age 62. The proportion is even greater (78 percent) if we focus on those cases in which *both* husband and wife receive pensions (Table 8.17). The more provocative finding, however, is that when the husband is only pension recipient among wives citing bad health, job loss, or caring for others, the proportions of married women exiting before age 62 are substantially above that of wives without any pension whatsoever.

[15] Among the retired workers in the New Beneficiary Survey, as reported elsewhere, married women have by far the greatest rate of exit before age 62 (60 percent). More than three-fifths of this subgroup (62 percent) had some kind of non–Social Security pension – their own or their husband's. More to the point, most of these pension recipients (two-thirds) actually had husbands who were the only pensioners in their marriage. That is, 41 percent of the husbands of the wives retiring before 62 were the only pension recipients. Wives who were the only pension recipient among this group amounted to a mere 15 percent.

Table 8.17. *Percentage of wives exiting before age 62, by pension recipient and primary reason for retirement*

	Pension recipients				
Primary reason	Wife only	Husband only	Both	All recipients	No pension
Job loss	69	70	78	71	61
Bad health	45	71	39	58	58
Caring for others	27	94	52	69	80
Husband's retirement	59	56	56	57	53
Tired of working	32	52	33	39	48
Total, all reasons	43	73	43	59	62

Even if there is *no* pension recipient, 80 percent of all wives exit before age 62 if having to care for others is their most important reason for doing so. Except when their husbands are the only pension recipient, nonrecipients among married women leaving for this crucial reason are more likely to exit before they reach age 62 than are recipients. This 80 percent among wives with no pension support exceeds by far the 69 percent of all other married women leaving before 62. Here again, the evidence suggests that pension receipt is not a crucial influence on wives who exit because they need to care for relatives or close friends. In this situation, wives leave the labor force before age 62 even if neither they nor their husbands are pension recipients. To be sure, some may have husbands who continue to work, thus making it possible for them to leave the labor force to provide the care.

8.5 THE POLITICS OF EARLY EXIT

The political issue that has succeeded the mandatory-age controversy relates to early exit. Some day there may even be debates over the need for a policy that discourages exit *below* a certain age. Current patterns and trends regarding incentives to exit (or disincentives to continue working) have moved to the foreground of the policy debate replacing compulsory retirement as an issue.

In explaining this change, we cannot rule out the role of political and other noneconomic incentives or that of sociocultural influences. Economic incentives (e.g., levels of anticipated retirement income, especially pension income) are not sui generis phenomena or "independent variables." Political pressures revolving, for instance, around the problem of youth unemployment have led to subtle and not-so-subtle techniques of removing "older" workers from the officially measured labor force.

But there are countercurrents in labor force developments. There is now a belated recognition by government and the private sector of a "labor gap" over the coming decades – a gap produced primarily as a result of declining fertility rates. These new demographic forces can move policy in an opposite direction (U.S. Department of Labor 1989). The "pool" of younger workers is shrinking, and when this is coupled with the current decline in the age at which older workers are exiting, a severely reduced rate of labor force growth (of about 1 percent per annum) is the result. That 1 percent growth rate in labor supply needs to be evaluated against a projected 2 to 3 percent growth rate in the economy. And all of these factors must, finally, be weighed against projections of an extremely poor productivity growth rate.

This impending labor shortage may result in a delayed "policy response" aimed at preventing the loss of qualified older workers to early exit caused by currently attractive exit incentives. The shortage may not be satisfactorily met through immigration and accelerated labor force participation by women under age 55 – which may already be plateauing.

The history of retirement in the United States involves a scenario of seemingly opposite or conflicting policy directions resulting from the *government's* efforts to raise age at exit or to restrain the drift toward early exit and the *employer world's* efforts to expand on and accelerate the rate of early exit.

The U.S. government – concerned, for example, about a Social Security Trust Fund "crisis" (whether contrived or real) in the near future – started to face the problem as early as 1978, when President Jimmy Carter signed amendments to the 1967 Age Discrimination in Employment Act that would raise the allowable compulsory retirement age from 65 to 70; later, the Carter Commission on National Social Security Policy pondered the question more deeply. By 1983, as a result of President Ronald Reagan's bipartisan commission, Congress (to the astonishment of many observers) legislated several measures designed to restrain the early exit trend and thereby lighten the pressures on the trust fund. Social Security is no longer so sacrosanct as in the past. Measures to be implemented toward the end of this decade or later include:

1. An increase in the "penalty" for retiring before age 65
2. A gradual increase in the age for "full" benefit to age 67 (it is now age 65)
3. An increased "bonus" or incentive to defer retirement
4. A lower penalty for continuing to work on a reduced-income basis while in receipt of "retired"-worker benefits.

The taxation of part of a retiree's Social Security income can be another potential disincentive for early retirement; the 1988 Catastrophic Medicare Act required a surtax on the income taxes of *only* the 65-plus population, contrary to the "traditional" mechanism of a payroll tax on only the working population of all ages, to pay for the support of the older population. In this case, however, the pressure of the senior citizens' lobby was sufficient to get the Act repealed shortly after it was enacted.

Light (1985) reminds us that Social Security will always be a "hot political issue" and a part of the continuing conflict concerning "who gets what, when, where, and how." Despite the public opposition (reflected through opinion polls) to changing Social Security into a means-tested program, eliminating it altogether and replacing it with private retirement-income plans, or raising the full-benefit retirement age from 65, Congress in 1983 nevertheless did make the changes potentially affecting retirement age.

These changes were in response to the recommendations of the presumably bipartisan National Commission on Social Security Reform, the members of which were appointed by the Reagan White House and Congressional Democrats and Republicans. One of the options the commission discussed for resolving the potential crisis of the system's retired workers trust fund was an increase in the retirement age for full benefits from the then current 65 (with no increase from 62 for "early retirement" benefits but with further actuarial reductions to benefits at that exit age).

The debate over retirement age actually focused on two points. First, the commission proposed *incentives* to defer labor force exit by raising the Deferred Retirement Credit (DRC) for each year the worker postponed retirement after age 65 gradually from 3 percent to 8 percent (reaching the full 8 percent in 2009). Republicans, according to Merton C. Bernstein, one of the consultants to the commission, pushed this proposal, and Democrats went along with the recommendation despite their concerns about its increased cost (Bernstein and Bernstein 1988:56). Second, and most controversial, was the *disincentive* recommendation, which proposed gradually raising the age for full retirement benefits to 67. All but one Republican commission member backed it, but the Democrats criticized it as unfair, claiming that the existing provisions of the Social Security Act (e.g., the DRC) would achieve the same objective and that age 67 for full benefits would actually mean a benefit reduction for some workers. Light (1985) lists labor, liberals, and the National Council of Senior Citizens (labor-backed) as among the groups opposing the increase in retirement age.

In the House of Representatives, the *only* commission recommendation that was debated was the increase in the retirement age. According to Bernstein and Bernstein (1988:5), "Congress decided to meet the one-third of the long-term projected deficit for which the commission did not make an agreed-upon recommendation by raising retirement age in two steps in the next century." (For a discussion of the arguments involved, see Chapter 8 of Bernstein and Bernstein in [1988], especially pp. 183–91.)

Another political thrust, in the United States at least, consists of a new form of "ageism" that may have certain implications for the issue of exit age. This new ageism contains two somewhat opposite images of the elderly: (1) as objects of resentment, because they are a "burden" on the "productive" population; and (2) as objects of envy because they have progressed more, economically, than young middle-aged and younger Americans. This is deemed unfair and inequitable. At times, this inequity is viewed as having been caused by the progress made by older persons in the United States.

This new ageism, as it makes further inroads among politicians, the media, and influential "public opinion" elements, could result in public policies aimed at keeping more older persons *out* of the retired population. In an effort to reduce the presumed burden of supporting older persons (and to meet the impending labor shortage), large segments of the "younger older" population may be encouraged to remain in the work force beyond current exit ages or may be discouraged from leaving it through the measures discussed earlier.

Some observers doubt that the recent changes in the Social Security provision will have much effect on the exit phenomenon (see Boaz (1987). This could be the case if early-exit "opportunities" in our private pension plans remain untouched. As long as employers sanction and prefer such possibilities, and as long as they, in so doing, benefit in the form of corporate tax savings and work-force size (or labor-cost) control, there is little chance of the legislative "reforms" of Social Security having much impact on that phenomenon.[16]

The future of the Social Security system continues to be under a cloud. In addition to proposals designed to reduce the costs of the system, there are even proposals to eliminate it altogether and rely instead on one or more forms of private-sector pensions and individual savings. Such proposals, it must be stressed, are unique to the United States. At the present time, they tend to be viewed as from the "radical-right fringe" and are

---

[16] The last time the U.S. government manipulated the Social Security system in order to cope with unemployment was in 1961, when there was a recession and unemployment was at 7 percent, a proportion deemed politically unacceptable at that time. Retirement under the system was lowered from 65 to 62, with reduced benefits, for men. Age-62 benefits had been available to women since 1956, but not as a measure to control unemployment.

not taken very seriously in the mainstreams of Republican and Democratic political circles or by their economic advisers. It should be noted,
however, that at one time raising the retirement age for full Social Security benefits was considered outlandish. But while (in 1981) the vast
majority of all Americans and those in the labor force aged 18 to 54 (85
percent of each sample) disapproved of reducing benefits for future retirees, only 58 percent rejected any gradual increase in the full-benefit
retirement age under Social Security as a way of helping the Social Security system.[17]

Would it be outlandish to speculate on the implications of a draconian
surgery on, or the actual elimination of, the retired-worker pension program under Social Security? In the event of that unlikely scenario, reliance on some form(s) of the private-pension approach, and on individual savings (made less attractive since incentives for Individual
Retirement Accounts were virtually eliminated under recent tax law
changes), might produce ideal retirement income resources, as the
extremist advocates of such approaches would have us believe.

If the critics (see, for example, Stein 1986) of the extremists' proposals
are correct in saying that the latter's schemes could not provide the level
of retirement incentives under current schemes (including continued
reliance on Social Security), or guarantee any protection from inexorable
inflation, then we need not concern ourselves with any potential problems associated with continuing trends of early exit.

But we do not know just how entrenched the practice of early exit –
especially before age 62 – is in the United States. Ekerdt, Bosse, and
Glynn (1985:405) of the Boston Veterans Administration's Normative
Aging Study claim that retirement itself is "now firmly embedded in the
life course . . . . Workers' intentions toward retirement may have a deep
keel keeping them in a long-held structure of expectation about later
life." The declining rate of labor force participation by persons as young
as 55 to 59 points up the "institutionalization" of early exit. What is still
not clear is just how strong these currents, or factors cited above, might
be in their future potential for veering that deep keel from the structure
of expectations.

The future of retirement-age policy will be affected by political and
value dimensions, especially as we move past the early years of the next
century. In 1979, Duke University's Richard Fox (in a paper prepared for
a National Research Council conference on the Future of Aging) wrote:

. . . given the upcoming conflict over the Social Security System and the moral
and fiscal quandary brought on by a decreasing number of young workers sup-

---

[17] Unpublished data from 1981 NCOA/Louis Harris survey.

porting an expanding number of old retirees, I can foresee demands so great as to appear revolutionary (or a reaction to these demands so strong as to represent an economic and moral reordering of basic social institutions).

Fox leaves out of his admittedly speculative statement the possible scenario of a *change* in retirement-age policy as one response to the projected burden on "a decreasing number of young workers." The changes in Social Security since 1979 (especially those made in 1983) may be a portent of such a shift. Indeed, if we witness additional legislation resulting in new costs for the older population, they could be interpreted as turns in a new direction that make it more expensive than in the past to spend a given number of years in retirement. Pension coverage appears to be declining among the employed (Andrews 1985). It still is not clear, however, how much workers indulge in a sort of cost-effectiveness analysis when making a decision about when to exit voluntarily. Be that as it may, there remains the persistence of the pattern already discussed: a sort of schizophrenia characterized by conflicting, inconsistent policy directions regarding retirement-age policy.

There is also the issue of the "politicization" of the retiree population as some sort of relatively homogeneous voter bloc, especially on the issue of retirement-age policy. Apart from the critiques of the notion or belief that they do constitute such a bloc, there is the confusion over the degree to which an already-retired population cares about retirement-age policy and/or whether older workers are actually a self-conscious group with an identity separate from workers of younger ages. To be sure, age-related organizations such as the American Association of Retired Persons have programs for and about employment-related problems for mature men and women. But it is not clear to what extent there is any objective or felt intra-organizational conflict between striving to keep older persons in the labor force, on the one hand, and striving to maintain and/or improve the welfare of the already-retired population on the other.

As for the politics of inter-generational relations, we must bear in mind that this is not the same as tensions based on social class, sex, ethnic, or racial differences. As Heclo (1988) has put it, "we are dealing with a phenomenon that involves (a) *family* (which includes young and old) [and] (b) a *time* dimension, i.e., the young eventually become old.

REFERENCES

Andrews, Emily. 1985. *The Changing Profile of Pensions in America.* Washington, D.C.: Employee Benefit Research Institute.

Bernstein, Merton C., and Joan Brodshaug Bernstein. 1988. *Social Security: The System That Works.* New York: Basic Books, p. 56.

Boaz, Rachel Floersheim. 1987. "The 1983 Amendments to the Social Security Act: Will They Delay Retirement? A Summary of the Evidence." *The Gerontologist* 27:151–5.

Ekerdt, David J., Raymond Bosse, and Robert J. Glynn. 1985. "Period Effects on Planned Age for Retirement, 1975–1984." *Research on Aging* 7:395–407.

General Accounting Office. 1986. *Retirement Before Age 65: Trends, Costs, and National Issues*. Washington, D.C.: GAO.

Graebner, William. 1980. *A History of Retirement: The Meaning and Function of an American Institution, 1885–1978*. New Haven: Yale University Press.

Heclo, Hugh, 1988. "Generational Politics." In: John Palmer et al. (eds.), *The Vulnerable*. Washington, D.C.: Urban Institute, pp. 388–411.

Kingson, Eric. 1981. *The Early Retirement Myth: Why Men Retire Before Age 62*. Report by the Select Committee on Aging, U.S. House of Representatives, October.

Light, Paul. 1985. *Artful Work: The Politics of Social Security Reform*. New York: Random House.

Meier, Elizabeth L. 1986. *Early Retirement Incentive Programs: Trends and Implications*. Washington, D.C.: Public Policy Institute, American Association of Retired Persons.

Mutschler, Phyllis. No date. *Corporate Inducements to Retire and Subsequent Retiree Income Status*. Working paper 12, Policy Center on Aging, Florence Heller School, Brandeis University.

    1986. *Siren Song: The Effect of Financial Incentives on Workers' Retirement Decisions*. Working paper 13, Policy Center on Aging, Florence Heller School, Brandeis University.

Packard, Michael D., and Virginia P. Reno. 1988. "A Look at Very Early Retirees." In: Rita Ricardo-Campbell and Edward P. Lazear (eds.), *Issues in Contemporary Retirement*. Stanford: Hoover Institution Press, pp. 243–72.

Rhine, Shirley. 1984. *Managing Older Workers: Company Policies and Attitudes*. Research Report No. 860. The Conference Board.

Sheppard, Harold L. 1977. "Factors Associated with Early Withdrawal from the Labor Force." In: Seymour Wolfbein (ed.), *Men in the Pre-Retirement Years*. Philadelphia: Temple University Press.

Shuman, Eric. 1983. "The Golden Handshake." *Dynamic Years*, March/April, p. 15

Standing, Guy. 1986. "Labour Flexibility and Older Worker Marginalization: The need for a new strategy. *International Labour Review* 125:329–48.

Stein, Bruno. 1986. "Phasing Out Social Security: A Critique of Ferrera's Proposal." In: Charles W. Mayer (ed.), *Social Security: A Critique of Radical Reform Proposals*. Lexington: Lexington Books, Chapter 2.

U.S. Department of Labor. 1989. *Labor Market Shortage*. Washington, D.C.: Department of Labor.

CHAPTER 9

Sweden: Partial exit

ESKIL WADENSJÖ

9.1 INTRODUCTION

SWEDEN is a late-exit country compared with most other countries, including all those included in this book. Workers in Sweden stay in the labor market for a longer period. This, however, is not the picture most people in Sweden have of the situation. The debate focuses instead on the trend toward earlier exit and the financial and long-term economic problems connected with this development.

In this chapter I try to contribute to the answers to the following questions: Why is Sweden a late-exit country compared with most other countries? and Why is there a trend in Sweden, as in most other countries, toward earlier retirement? I stress four factors here that may in part answer these two questions:

1. Compared with most other countries, Sweden has had a favorable labor-market development with low unemployment. This means that there has not been as much pressure on older workers to exit early in favor of younger workers as there has been in other countries.
2. Swedish social and labor-market policy has followed the work principle and not the cash support principle during most of this century. "Full employment for everyone" has been a catchword. This firm commitment to the work principle means that measures that lead to early exit have been avoided.
3. Since the 1930s Sweden has been strongly in favor of labor-market programs – for older workers as well as younger workers – as a central part of its policy to avoid unemployment. Public relief works, labor-market training, and mobility allowances are typical examples. This policy has been gradually stengthened in the postwar period.
4. Sweden has a pension system that facilitates part-time work for older workers. This system makes it possible for older workers to gradually decrease their number of working hours and may be a factor behind their relatively high labor force participation. At the same time, however, the total number of hours worked among older workers may be lower.

In this chapter I try to relate these factors to the pattern and the development of exit from the labor market in Sweden. Section 9.2 gives a short

284

overview of general developments in the Swedish labor market and presents in more detail the changes in labor-market participation and unemployment among older workers. In section 9.3 the policies of direct relevance for the exit of older workers from the labor force are presented. Section 9.4 shows how these policies are combined to form pathways for early exit, and section 9.5 analyzes the effects of these policies. In section 9.6 the political debate on labor-market policy and the prospects for the future are discussed.

9.2 LABOR-MARKET DEVELOPMENT IN SWEDEN[1]

As with many other industrialized market economies, the Swedish economy has experienced a period of stagnation since the first oil crisis. The decline in growth has been more accentuated than in many other European countries, and inflation has been high compared both with earlier periods and with that for important trade partners.

Even though the general economic development of Sweden follows that of other European countries, there are significant differences regarding the development of the labor market. In Sweden, labor force participation has increased during the whole period while open unemployment has remained at a low level. One factor contributing to this development is Swedish labor-market policy, which is more extensive and has somewhat different emphasis than in other countries. There are, however, two exceptions to this favorable labor-market development. Youth labor force participation has been decreasing for a long period, and not only because of better educational opportunities. Another group with a decrease in labor force participation is older men. On the average men leave the labor force at a younger age than in earlier decades, making their average working life shorter. The male retirement age is also much more flexible than in earlier decades.

9.2.1. Some characteristics of Swedish labor-market development[2]

A striking feature of the Swedish labor market is the development of labor force participation and employment. The labor force participation rate of those who are of an active age – 16 to 67 up to 1975, 16 to 65 since

---

[1] See, e.g., Wadensjö (1987) for an overview of long-run development of the labor market and labor-market policy in Sweden. For thorough studies of developments in the 1980s, see Flanagan (1987) and Standing (1988).
[2] The figures in sections 9.2.1–9.2.3 are from the Labor Force Surveys.

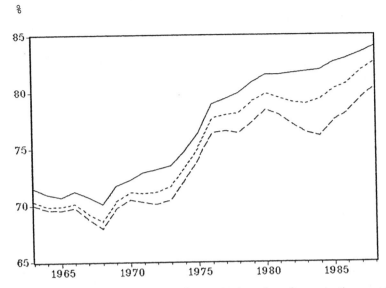

Figure 9.1. Labor force participation, employment ratio, and employment ratio except for those in jobs in labor-market programs, for the population of active age (16 to 67 up to 1975, 16 to 65 since). Key: ―――, labor force participation rate; - - - - -, employment ratio (percent of those of active age); – – –, employment ratio except for those in labor-market employment programs (public relief work, work with wage subsidy, sheltered workshop, youth teams, youth jobs) (percent of those of active age). *Source:* Labor Force Surveys; Information from the Labor Market Board.

1976 – has continuously increased and rose more than 12 percent between 1963 and 1988 (Figure 9.1). Even the employment ratio (employment as a percentage of those of active age) and the employment ratio excluding those in labor-market programs increased, although not as much.

In this area large differences exist between various demographic groups. For men between 20 and 59 years of age, the labor force participation rate has been more or less constant (at a very high level). For men aged 60 to 64, labor force participation has fallen quite noticeably – from 85 percent in 1963 to 64 percent in 1988. This fall is not as great as in other countries but is particulary striking in the Swedish labor-market context of higher and rising participation rates. For women, on the other hand, labor force participation has risen for all age groups between 20 and 64. This development is shown for those aged 25 to 64 in Figure 9.2. The labor force participation rate for women aged 60 to 64 is now 50 percent. Past the retirement age, the labor force participation for both men and women decreases sharply up to the 1980s.

%

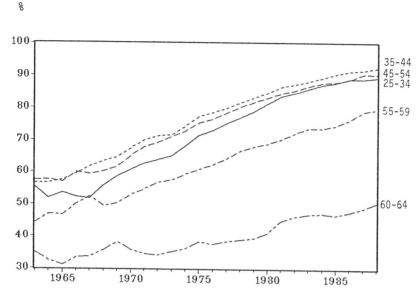

Figure 9.2. Labor force participation among women aged 25 to 64 from 1963 to 1988. The age group represented by each curve is shown at the right. *Source:* Labor Force Surveys.

Unemployment has increased in the past decades in Sweden. From a European perspective, however, unemployment in Sweden is still very low – 1.6 percent of the labor force was unemployed in 1988.

Figure 9.3 shows the development of unemployment over time. During every boom (1965, 1970, 1975, 1980, 1987–9) excluding the latest one, unemployment became slightly higher than it had been in the previous upswing. Also, though with one exception, unemployment tended to be higher during every recession than during the immediately preceding one. That exception was the recession at the end of the 1970s when not only did the labor-market policy programs increase but also industrial subsidy programs were introduced on a large scale.

As unemployment increased, its composition changed. In certain ways it became more unevenly distributed; in others, more evenly so. The difference between the unemployment of women and men has tended to diminish, and the male and female unemployment rates are now of equal size. Two possible explanations for this phenomenon are that women today are established in the labor market and that they are overrepresented in areas with growing employment. To a large extent, women work in the public sector, which has been expanding for a long time.

%

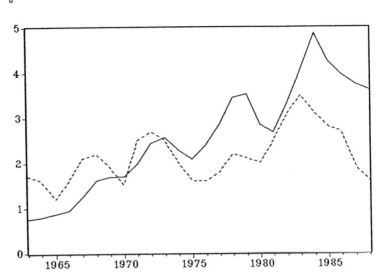

Figure 9.3. Unemployed and persons in labor-market programs as a percentage of those in the labor force. Key:————, in labor market programs; - - - - -, unemployment rate. *Note:* For calculating the share of the labor force in labor-market programs, those in labor-market training and vocational rehabilitation are included in the labor force. The labor-market programs included are labor-market training, public relief work (including subsidized recruitment places in the private and the local community sectors), disability policy programs (sheltered workshops, work with wage subsidy, vocational rehabilitation), and youth programs (youth jobs and youth teams). *Source:* Labor Force Surveys; Information from the Labor Market Board.

On the other hand, a division by age groups shows a markedly increased spread of unemployment. Unemployment for the oldest and the youngest groups has increased compared with other age groups. Unemployment among older workers, however, does not always mean that they are looking for a job. In many cases they have de facto exited from the labor force.

The labor force participation rate of females is now almost the same as that of males. In other respects the female and male labor-market situations differ. Women often work part-time, and their working hours are therefore on the average considerably shorter than men's. Part-time work has increased sharply among youths, who work as well as study, and among older persons (60 to 64) since the establishment of the partial pension system in 1976.

This short overview of the Swedish labor market indicates certain characteristics: rising labor force participation and low unemployment (compared with the 1960s, however, it is higher) and at the same time large shifts in labor-market participation as well as unemployment of different groups. Furthermore, the situation for women in the labor market both regarding labor force participation and unemployment increasingly resembles the situation for men (the same is true for wages, which are not treated here.) On the other hand, the situation for youths and older workers in the labor market has developed less favorably. The next part of this section treats the situation for older workers.

9.2.2   Labor force participation and unemployment among older workers

The labor-market development differs among sex and age groups. Even if we deal only with "older workers" – aged 55 or older – the variation is considerable, as can be seen in the following outline of the main development for older workers.

For men aged 55 and older, labor force participation has decreased continuously since the beginning of the 1960s (the first labor force survey was conducted in 1963). The older the age group, the higher the decline (Table 9.1; see also Chapter 2). In the first half of the 1960s around 50 percent of men aged 65 to 69 were in the labor force. This percentage continuously declined up to the beginning of the 1980s and is now around 15 percent. Part of this decline may be explained by the reduction of the ordinary retirement age from 67 to 65 effective on July 1, 1976, following in the footsteps of the central agreement between LO (The Swedish Trade Union Confederation for manual workers) and SAF (The Swedish Employers' Confederation) to lower the retirement age for all workers in companies who were members of SAF to 65 beginning July 1, 1973. Most of the reduction, however, must be explained by other factors. The participation rate was 16 percentage units lower in 1977 than in 1972, but the total reduction was 49 percentage units between 1963 and 1986. One easily ascertained factor behind this development is structural changes: The share of the self-employed decreased and among the employed the share of white-collar workers decreased. White-collar workers (and also blue-collar workers in the governmental and the municipal sector) already had contractual agreements on a retirement age of 65 years or lower long before 1976.

For those aged 60 to 64 the male participation rate decreased from 85 to 64 percent between 1963 and 1988. The decrease was gradual: the

Table 9.1. *Labor force participation rates, 1963–88*

Year	Men							Women						
	55–59	60	61	62	63	64	65–69	55–59	60	61	62	63	64	65–69
1963	93.8	88.0	86.9	85.9	83.3	78.9	53.5	44.2	37.0	38.1	39.5	34.0	25.4	15.1
1964	93.9	91.3	81.8	80.3	78.0	78.5	49.4	46.9	40.3	35.6	30.4	29.6	25.7	13.4
1965	92.8	90.5	90.7	80.5	77.8	74.2	47.2	46.6	36.0	36.7	31.5	24.2	25.3	15.4
1966	93.3	84.9	84.2	86.9	77.6	79.1	46.4	50.0	38.9	34.6	39.7	27.7	26.0	14.7
1967	94.2	90.3	82.3	81.1	85.5	76.0	45.6	52.3	46.3	36.0	32.0	26.9	25.2	11.1
1968	93.6	91.5	87.9	79.2	86.2	72.1	45.8	49.3	50.2	40.0	31.6	30.6	24.9	14.8
1969	91.9	88.6	83.0	80.4	77.2	72.3	42.1	49.9	47.6	44.8	34.8	32.7	29.7	15.9
1970	90.8	83.3	83.2	81.2	78.2	70.6	40.0	52.8	44.0	39.3	38.4	30.1	26.2	13.1
1971	90.9	81.4	82.0	79.1	74.7	72.7	38.0	54.6	45.1	39.8	35.5	27.9	23.2	12.6
1972	90.2	83.3	78.9	78.9	72.3	68.4	35.1	56.7	44.1	41.6	36.1	25.7	22.6	11.9
1973	89.3	83.1	78.9	77.2	71.7	68.4	32.5	57.4	46.8	43.5	35.0	28.7	21.3	11.3
1974	89.2	79.8	80.1	77.5	68.8	66.1	29.0	59.3	45.8	44.1	38.6	30.0	21.3	9.7
1975	89.7	82.0	77.4	77.0	67.6	65.5	25.3	60.8	51.5	44.6	41.8	30.4	22.9	8.8
1976	89.1	80.5	76.8	74.5	70.6	62.2	18.7	62.3	49.3	44.7	38.2	30.5	25.1	8.6
1977	88.7	78.4	74.0	67.0	66.3	62.7	15.5	64.2	53.6	44.3	37.3	32.7	24.5	6.9
1978	88.1	80.2	73.2	68.0	62.9	59.4	15.4	66.6	51.2	44.3	41.3	30.7	27.5	6.6
1979	88.1	79.2	74.2	69.8	62.5	58.9	17.4	67.9	51.3	47.4	40.7	33.1	24.3	5.5
1980	87.7	76.3	74.0	72.9	61.6	58.3	17.4	68.8	57.7	47.4	41.3	30.5	25.3	5.1
1981	87.8	73.5	73.2	69.8	64.1	58.0	14.5	70.2	59.9	50.6	48.5	33.1	28.0	5.8
1982	87.2	76.4	72.4	71.0	62.2	57.6	15.6	72.1	60.9	52.9	48.0	35.3	30.1	6.0
1983	87.2	75.5	72.3	68.1	62.2	57.9	14.2	73.6	64.8	52.6	49.5	35.0	32.2	6.0
1984	87.5	77.9	70.6	65.8	60.8	54.7	12.6	73.6	64.1	57.9	48.6	36.7	30.7	5.5
1985	87.6	77.1	73.9	62.5	60.8	52.2	12.3	74.5	63.2	54.8	50.1	38.0	29.2	4.8
1986	86.4	76.9	74.3	64.9	58.2	53.9	14.5	76.3	68.3	56.2	49.2	38.1	28.7	2.1
1987a	85.9	74.8	70.0	66.2	58.3	52.4	16.5	78.9	67.7	58.8	56.7	37.4	30.6	3.8
1988	85.9	75.9	68.6	66.2	58.9	51.6	14.8	79.6	64.0	59.0	54.2	43.6	32.4	6.4

aThe labor force surveys were changed in 1987, making the figures before and after not completely comparable.
Source: Labor Force Surveys.

higher the age, the larger the decrease. The declines in the five one-year age groups were 10, 18, 20, 24, and 27 percentage units. The decline of labor force participation in the group aged 55 to 59 was much smaller (7 percentage units) and was concentrated among those aged 58 and 59. The trends shown by the labor force participation rates are in some cases even more evident if the employment rates are studied. The unemployment rate has increased markedly, especially for those aged 62 to 64 (Table 9.2). In the 1987 and 1988 this trend was reversed, however. This may be explained by the low general unemployment but perhaps also by a change in the labor force surveys effective since 1987.

Several factors may contribute to the decrease in labor force participation and employment rates for older workers. In spite of the (in general) favorable development of the Swedish labor market, there may be structural changes that are negative for older workers. In the 1970s traditionally strong Swedish industries (steel, mining, ship building) that employed many older workers ran into severe crises and laid off many workers. Another, and probably more important, factor is that changes in the social security system and the contractual insurance schemes had made it much more advantageous than before to withdraw from the labor force. This issue is treated in detail later in this chapter.

For women aged 55 to 64 the development of labor force participation is the reverse of that for men. For women in this age group labor force participation rates increase steadily just as for younger women. Tendencies to exit earlier among those in the labor force (if existent) are much smaller than the general trend toward higher labor force participation among women.

The labor force participation for women aged 65 to 69, however, has gradually declined, and very few women aged 65 or older are now in the labor force. The factors behind this development are quite probably the same as those behind the corresponding development for men.

For women the increase in unemployment is still higher than among men for those aged 60 to 64 (up to 1987), especially among those aged 63 to 64. This is, however, mainly a statistical artifact or more correctly a social insurance effect (the statistical effect disappeared with the changes in the labor force surveys since 1987). The explanation for the increase in unemployment is that women in the municipal sector (e.g., health) retire at the age of 63 but when retiring they register at the employment office as job seekers. They do so not to get a job or unemployment insurance benefits but to get sickness cash benefits if sick. If they are members of unemployment insurance societies and registered as unemployed, they receive sickness cash benefits if they get sick, and sickness cash benefits provide higher compensation than pensions.

Table 9.2. *Unemployment as a percentage of the labor force, 1963–88*

Year	Men							Women						
	55–59	60–64	60	61	62	63	64	55–59	60–64	60	61	62	63	64
1963	2.0	2.0	1.6	4.4	2.9	0.5	0.0	0.9	0.8	1.3	0.8	0.0	2.0	0.0
1964	0.8	1.6	1.7	1.4	1.2	1.7	2.2	1.1	0.6	0.0	0.8	0.0	0.0	2.6
1965	0.8	1.0	1.0	1.0	0.4	1.1	1.7	0.6	1.0	1.5	1.6	0.0	0.0	1.3
1966	1.3	1.5	1.1	2.0	1.5	0.0	2.8	1.0	0.5	0.7	0.9	0.0	0.0	1.2
1967	1.6	2.9	2.8	2.1	3.4	3.9	2.5	2.1	1.1	0.6	0.8	4.0	0.0	0.0
1968	1.9	3.6	2.7	3.7	2.9	5.9	2.5	1.1	1.0	1.4	0.6	1.1	1.7	0.0
1969	1.4	3.4	2.6	3.0	1.7	4.9	5.6	0.5	1.6	0.5	4.2	2.3	0.0	0.0
1970	1.2	1.9	1.5	2.0	2.0	2.2	1.8	1.0	1.6	1.3	1.7	1.6	2.8	0.8
1971	1.9	2.8	2.6	2.5	3.3	3.6	1.8	2.1	3.0	2.0	3.0	3.3	2.9	4.4
1972	1.7	3.1	2.0	2.1	2.4	4.5	5.2	1.8	2.9	3.8	1.4	3.0	2.5	4.3
1973	1.6	2.8	2.3	2.7	2.3	3.5	3.2	2.0	2.8	1.4	3.2	1.4	5.9	3.3
1974	1.2	2.8	1.8	2.4	2.8	4.3	2.8	1.6	2.8	1.4	3.1	1.9	4.5	4.7
1975	1.0	2.3	1.2	1.6	2.8	2.9	3.2	1.0	2.0	2.0	1.0	1.6	1.4	5.5
1976	0.8	2.1	1.2	1.5	1.3	2.4	4.8	1.2	2.3	2.2	2.1	1.4	3.2	3.0
1977	0.6	1.9	1.2	1.6	2.1	2.7	2.3	1.5	1.8	1.6	1.6	0.9	2.5	3.2
1978	1.0	2.9	1.5	2.9	2.8	4.7	3.1	1.5	2.7	2.3	3.0	1.5	4.3	3.1
1979	1.0	3.0	1.8	2.3	4.1	3.2	3.8	1.8	2.9	2.0	2.6	2.6	3.7	5.0
1980	1.0	2.3	1.9	2.2	1.1	4.1	3.9	1.4	2.1	1.9	1.1	1.3	3.6	3.7
1981	1.6	3.0	2.2	3.0	2.3	5.3	3.9	1.0	3.0	1.4	1.5	2.9	7.6	4.8
1982	2.0	4.5	3.4	4.2	4.7	7.0	5.2	2.0	4.6	1.3	3.4	1.8	10.0	14.2
1983	2.4	5.9	5.7	4.7	5.6	7.7	7.1	2.3	6.1	3.4	2.7	4.1	12.4	13.2
1984	2.3	6.7	6.3	7.1	5.8	6.4	6.4	3.0	8.1	3.6	3.3	4.0	18.7	18.7
1985	2.3	5.1	3.3	5.2	4.9	7.0	6.2	2.4	7.8	3.1	4.4	4.4	14.7	19.6
1986	2.0	4.3	1.9	3.9	5.2	7.0	4.3	1.9	6.6	3.3	5.1	5.0	9.6	15.2
1987[a]	1.4	2.7	3.3	3.7	2.8	1.8	1.6	1.4	2.7	2.9	2.1	1.4	3.0	5.2
1988	1.1	2.2	2.1	3.5	1.5	1.6	2.1	1.2	2.3	1.6	1.8	2.0	2.9	3.9

[a]The labor force surveys were changed in 1987, making the figures before and after not completely comparable.
Source: Labor Force Surveys.

9.2.3 Working time and part-time work

As mentioned earlier, the labor force participation and employment rates have gradually increased in Sweden in the past decades. Up to the early 1980s, however, the total numbers of hours worked in the economy decreased. This means that the average number of hours per worker decreased even more. Since 1982 both the total and the average number of hours worked have increased. The total number of hours in 1988 was back to the level of 1966 and much higher than in the 1970s and the first half of the 1980s.

The long-run trend toward fewer hours worked per person comprises three factors. First, those in the labor force work on the average fewer weeks a year. Laws that increase the length of vacations step-by-step and make it easier to be free for studies or child care are important here. Second, those who work full-time on the average work fewer hours. Important factors behind this development are laws that have reduced the normal workweek to 40 hours and overtime regulations that are more stringent. The legal changes mentioned may be seen as a collective way to use part of the rising wages for leisure.

Third, among those employed, the number working part-time increased up to the beginning of the 1980s. The increase was particularly noticeable in the following three groups:

1. *Women.* Especially those who were new on the labor market worked part-time.
2. *Youths.* It became much more common to combine studies and part-time work.
3. *Older workers.* The part-time pension introduced in 1976 meant an increase in the number of part-time workers aged 60 to 64. However, the same development also applies to those 65 to 74.

Development after 1982 differs in several respects from that in the earlier postwar period. The average work week is increasing for both men and women. There are two exceptions, however: (1) Part-time work has increased among youths aged 18 to 19 as a result of the introduction of a part-time labor market program known as "youth teams." (2) For the oldest workers (65 to 74) the average working hours have continued to decrease.

Real wage decreases and lowered marginal taxes have been suggested as causes for the increase in working hours for those aged 20 to 64. For those 60 to 64 a decrease in the compensation level in the partial pension system during a period may have contributed. I return to this issue later.

9.3   SOCIAL AND LABOR-MARKET POLICY AND EARLY EXIT: THE BUILDING BLOCKS

9.3.1   *Social and labor-market programs for older workers*

Up to the postwar period, Swedish social policy was concerned with basic social security. Income compensation during unemployment, sickness, or old age, mainly given at a flat rate, was low in the national systems. The policy was firmly work oriented. Cash support, for example, was avoided for the unemployed in favor of labor-market programs. This was also the policy for older workers. The great majority continued to work up to the mandatory retirement age of 67, and even after retiring many complemented the low pension by working. White-collar workers, however, often retired at the age of 65 under pension schemes on the firm level or national collective agreements.

The policy changed in the postwar period. The compensation level was raised in the social insurance schemes in the 1940s and 1950s. The income replacement principle was introduced in all social insurance schemes. In the pension system this occurred when the national supplementary pension (ATP) system was introduced in 1960, with the first pensions paid out in 1963.

In the 1960s and 1970s it became easier and easier to get income compensation below the mandatory retirement age. Compensation for older workers who had exhausted their unemployment insurance compensation (starting in 1968) and disability pensions given to older workers for labor-market reasons (in 1972) are only two examples of that trend.

The national pension schemes are the financially most important, but several contractual pension schemes and other contractual insurance schemes are also of importance. These cover almost all employees and are organized on a national level. As complementary insurance schemes, they increase the compensation level and may also, which is of importance for our study, influence the age of exit from the labor market.

To summarize, in the past decades the work principle has still been in force for all but older workers, for whom several new pathways to early exit from the labor market have been opened. In the remainder of this section the various building blocks of the exit pathways are described as well as the labor-market programs that attempt to retain workers in the labor market.

9.3.2   *National social insurance schemes for older workers*

Several parts of the Swedish social insurance system were integrated when the National Social Insurance Act went into force in 1963. This act covers basic and supplementary old age, disability, and widow pensions as well as sickness insurance. When it was decided to introduce partial pensions in 1976, they were also included in the National Social Insurance Act.

National old-age pension. The age for receiving an old-age pension was 67 years up to July 1, 1976, and thereafter was 65 years. There have been several options both before and after 1976, however.

Until July 1976 it was possible to receive an early old-age pension from the age of 63, or to delay the pension up to the age of 70. In the former case, the pension amount was reduced by 0.6 percent times the number of months taken (maximum 48) prior to the pension age of 67, that is, up to 28.8 percent monthly for the duration of the pension (continuing after the age of 67). If the retirement was delayed, for each month of delay the pension was augmented by 0.6 percent.

In 1976, when the retirement age was lowered to 65, the rates were changed. The new interval became 60 to 70 years. If a person retires earlier than 65 his or her pension is now reduced by 0.5 percent a month. A delayed pension is still compensated by an increase of 0.6 percent a month.

The national supplementary pension scheme was established in 1960 and the first pensions were paid out in 1963. Participation is mandatory. This pension scheme supplements the old-age pensions as well as the disability and widow pensions. Supplementary pensions, which are consumer price indexed, depend on the number of years worked (30 years are required for a full pension) and the income during the 15 years with highest income. Incomes up to 7.5 basic amounts a year are the bases for granting pension. (The basic amount is a consumer indexed unit that is used in most social insurance programs. In 1989 a basic amount was set at 27,900 kronor). The total compensation from the national and the national supplementary pension schemes for most persons is about two-thirds of the average income during the 15 best years.

Disability pension. Disability pensions can be calculated by the same method as old-age pensions. This gives low pensions for those who have worked few years. Another possibility for calculation exists, however, if the person has been working or has received sickness cash benefits in the years before receiving a disability pension. In that case assumption points (expected income) are calculated for the years up to age 65.

The pension is calculated by using the assumption points and pension points from earlier years. Those who fulfill the conditions of 30 years' employment (or employment plus assumption point years) will receive income compensation equaling approximately two-thirds of their average gross income for the 15 years with highest income. The exception is, as with the old-age pension, those with the highest income (the scheme has a ceiling), but in practice they always have other supplementary pensions.

Formally, one can receive a disability pension in two different ways: (1) one can apply for a pension and (2) one can receive a pension after the initiative has been taken by the local social insurance offices. If one applies for one, it can be based on medical reasons, on medical and labor-market reasons, or on labor-market reasons alone. The local social insurance offices can initiate disability pensioning on medical grounds for those who receive sickness cash benefits from the health insurance or the employment injury insurance.

In most cases the application for a disability pension is approved by the pension committee of the Regional Social Insurance Society. In 1988 only 1.6 percent of the applications were rejected. This rate decreased from about 5 percent at the beginning of the decade. In the cases in which the local social insurance office takes the initiative for pensioning, few of the "applications" are not approved.

The requirements for obtaining disability pension have gradually become easier and easier. Since 1970 older workers could receive a disability pension for which labor-market considerations were weighed together with medical ones (those aged 63 or more were considered to be older; from January 1, 1974, the age was changed to 60). They no longer had to meet the same requirements regarding occupational and/ or geographical mobility as younger persons.

Two years after the 1970 change, that is, on July 1, 1972, the regulations were further altered. Medical reasons were no longer a necessary requirement for unemployed persons aged 63 and older (changed to 60 since January 1, 1974). The new alternative eligibility requirement for a disability pension is that older workers have used up their compensation rights from the unemployment benefit society (or have had cash unemployment assistance for a minimum of 450 days) and cannot support themselves with the same work that they did earlier or other suitable types of work.

As of January 1, 1977, the law was changed so that only disablement and not the cause of disablement is of relevance for the decision about a disability pension. This means, for example, that alcoholism is now accepted as grounds for granting a pension.

A comparison of the value of an actuarially reduced old-age pension and that of a disability pension shows that a disability pension is much more generous. An actuarially reduced pension drawn at the age of 60 gives a 30 percent lower pension than a disability pension. The difference is the same even after the age of 65.

Part-time pension. There are three possibilities for combining part-time work and a part-time pension:

1. It is possible to take a half old-age pension, for example, to work half-time and be retired half-time from the age of 60. The reduced pension is half of full retirement pension for the same age.
2. It is also possible to combine a disability pension with work. In 1963 three levels of disability pension were introduced – full pension, two-thirds pension, and one-third pension – the latter two for persons who retain some work capacity. On July 1, 1970, the three forms of pension were changed to full, two-thirds, and one-half pension. All pensioners with one-third pension on that occasion had their pension elevated to one-half.
3. In July 1976, a partial pension system was started. It is a separate pension system, financed by a special payroll levy but, like the other pension schemes, administered by the National Social Insurance Board and the regional social insurance societies. It is not possible to combine a partial pension with a part-time old-age or disability pension. It is possible to receive a partial pension if the following conditions are fulfilled: (i) The person has to be between 60 and 65 years old. (ii) The working time has to be reduced by at least five hours a week. (iii) The remaining working time has to be at least 17 hours a week. (iv) The person must have worked at least 10 years since he or she was 45 years old. (v) The remaining income after the reduction of working time may not exceed 7.5 basic amounts. (vi) The person has to reside in Sweden.

If the person who fulfills these conditions applies, he or she may receive a partial pension. The partial pension compensates for 65 percent of the income loss. For pensions granted from 1981 to 1987, the compensation was only 50 percent. On January 1, 1987, the compensation was raised to 65 percent for new pensions, and on July 1, 1987, the compensation rate was raised to 65 percent for partial pensions granted before 1987. The net income with partial pension in most cases will now be 80 to 90 percent of the income before pensioning.

It is possible to compare the value of a half early old-age pension, a half disability pension, and a partial pension assuming a reduction of the working hours from full-time to half-time. The difference between a disability pension and an early old-age pension is a maximum of 30 percent (if retirement is at the age of 60). The partial pension gives a higher reduction of income than the disability pension but a lower reduction than the early old-age pension.

A study by the National Social Insurance Board in 1984 (Riksförsäkringsverket 1984) shows the income after tax for the different alternatives compared with continued full-time work (Table 9.3). The compensation levels presented in Table 9.3, however, in many cases are not the total compensation. In many cases they are supplemented by compensation from contractual insurance schemes.

Table 9.3. *Net income in 1983 in different social insurance schemes as a percentage of gross income*

Scheme	Pensioned at age 63		Pensioned at age 60	
	100,000[a]	75,000	100,000	75,000
Partial (half-time) pension				
50 percent	82	79	82	79
65 percent	86	86	86	86
Half disability pension	90	89	90	90
Half early old-age pension	84	84	78	78
Half-time sickness cash benefits	96	96	96	96
Continued full-time work	100	100	100	100

[a] Yearly gross income in Swedish crowns.
Source: Riksförsäkringsverket (1984):75.

Sickness insurance. Everyone between 16 and 65 years of age in Sweden is insured against loss of income due to illness or injury through sickness benefits. If a worker misses work because of illness, he or she receives 90 percent of earned income. Sickness benefits are limited to a maximum of 90 percent of 7.5 basic amounts.

There is no waiting period, and a person may formally continue to get sickness benefits for an unlimited period (up to age 65). However, if a person has been ill for more than 90 days, it is the obligation of the local social insurance office to investigate to see if the person needs vocational rehabilitation. Additional measures could be a disability pension, an annuity from employment insurance, or a place in a labor-market program. In practice it takes much longer than 90 days to reach a decision about placement in a program. Of those given disability pensions on medical grounds, many receive sickness benefits for more than a year before being pensioned. Older workers are overrepresented among those with long periods of sickness pay.

For the majority, sickness benefits are supplemented by compensation from contractual insurance or from payment according to contractual agreement.

Occupational injury insurance. In 1977 a new occupational injury insurance scheme went into effect, replacing the old scheme that had been in existence since 1955. All employees, self-employed people, and employers are covered. The previous system did not include the latter two categories. The insurance scheme covers occupational accidents, occupational diseases, and accidents on the way to or from the place of work.

Compensation during the first 90 days after an accident comes through health insurance in the form of sickness benefits. The occupational injury insurance scheme covers expenses after this period. Prior to determination of a permanently reduced working capacity, sickness benefits continue to be paid, but are financed by the occupational injury insurance schemes. The sickness benefits from the occupational insurance scheme are higher than those from the health insurance scheme, 100 percent compared with 90 percent. In both cases the insurance schemes compensate only income losses up to 7.5 basic amounts.

If working capacity is permanently reduced by at least one-fifteenth, the injured person has the right to an annuity corresponding to the loss of income. The calculated loss must, however, be at least 0.25 times one basic amount. The income upon which the annuity is calculated is maximized to 7.5 basic amounts. The annuity is indexed by being calculated in basic amounts. If a person with an annuity is awarded a disability pension, only that part of the annuity that exceeds the pension is paid.

As is the case for disability pensions, terms are more lenient for older persons, who are subject to less strict requirements for geographic or occupational mobility in the labor market.

9.3.3 *Contractual insurance schemes: the LO-SAF area*[3]

Contractual insurance schemes cover most employees in the Swedish labor market. The exceptions are mainly those working at short-time, part-time jobs and some workers employed by small, unorganized firms. This section describes the insurance schemes that have been agreed upon between LO (The Swedish Trade Union Confederation for manual workers) and SAF (The Swedish Employers' Confederation), namely, insurance schemes for manual workers in the private sector.[4] In the next section some other important contractual insurance schemes will be presented.

Five contractually determined insurance schemes exist within the LO-SAF area. Four of them are of interest here since they may supplement the income compensation when someone makes an early exit from the labor market.

---

[3] See Edebalk and Wadensjö (1988).
[4] Edebalk and Wadensjö (1989) contains an overview of the contractual insurance schemes for salaried employees.

Severance pay (AGB). Severance pay, which was introduced in 1965, is divided into a taxable A-sum and a tax-free B-sum. Eligibility for the A-sum includes requirements for a certain minimum *length of employment* and a certain *age*. Eligibility for the B-sum requires in addition *continuous unemployment* (minimum of three months) within a certain time period after layoff.

The methods for calculating the A-sum and the B-sum have changed considerably over time. From the beginning, the A-sum was related to the years of employment in the company that made the layoff. This was changed to employment years in the industry and then to employment years in that part of the labor market where AGB insurance is normally taken. Since 1985, the size of the A-sum is related to age only.

On the other hand, until 1973, variations in the B-sum occurred only with respect to age. From 1973 to 1976, the B-sum was related to both age and the unemployment duration. Since 1978, the B-sum varies only in accordance with duration of unemployment. In general the B-sum amount is 1,000 Swedish crowns a month for a maximum of 27 months (39 months for those aged 60 or older when they are laid off). Unemployment insurance and the B-sum may give income compensation of over 100 percent. One important change since 1985 is that the time that one receives disability pension for labor-market reasons is counted as unemployment when calculating the B-sum.

Severance pay is often combined with unemployment insurance and a disability pension to facilitate early retirement, as discussed further in section 9.4.

Supplementary sick pay insurance (AGS). Supplementary sick pay insurance (AGS) came into effect in 1972. The AGS provides a supplement to sickness cash benefits or to a disability pension awarded for medical or medical combined with labor-market reasons. It thereby reduces the income loss for a person who receives a disability pension for those reasons.

A person who has a disability pension/temporary disability pension based on a medical diagnosis receives a monthly compensation that depends on his or her sickness cash benefit-based income.

The AGS compensation is tax-free. For a LO-worker with an average income, the AGS compensation is about the same as the B-amount in the AGB insurance scheme.

Since 1988 the employer pays the normal wage to the sick-listed employee for the first two weeks according to collective agreements. The social insurance system pays the sickness benefits for the same period to the employer.

Special supplementary pension (STP). During the latter half of the 1960s, LO became concerned with the issue of lowering retirement age, which was seen as one way of reducing inequities between blue-collar and white-collar workers. White-collar workers could retire at age 65, while the general retirement age was 67. A decision was reached between LO and SAF in 1971, and the pension scheme, STP, went into effect on July 1, 1973. According to this scheme, STP 1 was paid between the ages of 65 and 67, followed by STP 2 at age 67 as a complement to the national basic and supplementary pension (ATP). When the pension age in the national pension scheme was lowered from 67 to 65 years of age in 1976, the STP was changed to a supplement to the old-age pension from the national system.

The STP pensions depend on the number of qualifying years. This "earning-in time" is calculated in STP years, which must be between 28 and 64 years. An STP year is calculated by dividing the number of hours worked by 832. No more than 1.0 STP year can be earned in a calendar year.

The right to receive STP requires a minimum of three STP years. Further, at least three STP years shall have been earned between the ages 55 and 64, or at least 0.25 STP years between the ages 63 and 64. In general, 30 STP years are required for full STP.

The size of the pension depends on the number of years worked and on the income earned at the age of 55 to 59. The average of the three best years of this five-year period is calculated and called the "pension wage." Full STP constitutes 10 percent of the pension wage.

The total compensation from the STP is coordinated with other contractual pension systems. This means that someone who changes jobs, for example, from private to a municipal job or vice versa, gets credit for the total amount of time worked.

Labor-market no-fault liability insurance (TFA). The labor-market no-fault liability insurance (TFA) compensates principally in accordance with legal rules covering claims for damages caused by occupational injuries. What is important here is that TFA compensates for all income losses not compensated for from other sources. This means that TFA covers income losses for that part of the income that exceeds 7.5 basic amounts.

9.3.4 Contractual insurance schemes for other groups

The preceding section dealt with the contractually determined insurance schemes in the LO-SAF area, that is, insurance schemes for manual workers in the private sector. For other employees in the private sector and for all employees in the public sector, there are corresponding compensation schemes.

Nonmanual workers in the private sector have the same insurance scheme as manual workers for complementing the occupational injury insurance (TFA). For nonmanual workers in the private sector, there is also a severance pay scheme, AGE, which greatly resembles the AGB system.

The sickness pay schemes, however, are organized in a way that differs from the AGS system. Nonmanual workers in the private sector and all employees in the state sector get their (for some groups reduced) salary from the employer when they are sick also. The employer is compensated by the social insurance societies for that part of the compensation that follows the rules of the national social insurance. The complement to the disability pension is integrated with the contractually determined pension system and not with the sickness pay system as for manual workers in the private sector.

Employees of the state, counties, and municipalities have specific pension plans guaranteeing a higher compensation level than the national pension scheme. Those employed by the state have a supplementary pension system for both the old and the disabled. The general rule is that the old-age pensioner receives 65 percent of his or her last salary (the average of the salaries of the last five years calculated at the price level of the last year), plus 3.1 percent of one basic amount a month if 65 or older. The percentage is not calculated on the total salary for those with the highest salaries. The supplementary pension plan for governmental employees pays the difference between this level and the compensation from the national and the national supplementary pension schemes. For disability pensioners the percentage is still higher: 90 percent of the salary plus 3.1 percent of one basic amount a month.

Persons employed by municipalities and county councils have a pension plan that differs from that of the government sector only in minor details. In general, 90 percent of the final salary is guaranteed for disability pensioners, plus 3.6 percent of one basic amount a month.

Most salaried employees in industry get supplementary pensions according to the industrial supplementary pension scheme, ITP, which gives old age pensioners 75 percent of the portion of the final salary that is below 7.5 basic amounts and gives disability pensioners 80 percent. Both old-age and disability pensioners get 65 percent of the portion between 7.5 and 20 basic amounts and 32.5 percent of the portion between 20 and 30 basic amounts. If taking a partial pension, salaried employees in the private sector also get compensation for that part of the income that is over 7.5 basic amounts. The pension schemes for salaried employees in industry have been followed by other parts of the private sector.

The supplementary pensions introduced in this section have existed in the forms described here since the national supplementary pension system started at the beginning of the 1960s. Earlier, the pension schemes were organized in different ways.

9.3.5 Unemployment insurance[5]

State-supported unemployment insurance was introduced rather late in Sweden (in 1935) compared with other countries and was low for a long period. The work principle and labor-market programs with wages at the standard rate were strongly preferred to cash support. The replacement rate has been enhanced, however, in the past decades and is now high in an international comparison.

The combination of low total unemployment and an active labor exchange has resulted in few young and middle-aged persons being long-term unemployed. The labor-market programs have been used to place persons who risk long-term unemployment (if they refuse, they lose their compensation).

The regulations for older workers, however, have become gradually more lenient since the end of the 1960s. On July 1, 1968, the maximum compensation period was increased from 30 to 90 weeks for older workers. Prior to that, the compensation period had been unrelated to age. Older workers were defined as those aged 60 or older (55 or older for those laid off).

Simultaneously, a specific unemployment compensation scheme (*omställningsbidrag*) was introduced for those older workers who had exhausted their unemployment insurance benefits or for other reasons were not entitled to benefits. It was possible to remain on that support scheme up to the age of 67.

Of relevance here also is the introduction in 1972 of disability pensions for older workers who had exhausted their unemployment insurance benefits, described earlier.

In January 1974 a new support scheme (KAS) parallel to the unemployment insurance system was introduced. KAS replaced both the program introduced for older workers in 1968 and an old secondary support scheme for unemployed workers (local community-based but state-supported). The level of compensation in the KAS system is rather low. For

---

[5] See Björklund and Holmlund (1989).

older workers, recipiency of benefits from KAS for 90 weeks is a basis for receiving a disability pension.

The present unemployment compensation system has been in existence since 1974, providing a high compensation level for those who are members of an unemployment insurance society and, for older workers, also rather lenient requirements to test whether they are at the "disposal of the labor market." In practice, they are not obliged to move or change occupation. For younger workers the work principle is still valid.

9.3.6   Labor-market programs

As mentioned in the introduction to this chapter, one of the main principles in Swedish social policy is the work principle. Employment is strongly preferred to cash support. The labor-market policy that has been the centerpiece of this social policy was gradually developed during the present century. The labor-market policy in Sweden receives a larger share of governmental expenditures than equivalent programs in all other countries.

The labor-market policy consists of programs aimed at influencing the size and composition of labor demand (public relief works, subsidized employment, and sheltered workshops) as well as programs aimed at influencing the size and composition of labor supply (training and mobility allowances).

The policy is not restricted to certain age groups. With the exception of youth programs, labor-market programs are for persons of all ages. In practice, this policy has been somewhat modified for older workers. LO, the blue-collar union, objected to placing older workers in labor-market training programs or obliging them to move (the threat of stopping their unemployment benefits was used) in the late 1960s. The easier access to disability pensions mentioned earlier was introduced as a response.

However, this does not mean that older workers are excluded from labor-market programs. On the contrary, it is possible that their share in those programs has increased in the 1980s. The part of labor-market policy that increased most in the 1970s and 1980s is the disability policy, and older workers are overrepresented among the disabled.

Information about the age distribution in the various programs is not available in a uniform way, but an attempt at an overview is presented here.

The sheltered workshops, which since 1980 have been organized as parts of one conglomerate (Samhall), are designed for workers with disabilities that make them very difficult to place in the ordinary labor market. Many stay in sheltered workshops for very long periods even though

Table 9.4. *Share of the labor force in sheltered workshops (%) according to age in 1988*

Age	Males	Females
20–24	0.16	0.22
25–54	0.69	0.62
55–59	1.04	1.30
60–64	1.05	1.09
Total	0.68	0.59

Source: Labor Force Surveys; statistics from the Labor Market Board.

one of the goals of the program is to rehabilitate people and place them in the ordinary labor market. Table 9.4 shows the share of the labor force working in Samhall. As can be seen, older workers are overrepresented in that labor-market program.

Work with wage subsidy is the labor-market program for the disabled that has the most participants. As it is less expensive and more integrative, it is given higher priority and is expanding compared with work in sheltered workshops. Many remain in work with wage subsidies for long periods. Although there are no statistics on the age distribution of those in the program, statistics on the inflow to the program could be used. Table 9.5 shows the number of disabled persons placed in the program during one month.

Because many remain in the program for long periods, the flow statistics are an underestimate of the age of the participants. If we compare the flow data for work with wage subsidy and sheltered workshops, respectively, we find that the age distribution is about the same, and we already know that older workers are overrepresented among those in sheltered workshops.

A third program – labor-market rehabilitation – prepares workers for jobs (sheltered or otherwise) or training. The average length of participation in the program is short (three to four months), and the participants are younger in this program than in the others. However, there are a few participants older than 55 here as well.

Older workers are also placed in programs other than those for the disabled, especially in public relief work. Most participants in public relief work are young workers but older workers also participate in that pro-

Table 9.5. *Disabled workers placed in some labor-market*
programs in February 1989

Age	Work with wage subsidy	Shelterd workshops	Labor-market rehabilitation
<20	4	5	29
20–24	39	37	239
25–34	100	71	331
35–44	122	71	313
45–49	58	45	106
50–54	40	34	70
55–59	30	20	25
60–	9	5	0
Total	403	288	1113

Source: The Labor Market Board.

gram. The older workers' share of the participants corresponds to their share of those registered as applicants at the employment offices.

An important recent change in labor-market policy is the strengthening of employment security. This development started with special rules in the beginning of the 1970s for giving notice to older workers, making it more difficult and expensive to lay them off. The second step was the Law on Employment Security pass by the *Riksdag* in 1974. According to this law, layoffs have to be motivated, the period of notice increases with seniority, and reverse seniority is the rule at layoffs. This protection for older workers remains in effect up to ordinary pension age, 67 years before 1976 and 65 years thereafter. The reverse seniority order may be changed by agreement with the trade union. This law has strengthened the bargaining position of older workers.

A tentative conclusion is that the Swedish labor-market policy is one of the factors explaining the relatively late exit of older workers in Sweden. Without the labor-market programs, more people might have left the labor market and received compensation from the various social and occupational insurance schemes.

9.4 PATHWAYS OF EARLY EXIT

The various building blocks of social policy in Sweden presented in section 9.3 may be combined to facilitate early retirement in various ways. As shown in Table 9.1, many men and women leave the labor force

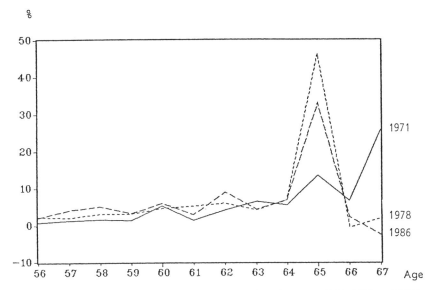

Figure 9.4. The share of a cohort leaving the labor force by age in 1971, 1978, and 1986: men. *Source:* Labor Force Surveys.

before the age of 65, the ordinary retirement age. For men there is a pronounced development over time in this direction. Many more men aged 55 to 64 are outside the labor force now than 10 or 20 years ago.

But we could also look at the picture from another angle. Figures 9.4 and 9.5 show the outflow rate per age group for three years, 1971, 1978, and 1986 for men and women, respectively. In 1971 there were two peaks in the male outflow rate: at the age of 67, the ordinary retirment age, and at 65, the age of retirement for salaried employees according to collective agreements (Figure 9.4). In 1978, after the change of the ordinary retirement age from 67 to 65, the only peak for the withdrawal from the labor force was at the age of 65. Almost 50 percent of the cohort left the labor force at that age. The picture is almost the same in 1986, but the share leaving the labor force at 65 is lower.

For women there were also two peaks of withdrawal from the labor force in 1971. They were at 67, the ordinary retirement age, and at 63, the retirement age for many in the health sector (Figure 9.5). In 1978 and much more in 1986, the exit from the labor force was higher at the age of 65, now the ordinary retirement age. In 1986 the pattern of withdrawal from the labor force was similar for men and women (Figure 9.6). Still, more women than men left the labor force at the age of 63, a fact

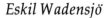

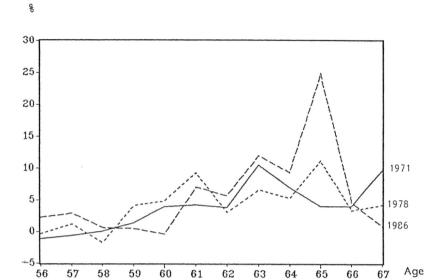

Figure 9.5. The share of a cohort leaving the labor force by age in 1971, 1978, and 1986: women. *Source:* Labor Force Surveys.

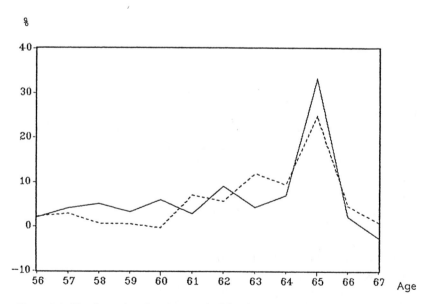

Figure 9.6. The share of a cohort leaving the labor force by age in 1986: men and women. Key: ————, men; - - - - -, women. *Source:* Labor Force Surveys.

that may be explained by the lower retirement age in the health sector (a new collective agreement in 1987 has now made the retirement age the same for men and women in the health sector; the new retirement age is 65). The increasingly similar labor withdrawal pattern for men and women that exists now as compared with earlier periods is explained mainly by changes in the female exit pattern. Those changes may be explained by the fact that women are less concentrated to areas with low retirement age than before, and that women who have entered the labor market later in life remain there longer in order to receive a higher pension (30 years of labor force participation is required for a full supplementary pension).

It is surprising that so many still leave at the age of 65. It is now possible to retire on the national old-age and supplementary old-age pensions at any time between the ages of 60 and 70. The pension is related to the age of pensioning in such a way that there are no economic reasons for retiring just at the age of 65. We must seek the explanation elsewhere.

One factor may be that many workers want to continue after the "retirement" age but that they are forced to leave at 65. The law of employment security gives protection only up to 65, and most firms, as a matter of practice, give notice to workers when they turn 65. Why do firms have this rule to terminate work contracts when the employees reach the age of 65? The explanation may be the prevalence of a seniority wage system that pays higher wages with advancing age. It is a system constructed to provide work incentives and motives to stay with the firm for younger workers. Such a system means that the value of the marginal product is lower than the wage at the time of "ordinary" retirement. The firms therefore adhere to the rule.

If that hypothesis is correct, what now needs to be explained is why many workers and an increasing share of the male workers leave before the mandatory retirement age. Let us now look at some of the pathways of early exit.

9.4.1   The ordinary early-exit pathway

The least frequently used of the five main pathways to early exit is to take an (actuarially reduced) old-age pension before the age of 65. In 1986, 6,194 men and 6,890 women aged 60 to 64 had full-time old-age pensions. These figures may be compared with the 63,586 men and 58,234 women of the same age with full-time disability pensions during the same year.

A delayed pension is even less frequent. Of *all* old age pensioners in 1986 (60 years or older), 6.6 percent had reduced pensions (had taken out a full or half old-age pension early) and 1.6 percent had enhanced pensions (had taken out full or half old-age pension late). Even if we study only the group aged 70 and older, we find that many more have a reduced than an enhanced pension. The majority of those who continue to work when they are 65 to 70 years old start to take out their old age pension at the age of 65, and the overwhelming majority of those who withdraw from the labor force before the age of 65 do not take out an old age pension before that age.

9.4.2   *The unemployment pathway*

Many workers who leave the labor force before the age of 65 do so through a pathway starting with a period of unemployment. In many cases the initial unemployment period is an integral part of a retirement plan.

As mentioned in section 9.3, it is possible for those aged 60 and older to get a disability pension for "labor-market reasons." Labor-market reasons means that a person has exhausted his or her right to compensation from the unemployment insurance society or from cash labor-market assistance. As older workers are entitled to unemployment compensation for 1 year and 9 months, it is possible for a worker who becomes unemployed at the age of 58 years and 3 months or older to receive income compensation up to the age of 65. If an older worker becomes unemployed as a result of a layoff, he or she is in most cases also granted severance pay (from the AGB-insurance if a manual worker, from the AGE-insurance if a nonmanual worker). The total compensation package is shown in Figure 9.7.

A typical case is the following: A firm wants to reduce its work force. According to the law of employment protection, the most protected (the last to go) are those with the highest seniority, generally the oldest workers. The firm wants instead to retain younger workers. As the older workers are the best covered by income compensation schemes, the trade union agrees to a deviation from the seniority rule, especially if the firm adds an extra severance payment to the older workers who leave. With extra severance pay of that kind, they may get an income compensation of over 100 percent.

In recent years the government has tried to make it more difficult to circumvent the employment protection given by the law to older workers. The employment offices are instructed to try to find jobs for older workers even if they have an "agreement" with the employer concerning disability pension for labor-market reasons, and since 1985 the local trade unions are not allowed to make agreements that break the seniority

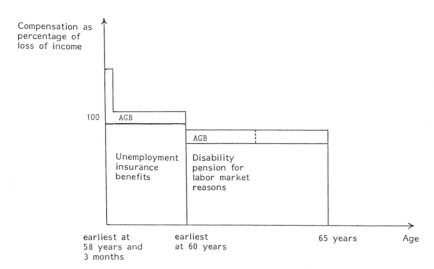

Figure 9.7. Pathways of exit from the labor force: the case of unemployment.

rule for those aged 57½ or older without permission from the national union. The severance pay statistics, however, show that the number of severance payments and thus the layoffs are still strongly concentrated to those aged 58 and older. The unemployment pathway is still open. Another factor has, however, worked to reduce the number of disability pensions awarded for labor-market reasons. The general upturn of the economy in the past few years has meant fewer layoffs and consequently fewer cases of labor-market pensions.

Of the 23,760 persons aged 60 to 64 who were granted a disability pension in 1985, almost half, or 10,663, got a disability pension for labor-market reasons. The share of the newly granted disability pensions given for labor-market reasons increased markedly in the 1970s and 1980s. With better labor-market conditions the number of newly granted disability pensions for labor-market reasons steadily decreased in the second half of the 1980s. In 1988, 20,653 persons aged 60 to 64 were granted disability pensions but only 5,424 of them were for labor-market reasons.

9.4.3   The health pathway

A third form of early exit is the health pathway. People leave the labor force with a disability pension granted on the basis of a medical diag-

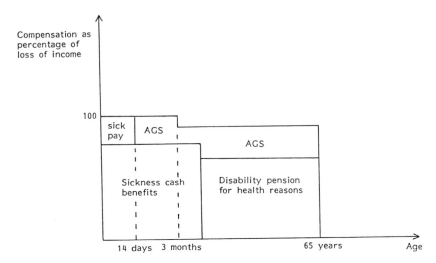

Figure 9.8. Pathways of exit from the labor market: the case of health.

nosis. Since 1970 labor market-related conditions are allowed to influence the pensioning decision for those aged 60 or older (until 1974, aged 63). Labor-market prospects may, in fact, also influence the decision for workers under the age of 60.

In many cases a period with sickness cash benefits precedes the decision to grant a disability pension. Sickness cash benefits are in most cases higher than the disability pension, so an individual has economic incentives to stay on sickness cash benefits. The social insurance office, however, can take the initiative to grant a disability pension. In most cases the final period with sickness cash benefits does not last much longer than one year. Not infrequently, the person may have had several long periods of receiving sickness cash benefits interrupted only by short periods of work. The total period with sickness cash benefits before a disability pension is granted may, therefore, be very long.

Both the disability pension and the sickness cash benefits for most persons are complemented by support from occupational insurances. This means that compensation in many cases is close to 100 percent. The system is shown in Figure 9.8.

It is not unusual for a company physician to initiate a disability pension for health reasons. When firms undergo comprehensive restructuring that ultimately leads to layoffs, it is standard procedure to investigate whether any of the employees are eligible for disability pensions. The firm may add an extra "severance" payment with this kind of pensioning. Concrete knowledge of this is scarce, however.

Disability pensioning has increased over time in all age groups with the exception of those under 30. The studies in this area indicate that the main explanation for the increase is the easier access and the higher compensation (see Hedström 1987; Wadensjö 1985). This does not mean that people are granted disability pensions for medical reasons without having any real cause; rather, many receive them who previously either could not get a pension or continued to work despite disabilities because of the low compensation.

In 1985, 51,000 persons were granted disability pensions, of whom 40,000 received them for health reasons. Of those, in turn, 13,000 were aged 60 to 64 and 11,000 were 55 to 59. In 1988 the corresponding figures were 54,000 disability pensions granted, of which 49,000 were for health reasons. Of the latter group 15,000 went to persons aged 60 to 64 and 13,000 to persons aged 55 to 59. Even if one takes into account that some disability pensioners have never been in the labor market, the health pathway is one used most frequently for early exit from the labor market.

Seen in the long run, the number of disability pensions granted for medical reasons is decreasing for all diagnoses except muscoloskeletal diseases. The expansion of pensions for this diagnosis is concentrated to the last few years and is parallel to the decrease in the number of disability pensions granted for labor-market reasons. It is not unlikely that persons granted pensions for labor-market reasons and those granted pensions for muscoloskeletal diseases have a labor-market situation very much in common.

9.4.4 *The occupational injury pathway*

The occupational injury pathway is the fourth pathway out of the labor market.

A person who leaves the labor market through the occupational injury pathway is compensated for all income losses. The system is shown in Figure 9.9.

For the first 90 days a combination of contractually determined sick pay, sickness cash benefits, and supplementary sick pay leads to 100 percent compensation. For the period after that, the occupational injury insurance scheme guarantees full-time income – the person may, for example, continue to work part-time or in a less well-paid position. The annuity covers the income loss here, as in other cases.

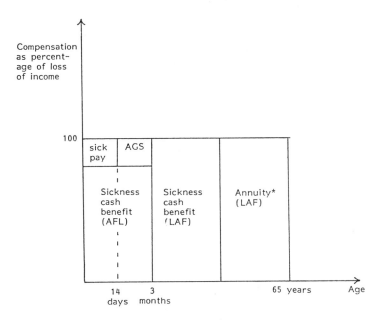

Figure 9.9. Pathways of exit from the labor market: the case of work injury. Note: AFL, National Insurance Act; LAF, work injury insurance. If a disability pension is received, the annuity shown is reduced accordingly.

Income compensation in the national system covers only that part of the income which is below 7.5 basic amounts. That part of the income above the limit of 7.5 basic amounts is covered by the TFA contractual insurance.

The development of the occupational insurance system has been explosive during the past few years. The costs were 1,813 million kronor in 1985 and 6,893 million kronor in 1988. The fund of the occupational insurance scheme had assets valued to 1,878 million kronor on December 31, 1985. On December 31, 1988, the fund had a net debt of 4,190 million kronor.

The costs for occupational injury cash benefits as well as the annuities have increased rapidly. The number of annuities (granted under the law of 1977) has increased from 13,562 in 1986 to 35,031 in 1988. For those aged 60 to 64, the figures are 3,682 and 10,045, respectively and for those 55 to 59, 2,391 and 7,158 respectively. Half of those with annuities are 55 to 64 years old (and about 15 percent are 65 or older). No statistics are available on how many of those with annuities are compensated for a full-time income loss and how many for a part-time income loss. Information is also missing on the number of persons who have an annuity combined with a disability pension, thereby reducing the annuity.

As a response to the rapid development, the National Insurance Board is now developing a new statistical information system, but this is not yet completed.

9.4.5 The part-time pathway

An important difference between Sweden and most other countries is that it is possible to combine part-time work with a part-time pension. Therefore, it is easier to make a gradual withdrawal from the labor force. This is the fifth pathway out of the labor market.

As described in the discussion of part-time pensions in section 9.3.2, there are three forms of partial pensions: half old-age pension, partial pension, and partial (two-thirds or one-half) disability pension. The first two are available from the age of 60; the third can be obtained without regard to age (16 to 64). A half old-age pension is also an option for those aged 65 to 69. Two of the pensions are in many cases supplemented with payments from occupational insurance schemes. For those with a part-time disability pension, the supplement is of the same kind as for those receiving a full disability pension for health reasons (it is not possible to get a part-time pension for labor-market reasons). For salaried employees in the private sector with a partial pension, the occupational pension scheme gives extra compensation for those with high income (more than 7.5 basic amounts).

It is also possible to combine a part-time disability pension and participation in a labor-market program, for example, a half-time disability pension and a half-time at a sheltered workshop (Samhall).

In section 9.3.2 it was shown that the compensation level is now highest for a person who gets a half disability pension and lowest for one who gets a half old-age pension. A half early old-age pension also means a reduced old-age pension after the age of 65. The differences in compensation are even higher because of the contractual insurance schemes. In many cases the income loss for those with a half disability pension is very small. To this comparison should be added that in 1981 to 1987, the compensation rate was lowered in the partial pension system. This meant that the short-run reduction in income was greater with a partial pension (working time reduced by 20 hours) than with a half old-age pension if retiring at the age of 63 or later. The compensation after 65, however, was also more favorable than with a partial pension.

Not everyone, however, can choose the pension with the highest compensation. A disability pension requires reduced health and the partial-

Table 9.6. *Persons aged 60 to 64 in various part-time pension schemes in 1980, 1986, and 1988*

	1980		1986		1988	
Pension scheme	Men	Women	Men	Women	Men	Women
Disability pension						
Two-thirds	1,393	2,501	1,106	2,240	1,051	1,598
One-half	4,109	2,770	7,134	5,932	7,402	6,213
Temporary disability pension						
Two-thirds	7	11	4	6	3	7
One-half	110	84	80	98	76	94
Half old-age pension	416	79	2,927	310	2,580	307
Partial pension	46,504	21,333	18,560	13,620	23,454	15,001
Total	52,539	26,778	29,811	22,206	34,566	23,220

Sources: Allmän försäkring 1981 and 1985/86. Information from the National Board of Social Insurance.

pension scheme also has some specific requirements. This explains why there are some persons who take the part-time pension with the lowest compensation rate.

The number of persons with various part-time pensions in 1980, 1986, and 1988 is given in Table 9.6. As can be seen, the total number of persons with a part-time pension decreased between 1980 and 1986. This is solely the result of a decrease in one of the schemes, the partial-pension scheme. This decrease is explained by the fact that the compensation rate in the partial-pension scheme was lowered from 65 percent to 50 percent for pensions granted between 1981 and 1987, leading to a drastically reduced inflow rate. The rise in the compensation rate to 65 percent on January 1, 1987, led to a new increase in the number of pensions. The number of persons with partial pensions increased from 32,180 in 1986 to 38,455 in 1988. This is, however, much lower than the levels of the early 1980s. On the other hand, the number with other forms of part-time pensions gradually increased in the 1980s. It will be interesting to see if this trend will change. Up to now the number has remained at the 1986 level.

The majority of those with partial pensions worked full-time before the reduction of working time. Although the most frequent working time after the reduction is half-time, the majority work more than half-time. Their working hours are evenly spread betwen 21 and 34 hours.

9.4.6 A comparison

The ordinary way out of the labor force is still the most frequently used. Almost 50 percent of the men leaving the labor force do so on reaching 65, and the female exit pattern is becoming increasingly similar to that for men.

The majority of those leaving at an age other than 65 leave earlier. Only a smaller part continue to work after 65, and the majority of those work part-time. Most of those who continue working after the age of 65 have a full-time old-age pension (there is no income test in the Swedish pension system). Only a few delay taking out their old age pension.

Many leave the labor force totally or partially prior to ordinary retirement age, most of them between 60 and 64. There are four main pathways: the health pathway (full disability pension for health reasons), the unemployment pathway (disability pension for labor-market reasons), the occupation injury pathway (annuity from the occupational injury insurance scheme), and the part-time pathway (three different pension schemes). In many cases the pension from a social insurance system is supplemented by compensation from other social security schemes and/ or contractual insurance schemes.

In the beginning of the 1980s the part-time pathway was the most common, but the lowering of compensation in the partial-pension scheme changed that. In the middle of the 1980s, approximately equal numbers of people exited through three of the pathways: the health, unemployment, and part-time pathways. The return to the earlier compensation rate in the partial-pension scheme in 1987 may lead to part-time withdrawal becoming the most frequent again. The generally good labor-market situation and the low unemployment level in the 1980s resulted in unemployment becoming one of the less frequently used pathways. In the last four years an increasing number have left the labor market by the occupational injury pathway. The statistics, however, are such that it is not possible to get comparable figures.

9.5 CONSEQUENCES OF EARLY EXIT

Up to now I have mainly discussed the consequences of early exit for the retiring individuals themselves. In most cases the income loss is small, and in some cases the exiters get more than full compensation.

The firm that the early pensioners leave often makes a gain as well. A seniority wage system often means that the early exit of an older worker is to the benefit of the firm (Lazear 1979). The wage is in many cases higher than the value of the marginal productivity for older workers in seniority-related wage systems. Further, when reducing the work force through layoffs, the firm in many cases prefers to keep younger workers in order to achieve a more flexible work force. The firm may pay extra severance pay to facilitate an agreement with the trade union regarding exceptions to the job security law. Social and occupational insurance schemes pay all or most of the compensation.

In many cases the local trade union is in favor of the older workers being laid off. Early retirement of the older workers means that the firm may retain (more of) the younger workers. In that way the local trade union may obtain a satisfactory solution for both groups: high income compensation for older workers and jobs for younger workers.

The problems are not on the micro- but on the macrolevel. An increase in early retirement means a decrease in the total labor supply. In the very short run this may result mainly in a decrease in unemployment, but in a few years it will lead to a decrease in employment. The unemployment rate is not determined by the size of the labor supply.

A smaller labor supply and thereby lower employment means lower tax proceeds and higher public expenditures. In particular the proceeds from wage-based taxes (payroll taxes and fees) decrease as employment diminishes. But most important is that public expenditures, especially income transfers, increase. Given the compensation rates in the income-transfer systems, this means that the tax rates and payroll fees have to increase. In a period of low productivity growth this implies that the net income growth for those in the labor force stagnates.

This explains why opinions concerning the early-exit option differ between the local and the central level. On the local level, most actors are generally in favor of the use of the early-exit option; on the central level the actors (goverment, national trade unions, national employer organizations) are against this solution. The government's policy is that a firm that wants to lay off workers should follow the rule of the law of employment protection, that is, lay off the younger workers. The idea is that the younger workers, with the assistance of the labor-market authorities, should move to vacancies (if necessary after retraining). Total employment would therefore be higher.

A typical feature of the Swedish system is the option of taking a part-time pension. The aim of that policy is to facilitate a gradual withdrawal from the labor force. The effects on the labor supply, however, are unknown. One effect may be that people who would otherwise have totally withdrawn from the labor force continue to work part-time. On the other hand, people who would have continued to work full-time may have reduced their working hours as a result of the law. The partial-pension system may also influence the number who work after age 65

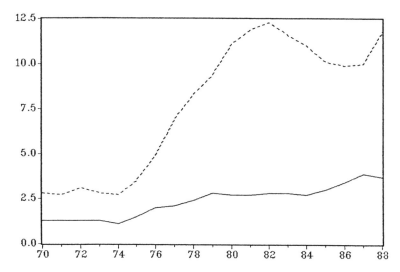

Figure 9.10. Percentage of the male population aged 45 to 54 and 55 to 64 with part-time employment. Key: ——————, men 45 to 54; - - - - -, men 55 to 64. *Source:* Labor Force Surveys.

and before age 60 (in the latter case to qualify for a partial pension). The political parties have not agreed in their evaluations of the partial-pension system, which explains the two changes in the compensation system: first down to 50 percent (decided by a non–Social Democratic goverment) and later up to 65 percent again (decided by a Social Democratic government).[6]

To enable a very preliminary evaluation, the long-run development of part-time work for those aged 55 to 64 in comparison with those aged 45 to 54 is given in Figures 9.10 and 9.11. For men aged 55 to 64 part-time work increased drastically with the introduction of part-time work in 1976. It diminished slightly after the reduction in the compensation from 65 percent to 50 percent in 1981 and went up again after the reintroduction of the 65 percent compensation rate in 1987. In the same period, the 1970s and 1980s, part-time work increased only slowly among those aged 45 to 54. This development took place in parallel with a decrease in full-time work among those aged 55 to 64 and a stable full-time employment rate among those aged 45 to 54. The decrease in full-time employ-

---

[6] See the first report from the governmental committee on the national pension system (SOU 1986:47). That report contains a proposal that the compensation in the partial pension scheme should be raised to 65 percent, but several members of the committee made a reservation against that proposal.

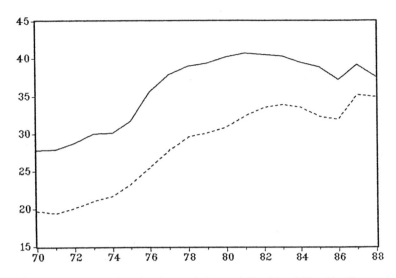

Figure 9.11. Percentage of the female population aged 45 to 54 and 55 to 64 with part-time employment. Key: ————, women 45 to 54; - - - - -, women 55 to 64. *Source:* Labor Force Surveys.

ment was especially strong in the years after the introduction of the partial-pension system and after the return to the 65 percent compensation.

Among women there is a parallel increase in the percentage with part-time work as a share of the population in the two age groups. At the same time the percentage of full-time employed increased considerably among those aged 45 to 54 but only a few percentage units among those aged 55 to 64. The full-time employment rate decreased slightly in the years after the introduction of the partial-pension system and again after the return to the 65 percent compensation rate in 1987. If we look only at those employed, there was a trend toward part-time work among those aged 55 to 64 compared with those aged 45 to 54.

The development described here shows that the partial pension scheme probably, at least to some extent, has resulted in a decrase of full-time employment. Only a more thorough study can show whether it also has meant a reduction in full-time early exit.

9.6 THE POLITICAL DISCOURSE AND PROSPECTS FOR THE FUTURE

The work principle is still the main principle of Swedish social policy for those of active age. People should have a job and not get cash support. Active labor-market policy is the preferred way to achieve this. However, for those over active age, the main principle is instead a high compensation related to earlier income. This leaves us with the crucial question: When is one over "active age"?

For many decades the dividing line was age 67 for all but the (severely) disabled. Old-age pensions could not be granted at an earlier age. Some groups, however, had a lower retirement age through collective agreements. The retirement age for salaried employees was generally 65. Groups such as military personnel and nurses and nurses' aids had an even lower retirement age. There has been a gradual closing of the gap in retirement age between different occupational groups. The lowering of the general retirement age to 65 in 1976 and an increase of the retirement age through revisions of the collective agreement are the factors behind that development.

On the other hand, the retirement age has been made more flexible for all occupations. To some extent this development has been planned. The introduction of the partial-pension system and increased possibilities for taking an early old-age pension are examples of that. Already in the beginning of the 1960s, early and delayed old-age pensions were introduced, and the partial-pension scheme was started in 1976. The flexibility downward has become more extensive than expected through a large-scale use of the system of disability pensions for labor-market reasons and a fast increase of disability pensions granted on the basis of a medical diagnosis. This unplanned flexibility is generally seen as a major problem for the pension system, and some steps have been taken to counteract this development. It has been made more difficult for an employer and a local trade union to agree on early exit through the unemployment pathway, and the labor market for the disabled (many of them old) has been given priority. However, the general development is still in the direction of earlier exit from the labor market for men.

The current discussion on the system of retirement and pensions revolves around the costs of the pensions. The changing age structure and the increasing costs for the supplementary old-age pensions are the main factors behind the increasing pension outlays. A low growth of productivity in the Swedish economy means that the payroll fees gradually have to increase, especially when the "baby boom" cohorts of the 1940s retire in the next century. A further increase in early exit may lead to even higher increases of the payroll fees.

There are several possible measures for diminishing the increases in payroll fees (see Wadensjö 1989): (1) a higher ordinary retirement age, (2) the right for people to continue working longer at their workplace (the present employment protection extends only up to the age of 65), (3) stronger economic incentives to take a delayed pension, and (4) more placement of older workers in labor-market programs (especially training programs that facilitate transitions to positions better suited to older workers). A governmental committee, *Pensionsberedningen,* has been working since 1984 on a major appraisal of the pension system. The committee presented its main report in November 1990 (see SOU 1990:76). However on December 14, 1989, prior to that report, the government presented a bill to the *Riksdag* proposing several changes in the social insurance schemes (for details, see Wadensjö 1990). The most important in this connection was a proposal to stop granting disability pensions for labor-market reasons only. The government bill was decided on by the *Riksdag.* From November 1991 disability pensions for labor-market reasons will not be granted. The debate on the retirement/pension system has already started, and it will quite probably be intense in the next few years.

Another issue in the present political discourse is the role of social insurance and contractual insurance schemes. There are proponents of a dual system in which the social insurance schemes give basic support at old age that is equal for all and the contractual insurance schemes are the income-related part. One important change is that such a system implies a greater funding and thereby increased savings, investment, and growth of the economy.

REFERENCES

Björklund, A., and B. Holmlund. 1989. "The Economics of Unemployment Insurance: The Case of Sweden." In: *FIEF Studies in Labor Markets and Economic Policy.* Oxford: Oxford University Press.

Edebalk, P. G., and E. Wadensjö. 1988. "Contractually Determined Insurance Schemes for Manual Workers." In: B. Gustafsson and A. Klevmarken (eds.), *The Political Economy of Social Economy.* Amsterdam: North Holland.

1989. "Arbetsmarknadsförsäkringar." *Report to ESO* (Ministry of Finance), Ds 1989:68.

Flanagan, R. J. 1987. "Efficiency and Equality in Swedish Labor Markets." In: B. Bosworth and A. Rivlin (eds.), *The Swedish Economy.* Washington D.C.: Brookings.

Hedström, P. 1987. "Disability Pension: Welfare or Misfortune?" *International Journal of Sociology* 16:208–20.

Lazear, E. P. 1979. "Why is There Mandatory Retirement?" *Journal of Political Economy* 87:1261–84.

Riksförsäkringsverket. 1984. *Delpension och rörlig pensionsålder. En uppföljning och utvärdering.* Stockholm.

SOU. 1986. *Delpension. Översyn med förslag till ändringar i delpensioneringen.* Stockholm.

1990. *Allmän Pension. Huvudbetänkande av Pensionsberedningen.* Stockholm.

Standing, G. C. 1988. *Unemployment and Labour Market Flexibility: Sweden.* Geneva: ILO.

Wadensjö, E. 1985. *Disability Pensioning of Older Workers in Sweden. A Comparison of Studies Based on Time-Series and Cross-Section Data.* Meddelande från Institutet för social forskning 15/1985.

1987. "Labor Market Policy and Employment Growth in Sweden." *Labour. Review of Labour Economics and Industrial Relations.* 1:3–23.

1989. "Varför har vi normal pensionsålder?" In: E. Wadensjö, Å. Dahlberg, and B. Holmlund (eds.), *Vingarnas trygghet. Arbetsmarknad, ekonomi och politik.* Lund: Dialogos.

1990. *Recent Labor Market Experiences of Older Workers in Sweden.* A Study Prepared for ILO. Swedish Institute for Social Research.

CHAPTER 10

Hungary: Exit from the state economy

JULIA SZALAI

10.1 INTRODUCTION

IN accordance with the international trend, people in Hungary, especially men, tend to give up their employment (i.e., their participation on a full-time basis in the state-controlled spheres of the economy)[1] some years earlier than the present regulations on retirement would suggest. (For details see Tables A.1–A.3 and section A.1 of the Appendix at the end of this chapter.) Nearly one-fifth (19.1 percent) of all male pensioners have retired before age 60 (that is, below the formal age of eligibility for an old-age pension).[2]

What are the explanations for this quite general behavior? Do the early exiters give up working, or do they only give up formal employment? How can one explain the fact that shortly after their entrance into the pension scheme, 17.9 percent of them seek part-time employment and again work in the formal economy while drawing pensions from social security? Do the rest of the men who exit early really give up working? If not, why do they withdraw from formal employment and intensify their work in the informal spheres of the economy? In addition, why do others, some 2.7 percent of those over age 60 (about 22,000 men) remain

---

[1] The terms "state-controlled," "formal," and "first" economy are used as synonyms throughout, as well as their counterparts: "informal," or "second" economy and "economy outside the scope of direct state control." For a more detailed description of the latter sphere as a specific product of the state-socialist economy, see section 10.3.

[2] This chapter deals only with the description of early exit of *men*. Comparison between men and women will be given occasionally to assist in understanding one or another phenomenon. That restriction of the scope of the chapter follows from the fact that the patterns, motives, history, and structure of both female employment and female retirement are quite distinct from those of men. The characteristics of female participation in the second economy, their role in the division of labor in the household, and their morbidity and mortality trends are also markedly different. A deep analysis of similarities and dissimilarities would have exceeded the framework of this chapter. Main trends of female employment are presented in Table A.3 of the Appendix.

in the formal labor force years after the age of eligibility for entry into the normal old-age pension system?

In this attempt to answer these puzzling questions, the main thesis is that early exit should be interpreted, first of all, as an expression of individualized struggle for autonomy under conditions of an exploitative and ineffective employment policy of the state-socialist regime. The main argument is that the increasing rate of early exit from formal employment does not mean an increasing rate of early withdrawal from work. On the contrary, the overwhelming majority of pensioners (both those who retired early and those who did so at the "ordinary" age of 60) still work hard. Some participate in various "branches" of the informal economy that depend on the efforts of households; others take up part-time employment, which usually offers much more flexibilty and much better working conditions than they had before. The two concepts of *employment* and *work* should therefore be strictly separated.

Motives for early exit from employment in Hungary must be understood in the context of employment policies (both of the state and of the firms), deteriorating health of middle-aged men, income constraints on the households caused by the generally low level of pensions, and people's desire for the relatively controllable types of work available in the informal economy. The interplay among the interests of the state, the firms, and the individuals must be considered if one is to give a relevant explanation of the phenomenon.

When speaking about differing or conflicting interests on the subject of early exit, I refer to people formally retiring from *full-time employment*, but not necessarily retiring from work. According to the regulations governing receipt of pensions, entrance into the pension scheme does not exclude either entering part-time employment or (even more frequently) extending activities in the second economy. It should be emphasized that, in fact, pensioners are the only group in Hungary who have the right to establish contracts for part-time employment with the firms of the first economy. The system of part-time work is otherwise practically unknown in that sphere.[3]

As we will see, the general behavior of pensioners is to work as much as they can. The only limit – though a very serious one – is their health.

---

[3]. The rate of part-time employment of the economically active population (those between ages 14 and 45) is negligible, affecting only 1.8 percent of those employed in state-owned firms (CSO 1985). Even that 1.8 percent is mostly a statistical artifact. The contribution of students at schools of vocational training and casual work is statistically registered as part-time work. Real, meaningful part-time work is done by outside workers (mainly women working at home for one or another firm), but the occurrence of that type of employment is sporadic.

In other words, a long workless period of retirement as a reward after decades of work is not regarded as a civil right by the society, and it also cannot be afforded in the present material conditions of the pensioners. A relevant factor in this situation is the role of traditions, which policy-makers, sometimes consciously but more often unconsciously, take into account. Retirement in Hungary must be seen in the social and cultural context of a former peasant society, where the general conviction, based on the "technological" needs of agricultural work, always dictated very rigidly that people were "useful members" of the community inasmuch as they contributed. Present-day pensioners – having extensive experience of agricultural "overwork" in the second economy, even during their period of active employment – follow the ancient rule: "I have to work on the field as long as I have arms and legs." The drive to work, of course, is seriously sustained by income needs, too. Since the level of pensions is extremely low (on an average, it has been equal to 57 percent of average earnings of those in full-time employment in recent years), the mere financial incentives to work are substantial.

Summarizing in brief the decisive social factors behind early exit, one has to speak of three main domains: the characteristics and peculiarities of employment in the formal sphere of the economy; the general health status of those in their mid-life period; and the special role of economic activities within the framework of the households in present-day Hungary. The structure of this chapter reflects these concerns.

First, we have to look at the history of the rapid extension, the basic features, and the conditions of formal employment in the state-controlled economy to understand why quite large and increasing groups of employees are seeking pathways of early exit from it.

The deteriorating health status of middle-age men seems to play an important role in early exit. But as we shall see, even people with chronically poor health (which entitles them to disability pensions) tend to work, albeit in spheres and conditions that better fit their skills, options, capacities, and aspirations.

The role of early exit should be put into a family context, too. Employment strategies of individuals are closely related to the general strategies of their households and have a part in the much broader framework of division of labor, tasks, and activities within the family. Those who withdraw from formal employment before the established retirement age tend to increase their participation in family agriculture or in the construction/repair work of the household (quite often on the basis of reciprocity arrangements in the community) and, instead of purchasing services, perform childcare, care for the sick or older members of the neighborhood, and so forth, thereby saving expenditures.

Extensive participation in the second economy is motivated by the underdevelopment of the pension scheme. People must work to keep their former standard of living after retirement. Those who cannot continue to work are very likely to drop to the lowest income groups of the society, suffering severe absolute poverty and sometimes even starvation.

A general overview of the basic regulations on retirement and the history of their modifications makes it easier to compare the characteristics of the group leaving the sphere of formal employment early with those of the other, larger group of "ordinary pensioners." It is hoped that the short outline provided gives a relevant context in which to analyze the few pathways of early exit available and to understand their social meaning. Information on some aspects of the way of life of pensioners (use of time, income level and distribution, additional sources of earnings available for retired people, types of work they do, and so forth) is presented to broaden the perspective provided by that description.

The last section aims at summarizing the present conflicts, political discourse, and alternative proposals that surround the issue of early retirement.

10.2 FULL EMPLOYMENT IN THE STATE-SOCIALIST SYSTEM

The restructuring of the social, economic, and political life of Hungary after World War II was based on some decisive principles and assumptions. Outstanding among these was the myth of a limitless number of formerly nonemployed people, in other words, the conviction that there was an ample reserve army of potential workers that would serve as the basis for rapid growth and prosperity of a socialist-type economy. Full employment as one of the distinct and principal features of the state-socialist system was declared an essential political goal in combating poverty and the uncertainties of unemployment, regarded as unavoidable under capitalism but never to be with us in socialism. Besides its political meaning, the overall priority given to the rapid increase of employment rates responded to many practical considerations, and it had its economical rationale as well. Altogether, they made the given policy not only convincingly attractive but even realistic, despite the fact that its built-in controversies (discussed later) could have been foreseen. To make clear the obvious relevance of that goal in the postwar period, we have to keep in mind some characteristics of the prewar society.

As a consequence of the historical development of capitalism in Eastern Europe, the social structure of Hungary in the 1930s was characterized by a painful duality and a high degree of symptoms of disintegration. The economic structure and weakness of capitalism meant that the urban-industrial part of the society functioned according to more or less adequate European standards of the time. It had a modern division of labor, well-developed income distribution, quite widespread use of services, and relatively good health standards, but it seemed to be *closed* for the greater part of the society. The urban-industrial world offered neither an adequate market nor an open way to promotion for about 52 to 60 percent of the society, namely, the agricultural-rural population. Agricultural laborers, servants of the large latifundia, peasant smallholders, and their families lived in extreme poverty with high rates of unemployment and low life expectancy and in an everlasting reproduction of uncertainties and crises. The prewar urban-industrial economy was unable to absorb that massive agricultural reserve army by offering a stable path for mobility, but it used it in a cyclical way that compromised any efforts made by families to build up their long-term strategies of living. That slow and uncertain way of development led to a disintegration of the social order, which was expressed in many aspects of the material, social, and moral disruption during the war.

Therefore the drives to construct stable, well-established bases for social integration and to overcome the disruptive factors of the prewar system enjoyed massive popular support after the war. Full employment was seen as the obvious and only way to create an adequate basis of living for each and every member of the society, and thus to achieve social integration and an everlasting victory over poverty. Thus the ideological-political goal had its foundation in reality and in people's aspirations: An extended employment policy seemed to serve economic and social purposes with an exceptionally high degree of harmony between the two. Nevertheless, the way that new employment policy was realized was full of controversies, and it contained at its start all those traps that led to a deepening social and economic crisis some decades later.

The crucial point here is that the rapid extension of employment was not rooted in an organic speeding up of the already existing branches and activities of the economy. Instead, the new economic policy arbitrarily identified its priorities in establishing formerly nonexistent branches of industry, especially heavy industry. The totalitarian system of economics arbitrarily forced the yearly growth of industrial production. All its regulations and administrative interventions were realized by exhausting agriculture, by exploiting individual and family resources, and by destroying all meaningful relations, in both the economic and the social order. The capital and the labor force required by that gigantic program were "directed" into industry in an extremely forceful way. (The two main resources of that policy were the households and the sphere of agricultural production.)

The goal of full employment was seen to be reached best by forcing its achievement through a number of means. These included economic and legal measures as well as strictly controlling (even forbidding and negatively sanctioning) any individual choices. Besides legal obligations, the main instrument of that policy was the redefinition of wages and salaries, both their content and their level, in 1946. In response to the extreme inflation that was destroying the functioning of the economy in 1944–5, a new currency was introduced in August 1946. Parallel with its introduction, the purchasing value of wages and salaries was centrally defined at a level equivalent to about one-third of their prewar counterparts. By that means, the state created the source for a high rate of accumulation in the hands of the state budget, which has been directly controlled since then by the central planning administration. The arbitrarily low redefinition of the wage level, which has remained with us continuously throughout the past decades, gave a "green light" to central expropriation of the surplus: Wages and salaries never rose over 12 percent of the yearly GNP.[4] Their outflow has remained a focus of strict central control even in the most liberal years of reforming the economy and "marketizing" it.[5]

One of the legitimizing arguments for leveling down personal earnings was the new responsibility of the state for delivering a number of services free of charge (or much below market prices) to those who took up gainful employment. Therefore, prices of education, health service, housing, transportation, and so forth have not been "built into" personal disposable incomes. On the other hand, eligibility rights for the over-

---

[4] On an average the net wage/salary share of the GNP is around 8 to 9 percent. The equivalent share in Western economies is about 30 to 40 percent. The artificial underevaluation of the labor force in production, with a significantly higher estimate of the income holders as consumers, describes one of the most essential features of state-socialist economies.w

[5] Here we see a fundamental structural element of the functioning of these economies. The liberal regulations introduced in 1968 released the so-called fixed labor economy of the firms, opened the channels in a formerly unseen way to individual choice for moves *within* the labor market of the state economy, and made space for second-economy activities. However, the strict central control over the income–outflow has not been reduced; the central administration has regulated, year by year, how much of its income the "marketized" and "independent" firm can spend for raising the wages/salaries of its employees. It is a different matter that the planned outflow differs regularly from the actual one (the latter exceeding the former in each year), and how the firms "play" within the "holes" of the never-perfect control. The regularity of the games between the firms and the central administration are a central part of the story. I will turn to that problem later, since that is the sphere where state social policy is used by the "independent" firm to shift burdens, to ease control, and to create some freedom for decisions on hidden and inner raises of earnings.

whelming majority of these services have been bound to full-time employment in the state economy. Two outcomes of this policy warrant mention here.

1. The priority given to the state economy is reflected in a number of negatively discriminating regulations for those working, for example, in cooperatives, not to mention those in the much reduced private sphere. The following examples illustrate this point. Until recently retirement age for cooperative members was five years higher than for state employees; earnings in agricultural cooperatives have traditionally been lower than wages-salaries in state-owned agricultural firms; until the mid-1960s private peasants had to pay the market price for hospital care or any use of the health care system. The forced cooperativization of the late 1950s and early 1960s opened the door for the peasants to enter the social security system and get free medical care. Private shopkeepers got the same right only in 1976.

2. Although the central redistribution of fundamental services aimed at meeting a number of true socialist goals of free and equal access, in reality the services have become extremely impoverished and their chronic shortage has contributed to a steady increase rather than a reduction of inequalities of access to them. Here there is no space to discuss the causes and consequences of that process, which I have written about elsewhere (see, for example, Szalai 1986). Two of the consequences should be emphasized, however. First, since these fundamental services have been delivered practically *exclusively* by the state, and rights for take-up could be deserved by employment, the need for them represented an "incentive" per se to accept any kind of employment, regardless of its adequacy for the individual. (That factor will be important in understanding why retirement is considered to be a "liberation," why people think of it in terms of regaining their autonomy.) Second, because of the poor quality and dysfunctions of the most basic services (preschools, education, health service, etc.) the additional value (i.e., "income in kind") of qualifying for them can be severely questioned. That additional value has remained a theoretical drive, while in reality, to get some access means to *spend* on those services from an income that has never been adequate to cover these expenditures. Housing is the best example of that deep controversy. The individual "solution" of the problem is the very intensive participation in the second economy, which is discussed later.

It is obvious that low wages on the one hand and the new eligibilities defined on the basis of labor force participation on the other have produced effective incentives to take up employment. The mere economic pressure of survival (in its very profound sense) has pushed all adult members of families into doing so, since even the so-called good wages of qualified male workers turned out to be inadequate to cover a family's costs of living. This way employment rates have been successfully increased within an extremely short period. The ratio of those in the adult population who have been employed for at least 10 years during their life rose from 63 percent in 1949 to 88 percent in 1980, while about 1,000,000 new positions for workers were created.

Two characteristics of that process that have special relevance to the issue of early exit will be mentioned here.

First, the realization of the new economic policy has been based on a radical change of property relations and of the mechanisms regulating distribution. The supremacy of state ownership and the creation of a far-reaching central planning/redistributive system of downward hierarchical regulations have been thought to ensure the best and most effective use of the resources by ex ante economizing and controlling the outflow of both sides of production (i.e., labor and capital). In this way, the interests of the firms have been fundamentally changed from those of firms acting under the control of a market system. The new state-owned enterprises became interested in extending the size of their labor force and the capital at their disposal[6] regardless of the consequences for productivity. Describing the emergence and reproduction of a shortage economy is not the task of this chapter.[7] But it is important to emphasize that the rapid restructuring and development of the economy was accompanied from the beginning by a permanent reproduction of the general shortage of both capital and labor, thereby reinforcing state interventions to overcome the problem by repeated direct administrative regulations. That feature of the state-socialist economy did not disappear even after important steps were taken to make some space for market forces by regulating the economy in a more healthy way and directing it toward more efficient functioning.

A distinctive sign of the dysfunctions of the system is the chronic labor shortage that became a crucial and painful constraint on the economy around the early 1970s, when the reserve army (in quantitative terms) had disappeared. That led to the forced industrialization of the countryside, resulting in a total exhaustion of resources around the end of the decade. It is important to mention here that the interest in increasing employment rates had deep effects on the composition of the labor force.

---

[6] That behavior turned out to be the most effective way to ensure good bargaining positions to influence the central planning agencies in their decisions about distribution of the resources of production. That has led in itself to an extreme concentration of labor and capital, and to an absolute overweight of huge firms, having several thousand employees. For example, 79.6 percent of the total labor force and 91 percent of the capital was held by 25 percent of the firms of the state-owned economy in 1985 (Szalai 1989).

[7] The best analysis and detailed description of it is given by Kornai (1982). He argues that chronic shortage is not an incidental, but a fundamental structural feature of these types of economies.

The pure quantitative increase meant a rapid growth of the absolute and relative weight of unskilled and semiskilled work (especially female labor) and of low-level white-collar jobs.

That general "hunger" of the economy for unqualified labor has been met basically by the former agrarian population (partially and most recently by gypsies), who had to leave agriculture (and/or their traditional occupations) without space and time for adaptation to the most difficult and hazardous unskilled (or low-skilled) work in industry, especially in heavy industry. An additional element relates to the chronic shortage of capital: The extension of workplaces has taken place without developing even the minimal requirements of occupational health and without elementary investments to serve the physical protection of the employees. Table 10.1 gives some insight into the extremely hard working conditions; I will turn to some of the very severe consequences on the health of those social groups later.

A second important feature of the forced-employment policy (that the artificially low wages have served successfully) has been that employment has meant full-time work in almost all cases. Part-time labor, as mentioned earlier, was not built in as a normal way of functioning. Its use came quite late, as an extra source for overcoming the chronic labor shortages of the economy via the reemployment of pensioners. (We come back to this problem when analyzing pathways of and motives behind early exit.) That aspect of the interest in extending forms of employment has been strengthened by the central wage policy. The somewhat more flexible way of increasing or decreasing reemployment rates gave some room for the firms to "play" with their internal wage distribution while fitting to the central control over the average level of wages. (The increase of the number of those with very low pay made it possible to raise the earnings of those in key positions much above the average.)

10.3 THE DEVELOPMENT AND EXTENSION OF THE INFORMAL (SECOND) ECONOMY

The policy of forced employment described in the preceding section has been twinned with another important element of state-socialist economic and social policy, namely, the rapid growth of the informal (second) economy. Its existence and involute interrelations with the highly controlled first (formal) economy have deeply affected labor force participation, as well as the reorganization of personal and family strategies of living.

Table 10.1. *Distribution of workers according to their working conditions,ᵃ by age and sex*

Age	Normal physical exertion		Extreme physical exertion	
	Other elements acceptable	Other elements disadvantageous	Other elements acceptable	Other elements disadvantageous
		Male workers		
Under 20	48.2	33.6	26.5	1.7
21–25	43.5	35.6	17.6	3.3
26–30	43.2	37.8	16.0	3.0
31–35	40.6	38.7	16.3	4.4
36–45	36.6	36.6	20.8	6.0
46–55	33.5	37.3	23.0	6.2
56–60	34.7	40.9	22.6	1.8
61 and over	54.1	30.6	14.4	0.9
All male workers	39.5	37.0	19.2	4.3
		Female workers		
Under 20	68.8	27.9	3.2	0.1
21–25	63.9	32.0	3.9	0.2
26–30	62.8	31.4	5.6	0.2
31–35	50.1	34.4	5.4	0.1
36–45	56.9	36.2	6.7	0.2
46–55	56.2	37.0	6.6	0.2
56–60	56.6	37.6	5.6	0.2
61 and over	50.4	43.5	6.1	0.0
All female workers	59.9	34.2	5.7	0.2

ᵃThe classification is based on official measurements of physical exertion and takes into account hazards of noise, dust, light, extremely low/high temperature, etc. Since these measurements are made by authorities having interrelated interests with the local firms, the above rates tend to underestimate the health hazards of industry. But even these measurements show that 65 percent of all unskilled male workers (who are relatively old: 42.7 percent are over 40) work under conditions of extreme physical exertion, whereas the relevant rate is only 15 percent among skilled workers (who are significantly younger: only 29.8 percent are over 40). (For a breakdown according to qualifications, see the source given below. Unfortunatley, cross-tabulations according to the age distribution *and* the working conditions within the groups of skilled, semiskilled, and unskilled workers are not published.)
Source: Data Collection on the Number, Ways and Earnings of Those Employed in State-owned Industrial Firms, CSO, Budapest, 1982.

The roots of the development of the informal economy are manyfold, but political causes played an important role. The 1956 revolution questioned on nationwide grounds the extremities of the way in which economic change and forced industrialization had been executed in the first half of the 1950s. Revolutionary masses refused radically and totally the "myth of the golden egg," that is, the sacrifice of their lives and minimal personal living standards to the supreme goal of future growth, accompanied by direct political oppression and persecution. The socialist promises of steady improvement of living conditions turned out to be lies during the Stalinist era. Claims for guarantees of material well-being formed the foci of the political demands of the revolution.

Therefore, one fundamental element of the compromise between the ruling Communist Party and the society was to work out some space for individual upward mobility, basically in material terms, while the primary goals of industrialization and forced economic growth (still regarded as distinctive principles of socialist development by the new leadership) were not given up. The opening of some channels of extra rewards for extra work seemed to be the bridging solution. In other words, the sources of macroeconomic growth (and exploitation) were not changed significantly. The depressed standard of wages and salaries remained with us, but some space for raising private consumption by using free time for work was opened.

The most important sphere of the informal economy has been small-scale agricultural production. The rapid increase of second-economy participation in this area cannot be understood without recognizing the widespread agrarian-peasant tradition of the Hungarian society, which the formal restructuring of employment has not abolished. Since the forced cooperativization of private lands after the revolution allowed the members to keep a small household plot (maximum one acre) for their own use, families started to organize their lives and the labor force participation of their members by combining the relative advantages of employment in the state sphere with membership in the cooperative sector, this way assuring for themselves relatively higher industrial-urban incomes and a parallel access to self-controlled agricultural production.

The second main branch of activities in the informal economy is centered around construction: 882,000 new privately owned flats (75 percent of all the new flats) were built exclusively by family efforts between 1971 and 1985, and 81 percent of the financial resources for expenditures on housing were covered by the private households in 1985 (overwhelmingly from their work in the informal economy). Another aspect of the spread of this type of second-economy participation is shown by the fact that 3 percent of the adult population is involved in one or another type of informal construction industry (in addition to their "normal" work in their first-economy workplaces) on any given workday of the year. That means that 374 million hours of work were devoted to these activities in 1986 (which equals about 4 percent of the yearly total work capacity used by the first economy).[8] Those activities generally involve not only the work of the whole of the family, but even that of neighbors and relatives, based on and regulated by a complicated form of long-term work exchange.

Besides the above-described main forms, the informal economy also embraces services, more traditional small-scale repair work, and industrial labor.

Some comprehensive data can give an impression on the overall extent of the development of the second economy, which became an integrated part of the life-style of the overwhelming majority of the adult society. Although it is quite difficult to measure just because of its informalities, various expert estimates (based on time-budget and income-survey data) report a 60 to 75 percent participation rate of the employed population in one or another form.

During the 1970s, 40 percent of the total agricultural production of the national economy was produced by the small household plots. In some branches of agriculture, export has been based almost exclusively on their products.

According to the data of the last country-wide representative survey on social stratification and living conditions in 1981–2 (CSO 1986), 59 percent of all households had a garden or small farm used for agricultural production and cultivated by the family itself; 55 percent of them produced some extra goods for sale, after covering the needs of the household.

Data from regular household surveys show that some 13 to 18 percent of the yearly income of families comes from activities in the second economy, in addition to the even more important (though unmeasurable) saving of expenditures by self-production.

The latest country-wide representative time-budget survey of 1986 gives us information on the amount of time devoted to the informal economy. The comparison of the results with those of the 1977 survey shows a significant increase, both in absolute and in relative terms:

Our data show that time devoted to small-scale agricultural production, to house-building activities in the informal economy, and to repair work has been

---

[8] Data on informal construction were calculated by Agnes Vajda and János Farkas, who gave an excellent description of the surprising achievements of the informal economy in one of their recent papers (see Farkas and Vajda 1988).

Table 10.2. *Work fund (measured in hours) of the society (on a yearly basis, in million hours)*[a]

	1977	1986	Rate of change between 1977 and 1986[b]
Working time spent in workplaces of the first economy	9,984.5	9,296.3	−7
Small-scale agricultural production of:			
Active earners	1,737.5	1,896.6	+9
Inactive population	632.0	1,137.0	+80
Dependents	384.8	375.7	−2
House-building activities (in the informal economy) of:			
Active earners	266.9	374.7	+40
Inactive population	33.7	79.6	+136
Dependents	21.0	17.2	−18
Total	13,060.4	13,177.1	+1

[a]See Time-Budget; Changes in the Way of Life of the Hungarian Society According to the Time-Budget Surveys of Spring, 1977 and Spring, 1986. CSO, Budapest, 1987. (The report was written by Istvan Harcsa and Béla Falussy.)
[b]1977 = 100.

increasing tremendously. It is well known that these types of work serve basically the reduction of expenditures of the households. However, agricultural production can contribute to the direct increase of earnings, since the ratio of sale is relatively high. Therefore the work-fund of the economy as a whole has not been decreasing. Remembering that the number of those economically active has been decreasing significantly [between 1977 and 1986], then our conclusion has to be a statement about a serious increase of workloads of the relevant social groups. We have to add that the share of activities in the second economy has been increasing significantly within the whole of the economy, since the ratio of time spent on them was 28.9 percent in 1977, and 35.5 percent in 1986 (CSO 1987).

Table 10.2 gives estimated data on a yearly macrolevel about the share of the two economies. It also presents an insight into the important changes that occurred between 1977 and 1986 in the participation of economically active versus dependent and inactive social groups.

As Table 10.2 shows, the performance of the inactive population (who are basically pensioners) increased dramatically, and that is perhaps the most important change during the period in question. Table 10.2 expresses very impressively how families started to "build" into their long-term strategies the stable existence and wide acceptance of the second economy, how they started to plan and economize the work and participation of their members, tending to follow an optimal division between the two economies.[9]

With regard to the extensive participation of pensioners in second-economy activities, we have to refer repeatedly to the already-mentioned motives for continuing to work after retirement. One of them is the serious income constraint created by the extremely low level of pensions, partially as a direct consequence of the depressed wage level. But another, equally important element is the search for autonomy. One often hears the reasoning that people give about their decision to retire: "I have *served* enough for the state. I want to work according to my *own* rules during the rest of my life." That mentality has an important impact on struggle for early retirement, in other words, on efforts to reduce the life cycle of dependency, and to extend that of self-(family-)regulated decision making. (I will present data and details on the role of those two motives, on the types of work available to pensioners, and on some aspects of their everyday life later.)

Nevertheless, health consequences of the long-lasting physical and psychical exhaustion caused by an overuse of working capacity have to be taken into consideration as probably the biggest price people have to pay under the given circumstances. In a way, one can say that great masses of people sacrifice their health for the relative material well-being and relative autonomy offered by the informal sector of the economy. The only way to achieve those goals is based on self-exploitation, which to a large extent follows (as already mentioned) from the peasant traditions of the society – namely, from a work ethic that never considers labor but only the relative shortage of capital. That leads to long working hours: According to time-budget data, the *whole* of the adult population

---

[9] A more detailed analysis of the components behind the dramatic increase of the second-economy performance of the inactive population shows that its main explanation can be found in the significant increase of both the rate of participation and the average duration of time spent on those activities by male pensioners. The rate of those men on pension who took part in informal agricultural work on an average day increased from 50.5 percent to 60.5 percent between 1977 and 1986. The rate of those working in the house-building sphere of the second economy showed an even more significant growth, i.e., from the 0.4 percent ratio of 1977 to 1.7 percent in 1986. The average duration of time devoted to agricultural work increased from 217 to 276 minutes, while that of house building increased from 198 to 284 minutes. (The number of male pensioners did not change dramatically in those years. Census data show a modest [10 percent] increase between 1980 and 1984.)

works 9.6 hours on a normal weekday on the average! Survey data show that even weekends and holidays, after 44 hours a week in the workplaces, are frequently used for productive work instead of recreation.[10]

The picture has to be completed, therefore, with a brief description of health standards, which have been rapidly deteriorating during the past two decades.

10.4   A BRIEF OVERVIEW OF THE HEALTH CONDITIONS OF THE SOCIETY

The steady deterioration of health of the Hungarian society is proved by a number of shocking facts. The most unquestionable ones are the data on mortality.

As Józan (1988), a leading expert, put it recently, the national average rates of mortality of the 1980s are below the standard of 1941. Hungary experienced a steady improvement of death rates in the first two decades of the post-war period. The turning point was around the mid-1960s, when the improvement of the yearly averages first stopped; then a gradual increase of the age-specific mortality indices took over the determination of long-term trends. The national average of 1985 was 34.4 percent higher than that of 1960. That means that the population loss of the 1980s was some 45,000 to 50,000 more year by year than it was 25 to 30 years ago.

The causes behind that disadvantageous trend are very complex. First of all, radical and rapid changes of the morbidity structure have to be mentioned. The very good performance of the first two decades was due to combating efficiently the most characteristic diseases of poverty, e.g., tuberculosis, epidemics caused by very low standards of hygiene, and extremely high rates of infant mortality. Those achievements could be produced relatively easily by the mere extension of access to screening, huge campaigns for organizing overall vaccination, and so forth – that is, by expanding services that did not require high rates of investment. Those achievements, however, led almost automatically to an increase of other health needs at the same time, namely, those that are generated by diseases characteristic of relatively developed societies. Cardiovascular diseases, cancer, and accidents took over the decisive weight within the causes of mortality, mirroring the shifts within the morbidity structure. The health care system, however, has not been able to cope with those changes in a flexible way. Although space does not allow me to

---

[10] The 1981–82 survey on social stratification reported that 57 percent of the 40-to 44-year-old heads of households spent their vacation on agricultural work, and 51 percent of them worked regularly during the weekend (CSO 1986).

Table 10.3. *Mortality rates by age and sex (number of deaths per 100,000 inhabitants in the relevant age groups)*

Age	Year						1985 mortality rates (as % of those in 1960)
	1960	1965	1970	1975	1980	1985	
				Males			
30–34	190	200	200	220	220	280	147
35–39	250	260	290	290	390	440	176
40–44	320	350	430	480	620	700	219
45–49	540	500	620	750	920	1,090	202
50–54	890	860	930	1,090	1,420	1,560	175
55–59	1,560	1,460	1,530	1,540	2,090	2,310	148
60–64	2,410	2,440	2,600	2,670	3,000	3,230	142
All males[a]	1,070	1,130	1,250	1,330	1,480	1,520	142
				Females			
30–34	130	100	90	90	100	120	92
35–39	180	150	140	140	170	190	106
40–45	250	230	230	240	280	290	116
45–49	400	350	360	390	440	440	110
50–54	580	520	540	600	640	660	114
55–59	900	870	850	860	980	990	110
60–64	1,560	1,430	1,410	1,400	1,530	1,480	95
All males[a]	960	1,000	1,080	1,160	1,240	1,260	131

[a]Including those under 30 and over 64.
Source: Demographical Yearbooks, CSO, Budapest.

describe its history, it has to be underlined that national expenditure on health care has remained at a very low level (around 3 percent of the yearly GNP during the whole period). The lack of adequate investments and of expanding the relevant facilities has in itself created painful gaps between needs and deliveries that have contributed to the increase of social inequalities in access, since legal entitlement for free medical care became a civil right in the meantime. (Those countries that have extended universalism with regard to health care have increased their expenditure on it to 7 to 12 percent of the yearly GNP in the past decades.)

Another aspect of mortality is shown in Table 10.3. As can be seen, the deterioration of death rates hits especially men.[11] The age cohorts at

---

[11] Female mortality rates have also started to increase, though with some "time lag" and with a smaller degree of unquestionable trend of deterioration. The life of women between 40 and 59 is at significantly higher risk, however, than it was 25 years ago.

highest risk are those between 35 and 55. The mortality rate of men aged 45 to 50 in the mid-1980s was 202 percent of the relevant rate for 1960; that of the group aged 40 to 44 was even worse: 219 percent.

It has to be added that the deterioration of mortality has accompanied a significant increase of inequalities among social groups. The influence of social class differentials is striking. The increase of age-standardized male mortality rates between 1970 and 1980 was produced *exclusively* by blue-collar workers. The risk of death was modestly decreasing for white-collar workers during those 10 years (by 4 percent), while its increase was sharp among blue-collar workers, exceeding a growth of 23 percent (Szalai 1986).

Regional and territorial differences have also been increasing. Men born in Budapest in 1982 have a chance of living two and half years longer than those born in small villages in the countryside. Men living in the upper-class area of the capital (2nd district) have a mortality rate similar to the national average of West Germany in the 1980s, whereas those living in the slum area (7th district) have one equal to the relevant index of Syria (Józan 1988).

Table 10.4 presents mortality differentials according to occupations in the age group at highest risk, namely, those aged 35 to 59. Taking the lowest and the highest ratios,[12] the multiplier showing huge inequalities of risks of death turns out to be not less than 8.39. Terroritorial and occupational differences expressing accumulated inequalities of living and working conditions are significantly high; if one looks just at the aggregated averages, the mortality rate of middle-aged rural blue-collar workers exceeds by 77 percent that of urban white-collar workers.

Cancer, cardiovascular diseases, and accidents produced 95 percent of all deaths among men aged 40 to 49 in 1985. The 19 percent share of accidents requires some extra attention, for two reasons.

First, the risk of accidents mirrors most directly the general lack of protection in various aspects of life and work. There is no space for detailed analysis of that fact, but the widespread use of 50- to 70-year-old machines in industry, the frequent practice of importing hazardous

[12] The lowest mortality rate of 122 occupations (in some cases, branches of occupations) was that of university lecturers living in the capital. Those at highest risk were the truck guards living in rural settlements. (Table 10.4 presents only a reduced number of occupations or branches published in detail in the source of reference.) Table 10.4 throws some light on the extreme inequalities of conditions of life between urban and rural settlements. Given the same occupation, higher rates of mortality tend to occur among rural dwellers. Unfortunately, there is not enough space here to elaborate in detail on the phenomenon of decisive inequalities of settlements, which is very characteristic for the historical development of Eastern Europe.

Table 10.4. *Mortality rates among 35- to 39-year-old men in given occupational groups (number of deaths per 100,000 men in the relevant occupational group)*

Occupation or branch of occupation	Place of residence		
	Budapest	Town/city in countryside	Village
Mining	863.93	1,045.47	1,244.40
Blue-collar work in steel industry	1,192.74	1,156.67	1,262.27
Industrial workers (average)	1,011.39	911.86	1,068.81
Blue-collar work in construction	816.76	937.70	1,233.63
Drivers	778.30	683.40	640.40
Truck guards	1,381.81	1,607.30	1,906.42
Unskilled work (general)	1,488.68	1,566.11	1,826.66
Engineers	536.88	625.00	586.20
Technicians	640.88	500.22	629.65
Party leaders; civil servants in higher positions	377.92	718.68	1,937.98
Physicians; dentist	530.58	442.27	571.75
Lecturers at universities	227.19	501.50	653.59
Teachers in primary and secondary education	888.73	416.66	774.19
Publishers; journalists	755.66	1,006.03	–
All blue-collar workers	1,088.13	1,054.98	1,255.99
All white collar workers	760.90	711.50	804.71

Source: Investigations on Mortality 4; Social, Economic and Occupational Differences in Mortality, CSO, Budapest, 1987.

chemicals because of their low price on Western markets, and the poor quality of roads that are inadequate to the requirements of expanded transportation have to be listed among the most important causes. It is true, on the other hand, that the exhaustion after 10 to 12 hours of work and the threatening degree of alcoholism have to be taken into account in describing a complex of factors that cannot be handled just by urgent improvements in health care, but require deeply rooted changes in economic and social policies in their broadest sense.

Second, the extremely high number of fatal accidents has to be regarded as an outcome of a long-term process of deterioration. Table 10.5 shows the steady increase of their ratios during the past 25 years. As can be seen, the relative increase has been the highest among those who are the focus of our present interest, namely, men aged 40 to 59. Nevertheless, the *somewhat* lower rate of increase among older men also has to warn us with regard to those consequences of overusing human capacities that I tried to demonstrate in the preceding section.

Table 10.5. *Deaths due to fatal accidents[a] in various age groups of the male population (number of deaths per 100,000 men in the relevant age groups)*

	Age			
Year	15–39	40–59	60+	All men
1960	23.5	23.4	69.2	28.2
1965	19.9	22.8	96.0	30.3
1970	20.8	32.3	119.6	37.5
1975	20.7	38.0	137.9	41.8
1980	22.9	52.2	176.3	50.1
1985	27.9	74.8	199.6	61.0
1985 as a percentage of 1960	119	320	288	216

[a]Except those occurring in transportation.

Finally, let me present the newest information on self-reported health. The last Microcensus (1984) asked people to compare their health with the general standard (the "average") in their age group. The sharp increase of the rates of "worse-than-average" answers among men over 30 seems to reflect the trends of real deterioration, reaching a point where 29 to 36 percent of men aged 50 to 65 reported poor health. (The ratios climbed somewhat over 40 percent among the elderly.) The other side of the coin is a steady decrease of rates of "better-than-average" evaluations in the subsequent five-year age brackets. Although these data involve value judgments and different cultural orientations as much as reflections of reality, they can be interpreted as true perceptions of exhaustion and decreased working capacity caused by health problems.

10.5   THE PENSION SCHEME IN GENERAL AND PATHWAYS OF EARLY EXIT

Before describing pathways of early exit, let me give a short account on the main features of the pension scheme in general. The present system is the outcome of a 40-year history. The state-socialist regime, in accordance with the aims and principles of its policy, has fundamentally reorganized social security as well as all other aspects of society.

Prewar Hungary was characterized by a great diversity of schemes of benefits and services, reflecting in their inner structure the duality of the society mentioned earlier. Relatively modern systems with high-quality services and benefits covered the upper strata of the urban population, and much less developed ones were in operation to meet the needs of the urban working class, whereas huge masses of the peasantry and of agricultural laborers were excluded from any type of coverage and benefits. The new system aimed at unifying rights and entitlements, but in a contradictory and dictatorial way. The basic principle of the new regulations was to urge people to take up employment in the so-called socialist spheres of the economy, first of all, in the state-owned firms. In other words, the new system of social security has been regarded much more as an additional important incentive to encourage the rapid increase of full-time employment than as a way of meeting various needs on the basis of civil right.

The 1951 Act on Retirement offered pensions exclusively for those who became employed in state-owned firms after 1945. Thereby it was extremely discriminatory against all those who remained in the much reduced private sphere (especially in agriculture), and even against members of cooperatives (though cooperatives have been regarded as "socialist" formations, but of a secondary type). That first act laid down some of the main principles that still prevail. It set retirement age at 60 for men and at 55 for women,[13] and requried at least 10 years of continuous full-time employment in the state-owned sphere of the economy for entitlement. Later modifications extended entitlements, and the discriminations against members of cooperatives and those working in the private sphere were gradually reduced and finally eliminated.[14]

The regulations in operation today were introduced by the 1975 Social Security Act. Its most important effect was the ultimate unification of regulations, which eliminated (at least in the legal sphere) the former political discrimination against those working in the "less socialist" (cooperative) and private economies. The new regulations reinforced retirement ages at 60 for men and 55 for women and kept the requirement of 10 years of full-time employment for entitlement. The scales of pensions are earnings-related and are progressive according to the duration of previous employment. The 10-year minimum entitles one to 33 percent of previous earnings, and the maximum pension (75 percent of the average of former wages/salaries) can be achieved by 42 years of employment. The base used for calculating retirement benefits is the

---

[13] For further comment on the history of ages of eligibility for retirement in Hungary, see section A.2 in the Appendix at the end of this chapter.

[14] Those working in the private sphere (either as owners or as employees) got the right to draw pensions as late as 1970.

Table 10.6. *Number and ratio of pensioners, by sex[a]*

	Males		Females	
Year	No. of pensioners	Pensioners among men over 60 (%)	No. of pensioners	Pensioners among women over 55 (%)
1960	184,743	31.3	195,724	18.0
1970	536,832	70.9	590,522	43.4
1980	700,788	92.8	962,701	67.0
1984	778,150	96.4	1,103,050	72.2

[a]Data present the aggregate number of persons covered by *any* type of pension scheme (normal old-age pension, disability pension, the so-called widow pension, etc.).
Source: Census data of 1960, 1970, and 1980 and Microcensus of 1984.

average earning of the three best years out of the last five. At the same time, incentives were introduced to encourage working full-time after retirement age: The amount of the pension is raised by 7 percent after each additional year one stays in employment over age 60 in case of male blue-collar workers and by 3 percent for male white-collar workers (the white-collar regulation was abolished again in 1981). These incentives obviously reflect a drive to ease the chronic labor shortage mentioned earlier; they serve to stimulate people to remain in the formal work force, with additional costs taken over by the state instead of the firms.

As an outcome of the gradual modifications, the number of pensioners increased very rapidly in the 25-year period 1960–84 (Table 10.6). (Unfortunately, data on pension receipt in the 1950s are not available as statistics were not published in those days.) As can be seen, the number of male pensioners was 4.2 times higher in 1984 than in 1960. Coverage is around 96 percent at the moment. The rate of increase has been even greater among women (the number of female pensioners in 1984 was 5.6 times their number in 1960); coverage at present is about 72 percent.

Table 10.7 gives some information on the costs and on the increase of per capita levels of pensions. Even these aggregate data indicate the main contradiction of the present pension scheme: While costs increase very rapidly, the level of pensions is very low. (The costs of pensions increased by 270 percent between 1975 and 1986, while per capita values were raised by only 180 percent.) The problem has become especially bothersome in recent years because of the 10 to 15 percent rate of infla-

Table 10.7. *Costs and per capita values of pensions*

Year	No. of pensioners	Per capita value of monthly pensions (forints)	Costs of pensions[a] (million forints)	Expenditures on pensions (% of GDP)
1970	1,380,300	765	12,984	—
1975	1,747,900	1,272	27,103	—
1980	2,018,000	2,267	55,979	—
1981	2,081,800	2,415	61,184	7.8
1982	2,130,800	2,647	68,541	8.1
1983	2,175,600	2,849	75,021	8.4
1984	2,215,300	3,109	84,053	8.6
1985	2,260,500	3,340	91,737	8.9
1986	2,299,400	3,557	99,315	9.1
		Rate of increase (1975 = 100)		
	132	280	367	

Source: Statistical Yearbooks (CS0) and Yearly Report on Social Security (Headquarters of Social Security).
[a]Social security expenditure.

tion. Since the scheme turned out to be incapable of valorizing its benefits, the gap between average pensions and average earnings has been increasing year by year: In 1986 the average pension equaled only 55 percent of the average monthly earnings, and despite moderate efforts of the state budget to compensate for the rapid rise of prices, 54.6 percent of the pensions remained below the declared pension minimum (3,000 forints) of the given year.

After characterizing the Hungarian economy as one with a permanent and widespread labor shortage as the general state of affairs, and indicating the relative underdevelopment of the entire pension scheme, it should not be surprising that the forms and pathways of early exit are relatively scarce. In fact, there are only two forms. The first is the dispensation of the usual retirement age, that is, a reduction of retirement age for a given set of extra-hard jobs. The second and more important form is the use of the disability pension as a pathway of early exit.

10.5.1 Early retirement for those in extra-hard jobs

The reduction of the retirement age for certain jobs goes back to the 1927 Act on Retirement, which introduced a special scheme for miners, including a dispensation of the regular age limit (age 65 for men at that time). As has been mentioned, the new regulations on pensions introduced after the war (in 1951) lowered the general age limit to 60 for men. At the same time, they "twisted" the dispensation into completing the pensions of those retiring from extra-hard work by adding a considerable amount. (Those regulations supported the efforts to expand employment as much as possible.) The number of jobs embraced by the 1951 regulations was increased to include work under hazards of radiation, in compressed air, and in extremely hot environments. But even with that extension, the list was relatively restricted, and the special regulations applied to only 64 occupations. Some jobs in transportation were added in 1959.

The present form of this pathway to early exit from the labor force was established by the new regulations redefining entitlements in 1973. They reflected the partial acceptance of people's desire to withdraw from the formal labor market and represented some concessions on the part of the central authorities. The present regulations declare that those who have worked at least 10 years continuously under extra-hard conditions are entitled to a reduction of retirement age by two years. Each five-year period of work beyond the 10 years increases the reduction by one more year. The list of the jobs in question has been extended again to cover about 100 occupations, including not only coal mining but also oil drilling, the steel industry, the most difficult jobs in dockyards, some types of textile work and bakery work, and some types of extremely exhausting work in health care (e.g., drivers of ambulances). In 1977 the twenty-second Congress of Trade Unions tried to achieve further extensions, but the government refused them. The argument was that the labor shortage made it impossible to accept "further liberalizations." If working conditions in some occupations improve in the future, these can be "dropped out" of the list, and that will allow "new" occupations to "get in." This way the coverage of the scheme has been stabilized. It accounts for about 4 to 4.5 percent of all new retirements (normal plus early) in any given year. Microcensus data show that about one-third of those pensioners who have retired earlier at any time have done so through the pathway of dispensation.

10.5.2   The disability pathway for early exit

The form of early exit that uses the disability pension is the one used most frequently. First, let me describe its regulations. The 1975 Act on Social Security defines as eligible those who have lost at least 67 percent of their former working capacity[15] because of permanent deterioration of their physical or mental health, and who otherwise meet the preconditions of retirement (e.g., at least 10 years of former employment). "Permanency" of deterioration means that they have been on sick leave for one year continuously, or if there was an interruption, their earnings before applying for a disability pension have dropped by at least 20 percent in comparison with the basis of calculation of a "normal" pension (i.e., average earnings of full-time work in the best three years out of the last five).[16]

The procedure of application for a disability pension is overbureaucratized.[17] The actual acknowledgment of the application frequently takes 6 to 12 months, and it is quite usual for the client to remain without *any* financial resources in the meantime.[18] In addition, applications are surrounded with suspicion and humiliation. The issue of disability is therefore one of the most contentious aspects of social policy, involving the defenselessness of both doctors and patients, not to mention the arbitrariness of the decisions.

The prevalence of conflicts is illustrated by the figures for 1985. Only half of the 71,300 new applicants for disability pensions (36,200 persons) were regarded as entitled. In 28,500 cases (40 percent of all applications) the degree of disability was considered to be below 67 percent.[19] The health status of only 6,600 applicants was considered serious enough to justify a decision of definite disability. For the remaining

---

[15] In case of miners the minimal loss has to be 50 percent.

[16] Sickness benefits reach a maximum of 75 percent of the "regular" monthly earning. Therefore the 20 percent loss can happen if one has been mostly out of work (but in employment) for several years.

[17] Since health and social security authorities try to reduce payments for sick leave, administrative regulations are put into effect from time to time if the take-up seems to be "too high." General practitioners are often blamed for being too liberal toward their clients. Therefore their interest is to "push forward" those patients who "overuse" their accepted "number of days on sick leave in their district," reported compulsorily in monthly returns. Needless to say, "acceptance" by the authorities is regulated by "norms of tradition," being highly responsive to labor-market shortages on the one hand and to the constraints of the state budget on the other.

[18] The payment of sick benefits stops automatically after one year.

[19] If the degree of disability is between 40 and 67 percent, the board refers the case to the general practitioner, who is expected to search for "relevant work for rehabilitation." It follows from the description of general working conditions that the firms usually cannot offer easy work, and because such jobs (if they exist at all) usually belong to the least rewarded segments of the economy, severely decreased earnings would result. The actual general outcome is that people with reduced working capacity try to remain in their former jobs, straining themselves and creating thereby a straightforward way to even more serious deterioration of their health. The mere "material interest" constructed by the trap of nonexistent forms of meaningful protection forces them to do so.

64,700 applicants, the decision required review after one or two years, since chances of future improvement were reported.[20]

Despite all the difficulties and conflicts, the number of new disability pensions is high and is steadily increasing. In 1985 this number was 404,900 (131 percent more than in 1970). Disability pensioners constitute some 21 percent of the total retired population and account for about two-thirds of cases of early exit.

The most frequent causes of disability, making up 63 percent of new entries into the scheme, are cardiovascular diseases, psychiatric problems (primarily neuroses), and various locomotor disorders.

Although it was mentioned earlier that receiving a disability pension does not necessarily mean that a person gives up working, the health problems seem to be quite serious. The two statements are not contradictory. High rates of application express above all a massive refusal to accept the working conditions of the "official" workplaces. People apply because (given their complaints) they cannot cope with the burden of shiftwork (especially night shifts) or with work on assembly lines, they cannot lift up 200 to 500 kilograms a day, they cannot adapt to the compulsory overtime ordered regularly by their bosses because of the hectic oscillation of stagnation and rush caused by permanent shortages of one or another component of production, and so forth. In other words, disability can often be interpreted as falling short of the requirements of *workplaces*, but not necessarily of those of *work*. All the conditions that people cannot tolerate in eight-hour work can be more or less acceptable on a part-time basis. In addition, part-time work has the advantage of liberating energies for their intensive participation in the second economy, as discussed earlier.

But individual interests in combining early exit with more flexible forms of work are just one side of the coin. Firms also have a massive interest in using the scheme. Since costs of sickness benefits and disability pensions are covered by social security, firms can "play" with the financial consequences. Central wage regulations allow them to hide the wages of workers on sick leave or in the process of applying for a disability pension. Firms can create a considerable sum from "saving" these wages for a while, by representing these workers among their actual employees. That sum remains with the firm and can be used freely for increasing the earnings of those who really do work. The widespread

---

[20] There are no data on suspension of disability pensions because of significant improvement of health. It seems to be a sporadic issue. In other words, conflicts center around the *first* decision on degree of disability. If once judged to be over 67 percent, than further reviews tend to confirm this level of disability.

shifting of burdens is the main form of evading the strict central regulations and control over wages. On the other hand, it contributes to the inflationary tendencies in the economy. Though there are attempts from time to time to stop that form of shifting by administrative rule, it seems to be one of the unavoidable consequences of artificial interventions of the state in matters of the economy.

10.6 SOME ASPECTS OF THE WAY OF LIFE OF RETIRED PEOPLE

As has been mentioned several times, early exit from full-time employment does not necessarily coincide with exit from work. On the contrary, the main social rationale of early exit, as we shall soon see, is to get better access to types of work that people hardly could combine with the rigid forms and regulations of formal employment.

These, then, are the important questions. What are the forms and outcomes of the silent struggle surrounding the issues of early retirement? Are there meaningful social differences with regard to typical ways people combine pensions and work? How much do people earn by extra work? A further set of questions should be raised regarding the interest of the firms, the state, and the families in these controversial issues regarding uncontrollable elements of the labor market. Their description should lead us to a better understanding of the present discourse and of proposals for both extending and restricting opportunities for early withdrawal from formal employment.

Table 10.8 presents data on social differentials of early, "ordinary," and "delayed" retirement between blue- and white-collar workers. If one keeps in mind that the main pathway of early exit is the disability pension scheme and that the health risks of middle-aged men are higher for laborers than for white-collars workers, then the findings in Table 10.8 will be quite surprising. The frequency of early retirement is somewhat lower, while that of delayed retirement is significantly higher, among laborers than among other male employees.[21] That finding underlines indirectly what has been said before about the social meaning of early exit: It is basically an expression of an ongoing social struggle, and white-collar workers seem to be more efficient in winning it. The explanations for postponing retirement lie partly in the incentives men-

---

[21] Not only the ration, but even the length of postponement of retirement, shows differences between the two groups: 67.2 percent of blue-collar workers postpone retirement by four or more years, while the relevant rate among white-collar workers is just 52.6 percent.

Table 10.8. *Early, ordinary, and delayed retirement of male employees*

	Percentage of those retiring		
Previous occupation	Early (under 60)	Ordinarily (at 60)	With delay (over 60)
White collar	24.3	33.8	41.9
Blue collar	22.5	29.8	47.7

Source: Microcensus of 1984.

tioned earlier that encourage workers to extend employment beyond the retirement age and in the construction of the pension scheme itself, which progressively and positively sanctions extra-long permanent employment (favoring especially those who remain in full-time work for more than 35 years).

Given the present pension scheme, retirement generally means a significant drop of the normal monthly revenue of the household. Pensioners, even with deteriorated health, therefore have good reasons to seek additional sources of income. They can do so in two ways. One is to take up employment shortly after entering the pension scheme. The other is to increase participation in the second economy, above all in agriculture.

According to the last Microcensus (1984), 24 percent of all male pensioners were employed in the first economy. Findings of the Income Survey of 1983 show a somewhat higher participation rate (26.1 percent on average). In most cases "employment" means part-time work, but in about 30 percent of them it is on a full-time basis. Regulations prescribe a ceiling (in working hours per year) for employing pensioners, but in some cases either the firm or the individual can apply for an exception to the rule. It is obvious that exceptions are usually made in occupations with a chronic labor shortage. The present rate of 30 percent is the outcome of a steady increase and reflects the effects of the economic crisis: Since social security has been unable to keep pace with the yearly inflation rate, the real value of pensions has been seriously decreasing, forcing people to extend their labor force participation.

Table 10.9 presents data on earnings from employment for the three large groups: former white-collar workers, agricultural workers, and nonagricultural workers. It can be seen that pensioners are able to supplement their pensions by 5 to 14 percent by reentering employment in the first economy. It has to be added, however, that their bargaining

Table 10.9. *Average sums (in forints) of pensions and of additional earnings (from employment) of male pensioners, by former occupation and by age*

	Former					
	White-collar workers		Blue-collar workers		Agricultural workers	
Age	Monthly pension	Average monthly earning	Monthly pension	Average monthly earning	Monthly pension	Average monthly earning
<59	4,870	460	3,726	252	2,483	296
60–64	4,976	465	3,546	463	3,029	422
65–69	4,632	508	2,999	419	2,570	346
70–74	4,133	404	2,724	291	2,399	311
75–79	3,464	248	2,500	198	2,195	112
80+	2,927	225	2,302	92	2,056	25
Total	4,512	433	3,147	326	2,470	261

Source: Situation of Old Aged People, CSO, Budapest, 1986. (The calculations are based on data of the 1983 Income Survey.)

position is improved relative to their former employment status. Since they take jobs that usually cannot be filled by ordinary workers (low-paid, low-skilled jobs, or jobs in workplaces requiring long-term practice), and they have the right to break the contract with the firm if they wish (which ordinary employees rarely can do without long-lasting disadvantageous consequences), they become honored members of the staff. Though their wages are low, they generally can negotiate much better working conditions and more flexible working hours, and they can refuse compulsory overtime. In addition (as already mentioned), their low wages help the firms to ease the strict central wage control and to "reserve" money to pay more to those they need most.

Though roughly one-fourth of male pensioners seek employment after retirement, that way of supplementing their incomes is secondary to the more widespread form of increasing participation in the informal economy. The latter is not only more common but is also more durable. After all, working hours in formal employment usually have to be reduced after age 70. Regular traveling to and from the workplace frequently becomes too exhausting, it requires too much to adapt to the quite rigid frames and machineries of the firms, and so forth. Agricultural work around the household, however, can fit the decreasing work capacity of the elderly much better. If they cannot do work in the fields, they find their role in poultry feeding, in the vegetable garden, and so forth. Division of labor within the household can be adjusted much more easily to their health and to their need to rest from time to time, and it also fits their cultural traditions much better. As can be seen from Table 10.10, work in agriculture decreases only slightly with age: 65 percent of those over 80 reported work on the household plot, a rate only 10 percent below the rate of the most active group, 60- to 64-year old pensioners.

Time-budget data also show a high (and increasing) rate of participation of pensioners in agricultural activities of the second economy. As shown in Table 10.11, both the frequency of participation and the amount of time devoted to those types of work increased between 1977 and 1986. Though agriculture is the most important "branch" of the informal economy, other work activities of pensioners in and around the household are also significant part of it. As has been noted already (see footnote 9), the importance of their participation in house-building activities has especially increased during those 10 years, reflecting the heroic efforts households make to balance the higher-than-average inflation rate in the construction market. They try to keep pace by extending work and saving money. The role of pensioners in those efforts seems to be more and more important. This supports what has been said earlier: The

Table 10.10. *Participation rates in employment and/or in agricultural work of the second economy by male pensioners, by age*

Age	Percent with additional income from employment	Percent taking part in second-economy agricultural work
<60	22.3	67.5
60–64	35.1	75.4
65–69	32.0	73.2
70–74	25.1	71.0
75–79	16.7	68.2
80–	8.4	65.0
Total	26.1	71.1

Source: Situation of Old Aged People, CSO, Budapest, 1986.

Table 10.11. *Rates of participation and amount of time devoted to various types of work by employed and retired men in 1977 and in 1986 (average weekday)*

	Employed (economically active) men				Pensioners			
	Participation rate (%)		Average duration (minutes)		Participation Rate %		Average duration (minutes)	
	1977	1986	1977	1986	1977	1986	1977	1986
Work at workplaces	67.9	63.3	341	307	13.6	4.1	59	17
Nonagricultural second economy	1.6	5.7	3	14	1.6	9.5	4	36
Small-scale agricultural production	34.6	37.7	58	68	50.5	60.5	106	154
Repair work inside or outside the house; traditional male housework, including construction	44.4	40.5	55	55	56.3	48.7	78	64

Source: The Economy of Time-Use and Various Types of Work (Report on the Time-Budget Survey of 1986/87); New Initiatives in Social Science; CSO and Institute of Sociology, Budapest, 1989.

fundamental function of early retirement (and retirement in general) is not to give up but to *extend* work. The real change that occurs upon retirement affects the control element, not the amount of work. People work hard (sometimes perhaps even harder than before), but for their own purposes and not "for the alien expropriator," that is, "not for the state."

In fact, the given state of affairs is not against all the interests of the central authorities. As long as people are capable of raising their incomes by extending work and exploiting themselves, the pressure on the state budget is eased in several respects. First, the loss of value of the pensions is a less burning issue. It seems to be easier to give people a chance to work more than to reorganize the present inefficient system of social security or to find resources for raising its budget. Second, state expenditures on housing have been decreased significantly during the past 10 to 15 years because of the efforts of families to build their own houses. Official reasoning is, in fact, quite cynical. It is openly admitted that the state wants to get rid of its responsibility to provide decent housing. If great masses of the population can manage without help, then the rest (who cannot) can be blamed for their own faults.

All in all, the interplay of the individuals' desire for more autonomy, the firms' desire for more flexible conditions of daily functioning, and the state's desire to get rid of its responsibilities with regard to "compulsory" state expenditures results in controversial discourses and proposals on early exit and on handling the social problems of the elderly in general.

On the one hand, the chronic labor shortage and the rapidly increasing costs of social security have led, from time to time, to central efforts to restrict the number of disability pensions and to try to force people to remain in formal employment. On the other hand, the growing unemployment that *accompanies* the general labor shortage creates an interest in extending pathways of early exit.

There are proposals for both restrictions and extensions. Those who object to the costs would like to raise the retirement age and introduce a scheme of partial pensions for those who would like to retire earlier. Those who fear unemployment (especially youth unemployment, above all because of its political dangers) argue for a consciously oriented "exchange of the generations" in the labor market, and they want to extend forms and pathways of early exit. An important argument for them is that the extension of the scheme is both legally and socially more acceptable and cheaper than introducing a decent scheme of unemployment benefits.

Firms of the first economy also behave ambivalently. On the one hand, with increasing economic difficulties they tend to fire older workers, citing their decreasing productivity. On the other, they also have an interest in employing pensioners part-time for reasons mentioned earlier.

The situation and decisions of the elderly reflect similar constraints. On the one hand, their fear of losing their jobs forces them to remain in full-time employment as long as they can. On the other hand, their motives for extending their participation in family work in the second economy make early exit enticing.

The delicate balance and smooth interplay of the complex of conflicting forces seems to be broken nowadays. The deepening economic crisis of the country, followed by a dangerous speeding up of inflation, has been accompanied by the introduction (in 1988) of a new system of personal income taxes oriented toward the "salvation" of the state economy, which has enlarged enormously the burdens of the households. They have tried to respond with an even greater intensification of their work in the second economy. There are symptoms, however, of an end of the countervailing capacity of the informal sphere. More and more groups in Hungarian society turn out to be unable to cope with the increased burdens and the parallel withdrawal of the state from the spheres of social protection. New community services and other initiatives, on the other hand, are not yet strong enough to fill the gaps. As a consequence, the number of people dropping below the poverty line has increased significantly in recent years. It goes without saying that large numbers of them are elderly people.

The issue of the shamefully low level of pensions, claims for valorizing them, and programs for urgent reforms of the social security system have been given high priority on the political agenda in the past two years. It seems quite probable that the first tasks of the coming new government will be to make efforts to stop inflation, to introduce regulations for helping the stabilization of the firms, and to put controls on wasteful spending of the state budget and the state-controlled social security funds.

It is hard to predict the short-term outcome of the changes with regard to the living conditions of the population, especially of those at highest risk at the moment. It is clear, however, that there are basically two alternatives for the future of Hungary.

A short-sighted economic policy enforced in the name of rapid stabilization might strengthen the position of those interest groups that would like to give overall priority to the urgent creation of a private market economy. Inherent in such a policy would be the great danger of an unstoppable disintegration of the society, reproducing the duality of prewar times by creating one world for those who can easily cope with changes toward a market-ruled system and another world for the "forgotten people."

But there are equal or even better chances for a modern East European version of social democracy. The latter should (and, it can be hoped, would) build its economic and social policy on those capacities, skills, solidarities, and working networks of the informal sphere, which have been developed on a large scale during the past two decades. After all, it can be a good start for the new political leadership to admit the surprising achievements of large groups of the society in their silent struggle against the totalitarian state, and to enhance the political representation of these groups in the development of the future of the country.

These last sentences were written one month before the election. Hungarian society is full of hopes and confusion. It is a good time to articulate alternatives and to argue for them. But it is an exceptionally bad time to make any "scientific" predictions. There are so many open questions, so many unsettled motives and struggles, that the best approach for the sociologist (as for anyone else) is that of mere personal curiosity. The rest will be presented by history.

APPENDIX

A.1   Early-exit trends in Hungary

During the past two decades, early exit from the labor market has been inspired by quite substantial changes in labor needs for production in a number of postindustrial Western societies. Looking at the statistical trends of employment by age in Hungary (Table A.1), one sees surprisingly similar structural changes. (The population figures for the same years are given in Table A.2.)

Since the "normal" retirement age for men is set at 60 in Hungary, "early-exit groups" are those aged 55 to 59 and 50 to 54. We can see that during the past 25 years employment rates have dropped by 23 percent and 10 percent, respectively, for these age groups. Even the group aged 45 to 49 has been modestly affected: The employment rate in this group declined from 95.4 percent in 1970 to 93.0 percent in 1984. (Because the five-year breakdown between ages 30 and 50 has been published only since 1970, comparison in this respect can be made only for the last 15 years.) Cohort data (Table A.3) show even more marked tendencies toward early exit. The group aged 40 to 44 in 1985 shows an employment rate 2.3 percent lower than that of the same group 15 years earlier when they were in their late twenties. The decrease over 15 years is 5.6 percent for those aged 45 to 49 in 1985.

In addition, and also in accordance with the international trends, female employment rates do not show a parallel decrease. On the con-

Table A.1. *Employment activity rates[a] by age and sex in 1960, 1970, 1980, and 1984*

	Males				Females			
Age	1960	1970	1980	1984	1960	1970	1980	1984
14	17.7	3.7	1.6	1.5	13.4	10.5	3.3	3.5
15–19	57.2	45.8	45.3	43.5	48.1	49.1 (50.6)	39.6 (45.3)	37.9 (40.8)
20–24	94.5	91.5	92.1	89.9	55.2	66.2 (81.0)	59.8 (88.7)	62.7 (88.0)
25–29	98.9	98.5	98.2	98.3	48.7	65.3 (78.7)	70.4 (92.4)	71.4 (93.2)
30–34		98.6	98.4	98.3		68.7	81.1 (90.7)	83.0 (92.6)
35–39	98.9	98.1	97.8	97.7	49.9	71.0	84.9 (88.2)	88.9 (91.9)
40–44		97.2	96.0	96.2		69.4	83.1 (83.9)	87.4 (88.1)
45–49	98.1	95.4	92.9	93.0	50.5	64.0	77.5 (77.6)	82.7 (82.8)
50–54	96.7	91.8	86.1	86.0	46.3	56.5	67.1	70.7
55–59	93.4	84.4	72.7	70.1	30.6	29.2	18.9	9.5
60–64	69.6	43.7	13.4	5.5	26.1	17.1	9.1	3.7
65–69	65.5	24.6	5.4	1.8	24.1	9.5	5.5	1.6
70–	51.3	10.7	3.1	1.0	18.6	3.5	2.3	0.3
Total	85.6	73.6	70.8	67.8	42.4	47.2	49.6	48.6

[a]Employment activity rates refer to those in full-time employment only. The rate of part-time employment of those in economically active ages is negligible in Hungary (see footnote 3 for details).

[b]Employment rates in parentheses include those on child care grant. The system of a social security cash benefit named "child care grant" was introduced in 1967 to help working mothers to stay at home with their children until the age of three years, while their workplace is protected. These young women can therefore be regarded as in employment, though temporarily out of it. Unfortunately, census data of 1970 do not separate those on child care grant from those already on disability pension. Since the more widespread take-up of disability pensions starts over 30, not even estimates could be made for older age groups of mothers on child care grant to include them among employed women. (The two distinct categories of disability pensioners and those on child care grant are covered by the label of "inactive population" for the year 1970.) That is the reason detailed data are available only for 1980 and 1984.

Source: Census data 1960, 1970, and 1980; Microcensus of 1984.

trary, the ratio of those potentially affected by early exit (i.e., those under 55, the official retirement age for women) has been rapidly increasing in the labor market (by some 25 to 30 percent) during the period of comparison.

Even cohort data show the extension of female employment. As one can see from Table A.3, for those aged 50 to 54 in 1985, the rate of full-time employment is only 0.3 percent lower than it was 15 years earlier, when they were in their "best" years (the relevant rate is 71.0 percent).

Table A.2. *Age distribution of the population, by sex, in 1960, 1970, 1980, and 1984 (in percent)*

	Males				Females			
	1960	1970	1980	1984	1960	1970	1980	1984
0–13	25.5	20.4	21.9	21.4	22.7	18.1	19.4	18.8
14	1.5	2.0	1.3	1.6	1.4	1.8	1.1	1.4
15–19	7.9	9.4	6.6	7.1	7.3	8.4	5.7	6.2
20–24	6.9	7.9	8.0	6.0	6.8	7.3	7.2	5.2
25–29	7.4	7.4	8.7	7.4	7.1	6.9	8.1	6.9
30–34	7.6	6.5	7.3	8.3	7.5	6.5	6.8	7.8
35–39	7.4	7.0	6.9	7.2	7.7	6.8	6.6	6.6
40–44	4.4	7.1	6.0	6.9	4.6	7.1	6.1	6.7
45–49	7.0	6.9	6.4	5.9	7.3	7.3	6.4	6.3
50–54	6.4	4.0	6.4	6.3	6.6	4.3	6.6	6.4
55–59	5.7	6.2	5.9	6.2	5.9	6.7	6.6	6.8
60–64	4.5	5.3	3.3	5.5	5.1	5.8	3.8	6.6
65–69	3.1	4.3	4.6	2.8	3.9	4.9	5.6	3.4
70–X	4.7	5.6	6.7	7.4	6.1	8.1	10.0	10.9
Together	100.0	100.0	100.0	100.0	100.0	100.0	100.0	100.0
Total population	4,804,043	5,003,651	5,188,709	5,151,650	5,157,001	5,318,448	5,520,754	5,506,850

Source: Population census of 1960, 1970, and 1980; Microcensus of 1984.

Table A.3. *Employment activity rate (full-time employment only) and changes of the relevant rates for five-years cohorts, by sex*[a]

	Employment activity rate			Rate of change		
Born in	1970	1980	1985	1970–80	1980–85	1970–85
			Males			
1951–55	45.8	98.2	98.3	+52.4	−0.1	+52.5
1946–50	91.5	98.4	97.6	+6.9	−0.8	+6.1
1941–45	98.5	97.8	96.2	−0.7	−1.6	−2.3
1936–40	98.6	96.0	93.0	−2.6	−3.0	−5.6
1931–35	98.1	92.9	86.0	−5.2	−6.9	−12.1
1926–30	97.2	86.2	70.1	−11.0	−16.1	−27.1
1921–25	95.4	72.2	5.5	−23.2	−66.7	−89.9
1916–20	91.8	13.2	1.9	−78.6	−11.3	−89.9
1911–15	84.4	5.3	1.1	−79.1	−4.2	−83.3
1906–10	43.7	3.7	1.1	−40.0	−2.6	−42.6
1901–05	24.6	2.8	0.6	−21.8	−2.2	−24.0
1900 and before	10.7	1.8	0.0	−8.9	−1.8	−10.7
			Females			
1951–55	49.1	69.8	83.0	+20.7	+13.2	+33.9
1946–50	66.2	81.1	88.9	+14.9	+7.8	+22.7
1941–45	65.3	84.9	87.4	+19.6	+2.5	+22.1
1936–40	68.7	83.1	82.7	+14.4	−0.4	+14.0
1931–35	71.0	77.5	70.7	+6.5	−6.8	−0.3
1926–30	69.4	67.4	9.5	−2.0	−57.9	−59.9
1921–25	64.0	18.8	3.7	−45.2	−15.1	−60.3
1916–20	56.6	8.7	1.6	−47.9	−7.1	−55.0
1911–15	29.2	5.1	0.5	−24.1	−4.6	−28.7
1906–10	17.1	2.1	0.3	−14.0	−2.8	−16.8
1901–05	9.5	1.8	0.0	−7.7	−1.8	−9.5
1900 and before	3.5	0.8	–	−2.7	−0.8	−3.5

[a]The two sets of data on the population – census of 1970 and 1980 – refer to the situation on the January 1 of the relevant year (census moment).

The 1984 Microcensus took October 1, 1984, as the date of reference. The error of estimation produced by the three-month shift of the data of reference is smaller, however, than what follows from the difference in the types of the surveys, namely, that the latter data are based on calculations of a representative sample.

Source: Census of 1970 and 1980; Microcensus (2 percent representative sample) of 1984.

Withdrawal from the labor force starts on a massive scale with eligibility for the "ordinary" old-age pension at the age of 55.

A.2   Retirement age limits in Hungary

The history of defining the age limits of retirement at the relatively low level of 60 for men and 55 for women has its roots in the political fights of working-class movements in prewar Hungary. Since the relatively weak trade unions were unable to stop the misuse of the funds of the main social insurance schemes by the central state (huge state investments and unfavorable state loans were financed from them, while the quality of benefits and services was often very poor), the working-class movements (especially of the social democrats) tried for a long time to extend the years of "enjoyment of the services" through legislation to allow earlier entitlement, thereby protecting the interests of the workers in contrast to the more powerful economy. (The actual age limits were 65 and 60 throughout the whole period of the 1930s and early 1940s.) Although the fights were not successful for a long time, the Nazis eventually expropriated the idea (as a means of political struggle against the leftist working-class movements), and legislation on lowering the age limits was introduced by the fascist government in 1944. There was not time for it to come into effect, since the war led to a total collapse of the country in 1945.

Strangely enough, the new Social Security Act kept the low age limits. The main purpose of doing so was to symbolize the commitment of the new regime to the old working-class movements. Nevertheless, there were other considerations. The highest priority of the economic policy of the period was the extension of employment by all means. The relatively low retirement age seemed to work well as a part of the "incentive package." Given the extremely low level of wages, considerations on the future increase of cost burdens did not play a part in the decision-making processes for a very long time. In fact, the actual rapid growth of social security pension costs started as late as the first half of the 1970s, when the first generations of "new" pensioners (namely those taking up full-time employment exclusively under the socialist era and thereby gaining entitlement for more "expensive" pensions) started to draw their benefits. It is not by chance, that the challenge of the old principles started at the same time. Any changes of the legislation on retirement ages, however, would require a general reform not only within the pension scheme itself, but would have far-reaching effects on the whole of the wage system, on taxation, etc. Therefore there has not been enough political strength until now to achieve a general reorganization. With the coming of a new government, important modifications much beyond the scope of legislation on retirement ages can be expected, as parts of political struggles over the principles and function of social security.

REFERENCES

CSO. 1985. *Employment and Earnings.* CSO, Budapest. 1987.

    1986. *Social Stratification, Living Conditions, Way of Life II.* CSO, Budapest.

    1987. *Time-Budget, Changes in the Way of Life of the Hungarian Society According to the Time-Budget Surveys of Spring, 1977 and Spring, 1986.* CSO, Budapest. (The report was written by István Harcsa and Béla Falussy.)

Farkas, János, and Agnes Vajda. 1988. *The Second Economy of Home-Building.* Manuscript, Budapest.

Józan, Péter. 1988. *Some Characteristics of the Health Status of the Population in Hungary in the 1980s.* Manuscript, Budapest.

Kornai, János. 1982. *The Shortage.* Budapest: Akadémiai Kiadó.

Szalai, Erzsébet. 1989. *Economic Mechanisms, Reforms and the Interest of Large Firms.* Budapest: KJK.

Szalai, Julia. 1986. *The Illnesses of the Health Care System.* Budapest: KJK.

CHAPTER 11

Pathways and their prospects: A comparative interpretation of the meaning of early exit

ANNE-MARIE GUILLEMARD AND HERMAN VAN GUNSTEREN

11.1 INTRODUCTION

DURING the past two decades, the labor force participation of men aged 55 to 64 has decreased, as shown by the comparative data in Chapter 2. This decrease has taken place very quickly in all seven countries covered by this study, except for Sweden. The chapters devoted to individual countries have focused on the main institutional pathways aging workers have taken to withdraw early from gainful employment. They have also shed light on the politics that have staked out these pathways and examined the consequences of this early-exit trend. It is now time to consider what general interpretations are suggested by the data presented in these country chapters. In doing so, we proceed along three lines.

First of all, what have we learned about how the welfare state, through its social policies, treats aging wage earners? What institutional mechanisms have served as the driving force behind this trend toward ever earlier exit from the labor force? Who have been the leading actors? Does this trend advance older workers' right to rest? Or is it "marginalizing" older people sooner as a result of the worsening situation in the labor market?

Second, what does this early-exit trend imply about the social organization of the life course? Is the transition from work to retirement merely being scheduled earlier? Or is it being transformed, as the life course is being reshaped and its basic tripartition is coming undone? Along with changes in the meanings of work and retirement as stages in the life course, are age groups and old age being socially redefined?

Third, we would like to comparatively analyze the debates now arising so as to assess the prospects of early exit. Will this trend be prolonged or reversed in the coming years? If the economy is its major determinant, do recent indications of a labor shortage signal an eventual reversal of this trend? Is there now a tendency to prolong people's working lives, as proposed retirement age reforms in certain countries seem to suggest? Such considerations are of ever greater import since governments in most of the countries under study have begun worrying about the current and future financial equilibrium of old-age insurance funds.

This comparative assessment is more speculative than the foregoing chapters. Its interpretations are hypotheses begging for further research; its comments are so many questions to be pursued by further investigation. We do not claim that these three lines of inquiry circumscribe the subject, nor that our answers represent a complete and noncontroversial account of the country chapters.

11.2 EARLY EXIT IN THE WELFARE STATE: INSTITUTIONS AND ACTORS

11.2.1 A similar dynamics

When comparing several countries, we are at first surprised by the diversity of the institutional arrangements used to open up pathways for the ever earlier exit of growing numbers of aging workers from the labor force. Beyond the differences, however, similarities can be observed in the dynamics underlying this trend.

Unplanned ad hoc pathways. What is most noticeable is that these new early-exit pathways have seldom been planned ahead. They are the unexpected consequences of a "tinkering" about (bricolage) that has involved combining marginal adjustments (usually thought to be temporary) in the welfare system with new ad hoc arrangements (such as preretirement programs). When deciding how to handle the problem of older workers who risk losing their jobs, social actors have drawn upon existing institutions, available resources, and self-evident cultural meanings. Usually, actors try to come up with sensible courses of action by putting together bits and pieces from what is available in this "repertory," which includes:

1. Unemployment insurance funds
2. Disability insurance funds
3. Public retirement programs

4. Private retirement programs
5. Programs for keeping older workers in the labor force or reintegrating them at the work place
6. Special preretirement programs, whether public, collectively negotiated, or private
7. Company-level arrangements offering incentives for early exit
8. Other welfare measures

While this repertory constitutes the space wherein decisions must be made, it seldom dictates the choice itself.

In many cases, welfare systems, though not originally intended to cover the specific risks of aging workers, have been changed so much that they have been assigned a crucial role in ensuring a passage from the working life toward retirement. This happened in France in 1972 when the guaranteed-income scheme for dismissed workers over age 60 was set up under the Unemployment Compensation Fund. Likewise in the Netherlands, disability insurance adopted, in 1973, new (broader than medical) criteria that took into account handicapped workers' "employability" in the local labor market – a measure that would be so frequently used to handle the cases of older wage earners.

The lack of planning in the opening of new early-exit pathways accounts for their extreme malleability. We can see, in each country, how they have been worked over again and again. Often, one program is phased out while another is unexpectedly started up, as in France when, as a result of termination of preretirement solidarity contracts, the number of jobless persons over 55 receiving special, long-term unemployment benefits rose spectacularly. This malleability, and instability, is evidence of governments' short-sightedness and of the dynamics (in particular of cost shifting) impelling the major parties toward early-exit arrangements.

Bridges between work and retirement. A second, common characteristic of early-exit arrangements is that they bridge the period between gainful employment and receipt of a public retirement pension. They are *intermediate* programs. Significantly, old-age insurance has not been the major institution providing for early exit. Instead, unemployment and disability insurance funds have been the preferred public means of doing so. Only Sweden (because of its partial retirement program) and, to a lesser degree, West Germany (thanks to some possibilities for retirement at 60) have used old-age insurance to redraw the border between work and retirement. True, in France, the age of retirement with a full pension was, in 1982, lowered from 65 to 60; but this measure only led to new intermediate programs spanning the period from 55 to 60. It did not significantly affect the boundary between work and retirement.

The following, brief account recalls the major intermediate arrangements used in each country under study. The reader will notice many similarities between the early-exit pathways used to bridge the time from work to retirement and will see how each country has pieced together responses out of the repertory at its disposal.

A summary of early exit in seven countries. France presents a relatively simple case since one of its major pathways has been continually in use. Indeed, the Unemployment Compensation Fund has provided ordinary or special benefits to early withdrawees under arrangements that have varied depending on contractual stipulations, the source of finances (whether the government or the fund itself), and age requirements. From 1982 to 1984, there were also specific preretirement arrangements for bridging the period between work and normal retirement.

In West Germany, early exit has developed thanks to legislation about the Old-Age Insurance Fund. Combined with other social services, arrangements under this fund have opened various early-exit pathways. The two principal combinations have been with unemployment compensation and disability insurance. For a limited time, there was also a preretirement program.

In the Netherlands, early-exit pathways have run through disability insurance, unemployment compensation, and contractual preretirement programs (VUT).

Great Britain has laid down rather narrow public pathways for early exit. When programs specifically for preretirement have existed (such as the Job Release Scheme), they have been tightly controlled. Early withdrawal calls for ample recourse to private pensions and a combination of various public welfare arrangements.

In the United States, which has passed a law forbidding age discrimination in employment and retirement, companies have offered enticing incentives to early withdrawees. Since the early 1980s, company-run Early Retirement Incentive Programs (ERIP) have opened the principal early-exit pathways. Of course, the legislation forbidding age discrimination runs counter to such private programs.

Sweden differs from the other countries as a result of both its active policy of integrating aging workers in the workplace and its adoption of a gradual retirement scheme whereby wage earners can modulate the time spent working as they grow older. Nonetheless, arrangements under public disability and unemployment insurance funds provide ways to get around this policy.

The situation in Hungary is considerably different from all others studied herein. It differs not only in terms of programs, political debates, and company-level decision making, but also with respect to the categories used to classify relevant data. This makes it all the harder to evaluate programs and do comparative research. This atypical situation forces us to assess, positively as well as negatively, the specific protection provided in liberal democratic societies to older wage earners who risk being "marginalized." It is surprising to observe that the early-exit trend has developed in Hungary too. Here, however, early exit primarily means leaving a job in the formal economy and finding gainful work in the underground economy. Early exit is not definitive departure toward a time of inactivity, whether well paid or not. This forces us to turn our attention back to Western countries in order to detect the return of older wage earners into the labor market or the "shadow economy." This reentry occurs to some degree in the United States (Burkhauser and Quinn 1989) but hardly at all in France, the United Kingdom, the Netherlands, and West Germany. The present comparative research project provides no definitive answers to the important question of what early exiters are doing. This is a topic for future research.

The social dynamics of opening new bridges between work and retirement. In many cases, these intermediate arrangements have, until recently, been impelled by an "agreement" that labor unions, employer organizations, and governments have, for various reasons, reached about the early exit in the context of an economic recession and rising joblessness. Labor unions saw such arrangements as a chance for freeing generations of wage earners with long working lives from work earlier than usual. They also thought that, given the scarcity of employment opportunities, jobs could thus be transferred toward young people. Employers saw such arrangements as a means of cutting the work force, if need be, and of "restructuring" firms, as necessary, while introducing greater flexibility in personnel matters. As for public authorities interested in acting on the supply of labor, they thought that such arrangements would free jobs while providing benefits to persons "at risk." All parties expected positive effects on the employment situation.

In this general agreement, employers played a leading role in drawing up various programs for spanning the period between the end of the working life and the start of life on retirement. In the Netherlands, for instance, companies, especially those in difficulty, were actively involved in opening a pathway through disability insurance for the definitive exit of older workers. In France, employers took the initiative by proposing the first such intermediate arrangement (the guaranteed-income dismissal scheme) and thus ensured their absolute control (through their power of dismissal) over definitive early withdrawal while making the Unemployment Compensation Fund bear the costs. The role of employers is even clearer in the United States: Public welfare subsystems (unemployment compensation, disability insurance, retirement) could not easily be adjusted so as to cover early definitive exit, and the 1986 law against age discrimination opposes such actions. Therefore, employers set up ERIPs and, when necessary, massively resorted to private pension funds to make definitive exit appealing to aging employees.

In general, employers have continually tried to cut back on the number of older workers by optimally using available social services and providing incentives, if need be, from their own budgets (for example, in Sweden and France), by offering severance bonuses, or, in Great Britain and the United States, by permitting early exit – without a concomitant reduction of benefits – under privately run retirement funds. Even in Sweden, firms trying to gain more flexibility in managing their work forces have found a way to get around programs for integrating older wage earners and protecting their jobs. They have been actively involved in opening new early-exit pathways through unemployment, health, and disability insurance funds.

Once started, early exit tends to develop on its own since it makes it easier to throw aging workers, who benefit from income replacement schemes, out of the labor force – even if, as in the Netherlands and Sweden, programs for protecting them exist. Insofar as it is possible to get rid of aging workers whose labor entails specific costs for firms (Standing 1986), the early-exit trend tends to become self-sustaining, thus "marginalizing" more and more older wage earners. Because they can leave the labor market under better conditions than other groups, these wage earners become the target when firms have to cut personnel or when public authorities want to act on supply in the labor market. Once this logic of substituting the labor of one age group for that of another has come into play, it is hard to put an end to it.

This self-sustaining trend explains an apparent paradox, namely, the contrast between the continual decrease in the labor force participation rates of persons over age 55 and the instability of early-exit pathways, many of which have come out of employment policies adopted to deal with a specific economic situation and have been enacted for a limited time (such as the guaranteed-income dismissal scheme and solidarity contracts in France, preretirement programs in West Germany, and the Job Release Scheme in Great Britain). Nearly everywhere, the same decision-making processes have led to drawing up, then doing away with or making changes in, early-exit arrangements. Actors try to "piece together" responses to the risks that older workers might be "marginalized." The arrangements enacted at any given moment are those in which all parties, including older wage earners, have interests. For the latter, early exit has to be a financial opportunity not to be missed. The failure of partial retirement programs everywhere except in Sweden provides evidence of this. Whenever early-exit arrangements are less appealing to wage earners than other arrangements, and furthermore, when they are hard for firms to manage, they are not successful. When all parties have an interest in them, they are increasingly used; and as a consequence, costs rise fast – so fast that efforts are made to shift them or contain them by restricting admissions.

As an outcome of this social dynamics, bargaining issues are narrowed down as actors concentrate mainly on the short-run question of who – which actor or which public body – will assume responsibility for the finances. The early-exit trend has, until recently, been considered to be a hard fact, a tough reality that no one could imagine controlling. Hence, collective actors have endeavored to manage costs in view of their interests, in other words, to avoid having to bear this financial load. As for aging wage earners, they switch from one type of payment to another, as they try to grasp whatever opportunities come up.

This social dynamics has also led to reorganizing institutions so as to, in general, replace one early-exit arrangement with another or, less often, to add one onto another. These are called, respectively, "instrument substitution" and "instrument cumulation."

Although the replacement of one pathway with another may be planned, it is usually the unexpected consequence of decisions about cost containment. In France, the Socialist government's 1982 decision to lower the retirement age from 65 to 60 and terminate the guaranteed-income schemes clearly illustrates a planned decision to compress early-exit costs by transferring beneficiaries to less generous coverage under public old-age funds. In the meantime, this "pathway substitution" created a context wherein new measures could be adopted that have led to the exit of workers between 55 and 60 years old. In most cases, however, this substitution is unplanned. For instance, when the French government decided to put an end to the costly solidarity preretirement contracts and, at the same time, make firms pay more for the remaining early-exit arrangements (the FNE preretirement program), employers took advantage of another measure (the suppression of the requirement of administrative approval for dismissals) in order to massively lay off workers over age 50. This cost them less than the FNE preretirement program, which could have been used to cover dismissed employees over age 55. In place of the preretirement solidarity contracts, a new early-exit pathway was opened up through ordinary unemployment compensation. In the Netherlands, the main pathway ran through disability insurance; but when this arrangement came under attack for being too generous, the pathway through unemployment compensation was increasingly used. Since such intermediate programs have come under review during recent social security reforms, contractual programs (VUT) based on collective agreements have become the main way to leave the labor force early.

Sometimes, the attempt to replace one pathway with another has amounted, in fact, to a cumulation of pathways. In West Germany the preretirement program, introduced in 1984 in order to shift the costs of early exit from the state onto firms, worked like an additional rather than an alternative arrangement. A major reason for not renewing these programs in January 1988 was that costs were not shifted as intended.

Early-exit arrangements have turned out to be less stable and less reliable than we might have expected, given their similarity to retirement pension systems. The fact that public programs have repeatedly been reworked is evidence of the vitality of the welfare state, usually believed to be in a crisis. It is also true, however, that the application of public early-exit arrangements has put the welfare state in trouble because of their considerable costs and also, more importantly, because of the confusion resulting from this cumulation of unplanned, ad hoc schemes. In effect, this confusion tends to undermine the welfare state's structure by mixing up various risks and coverage of them. For example, unemployment compensation has been made to work like a pseudo-old-age fund while retirement pension systems, at least in West Germany (and also in France where the retirement age was lowered), are forced to come to the rescue of jobless older persons. Disability insurance, too, has been used as a tool for socially managing unemployment.

11.2.2 What can be learned from differences between countries?

Institutions in the seven countries under study have responded differently to the plight of older workers facing unemployment. These differences can be grouped around three axes:

1. Whether older workers are compensated for lost jobs or are kept in the world of work (specifically through the adoption of appropriate measures of integration, rehabilitation, and job adaptation)
2. Whether private or public arrangements have been used to open up early-exit pathways
3. Whether early exit is an individual's choice, based on his or her interests and personal satisfaction, or a forced decision

Compensation versus integration. Comparing responses to this alternative helps us understand why Sweden is the only European country where early exit has not become a full-blown trend. In Sweden the boundary between work and retirement has not changed much. Whereas France and West Germany have clearly opted for compensating older workers for lost jobs, Sweden has made a special effort in favor of integrating the aged and handicapped. The Netherlands lies in between: Its policy for helping such workers stay in the labor force has been tempered, and can be evaded since broader measures have been adopted that compensate for the loss of either jobs or the fitness for work.

In Sweden, the only nation that actively seeks to prevent job loss among older wage earners rather than compensating them for it, the labor force participation rate of persons over age 55 has not decreased much during the past 15 years. As a consequence, Sweden has stabilized the boundary between work and retirement. The relative stability of older workers' rates of labor force participation is linked to the maintenance of the retirement system, thanks to the partial retirement program, as the regulator of definitive exit. This program, which allows for modulating the time persons spend working as they grow older, has forestalled exclusion from the labor market. Making the definitive withdrawal process gradual and more flexible has not simply resulted in lowering the exit age. The success of this partial retirement program can apparently be set down to Sweden's active employment policy, which includes measures reintegrating older wage earners in the workplace. For this reason, this program of partial retirement can probably not be directly carried over into other countries, where such active employment policies are lacking. In effect, attempts in Great Britain, France, and West Germany to develop partial retirement schemes have yielded few results and have often failed. One lesson to be learned from the Swedish example is that part-time or flexible retirement cannot become a major way out of the labor force if it is not backed up by an active employment policy that lets aging workers have the chance to continue working if they choose. Otherwise, early exit is not so much the wage earner's choice as his or her objective loss of chances for staying in the labor market. In this case, early withdrawal is a full exit that occurs as early as possible depending on the arrangements providing for it.

Several other conclusions about the redefinition of the boundary between work and nonwork can be drawn from the Swedish case. This boundary has been stable in Sweden thanks to coordinated actions in favor of integrating, or reintegrating, the aging in the labor force. In contrast, policies of compensating for the loss of jobs (or of the capacity to work) tend to accelerate and amplify the early-exit trend. A policy of integration in the labor market is not really consistent with one of providing generous compensation. In fact, as the Swedish case illustrates, the former is vulnerable to the latter: The Swedish partial retirement program has, since the early 1980s, been losing control over definitive withdrawal to disability insurance, whose conditions have been loosened for older jobless persons. These slacker conditions have been worked into companies' strategies. By means of disability insurance and severance pay, firms push out of production aging wage earners, who used to have the best job protection. A new early-exit pathway has thus been opened for getting around the policy of integration at the workplace. To a lesser degree, much the same process has taken place in the Netherlands, where relatively important measures for protecting aging employees at work have come to naught as a result of the continual expansion of compensatory schemes. The integration/compensation alternative admits of no compromise: The policy of integration is menaced whenever the logic of compensation is brought into play. Paradoxically, broadening compensation programs for unemployment or disability and expanding their benefits do not necessarily improve the protection of aging workers.

The case of the United States is noteworthy. Insofar as this nation, like Sweden, has not enacted special public programs for compensating older workers for loss of jobs or of the ability to work, we might think it is pursuing a policy of integration. But in contrast with Sweden's active integration policy, the United States has adopted an essentially different approach, namely, prohibiting discrimination on an age basis in matters of employment and retirement. The older person's right to a job has been legally reinforced and, as a victim of discrimination, he or she may win damages by suing. Beyond this proclaimed legislative intent to end such discrimination, there has been no active public employment policy in favor of older workers (apart from a few very limited measures). In these circumstances, private compensation programs have been set up to provide incentives for older workers to abandon their jobs. Only an active policy for maintaining and reintegrating older workers in the labor force enables aging workers to choose between going on retirement or continuing working.

Private versus public. As pointed out, early-exit pathways have often been made up of a combination of public welfare programs and private incentives offered by companies or provided under collective agreements. In this respect, there are two distinct groups of countries. The United Kingdom and the United States rely primarily on private schemes, whereas West Germany, the Netherlands (except for the VUT preretirement program), and France have developed major public programs, which seem to provide higher benefits than private ones.

Whereas the United States has chosen to protect older people by abolishing mandatory retirement and forbidding age discrimination, the three continental European countries have given priority to compensating older wage earners, even if this entails sacrificing their right to employment. The public ban on age discrimination in the United States has not halted the early-exit trend in the private sector. Instead, older workers are now laid off not simply because they are old and deserve a rest but because they are no longer useful or efficient (possibly but not necessarily as a result of aging). Protecting them from age discrimination has not significantly increased their chances of keeping or finding a job, and it definitely does not give them financial security. A system of legal rules and rights does not automatically form a financial safety net, and stretching out such a net tends to endanger the right to employment. In the three West European countries, programs insuring the income of older, jobless workers have apparently sped up the early-exit trend, since they forbid beneficiaries to engage in gainful employment. Furthermore, older people's chances of finding work have been restricted by the availability of adequate compensation.

The United Kingdom is a different case. It has developed public compensatory programs for older wage earners at risk, but with benefits so poor and eligibility criteria so tight that many workers prefer holding onto their jobs as long as possible and bargaining with their employers, either individually or collectively at the company or branch level.

An interesting mix of public and private arrangements has come out of situations where the outcome of *private* collective bargaining is *publicly* circumscribed. These public constraints need not be explicitly formulated in law. More often, as in Sweden and the Netherlands, the parties to negotiations are aware of, and accept, these constraints. The Dutch VUT programs are approved only if they provide benefits at least equal to retirement pensions. The outcome of private bargaining is thus publicly, albeit informally, circumscribed. In Sweden, collective bargaining seems to be effectively constrained by what would be publicly acceptable as an outcome. In the United States, private negotiations are not constrained by public expectations about the financial protection of the elderly. In the three Western European countries with compensatory public programs, the outcome of negotiations about early exit is random. Most of these programs almost automatically yield certain results; they do not contain limitations on program costs or participation. When costs start running up or when the number of applicants rises steeply, a new round of complicated political bargaining takes place to redesign the programs. However, since these are public, hence open to all citizens who meet requirements, the redesigned programs too will soon have to be reworked during another long, tough round of political bargaining. Public programs, though established so as to provide stable, reliable benefits similar to old-age pensions, are subject to unpredictable rounds of talks and unforeseeable interventions. They are, indeed, worked over again and again. Like private arrangements, they too have turned out to be unstable over time.

Individualization, choice, satisfaction. The subtle interweaving of individualization, choice, and satisfaction cannot be unraveled here. But some differences between countries can be pointed out.

Early-exit arrangements have become individualized in that the pathway taken from work toward retirement increasingly depends on the wage earner's individual characteristics and situation. In the European countries under study, admission under one of these arrangements normally depends on bureaucratic processes of program implementation wherein older workers have little room for making a personal choice or bargaining about the conditions. In the United States, the "individualized" offers that some firms make to older employees are usually on a "take-it-or-leave-it" basis; and the worker, were he or she to refuse, seriously risks being dismissed soon afterward. The German and Dutch pre-retirement schemes do, by and large, allow wage earners the choice to quit or go on working without risking dismissal or subsequently having to stand up under intense pressure. Much more frequently however, the "individualization" of definitive exit does not entail more individual choice.

Whether or not people are satisfied with early exit and its arrangements, before or after the decision to stop working has been made, is another matter. Satisfaction seems to depend on material resources and cultural meanings, which vary considerably from one country to another, but also probably between social strata. In West Germany, those eligible for early exit, whether under special preretirement or partial disability programs, seem to be satisfied with it. In France and the U.K., feelings are ambivalent. In Hungary, early exit is valued for, among other reasons, opening the prospect that pay from a job in the underground economy will be higher than wages in the official labor market.

11.3 EARLY EXIT AND THE SOCIAL ORGANIZATION OF THE LIFE COURSE

As a result of this comparative analysis of the new ways in which definitive exit is taking place, we can understand how the boundary between the working life and retirement is being redrawn and how transitions between these two periods are being redefined. We are thus led to study how old age is socially constructed and, more broadly, how the life course is reorganized.

Do the changes in definitive exit merely amount to a rescheduling of retirement? If so, retirement occurs earlier, in fact much earlier; but ages still follow each other in the same order, dictated by the threefold model of the life course: After the period of education comes work during adulthood, followed by a time of inactivity starting with old age.

According to another interpretation, changes in the boundary between the working life and retirement are evidence that the tripartition of the life course is no longer serving as a model. Our working hypotheses are grounded in this interpretation. Reorganizing the threshold for definitive exit is not so much a consequence of applying the logic of retirement to younger aging workers and thus rescheduling the life course as it is part of a process transforming the relationship between the welfare system and the life course, a transformation threatening the threefold model which has emerged since the start of industrialization. Under this model, the working life ends with entry into a retirement pension system, and the identity of old age is linked to being a retiree.

How has the early exit trend affected the passage from work to retirement? Several aspects call for attention:

1. Is this passage a gradual transition or a cutoff point?
2. Is it standardized or individualized? As Chapter 2 pointed out, definitive exit has gradually been made uniform in terms of the age of entitlement to a full retirement pension. Has early exit made the life course more flexible? more individualized? If so, stages in the life course will no longer follow each other in the uniform, foreseeable order essential to the threefold model, which placed everyone in a succession of hierarchically arranged stages within clearly marked bounds.
3. Who has made decisions about and exercises control over this passage? Do individuals still control their own definitive exit, as they did when they could decide, once eligible, whether or not to ask for retirement benefits?
4. Have the markers at the boundary between work and nonwork changed? The age of retirement has been the major milestone signaling entry into old age. But are other markers than chronological age (for example, functional criteria) now being used to stake out the life course?

The institutional arrangements, and their rules of eligibility, that have authorized shifting the boundary between work and nonwork indicate how the life course and old age are being socially reconstructed as a result of the massive early-exit trend. By comparing these arrangements, we can discover cross-national changes in the passage from the working life to retirement and thus raise theoretical questions about the social redefinition of old age, the distribution of work and free time over the life course, and the general changes under way in the latter's organization.

Two lessons can be drawn from the systematic examination of points of convergence between countries. Not only are public retirement systems losing the power to regulate definitive exit, but other welfare sub-systems are being used in their stead. Let us look at each of these points.

11.3.1 The retirement system's loss of power over definitive exit

A constant point standing out in the country chapters is that the early-exit trend has not only scheduled retirement earlier but also deeply affected the whole definitive exit process. Previously, definitive withdrawal from the labor force meant immediate admission into a public retirement pension system, usually on the basis of eligibility requirements having to do with age and the number of years worked. Nowadays, as evidence from the country chapters indicates, people are leaving the labor force long before entitlement to an old-age pension. Early exit has given rise to ad hoc systems of social transfers that usually have nothing to do with public old-age funds. Other institutional arrangements have taken up a place between work and retirement, and they – instead of these funds – now regulate definitive withdrawal. Whereas most persons, at least most men, used to stop working to go directly on retirement, a minority now do so in France, West Germany, and the Netherlands. Giving up one's job to go directly on retirement is still the prevailing model of definitive exit only in Sweden and Hungary. The aforementioned eligibility requirements no longer serve to set the boundaries between economic activity and inactivity.

In Great Britain, there were, in 1983, 700,000 jobless men aged 60 to 64 who could not draw public retirement pensions, since these are payable only at the age of 65 for males. Among them, 32 percent were on unemployment, 28 percent were receiving disability benefits, 12 percent were covered by the Job Release Scheme, 6 percent were drawing welfare, 17 percent had pensions from occupational retirement funds, and 5 percent had found other solutions (see Chapter 7).

In the United States, 62 is the earliest age of eligibility for a Social Security old-age pension. As a consequence, many aging persons who stopped working earlier are waiting for retirement thanks to, in particular, company programs eventually combined with limited coverage under unemployment compensation or disability insurance. The major incentive for early exit has been sizable bonuses paid by employers (ERIP) along with, in many cases, early pensions from company retirement funds.

In the French private sector, according to a 1981 definitive exit survey by the Ministry of Labor, a minority of older wage earners went directly from work onto retirement. To the mere 18 percent who had retired at the normal age (65) can be added 14 percent who, for various reasons, retired early with full or reduced pensions. In contrast, more than two-thirds (68 percent) were "preretirees," who stopped working early (i.e., before retirement) under intermediate arrangements related to welfare subsystems other than the old-age fund: 8 percent under company-sponsored programs and 60 percent under arrangements managed by the Unemployment Compensation Fund (see Chapter 5, Table 5.4).

France is the only country to have lowered the retirement age: in 1982, from 65 to 60. Did this restore the old-age fund to its function of regulating definitive exit? A positive answer would ignore the extension of "preretirement" arrangements under Unemployment Compensation to 55- to 59-year-olds. Although various arrangements have been terminated or made less attractive, the employment rates of persons over 55 have continued falling off since 1985. These persons, in ever growing numbers, depend on ordinary or special long-term unemployment benefits. Once ejected from the labor force, they thus manage to wait for retirement. In 1988 according to the Association Générale de Retraite des Cadres, only 26.5 percent of middle- and top-level white-collar workers were still working when they asked to start receiving a retirement pension, whereas 35 percent were under preretirement schemes and 20 percent were on unemployment. Furthermore, the number of applicants at retirement age who were already economically inactive was twice that of applicants who were still working. Although intermediate arrangements have changed, with preretirement benefits being replaced by ordinary unemployment compensation, there is still often the same waiting period between work and retirement.

Available data about West Germany (see Chapter 6, Table 6.2) also reveal that a minority of older wage earners pass directly from the labor force into retirement. Many new retirees had been drawing disability benefits: 40 percent in 1987. Furthermore, admission into retirement following a long period of unemployment compensation is frequent (about 10 percent). Direct admissions into normal retirement at 65 or "flexible" retirement at 63 ranged between 23 percent and 36 percent from 1980 to 1987, whereas in the 1960s they were over 50 percent.

In the Netherlands, eligibility for retirement, whether public or private, occurs at 65. The inactive men, who represented about 70 percent of 60- to 64-year-old males, were covered as follows (see Chapter 4, Table 4.5):

Preretirement programs (VUT) under collective agreements – 21 percent in 1983 and 32 percent in 1985

Disability insurance – 58 percent in 1983 and 50 percent in 1985
Unemployment – 11 percent in 1983 and 9 percent in 1985

The retirement system's loss of power over definitive exit is a crucial change. The generalization of public old-age pension funds has helped institutionalize the threefold life-course model by maintaining its chronology and standardizing the life course. Given the retirement system's importance in thus constructing the life course, what are the implications of its loss of power over definitive exit? Will the life course no longer be clearly organized in three successive stages? Whatever other conclusions may be drawn, this loss of power would seem to invalidate interpreting the early-exit trend as a mere rescheduling of retirement.

11.3.2   The new institutional arrangements and their implications

What welfare subsystems are taking the place of the public retirement system in regulating definitive exit? As already indicated, disability insurance and unemployment compensation funds are increasingly serving this purpose. Their logic and eligibility requirements are reshaping the passage between work and nonwork. In addition, contractual preretirement arrangements, often under collective agreements, are also used frequently.

The disability insurance pathway. Disability insurance provides one of the major ways out of the labor force in the Netherlands, West Germany, Sweden, and Great Britain. To open up this pathway, eligibility requirements for disability benefits usually had to be loosened. In some cases, this path has been connected to other arrangements, in particular unemployment compensation, so as to bridge the period until normal retirement.

In the Netherlands, early exit commonly passed, until the late 1970s, through disability insurance. This is still a well-trodden path. The number of beneficiaries increased 130 percent from 1973 to 1979, a year when nearly 60 percent of persons receiving such benefits were over 50 years old. This pathway was taken more and more often after 1973, when eligibility requirements were broadened so that partial, even minimal, disabilities could be reclassified as total if applicants were unable to find jobs in the local labor market adapted to both their qualifications and handicaps.

In the Federal Republic of Germany, there have been many early withdrawees under disability insurance, and this pathway has become a highway since 1976. By 1984, 48 percent of new admissions into the retirement system concerned persons who had received disability benefits. As in the Netherlands, this arrangement's success has come from broadening eligibility requirements beyond strictly medical criteria so as to take into account factors related to the labor market. Since 1976, partially disabled persons may receive full benefits if there are no suitable part-time jobs. As a result, this arrangement has been widely used by 55- to 59-year-olds, an age group that cannot enter the retirement system and whose position in the labor market is precarious. Although the tightening of eligibility requirements since 1985 has somewhat narrowed this pathway, it is still often taken.

In Sweden and Great Britain, disability insurance has not expanded as far as in the Netherlands and West Germany, even though it has been covering more and more early withdrawees.

In Sweden, eligibility requirements under disability insurance were loosened in favor of aging jobless persons, and "employability" became a criterion alongside medical ones. Since 1976, jobless persons at least 60 years old may claim disability benefits until normal retirement at 65 if they cannot find employment. It should be pointed out that introducing an explicit age stipulation under disability insurance has seldom occurred elsewhere. But companies have not missed the opportunity to work this arrangement into their personnel policies. This opportunity should not be underestimated since the target population is often less productive than other age groups and since this population, which has the best legal protection against dismissal, is able to receive benefits from a program that excludes it from the work force. Let us not forget, however, that early-exit pathways are not well trodden in Sweden.

In Great Britain, ever more aging workers have been withdrawing early under disability insurance, which, however, has not been purposefully reorganized or had its eligibility requirements broadened. Only a small proportion of older wage earners (mainly manual workers over 60) have been capable of negotiating this sort of coverage.

As these cases show, disability insurance has become a major early-exit pathway in countries where eligibility requirements include, besides purely medical criteria, the "employability" of aging workers. Disability is thus redefined in economic rather than medical terms. Outside Sweden, where jobless wage earners over age 60 can receive disability benefits for reasons related to conditions in the labor market, an age requirement has rarely been introduced as the main criterion in disability insurance.

Since explicit age stipulations have seldom been used under disability insurance, we can draw the conclusion that functional markers rather than chronological milestones are now being more frequently used to stake out the end of the life course. The replacement of retirement by disability insurance has involved redefining the criteria used to determine definitive exit. In effect, definitive exit is no longer linked to the age of entitlement to a full retirement pension but rather to the individual's fitness for work. This change might reflect a departure from the chronological pattern and thus result in an inevitable "destandardization" of the life course.

Since people's ability to keep working as they grow older depends on their socioeconomic category, these functional criteria generate major differences among individuals with regard to the timing of the passages between stages in the life course. Furthermore, a new social construction of old age seems to be emerging: Older workers are no longer simply said to be close to the age of entitlement to rest with a pension; instead they are being labeled as unable to work. When, as in West Germany or the Netherlands, nearly half of those who reach retirement age have previously been managed by disability insurance programs, economic inactivity no longer means the right to rest. It means being unfit for employment.

The unemployment compensation pathway. Unemployment compensation is another welfare subsystem decisively redefining the boundary between the working life and life after work. Toward the mid-1970s, special procedures were adopted in France, the Netherlands, West Germany, Great Britain, and Sweden for compensating older workers for lost jobs.

In France, arrangements under unemployment compensation were a principal means of managing a massive early-exit trend. A guaranteed-income scheme was set up in 1972 for persons over age 60 who were dismissed from their jobs, and this was extended in 1977 to those who resigned. In 1982 other arrangements relayed these schemes to 55- to 59-year-olds. Under agreements between the government and firms, wage earners at the age of 56 years and 2 months (and sometimes at 55) could be dismissed with special National Employment Fund allocations until normal retirement. More recently, government attempts to contain the costs of preretirement have caused a groundswell in the ranks of the aging long-term jobless who receive ordinary unemployment benefits.

The Netherlands adopted new rules in 1975 stipulating that recipients of unemployment benefits between ages 60 and 64 would continue being covered until the legal retirement age of 65. Under these new rules, people can stop working at 57½. Unemployment insurance and welfare assistance successively provide them with benefits until 65.

West Germany has gradually loosened the conditions for providing unemployment benefits to the jobless over 54. Since 1987, persons aged 57 years and 4 months who are dismissed from their jobs can receive unemployment benefits until 60, the age when the "long-term unemployed" become eligible for a normal retirement pension. Hence, the so-called "59er" rule has become a "57er" rule. In 1986, 11 percent of new retirees had exited from work early under unemployment compensation.

In Sweden, the unemployment and disability insurance funds have been combined so as to open a definitive exit pathway as early as age 58 (with unemployment benefits until 60 and then disability benefits until 65, the normal retirement age). In comparison with other countries however, this pathway is still seldom followed.

In Great Britain, no special protection has been offered to the aging jobless; nor has any special pathway been opened for early exit through unemployment compensation. However, unemployment assistance compensation for cases of long joblessness is often provided to supplement the incomes of "discouraged" aging wage earners (Laczko 1987) who have stopped working either as a result of partial disability or thanks to the early receipt of occupational old-age pensions. Early-exit routes in Britain often pass through occupational pension funds.

In all five countries, the same process is under way. Better benefits are provided to the aging jobless. Unemployment compensation, which used to be based on eligibility requirements having nothing to do with age, has become "age-specific." Meanwhile, making it easier for older workers to receive compensation also makes it easier for companies to dismiss, first of all, those who benefit from such better coverage. Firms can thus get rid of these persons at lower economic and social costs. Adopting measures that compensate older wage earners for lost jobs reinforces age discrimination in the labor market, all the more so when the economic situation worsens.

Does the use of age requirements to turn unemployment compensation into an early-exit pathway mean that such criteria are still the major means used to stake out the life course? There are significant differences between the chronological milestones incorporated in public retirement systems and the criteria introduced in unemployment compensation funds. The latter are variable and are continually changed. They cannot, therefore, serve as standardized chronological milestones marking the passage from the working life to the age of retirement. The age requirements under unemployment compensation do not mean that everyone has the right to rest sooner. Instead, they are evidence that aging workers are less and less secure in the world of production, a precariousness that varies as a function of the industry, qualifications, and training. Behind these ad hoc, variable age requirements, we can glimpse another phenomenon: the reassessment of the functional definition of age. There is no longer any precise chronological boundary between work and non-work. The new bounds are being directly modulated as a function of the labor market and of the definition of ages, in particular in relation to employment. As a consequence, the working life ends unforeseeably for everyone. Even when optional (as under the now terminated French guaranteed-income schemes), the unemployment compensation pathway depends mainly on the employer and his power of dismissal, not on employees and their claim to rest.

The growing importance of both unemployment compensation and disability insurance as a means of regulating definitive exit has two major implications for the life course. First of all, the receipt of such social transfer payments entails surrendering the right to a job. In contrast, retirement systems generally separate the right to employment from the right to a pension. In most countries, one does not have to give up working in order to receive a public old-age pension. Second, replacing the retirement income system with these two other arrangements has opened a gap between the second and third stages in the life course. Wage earners have lost control over the definitive exit process. After the working years comes a time when one is denied the right to a job and forced to stop working. At the same time, one can no longer clearly foresee the passage toward the last stage in the life course. The chronological milestones of retirement have been swept away and, with them, any principle providing for an orderly transition from work to nonwork. While there is more flexibility in organizing the end of the life course, the exit process is increasingly regulated by the labor market and companies' employment policies.

The closing of the preretirement pathway. Analyzing the meaning of the institutional arrangements used to manage early exit would not be complete without mention of "preretirement," the third principal pathway out of the labor force: solidarity preretirement contracts in France, the Preretirement Act in West Germany, the Job Release Scheme in Great Britain, and the VUT in the Netherlands. Such programs are mainly intended to improve the situation in the labor market by proposing voluntary early retirement to aging wage earners and, in many cases, by requiring that these departures entail new hirings of jobless young people. Whether part of public policy or of collective agreements, they tend to manage definitive exit similarly to old-age funds: Age remains the essential eligibility requirement, and the choice of whether to take retirement early is mainly left up to the individual. Although eligibility requirements fluctuate with conditions in the labor market, preretirement provides for an orderly passage out of the work force without placing beneficiaries in successive, precarious positions of dependency on ordinary unemployment compensation, disability benefits, or other welfare payments.

Significantly, preretirement schemes have been abandoned in France, the United Kingdom, and West Germany. Only the Dutch VUT program is still in effect, although it, too, is being called into question.

This abandonment corroborates the interpretation presented at the start of this chapter. The early-exit trend does not merely mean that the age of retirement is being lowered. The expiration of preretirement programs, along with the retirement system's loss of power over definitive exit, might well be evidence of the departure from the chronologically patterned life course, since these programs, like this system, use chronological criteria to regulate withdrawal from the labor force.

11.3.3 *Toward the deinstitutionalization of the life-course model?*

Although, at first glance, we might think that the foregoing changes amount to nothing more than setting the schedule of retirement ahead, they turn out to be part of a thoroughgoing reorganization of the end of the life course. The retirement system's loss of power over definitive exit is evidence of changes in the linkage between the life course and welfare subsystems.

The Swedish case, in contrast, illustrates the maintenance of a tight linkage between the retirement system and the tripartition of the life course. Whenever the public retirement system maintains its power over definitive exit, the social organization of the end of the life course stays more or less the same, and the bounds marking the entry into old age do not change much.

In all the other countries however, much more than the schedule of retirement has come under question: The very ways in which people pass from one stage of life to another, as well as the bounds marking stages, have been deeply affected.

The welfare subsystems (principally unemployment compensation and disability insurance) that have replaced retirement have their own logic for regulating the passage from work to nonwork. As a result, the life course's chronological milestones are being torn up, and functional criteria are increasingly staking out the later years of life. This is especially noticeable when disability insurance replaces retirement. Another observation reinforces this conclusion: The 1986 U.S. law against age discrimination in employment can be interpreted as indicating a different organization of the life course. While less importance is placed on chronological age, greater stress is laid on functional criteria based on the individual's capabilities and effectiveness, since only these criteria can now be legally used by employers to dismiss or retire employees.

Although the end of the life course no longer follows a normative schedule, it can hardly be said to be individualized, for the individual has not gained more control over it. The majority of early withdrawals are not voluntary, definitely not in France (Guillemard 1986) and the United Kingdom (Casey and Laczko 1989). Only in West Germany has individual choice been somewhat maintained. In fact, the early-exit trend is tied to conditions in the labor market and companies' strategies.

Taking away the chronological organization of the life course entails destandardizing it. The threefold model, which places everyone in a continuous, foreseeable trajectory of successive stages, statuses, and roles, is coming apart. The end of the life course is becoming variable, imprecise, and contingent, since chronological milestones are being torn up. Nowadays, no one working in the private sector knows at what age and under what conditions he or she will stop working. Retirement as a social situation and a system of transfers no longer constitutes the horizon where everyone foresees the pathway to be taken, one day, out of the labor force toward old age.

Evidence of this deinstitutionalization of the life-course model also comes from the confusion about the meaning of the third stage of life. Under the threefold model, retirement is the unifying principle that gives a homogeneous meaning and identity to the third stage starting after definitive exit. However, very few of the "young old" – 55- to 65-year-olds who no longer work – now identify themselves as retirees. There is clear evidence of this in France and Great Britain. One-quarter of the jobless British population between 60 and 64, and only 12 percent between 55 and 59, classify themselves as retirees; the rest say they are unemployed or "discouraged" workers no longer looking for a job (Casey and Laczko 1989). The social construction that closely associated definitive withdrawal, old age, and retirement is breaking up (Guillemard 1983). The meaning of the last stage of life is blurred.

Behaviors too are indicating that the threefold life-course model is coming undone. Some "young retirees" expressing concern about their social usefulness are, in effect, objecting to the strict division of functions (education/work/retirement) on an age basis. This behavior is challenging the specialization that makes the third stage of life the time of leisure and inactivity. These preretirees are trying to reduce differences between age groups by shifting the boundary between work and nonwork, as they perform many voluntary, unpaid activities that make them redefine the meaning and significance of work. They are giving new importance to "free work," as distinguished from gainful employment. They are thus supporting another model for organizing the life course wherein functions are no longer compartmentalized by age group. Free time, education, and work are all present in their activities. Evidence of this can be found in data for France, the Netherlands, and Great Britain.

How paradoxical that the early-exit trend has undermined the tripartition of the life course, whereas these pathways were initially legitimated by the radical distinction between an adult life devoted to work and an old age devoted to the inactivity of retirement.

The tendency to deinstitutionalize the end of the life course may partly be linked to a changing relationship with time itself. In effect, our societies may no longer be managing time so much as refusing it (Roussel and Girard 1982). The reworking of the transition toward definitive exit may thus reflect the new requirements of the socialization process in societies that are tending toward the ephemeral.

11.4 THE PROSPECTS OF EARLY EXIT

The social dynamics that led to the "agreement" among labor unions, employer organizations, and governments about the early exit of aging wage earners is losing force. These parties' positions are no longer the same as during the recession with its high unemployment rate. Their arguments are now diverging. Interests are conflicting, and disagreements are arising in a context of economic recovery and in the perspective of the inevitable aging of the population. The situations in the Netherlands, West Germany, France, and Great Britain illustrate this especially well.

Governments have become aware that lowering the definitive exit age makes it hard to balance the books of retirement funds at a time when the latter have to find the means of dealing with the aging of the population. Hence, most governments are now attempting to halt the early-exit trend. To this end, they are reforming public retirement systems. One measure being worked out in several countries, and already adopted in West Germany and the United States, gradually raises the age of retirement with a full pension. Another measure under study is to make retirement systems more flexible so as to provide for part-time retirement (as in West Germany, France, and the United Kingdom) or flexible retirement (as under a Swedish proposal that would enable wage earners to go on retirement when they choose between 65 and 70) (Jacobs 1990).

Given the data assembled in this book, we doubt that such measures, by themselves, can reverse the tendency to lower the age of definitive exit. In fact, definitive exit is already taking place well before the retirement age, and it is no longer regulated by the eligibility requirements of public retirement systems. As a consequence, changing the retirement age risks being ineffective if it is not accompanied by other measures that better protect older wage earners and integrate them in the world of work. Such public employment policies have not been significantly developed, however. Apparently, only France has undertaken a few, very timid steps toward helping jobless aging persons go back to work.

As for firms, the economic recovery and the prospect of a shortage of labor (particularly skilled labor) do not suffice to change their strategies based on the elimination of aging wage earners. The need to reduce the work force has not been the only reason that companies have given priority to laying off older workers. The quest for more flexibility in personnel matters, the decline of the norm of a lifelong job, and the demand for a more adaptable work force are so many factors that still motivate many firms to adopt "substitution strategies" for replacing older wage earners. Given the current context of economic recovery, however, companies are no longer willing to pay so much for early-exit arrangements as they previously were when they wanted to keep the "social peace." More importantly, they expect that such arrangements should have more qualitative effects on "restructuring" the work process. To this end, they are trying to control them more directly. One piece of evidence of this new position comes from the nonrenewal of the Preretirement Act in West Germany.

Even though the early-exit trend emerged out of the strategies that actors adopted to deal with a downturn in the business cycle, it is not about to be reversed as reforms are passed that affect the retirement age or as the recession ends, for major changes have occurred in the latter's wake. This trend has affected the social construction of the life course and conceptions about the distribution of work and nonwork over the life course. It has also had effects on the welfare system and undermined its consistency. What used to be obvious for everyone is no longer so. In particular, this trend has aroused doubts about the relevance of age as a criterion for setting the date of definitive exit. Wage earners are now aware that the age of entitlement to social transfer payments can become a cutoff point that is not in their interests and does not preserve their freedom to choose. Companies have realized that age is a rigid criterion contrary to individualized ways of managing human resources in line with the quest for efficiency in a less Tayloristic system of work.

The new reality, for which there is evidence in the various countries under study, suggests two possible futures for older wage earners.

In the first, employers (seeking to obtain more flexibility in work), employees (worried about their security), and governments (attempting to control social spending and maintain balanced public pension systems) will try to strike a new compromise, which would most likely involve revising the concept of retirement and setting up a system that would make work more flexible while guaranteeing incomes but not reducing wage earners' room for decision making. Although several proposals suggest that such a compromise might be reached (Standing 1986), this future is not yet certain. Realizing it supposes active state interventionism.

If no compromise is reached, actors will adopt strategies that are less and less compatible. Governments will reform public pension systems so as to control costs. As a consequence, eligibility for retirement will occur later and be less advantageous financially. Companies, in order to modernize, will continue getting rid of certain fractions of their aging work forces. If this is the future, the early definitive exit trend will be prolonged, but its financial and social costs will probably be borne by aging wage earners in precarious circumstances. For example, they will receive fewer unemployment benefits or will have their old-age pensions reduced because they left the labor force before the age of entitlement to a full pension. This not very reassuring prospect, mentioned in the chapters about Great Britain, France, and West Germany, screams for the attention of all actors, including public authorities. If no actions are taken to avoid this future, a new era might begin as developed industrial societies, having dealt with the problem of unemployment among young people, have to face the consequences of excluding older workers from the labor force at a time when they make up a growing percentage of the available pool of labor. It would thus be impossible to manage the inevitable aging of the populations in these societies.

REFERENCES

Burkhauser, R., and J. Quinn. 1989. "Work and Retirement: The American Experience." In: W. Schmähl (ed.), *Redefining the Process of Retirement in an International Perspective*. Berlin: Springer, pp. 91–113.

Casey, B., and F. Laczko. 1989. "Early retired or long term unemployed? The situation of non-working men aged 55–64 from 1979 to 1986." *Work, Employment and Society*, no. 4, pp. 509–26.

Guillemard, AM. 1983. *Old Age and the Welfare State*. London: Sage.

Jacobs, K. 1990. "Les Retraites partielles: une comparaison europiénne." In: M.I.R.E. (ed.), *Chroniques internationales du marché du travail et des politiques d'emploi 1986–1989*. Paris: Documentation Française, pp. 109–19.

Laczko, F. 1987. "Older Workers, Unemployment and the Discouraged Worker Effect." In: S. di Gregorio (ed.), *Social Gerontology: New Directions.* London: Croom Helm, pp. 239–51.

Roussel, L., and A. Girard. 1982. "Régimes démographiques et âges de la vie." In: *Les âges de la vie, actes du septième colloque de démographie,* vol. 1. Paris: Presses Universitaires de France, pp. 15–23.

Standing, G. 1986. "La flexibilité du travail et la marginalisation des travailleurs âgés. Pour une nouvelle stratégie." *Revue Internationale du Travail* 125:363–83.

Index

389